THE HUMBLEST MAY STAND FORTH

Studies in Rhetoric/Communication
Thomas W. Benson, Series Editor

THE HUMBLEST MAY STAND FORTH

Rhetoric, Empowerment, and Abolition

JACQUELINE BACON

UNIVERSITY OF SOUTH CAROLINA PRESS

Material from chapters 3 and 5 appeared in the articles "Taking Liberty, Taking Literacy: Signifying in the Rhetoric of African-American Abolitionists," *Southern Communication Journal* 64 (1999): 271–87, reprinted with the permission of the Southern States Communication Association; and "'Do You Understand Your Own Language?': Revolutionary *Topoi* in the Rhetoric of African-American Abolitionists," *Rhetoric Society Quarterly* 28.2 (spring 1998): 55–75, reprinted with the permission of the Rhetoric Society of America. Material from chapters 4 and 5 appeared in the article "'God and a Woman': Women Abolitionists, Biblical Authority, and Social Activism," *Journal of Communication and Religion* 22 (1999): 1–39, reprinted with permission of the Religious Communication Association. Quotes from Audre Lorde in chapter 6 are printed with permission from *Sister Outsider,* by Audre Lorde, copyright 1984, published by the Crossing Press, Santa Cruz, California.

Published in Columbia, South Carolina, by the
University of South Carolina Press

Manufactured in the United States of America

06 05 04 03 02   5 4 3 2 1

Library of Congress Cataloging-in-Publication Data

Bacon, Jacqueline, 1965–
    The humblest may stand forth : rhetoric, empowerment, and abolition / Jacqueline Bacon.
        p. cm. — (Studies in rhetoric/communication)
    Includes bibliographical references and index.
    ISBN 1-57003-434-6 (alk. paper)
    1. Speeches, addresses, etc., American—African American authors—History and criticism. 2. Speeches, addresses, etc., American—Women authors—History and criticism. 3. Rhetoric—Political aspects—United States—History—19th century. 4. Power (Socialsciences)—United States—History—19th century. 5. Antislavery movements—United States—History. 6. African American women abolitionists. 7. Women abolitionists—United States. 8. African American abolitionists. I. Title. II. Series.
PS407 .B33 2002
815'.409896073—dc21   2001006912

To the congregation of St. James' Episcopal Church, Austin, Texas

Contents

Editor's Preface

Jacqueline Bacon's *The Humblest May Stand Forth* is an analysis of the abolitionist rhetoric of African American men, white women, and African American
women in the decades preceding the American Civil War. Professor Bacon
argues that the muted and marginalized status of these advocates did not silence
them, but that, on the contrary, they used their situations to create distinctive
challenges not only to slavery, but also to conventional rhetorical practices, and
that in so doing they also challenged mainstream notions of rhetorical theory and
rhetorical history.

For the abolitionists marginalized by race and gender, the very act of advocacy was a powerful rhetorical appeal, claiming as it did the capacity, the right,
and the duty to engage in public discourse, despite the widely shared assumption
that only white men possessed the authority to inhabit the public sphere. Bacon
analyzes the rhetoric of the African American abolitionists David Walker,
William Whipper, William Watkins and his son William J. Watkins, Frederick
Douglass, Charles Lenox Remond, Maria Stewart, Sarah Douglass, Sarah
Remond, Frances Ellen Watkins, Sojourner Truth, and Harriet Jacobs; and the
white female abolitionists Lydia Maria Child, Angelina Grimké, Sarah Grimké,
Abby Kelley, and Lucretia Mott. She then shows how from the mid-nineteenth
century through the twentieth century, the rhetorics developed by these advo-
cates were used as a resource by other activists such as Ida B. Wells, Archibald
Grimké, Malcolm X, and Audre Lorde.

Professor Bacon argues that organized African American agitation to abolish slavery was well underway in the late eighteenth century and that it had
important influences on the direction of white abolitionist rhetoric. But the
influences among various groups of abolitionists were mutual. Once white
reformers formed organized abolition efforts, writes Bacon, they made use of but
assumed they should guide and control the abolitionist work of females and
African Americans. Hence, the abolitionist rhetoric of African Americans and
women was shaped in resistance not only to slavery but also to the prejudices and
preferences of white male abolitionists.

In this illuminating and inspiring study, Professor Bacon explores the continuing challenge posed by these activists, who struggled against silence and enslavement, reminding us of the surprising ways in which, "If silence and slavery are linked, so are freedom and rhetoric."

Thomas W. Benson
Pennsylvania State University

Abbreviations

In the citation of works, short titles are generally used. Organizations, periodicals, and works frequently cited are identified by abbreviations:

AASS   American Anti-Slavery Society.

BAP   Ripley, C. Peter, et al., eds. *The Black Abolitionist Papers.* 5 vols. Chapel Hill: University of North Carolina Press, 1985–92.

DWA   Walker, David. *David Walker's Appeal, in Four Articles; Together with a Pre–amble, to the Coloured Citizens of the World, But in Particular, and Very Expressly, to Those of the United States of America.* 3d ed. 1830. Reprint, ed. Charles M. Wiltse, New York: Hill and Wang, 1965.

FJ   *Freedom's Journal* (New York).

ILSG   Jacobs, Harriet A. *Incidents in the Life of a Slave Girl: Written by Herself.* ed. Lydia Maria Child. 1861. Reprint, ed. Jean Fagan Yellin. Cambridge, Mass.: Harvard University Press, 1987.

Lib   *Liberator* (Boston).

NASS   *National Anti-Slavery Standard* (New York).

NS   *North Star* (Rochester, N.Y.).

PY   Grimké, Sarah Moore, and Angelina Emily Grimké. *The Public Years of Sarah and Angelina Grimké: Selected Writings, 1835–1839.* ed. Larry Ceplair. New York: Columbia University Press, 1989.

Quotations from Lydia Maria Child's works are cited in the text by abbreviations:

A   *An Appeal in Favor of That Class of Americans Called Africans.*

AA   *Authentic Anecdotes of American Slavery.*

C   *Correspondence Between Lydia Maria Child and Governor Wise and Mrs. Mason, of Virginia.*

PI   *The Patriarchal Institution, as Described by Members of its Own Family.*

RW   *The Right Way the Safe Way, Proved by Emancipation in the British West Indies and Elsewhere.*

Quotations from Frederick Douglass's works are cited in the text by abbreviations:

FDP   *The Frederick Douglass Papers.*
MB   *My Bondage and My Freedom.*
N   *Narrative of the Life of Frederick Douglass, An American Slave: Written by Himself.*

Quotations from Angelina Grimké's works are cited in the text by abbreviations:

ACW   *Appeal to the Christian Women of the South.*
LCB   *Letters to Catherine* [sic] *E. Beecher.*

Quotations from Sarah Grimké's works are cited in the text by abbreviations:

E   *An Epistle to the Clergy of the Southern States.*
LES   *Letters on the Equality of the Sexes, and the Condition of Woman.*

Quotations from Maria Stewart's works are cited in the text by abbreviations:

R   *Religion and the Pure Principles of Morality, the Sure Foundation on Which We Must Build.*
MWS   *Maria W. Stewart, America's First Black Woman Political Writer: Essays and Speeches.*

Acknowledgments

Recalling in 1893 his decision to undertake the publication of the newspaper the *North Star* almost fifty years earlier, Frederick Douglass describes the aid of his friends in England. "For [their] prompt and generous assistance," Douglass remarks, "I shall never cease to feel deeply grateful, and the thought of fulfilling the expectations of the dear friends who had given me this evidence of their confidence was an abiding inspiration for persevering exertion." These words aptly capture my feelings about those who have generously assisted me throughout the process of researching and writing this book.

First and foremost, my husband, Glen McClish, has been a tireless supporter, listening to my ideas, offering continual encouragement, providing advice and editorial assistance, and motivating me in my work. I am blessed to have such a partner in my life and work. Linda Ferreira-Buckley has been a constant source of aid and friendship, as well as an inspiring example of the best of the academic profession. Joe Moldenhauer, Michael Winship, Susan Sage Heinzelman, and Nan Johnson responded to an earlier version of this study with enthusiastic comments that helped me in the process of revision. My parents, Gary and Wynne Bacon, taught me the lessons of perseverance, tolerance, and dedication to intellectual pursuits that have made my scholarly achievements possible. In addition, my father aided me in my research, discovering valuable resources that have greatly enhanced this work; and my mother read parts of drafts and provided useful insight. My parents-in-law, Leonard and Elaine McClish, have continually supported me with their love and encouragement. Many friends have encouraged and inspired me as I devoted myself to this project. In particular, I would like to thank Una and Milton Flemings, Joan Burton, Dave Stinchcomb, Larry Clay, Mity Myhr, Christa Dieckmann McDaniel, the late Dick Hossalla, and the members of Integrity/Austin.

Barry Blose, acquisitions editor at the University of South Carolina Press, offered welcome advice and assistance, and the suggestions of three anonymous readers for the press helped me improve this study greatly. I also appreciate the generous assistance of librarians at the University of Texas at Austin; the University of California, Berkeley; and Southwestern University.

Finally, I thank the people of St. James' Episcopal Church, Austin, Texas, who sustained my mind and soul with fellowship, support, and love. They have been and continue to be my "abiding inspiration for persevering exertion."

THE HUMBLEST MAY STAND FORTH

1

Slavery and Silence, Freedom and Rhetoric

In an 1850 speech in Rochester, Frederick Douglass reveals an essential component of slavery:

> Why is it that all the reports of contentment and happiness among the slaves at the South come to us upon the authority of slaveholders, or (what is equally significant), of slaveholders' friends? *Why* is it that we do not hear from the slaves direct? . . .
>
> . . . There comes no *voice* from the enslaved, we are left to gather his feelings by imagining what ours would be, were our souls in his soul's stead.
>
> If there were no other fact descriptive of slavery, than that the slave is dumb, this alone would be sufficient to mark the slave system as a grand aggregation of human horrors. (*FDP,* 2:258–59)[1]

A former slave, Douglass knew from experience that silence was a powerful tool of the slaveholding regime that prevented slaves from relating the harsh details of their lives. Yet his commentary on slavery's silencing power is not restricted to the condition of literal enslavement. Douglass suggests, too, that society often threatens to silence those who are marginalized in a variety of ways. Others may claim to speak for them and to represent their concerns. Various channels of communication, such as the mainstream press, may ignore their voices. Marginalized rhetors may be advised to adopt particular styles of communication to fit societal expectations or to persuade only in contexts controlled by others. Thus even when they are not literally silent, those who are oppressed in society may encounter restrictions that threaten to render them, in effect, voiceless.

Douglass's own experience illustrates how these forces can combine to present obstacles to marginalized rhetors who wish to speak for themselves. White leaders often advised Douglass to shape his rhetoric in response to various preconceived notions of what would be "appropriate" and "believable" for an African American and former slave. As an aspiring editor, Douglass was discouraged by white abolitionists from creating his own newspaper, in which he could control his own rhetoric and publish the writing of other African Americans. Yet Douglass's life and rhetoric also demonstrate that marginalized rhetors need not be silenced—that they can speak on their own terms; can take control of their rhetoric; and can negotiate, resist, and even overturn the restrictions that they face. Douglass became more independent from his white mentors as his career progressed, challenging their expectations, founding and editing three newspapers, and rejecting the presumption that he conform to widely held stereotypes.[2] Through rhetoric, then, those who are oppressed can fight the unjust conditions under which they must live.

Douglass also recognized that voices may be silenced not only in their own time, but may also be lost to future generations if scholars and historians do not diligently seek sources that are often overlooked, question traditional historical narratives, and reject biased assumptions. In an 1854 address to the literary societies of Western Reserve College in Hudson, Ohio, Douglass maintains that although the "facts" of history prove that the "destiny" of African Americans is "united to America and Americans," scholars are the gatekeepers who influence how America perceives this history: "The future public opinion of the land . . . whether just or unjust, whether magnanimous or mean, must redound to the honor of the Scholars of the country or cover them with shame" (*FDP*, 2:524–25). Speaking in Rochester the following year, Douglass demonstrates how history must be challenged and revised in order to provide a place for previously overlooked figures. Douglass questions commonly held beliefs about the antislavery movement—such as the notion that William Lloyd Garrison "discovered its principles, originated its ideas, [and] framed its arguments" (*FDP*, 3:19–20)—and calls attention to overlooked antislavery activists whose efforts preceded Garrison's.

When I began to study abolitionist rhetoric, I had not yet encountered Douglass's profound association of silence and slavery or his suggestions that scholars must challenge traditional views in order to discover voices that have been lost. Yet, reading eyewitness accounts of the movement and the early annual reports of the American Anti-Slavery Society (AASS), founded in Philadelphia in 1833, I began to sense troubling silences. First, I discovered that these sources provide only a partial history of the struggle against slavery in antebellum America. I knew that in the 1830s abolitionists who were women or African Americans spoke and wrote against slavery, but most of the speakers whose words were preserved in the minutes of the early AASS meetings were white men. Although the Reverend Samuel May remarked at the 1853 AASS meeting that three women—Lucretia Mott, Esther Moore, and Lydia White—had spoken powerfully at the 1833 convention at which the AASS was founded, he acknowledged that these women were not mentioned in the published account of the meeting. Both May and fellow AASS member Oliver Johnson later recalled that Mott's ethos in her speech at the 1833 convention was informed by deference and hesitation, suggesting both the constraints on the speech of female abolitionists and the potential biases of accounts of women's rhetoric written by their white male abolitionist contemporaries.[3]

The minutes of early AASS meetings also reveal that the expectations of white male abolitionists often influenced the activism and the rhetoric of their female or African American colleagues. Women abolitionists are mentioned only as participants in "ladies' antislavery societies," subsidiary organizations expected to aid male abolitionist organizations and to defer to their leadership. Although at the sixth annual meeting in 1839, women were granted official membership in the AASS, the rights to vote and hold office, and formal acknowledgment of their speech, the heated controversy over these privileges at the meeting indicates continuing sexism on the part of many male abolitionists. Similarly, although some African American male abolitionists were members of the AASS since its founding, their participation and their voices also appear to have been restricted in the organization. Brief comments were offered by African American abolitionists Robert Purvis, David Ruggles, and Theodore Wright at early AASS annual meetings, yet these remarks are much shorter than the lengthy comments of white abolitionists. Significantly, too, Ruggles prefaces his 1834 remarks by "ask[ing] permission to say a few words," a request not made by white speakers. Not until the minutes of the Society's fifth annual meeting in 1838 did I find a sustained speech of an African American abolitionist, physician James McCune Smith.[4]

In addition, the AASS reports suggest that white abolitionists often presumed to speak for their African American colleagues rather than allowing them to define and articulate their concerns. Eyewitness accounts of slavery at the meetings were provided not by former slaves or their family members, but by white men such as James Thome and H. B. Stanton, who had lived or traveled in the South or had heard the testimony of southerners, or by former slaveholders such as James Birney. On subjects such as colonization—a scheme that proposed sending free African Americans to Africa—or the ability of freed slaves to become productive members of American society, white speakers offered pronouncements in which they claimed to speak for African Americans.[5] Although the hardships of slave wives and mothers were frequently discussed, African American women were not mentioned as speakers on these subjects. Indeed, they were not explicitly identified at all in AASS reports as participants in the movement.

Douglass's implication that historical accounts are often incomplete also proved relevant as I researched the antebellum antislavery struggle. Until recently, most historical accounts of the abolition movement have focused on organizations such as the AASS and its principal post-1840 rival, the American and Foreign Anti-Slavery Society (AFASS), societies whose leadership was primarily white and male. In these studies, women's participation—when considered at all—is discussed in terms of their work within these organizations, their assistance to white male leaders, and the responses of white antebellum society to their activism. Studies of individual abolitionists have traditionally featured such notables as William Lloyd Garrison, Samuel Joseph May, Theodore Dwight Weld, Elizur

Wright, Ralph Waldo Emerson, and Henry David Thoreau. Although many historians and biographers have studied Frederick Douglass, only recently have other African American abolitionists received extensive critical attention.[6]

Yet I knew that, in spite of the limitations of traditional accounts, antislavery persuasion includes much more than the rhetoric of well-known figures such as William Lloyd Garrison and discourse that has been traditionally associated with the abolition movement. White women and African American men and women also were involved in the abolition movement and often spoke and wrote against slavery. In addition, the ways marginalized abolitionists marshaled power demonstrate that agency did not belong only to those whom society considered influential. I wanted to recover the voices of various abolitionists who often seemed to be silenced within traditional accounts of the antislavery movement and to explore their rhetoric—not only such well-known figures as Frederick Douglass, Sojourner Truth, and Angelina Grimké, but also those whose names are less familiar to contemporary scholars. The voices of many women or African American abolitionists have been lost and deserve attention. This effort not only is crucial to the study of the discourse of marginalized Americans throughout history, but also to the broad understanding—both in the academy and in society at large—of the rhetoric of those who continue to be marginalized in America today.

My study features two interrelated contentions about abolitionist rhetoric. First, the rhetoric of abolitionists who were African Americans or women—when viewed on its own terms—expands our conception of the domain of abolitionist discourse. In particular, their rhetoric challenges scholars to shift attention from well-known organizations such as the AASS and widely studied figures such as Garrison, to broaden the scope of what should be considered antislavery persuasion, and to examine the particular factors that shaped the activism of female or African American abolitionists. Second, because they were marginalized both within American society and within the abolition movement, abolitionists who were women or African Americans developed a diverse, empowering, and theoretically complex array of rhetorical strategies in order to assume agency within a society that did not grant them full equality. Their rhetorical practice demonstrates that conventional categories and modes of persuasion are not only the province of those with linguistic or political power in society. Correspondingly, I explore the ways in which traditional approaches to rhetoric need to be challenged, questioned, and expanded in light of the persuasion of these rhetors. Their discourse demonstrates that conventional assumptions about rhetorical theory and practice must be revised to account for the persuasion of those who are marginalized in society.[7] I provide here preliminary discussion of each of these components of my approach.

To find texts of abolitionist rhetors who were women or African Americans, I needed to question traditional histories of the abolition movement, to look beyond organizations such as the AASS, and to challenge historical assumptions derived from the experience of white male abolitionists such as William Lloyd Garrison. My work was aided by scholarship that explores the roles of previously neglected abolitionists. Although most historians have until recently overlooked the contributions of female or African American abolitionists to the antislavery movement, groundbreaking work to correct these omissions was begun by scholars in the 1960s and 1970s. Benjamin Quarles, William and Jane Pease, George Levesque, and Robert Dick explored the contributions of African American abolitionists; and scholars such as Blanche Glassman Hersh, Gerda Lerner, and Katharine Du Pre Lumpkin examined the contributions of white women to the abolitionist movement.[8] These studies feature well-known figures such as Frederick Douglass and Angelina Grimké but also establish the important contributions of other female or African American abolitionists, who spoke and wrote against slavery in a variety of settings. Scholarship of the 1980s and 1990s has continued to address historical omissions, providing alternative accounts that incorporate the work of abolitionists who were African Americans or women.[9] Studies of some of the previously neglected figures in the antislavery movement feature white women abolitionists such as Lydia Maria Child, Abby Kelley, and the Weston sisters; African American male antislavery activists such as Henry Highland Garnet, Samuel Ringgold Ward, and Jermain Wesley Loguen; and African American female abolitionists such as Sojourner Truth, Maria Stewart, and Harriet Jacobs.[10] Recent studies also have provided a new context for Frederick Douglass's antislavery contributions by exploring his interactions with other African American abolitionists and by reexamining his relationship with white mentors and audiences.[11]

To explore fully the work of these and other marginalized abolitionists—as well as locate little-known primary texts—I began to explore antebellum female and African American abolitionist organizations. In addition, I found that a focus on societies formed solely to combat slavery excludes significant contributions of some of the marginalized abolitionists. African American abolitionist activity in particular was often incorporated in societies not exclusively dedicated to abolition whose goals were also educational and religious. The recent work of historians inspired me to research the abolitionist activity of female antislavery societies, African American benevolent societies in northern states, and African American churches.[12] Because these studies demonstrate the inaccuracy of the traditional assumption that the organized abolition movement began in the 1830s, I began to search for abolitionist activity that predated the involvement of white male abolitionists such as Garrison. This effort introduced me not only to pre-1830 abolitionist texts but also to African American newspapers that regularly criticized slavery, including *Freedom's Journal,* which began publication almost four years prior to the appearance of William Lloyd Garrison's *Liberator,* usually considered the groundbreaking abolitionist periodical. I was indebted in my search to various scholars whose collections of primary texts provided me with rhetoric by African American abolitionists otherwise not readily accessible.

To understand the constraints on the speech of abolitionists who were women or African Americans, one must focus on antebellum formulations of gender and race. I discovered that it was necessary to consult primary sources whenever possible to determine how notions of race and gender were articulated by antebellum Americans. Popular formulations of women's appropriate roles and the rhetorical intricacies of antebellum defenses of slavery are best understood by reading the original texts themselves. I turned to popular writings on gender and race from the antebellum period, such as Thomas Jefferson's *Notes on the State of Virginia,* Catharine Beecher's domestic manuals, and influential proslavery tracts. I also began to explore less popular texts that illuminate antebellum thought on gender and race. Editorials and letters in newspapers reveal dominant antebellum formulations of race and gender as well as the responses to these notions by women and men, both white and African American. I also searched for periodical articles written for women, speeches given to female or African American organizations, constitutions of antislavery societies with primarily female or African American membership, and private letters written by African American or female abolitionists. Autobiographical accounts such as Frederick Douglass's *My Bondage and My Freedom* and Harriet Jacobs's *Incidents in the Life of a Slave Girl* elucidate—both implicitly and explicitly—the ways antebellum perspectives about gender and race affected the day-to-day lives of antislavery activists.

Secondary sources also proved useful in my investigation of antebellum notions of gender and race. I was continually aware, however, that historians often disagree about issues that profoundly affected the experiences of nineteenth-century women, such as the way antebellum Americans conceptualized the "public" and the "private" or nineteenth-century views of women's appropriate roles in society. I found, too, that the work of scholars of gender is continually being updated and challenged. For example, Barbara Welter's *Dimity Convictions: The American Woman in the Nineteenth Century* and Carroll Smith-Rosenberg's *Disorderly Conduct: Visions of Gender in Victorian America*—groundbreaking texts that illuminate aspects of nineteenth-century formulations of gender—have been challenged and expanded by more recent research about the complex role of women in antebellum America by scholars such as Nina Baym, Gillian Brown, and Mary Ryan. These works, which focus on white women, have in their turn been challenged by studies such as Paula Giddings's *When and Where I Enter: The Impact of Black Women on Race and Sex in America,* Dorothy Sterling's *We Are Your Sisters: Black Women in the Nineteenth Century,* and Deborah Gray White's *Ar'n't I a Woman? Female Slaves in the Plantation South.*[13] I draw on secondary studies such as these as well as on primary sources to expand conventional accounts of antebellum women's experiences.

As these studies have challenged traditional assumptions about women's experiences based primarily on the experiences of white—and often upper-class—women, scholars have also begun to question the conventional notion that racism only affects the lives of people of color. Traditionally, they propose, discussions of race in America focus only on those who are not white. Yet recent studies of "whiteness" demonstrate that although white people do not always perceive the influence of societal constructions of race in their lives, their perspectives and experiences are fundamentally shaped by their racial identity, which is a position of privilege in society. This growing body of scholarship is germane to an understanding of the position of nineteenth-century white women abolitionists, in particular, whose lives were simultaneously influenced by the sexism of their society and by their privileged position—in terms of race—that separated them from their African American male and female colleagues and shaped their perceptions of them.

To analyze the rhetoric of abolitionists who were women and African Americans, I focus on the rhetorical strategies that allowed them to negotiate and overcome the obstacles they faced and to assume agency. First and foremost, my analytical approach is guided by a focus on the texts themselves, which I emphasize and feature throughout the study. Douglass's commentary serves as a warning that one must analyze this rhetoric on its own terms, that the voices of these marginalized rhetors must not be silenced by an analytical framework that threatens to replace, reduce, alter, or control the primary texts themselves. In other words, theory should enhance but not replace or overpower the persuasion of the rhetors I study. Henry Louis Gates warns that texts cannot "speak for themselves" when they are analyzed in terms of critical theories "borrowed whole" from other traditions.[14] I do not try to fit texts neatly into theoretical categories; conversely, my analysis is deeply rooted in the primary texts themselves. I wish for the reader to encounter these abolitionists "speaking for themselves," not through me or through particular theoretical lenses.

Yet theoretical principles are germane to my rhetorical analysis. Allowing the rhetoric of the abolitionists I study to dictate what theories are relevant rather than choosing only those texts that conform to particular analytical tools, I borrow from rhetorical approaches that help elucidate certain features of the discourse of African American or female abolitionists. Often, the rhetors I feature marshal strategies that can be understood in part in terms of traditional rhetorical theories. Kenneth Burke's studies of language and rhetoric illuminate aspects of the rhetorical strategies of abolitionists who were female or African American, particularly his theory of language that invokes identification and difference and his analysis of rhetoric based on social and cultural hierarchies. Because African American or female abolitionists often were able to find authority through religion and evangelism, theories of religious rhetoric also inform my study. In particular, I draw on traditional studies of the jeremiadic form in America, such as those of Sacvan Bercovitch and Margaret Zulick.[15] These and other theoretical approaches inform my analysis.

I also draw on less conventional theoretical models, particularly those developed to account for the persuasion of those who are marginalized in society. For instance, muted group theory—an approach to language developed to understand the communication of those whose discourse is often silenced—is an analytical framework that is germane to this study. Developed by linguistic anthropologists Edwin and Shirley Ardener and communication theorist Cheris Kramarae, muted group theory posits that the control of language by dominant members of a society leaves other individuals in a "muted" position. The linguistic models of those in power claim to define marginalized members of society without acknowledging their perceptions, leaving them "voiceless" in terms of the dominant group's discourse. Mutedness does not connote silence, however; instead muted rhetors must adopt linguistic strategies that allow them to speak for themselves in spite of their marginalized position. Their discourse may take a variety of forms. Muted groups may rely on the dominant group's linguistic or rhetorical models, encoding their particular concerns—even those that threaten prevailing beliefs—in an "acceptable" form. From within these dominant models, members of muted groups may find ways to challenge the ideological bases of the dominant group and offer alternative standards. Members of muted groups may also choose models outside of the dominant discourse through which to express themselves. These alternative forms may offer members of muted groups more flexibility to express their concerns because they are not judged in terms of traditional models based on the experiences of the dominant group. Through such alternative channels, muted rhetors may offer powerful arguments even as they are excluded from traditional persuasive roles. Muted group theory, then, acknowledges that the discourse of muted rhetors is variable—incorporating traditional cultural assumptions as it undermines them, featuring conventional and unconventional linguistic patterns, and fashioning alternative forms of discourse outside of traditional discursive boundaries.[16]

My exploration of the rhetoric of women abolitionists is also informed by the feminist studies of Karlyn Kohrs Campbell and Jean Fagan Yellin on antebellum women's speech and writing. Yet traditional feminist theory, although very useful in analyzing white women's rhetoric, is often inadequate for an examination of the discourse of African American women. Studies of African American women reveal that feminist theory is often based primarily on the experiences and perspectives of white women, frequently ignoring the particular influences of both racism and sexism in the lives of women of color. Thus I draw on the work of African American scholars such as Patricia Hill Collins and bell hooks, who focus on the particular experiences and concerns of African American women, in my analysis of African American women's rhetoric.[17]

My study also draws on theoretical studies of the rhetoric of African American men and women. General studies of the jeremiad prove insufficient for analysis of African Americans rhetors' deployment of this genre. Studies of the particular form of the African American jeremiad, elucidated by David Howard-Pitney and Wilson Jeremiah Moses, inform my exploration of the religious rhetoric of African American male and female abolitionists. Because feminist theology, like feminist theory in general, often privileges the experiences of white women, my exploration of African American women's religious rhetoric draws on studies both of the roles African American women assume through religion and their views of theology and Scripture. My analysis of the speeches and writings of African American abolitionists also relies on the studies of Henry Louis Gates, Claudia Mitchell-Kernan, and Roger Abrahams on African American rhetoric, particularly the rhetorical act of signifying.[18]

Although relevant to my study, none of these theories—either traditional or nontraditional—constitutes a defining approach to the rhetoric of abolitionists who were African American or female. Nor do I assume that these rhetorical frameworks are sacrosanct categories that should be adopted wholesale or uncritically. Throughout this study, I explore the limitations of theoretical perspectives for my analysis, limitations that not only should be acknowledged but that also can help challenge and revise conventional theoretical tools. Significantly, the rhetoric of the abolitionists featured in this study often demonstrates the shortcomings of particular rhetorical theories, suggesting that the persuasion of marginalized members of society may challenge, expand, or revise theoretical categories.

The questions I engage in my analysis resonate with current discussions within the field of rhetorical studies. Scholars are exploring the functions of public discourse in American history, focusing on the often conflicting norms, ideals, and anxieties influencing Americans' views of public argument; the ways Americans' perceptions of themselves, the nation, race, and gender are shaped by public discourse; and the connections between public rhetoric and power, violence, authority, and social change. Kimberly Smith's history of how rational public debate came to be associated with democracy for nineteenth-century Americans; James Perrin Warren's exploration of the connections among power, language, and cultural transformation in antebellum America; and Stephen Browne's analysis of how violence functions discursively in Angelina Grimké's antislavery persuasion highlight the significance of these issues for studies of antebellum rhetoric. Because norms of democratic politics were not established in the antebellum period, Smith argues, the discourse of the time reveals implicit questions and anxieties about public argument and its connection to democracy, violence, emotion, and the prevailing social order.[19] My study of how abolitionists who were women or African Americans assumed the agency to argue publicly, challenging and expanding conventional discursive categories, contributes to this scholarly inquiry.

My project is also connected to examinations of the public sphere that emphasize the way race, gender, power, and access influence public argument in American culture. Jürgen Habermas's influential notion of the public sphere has been challenged by scholars who question his idealistic conception of an open and accessible realm in which rationality, equality, and enlightened discourse prevail. They also question his separation of the private from the public and his failure to account for the exclusion of certain groups, such as women or African Americans, from the public sphere.[20] Revising Habermas's model, Nancy Fraser suggests that "stratified societies" yield "a plurality of competing publics," including "subaltern counterpublics" constituted by "members of subordinated social groups." Fraser and Lisa Gring-Pemble suggest this alternative notion allows for the consideration of practices and issues that are often denoted private but which in reality shape public discourses and identities. Houston Baker and Michael Dawson describe an African American counterpublic, in which institutions such as the church and the African American press generate forceful discourse and activism.[21] Female or African American abolitionists often argued within a variety of counterpublics, including all-female groups, African American organizations, and groups led by primarily a white male leadership, such as the AASS. My analysis considers the roles of these contexts in shaping discourse, the varying access to power and authority available in different arenas, and the ways seemingly private or personal considerations influenced the public rhetoric of these marginalized abolitionists.

Certain practical considerations bear on this study, as well. I focus on oratory and nonfiction prose, including tracts and autobiographical accounts such as slave narratives. The process of narrowing the large and diverse field of potential texts fitting this description presented me with several theoretical challenges. Although I rejected the traditional historiographical assumption that the organized abolition movement arose in the 1830s as inaccurate because it is based on a perspective that privileges the thought and activism of white abolitionists, I had to draw chronological boundaries for this study. Although the historical record indicates that African American rhetors addressed slavery as early as the late eighteenth century, noteworthy developments of the late 1820s make it a productive point of departure.[22] During this period, historian Peter Hinks argues, African Americans organized beyond their localities to form a "tight-knit union of interest among free black communities" in different cities, building on and solidifying national connections and networks that had been developing since the Revolution and that intensified during the 1820s. This unified activism took a variety of forms and was spurred by various factors. African American protest against colonization intensified in the late 1820s as the colonization movement in the white community gained prominence. Violence against African Americans and restrictions of their civil rights in the 1820s also spurred activism. Many African American organizations that incorporated antislavery within their goals, such as the Massachusetts General Colored Association (MGCA), were founded in the mid-1820s; and the first African American newspaper, *Freedom's Journal,* founded in 1827, gave African Americans a national forum for debating and discussing slavery and other issues.[23] For these reasons, I have chosen texts written in and after the late 1820s.

Finding an end point for my selection of texts was less difficult. The Civil War altered the American landscape for men and women for all races and offered new avenues for activism against slavery, including military service and assistance to African American soldiers and freed Southern slaves. I have concluded my selection of texts with Harriet Jacobs's 1861 *Incidents in the Life of a Slave Girl*.

Bibliographic and textual problems arise with respect to various texts featured in this study. Often published versions of nineteenth-century speeches are not verbatim transcriptions but third-person accounts of a speech—sometimes, but not always, including direct quotes in the summaries—written by white newspaper reporters. Not surprisingly, different accounts of a speech may vary, and we have no way of determining how faithful particular accounts are. Journalist John Dennett suggests in an 1866 article that readers should be skeptical of the accuracy of third-person accounts of speeches: "[Reporters] are guided by their own notions, and these are not always either judicious or severe. Frequently they bring away only what they can readily remember, and what is not worth the pains of remembering at all." Even stenographically transcribed versions of a speech, John Blassingame warns, may not be completely accurate—although he adds that the proceedings of many antislavery meetings were transcribed by respected stenographers. He also notes that certain factors mitigated against calculated misrepresentations, including orators' criticisms of inaccurate reports and contact between reporters and speakers in which the former requested written copies of a speech or asked for repetition of certain passages.[24]

A figure such as Sojourner Truth, who never learned to read or write, presents additional problems. Her 1850 *Narrative of Sojourner Truth* was dictated to the white female abolitionist Olive Gilbert, who presents Truth's history in the third person, occasionally offering interpretations that she identifies as her own. It is impossible to determine to what extent Gilbert influenced the *Narrative*. In addition, newspaper reports of her speeches are problematic. Although newspapers were read to her and she dictated letters to editors, the significantly varying reports of her famous speech at the 1851 Woman's Rights Convention in Akron, Ohio—most often associated with the refrain "Ar'n't I A Woman?"—highlight the difficulty of determining the accuracy of accounts of her rhetoric.

These problems cannot be completely solved. Because textual questions are best answered by editors of abolitionist works, I defer in many cases to the judgments of scholars such as Blassingame, C. Peter Ripley et al., and Larry Ceplair, whose collections include speeches of the abolitionists I consider and who have chosen accounts that they consider most accurate.[25] For relatively unknown speeches not available in edited collections, I rely on newspaper accounts or other published versions I discovered in the course of my primary research. In the particular case of Truth's 1851 Akron speech, I analyze parallel passages from three accounts, using intertextual references to suggest the most complete account of the speech—albeit mediated—available to readers. Yet any method that attempts to uncover accurate versions of a speech is necessarily speculative. Although I acknowledge this difficulty, I am confident that my analysis of these speeches enhances our understanding of the rhetoric of women and African

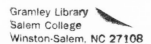

American abolitionists. And to exclude any version that might not be completely accurate would further silence voices that cannot otherwise be heard. Indeed, many nineteenth-century Americans encountered this rhetoric only through these secondhand accounts, making them important antebellum antislavery documents that reflect—at least in part—the rhetoric of abolitionists who were women or African Americans.

Because many antebellum women and men, white and African American, argued against slavery, I could not consider every abolitionist who was female or African American, nor could I analyze all of the texts produced by various rhetors. I have chosen figures and texts that are "representative" of this group of abolitionists in the sense of Kenneth Burke's notion of a "representative anecdote": examples that provide "a solid point of departure" for the creation of "analytic instruments" and "terms of analysis."[26] In other words, I do not imply that my selection of figures and texts delineates all of the discourse of abolitionists who were women or African Americans, but rather that their rhetoric provides a rich and diverse foundation for analysis, suggests the range of this discourse, and invites further study by scholars. My analysis features the rhetoric of African American male abolitionists David Walker, William Whipper, William Watkins and his son William J. Watkins, Frederick Douglass, and Charles Lenox Remond; white female abolitionists Lydia Maria Child, Angelina Grimké, Sarah Grimké, Abby Kelley, and Lucretia Mott; and African American female abolitionists Maria Stewart, Sarah Douglass, Sarah Remond, Frances Ellen Watkins, Sojourner Truth, and Harriet Jacobs.

I divide my analysis into chapters based on these three subgroups—African American men, white women, and African American women—because race and gender pose particular constraints and intersect in unique ways for rhetors from each group and because they often adopt similar strategies in response to these obstacles. Although these groupings are useful for rhetorical analysis, they do not represent the only associations among these abolitionists. Abolitionists from different groups often interacted with one another, adopted common strategies, and influenced each other's discourse. Sojourner Truth, for example, interacted with white female abolitionists and with Frederick Douglass, and Lydia Maria Child edited and wrote an introduction for Harriet Jacobs's *Incidents in the Life of a Slave Girl.*[27] Similarly, I do not mean to imply that members of each of these groups were subject to the same effects of prejudice. All nineteenth-century African Americans encountered racism, although not always through the institutions of slavery or servitude. Similarly, racism was experienced differently for African American men and women. Nor do I suggest that the members of each group shared similar opinions on contemporary issues. Clarence Walker aptly notes that a community that is "formed in response to oppression" is not necessarily a "constructive community" in which members agree on fundamental issues.[28] Therefore, although I refer to the antebellum African American community, I adopt the term "community" in the specific sense of a group of people who, because of common restrictions on their freedom and civil rights, organized together and developed societal institutions to empower themselves and fight for their rights. Although African American organizations often adopted common practical strategies, disagreement was not uncommon; and I address these differences in the study when relevant.

In chapter 2, I begin the process of recovering the voices of African American or female abolitionists by critically examining traditional historical perspectives on the abolition movement and suggesting the ways in which they ignore the concerns and experiences of these abolitionists. This critique suggests that we need alternative accounts of the abolitionist movement that not only incorporate the activism of the abolitionists but also reveal the ways in which they were marginalized in the abolition movement and in antebellum society; the ways in which they overcame these limitations within the movement; and the alternative abolitionist organizations and media they created so they could fight slavery on their own terms. I provide brief historical accounts of the antislavery work of African American men, white women, and African American women—both within the movement dominated by white men and in alternative organizations and associations.

Chapters 3, 4, and 5 present analysis of selected rhetorical texts by African American men, white women, and African American women, respectively. Because my aim is to suggest the range of this discourse—both thematically and theoretically—rather than to examine exhaustively the work of any one figure, my analysis in these chapters is centered on rhetorical strategies revealed in various works and on the ways they conform to and challenge theoretical assumptions rather than on a comprehensive analysis of any one text. Although each of these chapters focuses on one of the subgroups of abolitionists I feature, they are interrelated. Throughout my discussion of the rhetorical strategies of African American men, white women, and African American women, I examine the ways in which they frequently adopted similar strategies as well as highlight significant differences that render the rhetoric of each group unique.

The rhetorical approaches adopted by the abolitionists featured in this study evoke intriguing questions for Americans at the outset of the twenty-first century. More than one hundred years after orators such as Douglass and Truth spoke, what are the rhetorical obstacles that continue to face marginalized rhetors? How have societal expectations for these rhetors changed? How do the rhetorical strategies of marginalized rhetors of the late nineteenth and twentieth centuries connect to those of the abolitionists, and how have alterations in American society given rise to new strategies? Chapter 6 addresses these questions by exploring the discourse of four African American rhetors: Ida B. Wells, late nineteenth-century journalist, civil rights crusader, and antilynching activist; Archibald Grimké, a lawyer, politician, and active speaker on African American rights in the early twentieth century (who was also the nephew of Angelina and Sarah Grimké); Malcolm X, the influential Black Muslim spokesman for militant protest; and Audre Lorde, an African American feminist poet and activist who spoke and wrote in the 1970s and 1980s. The rhetoric of these figures represents the legacy of the marginalized abolitionists.

In 1852, William G. Allen, one of three African American professors at New York Central College in McGrawville, spoke to the institution's Dialexian Society on orators and oratory. His speech articulates the converse, in effect, of Frederick Douglass's comments about silence and slavery. "Orations worthy the name must have for their subject personal or political liberty," Allen maintains, "and orators worthy of the name must necessarily originate in the nation that is on the eve of passing from a state of slavery into freedom, or from a state of freedom into slavery. How could this be otherwise? Where there is no pressure, the highest efforts of genius must lie undeveloped." Significantly, Allen more explicitly connects the experience of oppression to powerful rhetoric: "I was about to say, that orators worthy the name, must originate among the oppressed races, but on turning to the pages of history, I was reminded of the fact, that all races, with scarcely an exception, had, at some period of their existence, been in a state of thraldom."[29] The most powerful oratory, then, arises from oppression, and rhetoric is fundamentally connected to the transition from slavery to freedom. If, as Douglass maintains, "there comes no *voice* from the enslaved," it is also true that it is an act of freedom and resistance to oppression to speak for oneself, to determine one's own discourse. If silence and slavery are linked, so are freedom and rhetoric. In this latter conjunction lies an additional significance of the rhetoric of the white women and African American men and women who argued against slavery. They did not just argue for freedom; they gained freedom themselves through their persuasion. Let us keep this transformation in mind as we begin the process of exploring their rhetoric.

2

Recovering the Voices of Marginalized Abolitionists

Abolitionists who were African Americans or women were marginalized not only in their own time. Historians have also silenced their voices by predicating their accounts of the antislavery movement on the experiences of white male abolitionists. To recover the voices of marginalized abolitionists, we must challenge historiographical assumptions that neglect them and create alternative accounts that allow us to explore their rhetoric and activism. We must also focus on the unique experiences, concerns, and beliefs that shaped the rhetoric of female or African American abolitionists. Speaking against slavery, these rhetors faced obstacles as marginalized members of antebellum society and of many antislavery organizations, negotiated these restrictions to work within the abolition movement dominated by white men, created alternative avenues for activism, and resisted and redefined societal assumptions and expectations.

TOWARD ALTERNATIVE HISTORIES OF THE ABOLITION MOVEMENT

Hayden White maintains that historians mediate and organize events by characterizing them as elements of a "story" that has a "discernible beginning, middle, and end."[1] Most scholars of the abolition movement, who focus primarily on its white male leaders, designate the early 1830s as the beginning of a new and influential phase of the organized abolition movement. Although there had been organizations of white males who opposed slavery in various states prior to this time—both in the North and South—historians mark a shift in the early 1830s for three major reasons. Many white male reformers shifted their support in the early 1830s from proposals for gradual emancipation to the immediate abolition of slavery; they turned away from colonization, a plan that proposed expatriating free African Americans, and began to harshly oppose it; and they started to formulate more militant and uncompromising criticisms of slavery.[2] These accounts of the abolition movement identify a variety of precipitating events—those events White calls "inaugural motifs"—that mark this chronological boundary.[3] These "inaugural motifs" include William Lloyd Garrison's establishment in 1831 of the *Liberator,* a weekly antislavery newspaper which advocated immediate abolition and condemned colonization; the British precedent for the idea of immediate abolition; and the organization by white reformers of antislavery societies to promote immediate emancipation and oppose colonization, beginning in 1832 with the New England Anti-Slavery Society. The goal of establishing a national society dedicated to these principles was realized in December 1833, when abolitionists gathered in Philadelphia to form the AASS. Historians have generally agreed with the assessment of AASS members, who believed that their position represented a dramatic new conception of antislavery. As the *First Annual Report* of the AASS declares, "Till the organization of the New-England Anti-Slavery Society in 1832, there was scarcely a rill of pity for the slave which was not diverted to the EXPATRIATION OF THE FREE."[4]

Recent scholarship on the work of African American abolitionists challenges this narrative on a variety of counts.[5] First, the focus on white reformers both prior to and after the 1830s neglects the work of African American abolitionists in various Northern states. As early as the late eighteenth century, leaders such as Absalom Jones, Richard Allen, and Cyrus Bustill began speaking and organizing against slavery; petitioning the government to abolish the slave trade; creating plans for emancipation; and establishing societies such as the Free African Society of Philadelphia (1787), the African Society of Boston (1796), and the African Masonic Lodge in Boston (1797), which included antislavery resolutions among their goals. By the 1820s, abolitionist activity among African Americans in a variety of cities was strong, and organizations were formed specifically to fight southern slavery and northern segregation, such as the Massachusetts General Colored Association (MGCA), founded in Boston in 1826. In addition, the publication in New York of *Freedom's Journal,* the first African American newspaper and an organ that regularly published articles critical of both colonization and slavery, predated the *Liberator* by nearly four years. By the late 1820s, the increasing activism in major cities in the North and the development of connections between African Americans in different cities through *Freedom's Journal* led to the Negro Convention Movement, a series of national gatherings of African American leaders beginning in September 1830 to discuss issues such as slavery, colonization, education, and moral uplift. It is important to note that, like white reformers, many African American abolitionists did not publicly argue for immediate abolition prior to the 1830s—articles in *Freedom's Journal,* for example, often supported gradual abolition. Yet the activism of African Americans prior to the 1830s did not merely mirror white antislavery activity and deserves to be studied in its own right.

In particular, the opposition to colonization of African American abolitionists in northern states predated similar activity by white reformers and influenced the views of white abolitionists. Although some African Americans supported emigration from the United States, most opposed white-sponsored plans to colonize free African Americans in Africa. African American opposition to colonization began immediately following the founding of the American Colonization Society (ACS), formed in 1816 by white reformers. Most African Americans felt that they were Americans and that their destiny was linked to the United States. They questioned the value of colonization in ending slavery and even suspected that the removal of free people of color would strengthen slavery (a belief supported by the membership of many slaveholders in the ACS), and they resented the rhetoric of the ACS, which portrayed free African Americans as depraved and argued that whites could never coexist with them peacefully.[6] In the pages of *Freedom's Journal* as well as in published works such as David Walker's forceful and controversial *Appeal to the Coloured Citizens of the World*, first published in 1829, African Americans publicly argued against colonization.

Similarly, the assumption that Garrison and his followers were the first to use harsh and militant language against slavery and colonization overlooks the many powerful antislavery arguments offered by African American reformers prior to Garrison's radical rhetoric. African American antislavery and anticolonization rhetoric of the late 1820s was strong, harshly critical of American society, and, in some cases, militant. An example from Walker's *Appeal* serves to illustrate this point: "The man who would not fight under our Lord and Master Jesus Christ, in the glorious and heavenly cause of freedom and of God—to be delivered from the most wretched, abject and servile slavery, that ever a people was afflicted with since the foundation of the world, to the present day—ought to be kept with all of his children or family, in slavery, or in chains, to be butchered by his *cruel enemies*" (*DWA*, 12).[7] This passage also demonstrates that the rhetoric of Garrison and his white colleagues did not constitute the first publicized appeals for immediate abolition. Throughout, Walker's *Appeal* suggests that if abolition is not effected immediately, slaves will, with the help of God, take violent action to gain their freedom. Although historians have often presented Walker's arguments as atypical of their time, Peter Hinks maintains that this perspective is inaccurate. Indeed, harsh rhetoric about God's vengeance for American slavery was offered by African American spokesmen as early as the late eighteenth century.[8]

Contrary to the usual assumption that Garrison and his white colleagues and followers "began" the militant phase of antislavery activity, white abolitionists were in fact influenced to shift their earlier views through their contact with African American abolitionists. African Americans in Baltimore, Philadelphia, and Boston—particularly David Walker—had a profound effect on Garrison. His sons, Wendell Phillips Garrison and Francis Jackson Garrison, proposed in their biography of their father that "some of [Garrison's] colored friends in Baltimore" convinced him to reject colonization.[9] To recover the voices of African American abolitionists, then, we must look beyond traditional chronological boundaries and historical accounts to explore the groundbreaking antislavery work of African American abolitionists in the late 1820s.

Traditional accounts of the unfolding of the abolitionist movement—the "transitional motifs" that White explains transform historical events into parts of a "process"—also limit our understanding of the abolitionist activity of African Americans and women.[10] Historians generally identify two issues that divided abolitionists and altered the course of the antislavery crusade. First, disagreements over the scope of the movement and what issues should be addressed split white reformers into two camps. Followers of Garrison were characterized by their opposition to voting and to all other political activities because of their view that society's institutions, including the government, had been corrupted by slavery's influence. This group associated slavery with a larger constellation of issues of oppression, eventually including the degradation of women. A second group, including such abolitionists as Lewis and Arthur Tappan, supported collective activity in the larger society, including working within institutional frameworks such as the church and, in some cases, political parties. This faction questioned the Garrisonians' incorporation of so-called "extraneous issues" such as women's rights in the antislavery platform. Although members of both factions worked together under the umbrella of the AASS during the 1830s, by 1840 the two wings could no longer coexist within one national organization, and the national society split, with the Garrisonians retaining control of the AASS and their opponents forming the American and Foreign Anti-Slavery Society (AFASS). Although the "woman question" in general and the election of Abby Kelley to the business committee in particular drove those who opposed Garrison to leave the AASS at the 1840 meeting and form the AFASS, this issue was only part of a multifaceted disagreement over the movement's goals and boundaries.

Another important "transitional motif" addressed by historians involves abolitionists' perspectives on violent antislavery action. Traditionally historians have looked at these changes in terms of the movement's white participants, emphasizing the ways in which events shifted their attitudes. They note that although antislavery thought of the 1830s and early 1840s was generally pacifist in nature, a shift subsequently occurred. Abolitionists began to doubt the efficacy of moral opposition to slavery alone and often became willing to embrace violent means to bring about abolition. Significant events changed this perspective, including the expansion of slavery through the 1845 annexation of Texas; violence in the mid-1850s in Kansas over whether slavery would be permitted in the territory; and the 1859 raid on the federal arsenal in Harpers Ferry, Virginia, by the radical white abolitionist John Brown, who proposed to arm slaves for insurrection. Finding themselves sympathetic with John Brown or enraged at the increasing power slavery wielded in the nation, some white abolitionists questioned their original reliance on peaceful or nonresistant means to their desired end.

The Fugitive Slave Law of 1850, legally binding Northerners to assist slaveholders in capturing fugitives, was considered a turning point by many white abolitionists. Ralph Waldo Emerson explained in speeches on the 1850 law that he had "lived all [his] life without suffering any known inconvenience from American slavery"—in fact, "it was like slavery in Africa or in Japan for [him]." This law, however, forced him to "hunt slaves" and made "citizens in Massachusetts willing to act as judges and captors." Slavery had become more "aggressive and dangerous," Emerson protested, making it his "duty"—and not an "option"—to exhort abolitionists to "defend the weak, and redress the injured."[11] White abolitionists found that they had to take a position on a question that, for the first time, directly involved them. By the late 1840s and the 1850s, even the stalwart pacifist Garrison and his fellow nonresistant Samuel May had developed complex responses that acknowledged the potential value of violence under certain circumstances.

These "transitional motifs," however, do not accurately reflect the experiences or convictions of abolitionists who were women or African Americans. The account of the tensions between the Garrisonians and their opponents over the range of the antislavery movement proves inadequate for an analysis of the work of those abolitionists who were outside of the white male leadership. For practical reasons, many abolitionists who were African American or female worked within one faction of the movement. Yet because these factions were controlled by white men, who formulated policy for the national antislavery organizations, white women and African American men and women were usually given a secondary role, and their concerns were often insufficiently represented. For example, the issue of whether other reforms should be included within the movement's scope had different connotations for African Americans and white women than for the white men who formulated antislavery goals. African American men who were involved with defining the abolitionist agenda necessarily took a concrete rather than an abstract perspective on the issue of the movement's scope. Because to African Americans the movement involved their own freedom and civil rights, they often perceived other reforms supported by the Garrisonians as distractions. Although many white Garrisonians also objected to the emphasis on what they perceived as secondary issues, for the most part they were willing to defer to Garrison's leadership. But African American male abolitionists became impatient with what they felt were obstacles to practical antislavery action. In 1855 Frederick Douglass criticized the Garrisonian-led AASS for denouncing the Constitution and the Union, which he maintained was unwise and inexpedient, putting obstacles in the way of emancipation (*FDP*, 3:43). Although he was a supporter of women's rights, Douglass disapproved of the introduction of the issue into the antislavery movement, remarking, "Thus was a grand Philanthropic movement rent asunder by a side issue, having nothing, whatever, to do with the great object which the American Anti-Slavery Society was organized to carry forward. . . . The battle of Woman's Rights should be fought on its own ground; as it is, the slave's cause, already too heavy laden, had to bear up under this new addition" (*FDP*, 3:39–40).[12]

Because they desired a more single-minded focus on abolition, many African American male abolitionists gravitated after the 1840 split in the AASS ranks to the alternative contingent, represented by the AFASS. This wing of the movement, however, was also problematic because of the racially exclusionary policies of various political parties this faction favored, such as the Liberty Party and the Free Soil Party. Although African Americans such as Henry Highland Garnet were involved with the organization of the Liberty Party, various issues demonstrated problematic tendencies to endorse racial separation. These included its failure to nominate African American candidates for public office; the vice-presidential nomination in 1844 of Thomas Morris, an opponent of African American suffrage; and the association with the Free Soil Party, which opposed only the expansion of slavery, but tolerated its presence in states where it already existed.[13]

Another traditional "transitional motif" involves the notion that the movement divided in 1840 primarily over whether women's participation should or should not be part of the abolitionist agenda. Although accurate in part, this perspective does not fully account for the complex experiences of abolitionist women. For both white and African American women, women's rights was not an abstract reform separate from their abolitionist work; their very participation in the movement was at stake in this debate. Although white male abolitionists might advise white women to address the cause of the slave before other issues, their white female colleagues found that they could not ignore the "woman question." Their public activism was itself an assertion of women's rights. Angelina Grimké informed Theodore Dwight Weld and John Greenleaf Whittier, "If we are to do any good in the Anti Slavery cause, our *right* to labor in it *must* be firmly established. . . . [W]e cannot push Abolitionism forward with all our might *until* we take up the stumbling block out of the road. . . . [H]ow can we expect to be able to hold meetings much longer when people are so diligently taught to *despise us* for thus stepping out of the sphere of woman!"[14]

Neither does the conventional formulation of the "woman question"—that women's rights represented a "separate" goal incorporated within the antislavery agenda—explain the particular experiences of African American women. White female abolitionists gave priority to questions of women's rights in order to defend their own public persuasion, but their perspectives often did not align with those of their African American female colleagues. Separating sexism from racism was (and remains) a fundamental philosophical problem for African American women because it negates the ways in which sexism and racism intersect in their lives. Scholars such as bell hooks, Paula Giddings, and Valerie Smith assert that sexism and racism are interrelated obstacles that African American women negotiate in their lives, and they reject many of the either/or choices posited by those who have focused solely on the experiences of white women. Antebellum African American women did not view the struggle for women's rights in the same way as their white counterparts. For them, it was fundamentally connected to the struggle for freedom and civil rights. As a result, they did not define women's roles in terms of the either/or choices formulated by white reformers. They did not perceive conflicts between domesticity and work outside the home, between femininity and community uplift, between religious ideals and activism. Thus, while white leaders and white women clashed over women's role in the abolition movement, African American female abolitionists charted their own course.[15]

One issue for African Americans, both male and female, that was not "extraneous" to the antislavery movement was the elimination of prejudice and segregation. Yet white abolitionists often failed to understand or to address their African American colleagues' concern with the problem of prejudice and their commitment to fighting it. White abolitionists often viewed the fight against slavery as separate from the elimination of prejudicial restrictions of northern society—and they perceived the abolition of slavery as the primary goal. African American activists, though, saw prejudice and slavery as inextricably linked and advocated measures to end prejudice as direct action against slavery. In an 1842 editorial, African American journalist Stephen Myers asserted that if white abolitionists would "break down prejudice . . . by taking our youth and instructing them" in trades, they would "make a powerful thrust at slavery." He criticized white abolitionists' unwillingness to address racism—including their own—as part of the antislavery movement. "Now we ask if the prejudice which exists at the north is not akin to the slavery of the south?" Myers demanded. "*We* firmly believe it to be so, and if the prejudice of the northern abolitionists will not permit them to take as apprentices colored boys . . . *we also believe* that the influence of their example is more injurious to colored people at large, than the disinclination of the slave holder to release the victims of his avarice."[16] Because their perspective on prejudice was not shared by white abolitionists, traditional historical accounts do not address these appeals for an end to prejudice and segregationist policies in the North. These arguments should be considered integral to—rather than separate from—the antislavery rhetoric of African American abolitionists.

The assumptions of historians regarding abolitionists' beliefs about the use of violence in the movement also require revision. The traditional notion of a shift following events of the 1840s and 1850s does not accurately reflect the perspectives of African American abolitionists. Although many African American abolitionists favored nonresistance in the 1830s, David Walker's *Appeal* and Nat Turner's slave revolt in Southampton County, Virginia, were precursors of later militant thought. A modification in the perspective of many African Americans began in the early 1840s, preceding the change in the white abolitionist community. The conventional focus on white abolitionists neglects the unique factors influencing this earlier shift, including increasing racial violence in northern cities, disillusionment among African Americans about the efficacy of moral suasion, and the influence of a new generation of African American leaders.

In addition, the African American response to the resistance of those who sought to recapture fugitive slaves differed significantly from the views of white abolitionists. Although they were disturbed and angered by the increasing national power of slavery solidified in the Fugitive Slave Law of 1850, it was not the first such statute to threaten African Americans in the North—and it was not the first time they were faced with the practical question of assistance to fugitives. The Fugitive Slave Law of 1793 had similarly interfered with their liberty, making slavery "aggressive and dangerous"—to use Emerson's words on the 1850 statute—to all African Americans. This earlier law proclaimed that a purported fugitive slave could be seized anywhere in the country without a warrant, presented to a judge, and—if it could "proved" that the person in question had escaped—taken into custody. The civil rights of all African Americans were threatened by such a law. Thus even during the 1830s, when most abolitionists supported nonviolent action, the question of resistance demanded a response from African Americans because, Carol Wilson notes, "concern for the safety of individuals in [their] community was perhaps more immediate" for them than for their white colleagues.[17]

African Americans generally agreed that they would disobey any fugitive slave law, but the question of physical resistance to slavecatchers drew debate, some arguing in theory that a nonviolent position must be maintained, others claiming that physical defiance was valid. Many African Americans, though, did not view support for nonresistance and the endorsement of potential violence as mutually exclusive. In their conception, the demand in certain situations for self-defense or militant action was not inconsistent with a general approbation of peaceful protest and Christian principles. Augustus William Hanson, an Episcopal clergyman of West African descent, wrote in a letter to Garrison, "I would under no circumstances exercise physical force to the infliction of injury upon any fellow being. [Yet] I do not believe that I should commit sin—that is transgress the law of God—by the exercise of the same physical powers merely to restrain that fellow being from inflicting an injury upon me." A committee of African American Philadelphians who met after the passage of the 1850 Fugitive Slave Law resolved that although they generally supported obedience to American laws, a militant response was demanded to a law "so repugnant to the highest attributes of God, justice and mercy." "We deem it our sacred duty," they asserted, "a duty that we owe to ourselves, our wives, our children . . . as well as to the panting fugitive from oppression, to resist this law at any cost and at all hazards."[18]

Various organizations worked to carry out this "sacred duty." Although some whites worked with African Americans through the Underground Railroad and vigilance committees in cities such as New York, Boston, and Detroit, the predominant support for the assistance of fugitives in the 1830s and 1840s was concentrated in the African American community.[19] For the most part, the support of white abolitionists emerged later; and, William and Jane Pease suggest, their views were molded by their African American precursors: "Blacks were major shapers of the policies and methods which after 1850 many white abolitionists accepted and made their own. Thus the pattern of black resistance to both fugitive slave laws [of 1793 and 1850] remained the same, although it intensified . . . with the passage of the 1850 law. By contrast, the basic form of opposition by whites changed sharply in 1850, following a path new to them, but blazed by blacks during the twenty years preceding."[20]

The leadership of African American abolitionists in organizations such as the vigilance committees suggests that we must look beyond organizations like the AASS or the AFASS to understand fully the work of marginalized abolitionists. Because antislavery societies dominated by white men did not always reflect their concerns, even those white women and African American men and women who were affiliated with these organizations often chose additional outlets for their antislavery activity. James McCune Smith told the 1855 gathering of the National Council of the Colored People at the First Colored Presbyterian Church in New York that they could not depend solely upon white organizations to address their goals: "Our people must assume the rank of a first-rate power in the battle against caste and Slavery . . . and with God's help we must fight it ourselves. Our relations to the Anti-Slavery movement must be and are changed. Instead of depending upon it, we must lead it."[21] African American organizations offered opportunities for such leadership.

In addition to their work to assist fugitives, African American abolitionists met separately from white leaders to debate such issues as the segregation of public transportation and education. Both white and African American women found that all-female antislavery societies—although they were often officially considered "auxiliary" to male organizations—allowed for female leadership and alternative perspectives on antislavery tactics. While abolitionists such as Garrison and his supporters and opponents debated what was relevant to the abolition movement and what was "extraneous," abolitionist women raised funds for schools and for the relief of poor African Americans in the North, and African American women petitioned in Boston against segregated schools.[22] Traditional historical perspectives of the abolition movement do not account for these avenues for leadership and activism.

In particular, historians have often excluded African American organizations from their accounts of abolition because many of these societies were not devoted exclusively to abolitionist activity, incorporating antislavery within an agenda that addressed issues of civil rights, prejudice, and self-help. For African American abolitionists, these issues were fundamentally connected to abolition. C. Peter Ripley et al. propose that we cannot search for African American abolition solely in organizations explicitly devoted to the cause: "Black abolitionism possessed a seamless quality, fusing a variety of concerns, which gave the movement a practical and intellectual continuity that few white reformers appreciated. A black temperance gathering could adjourn and immediately reconvene as an antislavery meeting with no change in tenor or participants. . . . A black vigilance committee, while aiding fugitive slaves, could also organize a petition campaign for black voting rights. The range and continuity of these activities helped broaden the meaning of black abolitionism to include much of northern black life, institutions, and culture."[23] To consider African American abolition effectively on its own terms, we need to expand our historical framework to include such contexts.

In particular, "self-help" or "racial uplift"—moral advancement through education, economic self-sufficiency, and religious commitment—was, in many cases, part of the antislavery agenda of African American abolitionists. Self-help, African American activists maintained, was a weapon in the fight against slavery. Samuel Cornish warned free African Americans in an 1837 editorial in the *Colored American,*

> Should we prove unworthy [of] our few privileges, we shall furnish our enemies the strongest arguments, with which to oppose the emancipation of the slave. . . .
>
> On the other hand, should we establish for ourselves a character—should we as a people, become more religious and moral, more industrious and prudent, than other classes of community, it will be impossible to keep us down. . . .
>
> . . . We owe it to ourselves and we owe it to the poor slaves, who are our brethren.
>
> On *our* conduct, in a great measure, *their* salvation depends.[24]

Similarly, in his 1855 autobiography, *My Bondage and My Freedom,* Frederick Douglass directly connects the moral elevation of free people of color in the North to the fight against slavery, noting that "one of the best means of emancipating the slaves of the south is to improve and elevate the character of the free colored people of the north" (*MB,* 398).

Although, as Douglass's and Cornish's remarks demonstrate, advocacy of moral reform is often a component of antislavery rhetoric, historians often overlook the significance of self-help rhetoric for African American abolitionists. Historical accounts frequently separate self-help rhetoric from explicitly antislavery discourse, proposing that antebellum African American leaders chose *either* to highlight individual moral regeneration and assimilation to the values of white America *or* to support action, resistance, and even militancy in the fight against slavery. Scholars have often separated the self-help rhetoric of antebellum African American leaders from abolitionist texts and represented it as individualistic, primarily focused on self-improvement or the quest to emulate white Americans rather than on social activism.[25] An alternative history of the abolition movement that considers African American abolition on its own terms must resist this false dilemma and explore how self-help rhetoric can function as strong, even militant abolitionist persuasion.

For a variety of reasons, then, traditional histories of the abolition movement do not provide an adequate framework for understanding the contributions of the abolitionists I feature in this study. Without a clear understanding of the unique experiences, goals, and priorities of abolitionists who were African American or female, we lack the context for understanding their antislavery rhetoric. These rhetors faced particular constraints—imposed both by society at large and by other abolitionists—yet they negotiated these restrictions, resisted limiting assumptions, and offered powerful arguments against slavery. Their experiences must be fully explored to evaluate their rhetoric. Such an examination must take into account the position of these rhetors within the abolition movement and within society; their unique perspectives on gender, race, slavery, freedom, and reform; the rhetorical restrictions they faced due to the expectations and prejudices of audiences and abolitionist leaders; and the traditional and alternative channels through which they chose to persuade.

"TO PLEAD OUR OWN CAUSE":
AFRICAN AMERICAN MALE ABOLITIONISTS

In antebellum society, among both southern supporters of slavery and many northern whites, prejudices against people of African descent were bolstered by racial theories grounded in religion and science.[26] The religious justification for a belief in racial hierarchy rested on interpretations of various Old Testament passages. Those of African descent were the "seed of Cain," it was argued, and thus were "cursed." Josiah Priest described this theory in his 1851 *Bible Defence of Slavery:* "[Some] have imagined, that the mark set upon *Cain* by the Divine Power, for the crime of *homicide,* was that of *jet,* which not only changed the color of his body, but extended to the blood and the whole of his physical being, thus originating the negro race." An alternate—and more commonly cited—biblical argument involved Noah's curse on Canaan, the descendents of his son Ham (Gen. 9: 22–27), whom proslavery writers maintained were Africans. Louisiana physician Samuel Cartwright, for example, argued in 1843 that the biblical descriptions of Canaan in the Hebrew matched the physical and mental characteristics of Africans. Thus those of African descent, the argument held, were cursed to serve the whites, the progeny of Ham's brother Japheth.[27] Although not all Old Testament social conventions—such as the sanctioning of polygamy—were considered binding, antebellum apologists for slavery claimed that slavery differed from these practices. Slavery was not outlawed by the New Testament, they asserted, because Jesus did not condemn it and because the epistles mention slavery—such as in Paul's letter to Philemon—without forbidding the practice.[28]

These religious justifications of racist views coexisted—and, in some cases, were combined—with antebellum scientific thinking. Enlightenment philosophers had proposed that those of African descent were fundamentally different from—and inferior to—whites. This view was expressed by Thomas Jefferson in his *Notes on the State of Virginia,* first published in 1787, which draws particular attention to physical distinctions. Jefferson and nineteenth-century proslavery writers such as Cartwright, George Fitzhugh, Josiah Nott, and Thomas Dew maintained that those of African descent were intellectually inferior to whites in reason, imagination, and creativity; less susceptible to deep emotions—such as grief or love for others—than whites; innately lazy, stubborn, and intemperate; and ruled by sensuality.[29] By the mid-nineteenth century, anthropological and "scientific" claims were marshaled to support these contentions. Ostensibly basing his conclusions on ethnology, Cartwright argued that the physical features of those of African descent proved that they were animalistic, unreflective, endowed with "servile mind[s]," and "unable to provide for and take care of [themselves]."

Thus slavery was "necessary," he and other proslavery rhetors proposed, to "elevate" or to "protect" those of African descent. "The compulsive hand of arbitrary power," Cartwright asserted, was requisite to allow them to "lead a life of industry, temperance, and order." By the 1860s, Darwinism was combined with theories of inferiority to support the institution of slavery. Because of their purported weakness, Fitzhugh argued, the "weaker" Africans would be "displaced and exterminated by the stronger and more hardy" without the "protection" provided by slavery.[30]

These prejudices affected the lives of all African Americans, slave and free. Many free African Americans refused to remain silent and allow their humanity and destiny to be defined by this oppressive discourse. Early in 1827, free African Americans in New York met to create a forum that would allow them to dicuss slavery, colonization, and other issues on their own terms. The result was *Freedom's Journal,* the first African American newspaper, which began publication on March 16, 1827; Samuel Cornish, a minister who had organized the First Colored Presbyterian Church in Manhattan in 1821, and John Russwurm, one of the first African American college graduates, were chosen by the group to edit the paper. Outlining the "motives" underlying their endeavor in their lead editorial, "To Our Patrons," Cornish and Russwurm highlight the ways in which free African Americans are marginalized, particularly because others presume to speak for them, frequently in ways that demean them. Their newspaper, they assert, will help African Americans resist others' definitions of them and voice their own concerns:

> We wish to plead our own cause. Too long have others spoken for us. Too long has the publick been deceived by misrepresentations, in things which concern us dearly. . . .
>
> . . . Is it not very desirable that [our friends] should know more of our actual condition, and of our efforts and feelings, that in forming or advocating plans for our amelioration, they may do it more understandingly?[31]

Because of the many public debates concerning issues of importance to them, the editors declare that the time is right for their project. *Freedom's Journal* would bring the rhetoric of African Americans to both white and African American readers.[32]

Cornish and Russwurm admit in their opening editorial to "feel[ing] all the diffidence of persons entering upon a new and untried line of business." They faced difficulty, however, not merely because their endeavor was unprecedented. The force of prejudice in the North during the 1820s and 1830s was strong, leading to rising violence against African Americans, a restriction of their civil rights in various states, and their exclusion from many public institutions. The popularity of the colonization movement suggested that the "solution" to the problem of prejudice was not to eliminate white misconceptions, but to remove African Americans from the country. Cornish and Russwurm aptly note that prejudice rendered them marginalized not only in society as a whole, but also within the community of whites presumably sympathetic to their concerns: "Our friends, to whom we concede all the principles of humanity and religion . . . seem to have fallen into the current of popular feeling and are imperceptibly floating on the stream—actually living in the practice of prejudice, while they abjure it in theory, and feel it not in their hearts." Yet *Freedom's Journal* gave African Americans a voice to participate in debates about issues that affected them and the agency to offer alternatives to others' perceptions. For two years the paper provided a forum for African Americans to "plead their own cause" to a wide audience throughout the United States, particularly in the North but also in some southern cities, as well as in Haiti, Canada, and England.[33]

Articles critical of slavery appeared in *Freedom's Journal,* but its columns were open to discussion of a variety of other subjects, including education, civil rights, and religion. This multifaceted approach fit with the aims of the abolition movement in the African American community. Free African Americans perceived many goals as integral to the antislavery effort, including promoting temperance, economy, and educational improvement; opposing colonization; affirming the citizenship of African Americans in American society; and fighting segregation and other barriers to economic and social equality. Thus many African American community organizations in the North, such as churches and literary societies, were perceived as part of the antislavery effort.[34] The MGCA, for example, was devoted to the twin goals of opposing slavery and fighting segregation in the North.

Although African American men also participated with white reformers in antislavery societies such as the AASS during the 1830s, their agency was often limited within the white-dominated movement. African American abolitionists found that their white colleagues were often influenced by traditional prejudices about race and were hesitant to grant them leadership.[35] In spite of the theoretical commitment to equality for African Americans shared by both of the major abolitionist camps, many white antebellum reformers believed in fundamental racial differences, often holding a view that George Frederickson calls "romantic racialism," which proposed that African Americans were more "innocent," "childlike," and innately religious than whites.[36] This view led to paternalistic and condescending treatment of African American abolitionists by their white colleagues. Often, too, white male abolitionists succumbed to their racial anxieties, restricting their contact with African Americans or excluding them from social or professional situations.

William J. Watkins relates a telling experience in an 1854 editorial in *Frederick Douglass' Paper.* After applying for an advertised job as a clerk, Watkins found that the employer's professed abolitionist principles were entirely abstract:

> I was recommended to the advertiser . . . and was told he was a good Abolitionist. I went into his countinghouse. . . . I made known my business. He looked at me and laughed, and virtually informed me I had mistaken my vocation. I told him I approached him as a friend, and that I took him

to be an Abolitionist. . . . He was the victim of an exigency he did not anticipate. He tested my ability, and . . . he frankly replied, your COLOR IS THE ONLY OBJECTION. He told me the *time had not come yet* for colored men to apply for such situations; the prejudice against them precluded the possibility of success. But, said I, do you not cater to this wicked prejudice, when you "thrust me out on account of my complexion?" He sympathized with me, and was willing to do anything else for me in his power. I left him, having formed a rather unfavorable opinion of *his* Abolitionism.

Prejudice could not be conquered, Watkins asserted, if abolitionists "lack[ed] the moral courage to *actualize* their ideas" and to "live out practically the doctrines they so faithfully promulgate."[37]

As Watkins's comments suggest, African American men did not let this treatment go unchallenged. They frequently voiced their concerns about the effects of prejudice on the abolition movement, stressing that African Americans' full participation in organizations like the AASS could not be achieved as long as racism was present. In 1836, Presbyterian clergyman Theodore Wright challenged members of the New York State Anti-Slavery Society—in a roundabout way—to examine the way their prejudices hindered true cooperative effort: "Let me . . . request this delegation, to take hold of this subject [of prejudice]. This will silence the slaveholder, when he says, where is your love for the slave? Where is your love for the colored man who is crushed at your feet? Talking to us about emancipating our slaves when you are enslaving them by your feelings, and doing more violence to them by your prejudice, than we are to the slaves by our treatment!" Publisher Benjamin Roberts put the matter more bluntly in an 1838 letter to white abolitionist Amos Phelps, an agent of the Massachusetts Anti-Slavery Society: "I am aware that there has been and *now is,* a combined effort on the part of certain *professed* abolitionists to muzzle, exterminate and put down the efforts of certain colored individuals effecting [*sic*] the welfare of their colored brethren. . . . I was not aware that so many hypocrites existed in the [Massachusetts] Anti slavery society. According to what I have seen of the conduct of some, a black man would be as unsafe in their hands as in those of Southern slaveholders."[38]

As Wright's and Roberts's comments imply, prejudice affected both the attitudes of white abolitionists toward biracial membership in antislavery societies and the roles given to African American abolitionists within these organizations. White abolitionists felt ambivalent about their African American colleagues, accepting their participation with what the Peases call a "patronizing tolerance." Their attitude is aptly illustrated by Lydia Maria Child's 1836 condescension: "It is true that a very small number of intelligent colored people do belong to our societies. The very circumstance of their feeling an interest in their degraded brethren is an indication of moral worth. When such men and women ask to give a portion of their hard earnings to a righteous cause, who could justify us in refusing their offer?" Benjamin Quarles notes that in speaking of their "above-average" African American colleagues, white abolitionists lavished praise "as if in surprise that [they] revealed any ability at all." In a letter to her sister Deborah, Anne Warren Weston suggested that abolitionist Charles Lenox Remond's "high breeding" was exceptional in comparison to the presumably more typical demeanor of his sister Sarah Parker Remond: "Miss R on the contrary has many of the manners & ways supposed to be peculiar to her race."[39]

Given such views, it is not surprising that the African American male members of antislavery societies such as the AASS seldom were granted leadership or decision-making roles. White abolitionists expected African Americans to defer to their policy decisions. Such preconceptions are aptly illustrated in the employment of African American workers in the antislavery societies. Assigned subordinate roles, they were appointed office assistants rather than managers, excluded from editorships of the newspapers of the antislavery societies, and overlooked as speakers for certain important lecture series. In 1855, James McCune Smith expressed anger in a letter to *Frederick Douglass' Paper* over the treatment of African American and white agents for the *Liberator*—those assigned to promote and circulate the paper. In the early days of the periodical, Smith relates, "five-sixths of the most active agents . . . were colored men." Yet in 1835, after the paper had become more established and successful, white abolitionists were appointed as agents—and, unlike the early African American agents, were compensated. "Where are the colored gentlemen agents now?" Smith demanded. "Out of the forty who had stood by the *Liberator* and upheld it in the day of its struggling adversity, was there no one fit for the office of agent when that office *paid*? There were dozens, but they were passed over whenever money began to flow in, and white men placed in their stead; and this course of conduct . . . has ever marked the subsequent history of the 'host.'"[40]

Although white abolitionists did not always treat their African American colleagues as equals within the movement, they realized the value of African American antislavery rhetors to the cause. By the late 1830s, the AASS began to hire African Americans as "agents"—part of the society's team of public speakers who lectured publicly on organized tours. John Collins, agent for the Massachusetts Anti-Slavery Society, wrote to Garrison in 1842, "The public have itching ears to hear a colored man speak, and particularly *a slave*. Multitudes will flock to hear one of his class speak. . . . It would be a good policy to employ a number of colored agents, if suitable ones can be found."[41] Former slaves joined the ranks of the antislavery agents by the mid-1840s, offering their experiences as direct testimony of the evils of slavery.

As Collins had predicted, these orators were popular. However, as John Sekora remarks, the significance of Collins's adjective "suitable" should not be overlooked. White male abolitionists and white antebellum audiences had particular expectations for these orators, and they were often treated accordingly. Organizers of lecture tours, for example, gave African American agents much less freedom than their white counterparts. In his discussion of Douglass, Sekora lists revealing discrepancies in the treatment of antislavery agents:

> Black anti-slavery agents did not receive as much pay as white, and Douglass was rebuffed when he asked . . . for equality of salary or conditions. White speakers generally rode to the lectures; Douglass walked. White speakers carried the money from sales and contributions; Douglass could not. White speakers would introduce themselves; Douglass could not. . . . White speakers would themselves determine the content of their addresses; Douglass could not. White speakers had arrangements made for their lodging; Douglass made his own. . . . [AASS secretary Maria Weston Chapman] believed she was applying the lessons of the British anti-slavery societies. . . . They kept black spokesmen on a very short leash. . . . As policy Chapman ordained that black agents not have money to carry, preferring to send salaries home to their wives and to arrange always for a white agent to hold the funds for the journey.[42]

White abolitionists and audiences also held expectations about the rhetoric of African American abolitionists. African American orators were not supposed to offer independent arguments against slavery; their race itself—and, in some cases, their status as former slaves—was the draw for audiences. In *My Bondage and My Freedom,* Douglass recalls that in his early years as an antislavery orator, both audiences and white speakers with whom he shared the platform downplayed his words, suggesting that his presence on the platform constituted his argument against slavery:

> I was a "graduate from the peculiar institution," Mr. Collins used to say, when introducing me, *"with my diploma written on my back!"* . . .
> . . . Many came, no doubt, from curiosity to hear what a negro could say in his own cause. I was generally introduced as a *"chattel"*—a *"thing"*—a piece of southern *"property"*—the chairman assuring the audience that *it* could speak. (*MB,* 365–66)

White audiences and abolitionists, Douglass indicates, saw African American rhetors as secondary to white orators: "Mr. Garrison followed me, taking me as his text; and now, whether I had made an eloquent speech in behalf of freedom or not, his was one never to be forgotten by those who heard it" (*MB,* 364–65). The African American abolitionist was supposed to *be*—rather than to *create*—a "text" that would be analyzed and debated by white rhetors.

White abolitionists' and audiences' patronizing assumptions influenced both the presentation and content of African American abolitionists' speeches. In *My Bondage and My Freedom,* Douglass recalls that leaders suggested that his polished speech might lead audiences to doubt he had been a slave. Douglass relates that he was advised that his audiences would be suspicious if he seemed too eloquent: "'People won't believe you ever was a slave, Frederick, if you keep on this way,' said [white lecturer George] Foster. . . . It was said to me, 'Better have a *little* of the plantation manner of speech than not; 'tis not best that you seem too learned'" (*MB*, 367). It would seem that Foster's point reflected a significant bias on the part of white auditors; by 1844, many observers *were* skeptical that he had ever been a slave.[43] Appearing too educated aroused hostility among audiences as well. As Douglass told an English audience in 1847, "The hatred of the American [is] especially roused against the intellectual coloured man. When he is degraded, they can bear with him; he is in the condition which they think natural to him; but if he is intelligent and moral . . . an American would not tolerate him" (*FDP*, 2:5). The African American abolitionist John Swett Rock confirmed this assessment, remarking that educated African Americans "suffer[ed] the more keenly" for their talents, fostering "the embittered prejudices of the whites."[44]

White abolitionists suggested that African American orators yield to such expectations, offering only facts and avoiding analysis. Douglass describes such advice:

> "Let us have the facts," said the people. . . . "Give us the facts," said Collins, "we will take care of the philosophy." Just here arose some embarrassment. It was impossible for me to repeat the same old story month after month, and to keep up my interest in it. . . . I was now reading and thinking. New views of the subject were presented to my mind. It did not entirely satisfy me to *narrate* wrongs; I felt like *denouncing* them. I could not always curb my moral indignation for the perpetrators of slaveholding villainy, long enough for a circumstantial statement of the facts which I felt almost everybody must know. (*MB*, 367)

John Blassingame and Gregory Lampe argue that Douglass did not restrict his remarks to personal testimony even in his early speeches. In addition, Douglass was selective in what he revealed, often emphasizing his experiences after his escape rather than details of his slave life that might lead to his recapture. Yet audiences, Blassingame notes, wanted and expected to hear about the personal experiences of Douglass and other former slaves. This presumption conforms to the stereotypical notion held by many white Americans at the time that people of African descent were not capable of abstract reasoning, a perspective voiced by Jefferson in *Notes on the State of Virginia*, in which he declares, "I think one could scarcely be found capable of tracing and comprehending the investigations of Euclid."[45]

Although they were tolerated in this limited speaking role, African American abolitionists who wished to persuade through writing were often discouraged. According to William Andrews, Frederick Douglass suspected the reason for such attitudes: "The very idea that blacks should confine themselves to the role of speaker in the movement smacked of a certain patronizing attitude among whites, if not an assumption that blacks were somehow constitutionally better suited to speak than to write." But white abolitionists were compelled to acknowledge the popularity of slave narratives and to incorporate such narratives into their publishing agendas. This "sponsorship," however, included tight control; white abolitionists often edited slave narratives and included letters verifying the authors' identity. Given the skepticism such texts would engender, white sponsors suggested that slave narrators also avoid "philosophy" and stick to verifiable facts and objective testimony. This requirement led slave narrators to offer self-conscious statements explaining that they would merely narrate rather than persuade. In the introduction to his 1842 narrative, former slave Lunsford Lane declares, "I have not, in this publication attempted or desired to argue anything. It is only a simple narration of such facts . . . as I thought would be most interesting and instructive to readers generally." Elizur Wright's review of Charles Ball's 1836 narrative similarly highlights the objective nature of the text: "If it is a mirror, it is of the very best plate glass, in which objects appear so clear and 'natural' that the beholder is perpetually mistaking it for an open window without any glass at all. . . . Though it comments with just severity upon some of the atrocities of slavery, it broaches no theory in regard to it."[46] Writers of slave narratives who wished to offer arguments in addition to facts had to be particularly creative in negotiating the tensions posed by white expectations.

As Douglass suggests in his comment that he soon tired of offering only "facts" rather than "arguments," African American abolitionists were often irritated by the restrictions placed on them by their white colleagues. Many continued to work with white abolitionists, but by the 1840s they frequently began to seek more independence and to create additional outlets for their activism in which they could assume more agency. Thus African American activists often worked within primarily African American organizations as well as in the larger white-dominated movement. In effect, they argued within a white public sphere as well as in the black public sphere or counterpublic described by Baker and Dawson.[47] In addition, the revival of a strong African American press became a priority in the late 1830s and 1840s. After the demise of *Freedom's Journal,* African Americans had thrown their support behind white-run periodicals such as the *Liberator.* They were discouraged by white abolitionists from establishing other papers that would presumably stretch the financial resources of the movement. But in 1837, Samuel Cornish took over the two-month-old *Weekly Advocate,* renamed it the *Colored American,* and proclaimed—as he and John Russwurm had in 1827—that African Americans needed a forum in which they could speak for themselves. In his editorial "Why We Should Have a Paper," he argues, "Colored men must do something . . . they must establish and maintain the PRESS, and through it speak out in THUNDER TONES."[48]

White abolitionists often were angered when African Americans asserted their independence. In an 1855 letter to Frederick Douglass, African American clergyman and abolitionist Jermain Wesley Loguen disclosed how many "willing to work in the name of the slave" refused to accept self-determination on the part of their African American colleagues: "The colored man is 'all right'; he is a "good *nigger*" so long as he will worship at their shrine . . . but let him only presume to think and act for himself, like an independent and accountable being . . . and he is no longer a 'good *nigger*'!"[49] Douglass's own experiences had already demonstrated the unfortunate truth of Loguen's assessment. In 1847, Douglass decided—against the wishes of Garrison and his supporters—to publish an anti-slavery newspaper, the *North Star.* Garrisonians were concerned that the paper would compete with established organs such as the *Liberator,* but, more significantly, Douglass's decision to establish independence from white control created a deep tension with the Garrisonians. In *My Bondage and My Freedom,* Douglass recalls the reasons given to discourage him from his plan: "First, the paper was not needed; secondly, it would interfere with my *usefulness* as a lecturer; thirdly, I was *better fitted* to speak than to write; fourthly, the paper could not succeed" (*MB,* 389–90; emphasis added). These hints that Douglass defer to white leadership rather than presume to define his own agenda were echoed in Wendell Phillips's comment to Samuel May: "Douglass ought to speak to his race thro' our columns & use his mighty voice to get circulation for the National organ [the *Liberator*]."[50]

But white abolitionists' presumptions did not curb independent African American activism such as the establishment of periodicals. In spite of white opposition to the *North Star,* Douglass asserted, as had his predecessors Russwurm and Cornish, that African Americans needed a forum in which they could establish their concerns in print. He did not, he assured readers, begin the *North Star* because he felt "distrust" of white abolitionists or doubted their "zeal, integrity or ability." Yet African Americans needed a periodical that they controlled that reflected their particular perspectives: "Such a Journal . . . would do a most important and indispensable work, which it would be wholly impossible for our white friends to do for us." "The man who has *suffered the wrong* is the man to *demand redress,"* he maintained; "we must be our own representatives and advocates, not exclusively, but peculiarly—not distinct from, but in connection with our white friends."[51] In the columns of the *North Star* and its successors *Frederick Douglass' Paper,* published from 1851 to 1860, and *Douglass' Monthly,* published from 1858 to 1863, African Americans could be their "own representatives and advocates."[52] Continually asserting their right to speak throughout the decades from the late 1820s to the early 1860s, African American men negotiated the obstacles facing them as rhetors and refused to remain silent. "Too long have others spoken for us," Cornish and Russwurm maintain in their first editorial in *Freedom's Journal,* and the African American male abolitionists that followed them agreed. To "plead their own cause," they assumed editorships; mounted the platform; and published tracts, narratives, and articles in antislavery periodicals. Confronting restrictions that threatened to silence them, they took agency and created powerful arguments.

"TRUE WOMANHOOD," REFORM, AND RHETORIC: WHITE WOMEN AND ABOLITIONIST WORK

For both white and African American women, conventional antebellum ideals of womanhood presented obstacles to public participation in reform movements. Yet these restrictions differed greatly due to the ways race and gender intersected uniquely for the women in each group. Particular ideals of femininity and women's proper role in society were influential among white antebellum Americans, and these conceptions of womanhood affected white women's work for reform. Historians and scholars of gender have frequently articulated the influence of antebellum femininity—often described in terms of the so-called "Cult of True Womanhood"—on white women's lives.[53] Although, as scholars have noted, the day-to-day experiences of most antebellum women did not match this ideal,[54] gendered rhetoric of early nineteenth-century America influenced social expectations of white women's behavior.

The rhetoric of "woman's sphere" posited that God-given male and female roles placed men and women in different—and separate—realms. This rhetoric sharply divided the home and the larger world, the former a "sanctuary" that counteracted the hardships and adversity of the latter. A woman's place was in the home, and her responsibility was to render it a haven for male family members who ventured into the realm beyond. "M. A. H." assures men in a contribution to the 1833 *Ladies' Magazine and Literary Gazette,* "Our sphere is far removed from scenes of contending ambition, and we would never willingly relinquish the peaceful serenity of domestic life for the turbulent arena of political emulation. It is alike our duty and our happiness to . . . cast around your homes a halo of affection, whose holy light shall make you forget the trials and perplexities which often darken your course."[55]

The woman who would create such an ideal home is described in "On the Duties of Wives," published in the 1806 *Christian Monitor:* "The wife, then, should be faithful and constant, humble and obedient, prudent and discreet, tender and kind, affectionate and pious." An article published thirty years later in the popular women's periodical *Godey's Lady's Book* advises that all women should cultivate "sincerity, discretion, a well-governed temper, forgetfulness of self, charitable allowance for the frailty of human nature." The requisite qualities included submission to husbands, as the author of "On the Duties of Wives" remarks, which was enjoined both by the dictates of "reason" and "religion." Because of their influence in the redemptive realm of home and family, the discourse of domesticity suggested that the "True Woman" was morally superior to men. *Godey's Lady's Book* notes, "Woman is of a texture much finer than man: all her soul is a melody of love, sweet, profound, lasting. Woman is a ray created by God to illumine the obscure and rough shades of this world." This rhetoric posited that women could "redeem" men by exerting their moral authority, an influence that men would not resist. A wife, John Bolles comments, "has access to her husband when his feelings and affections are melted and softened into unusual plasticity—and are ready, from her kind hand, to receive their form and pressure." By providing "aid and counsel" when her husband is prey to "ambition" or "interest," Bolles adds, a wife could remind her husband of "the voice of conscience."[56]

Because the ideal woman was submissive, noncompetitive, modest, and unassuming, she was unsuited for the world outside the home—the world of politics and business, where competition, confidence, and aggression were needed. Contributor "G." to the *Ladies' Magazine and Literary Gazette* declares, "It is impossible not to see that the two sexes are called to occupy very different stations. Men are destined to the public stage; women to domestic life." "True Women" should be educated—even in such seemingly masculine subjects as civics and history—so that they could be fit wives and mothers, but such training recognized the conventional boundaries between the home and the outside world. As "G." reminds female readers, "It is not the learning which makes the woman unlovely, but the affectation which accompanies it. Remember your duties; remember your stations, and you may be as learned as you please."[57]

Public argument, thus, was removed from proper female behavior. Catharine Beecher, the influential writer of domestic and educational manuals, maintains in her 1837 *Essay on Slavery and Abolitionism, with Reference to the Duty of American Females* that although "a man may act on society by the collision of intellect, in public debate," the public sphere must be eschewed by women, because "whatever, in any measure, throws a woman into the attitude of a combatant, either for herself or others . . . throws her out of her appropriate sphere." Woman's influence on the views of others should be indirect, embodied in her behavior and moral qualities rather than in any rhetorical activity. *Godey's Lady's Book* advises that a woman instructs more effectively through "examples" than "either precept or admonitions." In the *Ladies' Magazine and Literary Gazette,* "G." counsels, "Men must force their way by resolution and activity; women win most by modesty and retirement." Instead of participating in rhetorical exchanges, in which opposing sides are advocated, women were expected to mediate debates. For a woman, "political preferences" should be irrelevant to social intercourse, implies the author of "The Women of '76," an essay in *Godey's Lady's Book:* "Women, even in ordinary times, [are] the messengers of peace between those who might otherwise be estranged; and bitter days must those be when these gentle mediators are unable to preserve the courtesies, if not the spirit of peace, between men of different parties."[58]

Antebellum religious ideology further limited women's rhetorical activity. Religious leaders cited both Old and New Testament passages to elucidate the proper relation of women to men, the exclusion of women from positions of religious authority and from public roles in society, and the restriction of women's duties to the domestic sphere. Because the prevailing antebellum view of biblical authority posited that the Bible was literally correct and unambiguous,[59] scriptural passages about women had considerable authority. Commentators refer to Gen. 2:18–3:24, which relates the creation of Eve from one of Adam's ribs; describes her as Adam's "help meet"; and chronicles her temptation, sin, and punishment by God. The author of "On the Duties of Wives" advises women to heed God's dictate to Eve in Gen. 3:16: "Obedience of wives is the commandment of God himself; 'thy desire shall be to thy husband,' says he; 'he shall rule over thee.'" This relation of husband and wife is, by extension, the model for the relation of men and women in society. Because of the "natural superiority of man," obedience in the home must be combined with "quietness and HUMILITY" in the public sphere: "The virtues of a woman were not meant to glare in the dazzling lustre of publick business."[60]

Two Pauline passages reiterate the dictates of Genesis and explicitly connect them to the exclusion of women from preaching and public speaking:

> Let your women keep silence in the churches: for it is not permitted unto them to speak; but they are commanded to be under obedience, as also saith the law. And if they will learn any thing, let them ask their husbands at home: for it is a shame for women to speak in the church. (1 Cor. 14:34–35)

> Let the woman learn in silence with all subjection. But I suffer not a woman to teach, nor to usurp authority over the man, but to be in silence. For Adam was first formed, then Eve. And Adam was not deceived, but the woman being deceived was in the transgression. (1 Tim. 2:11–14)[61]

Antebellum religious commentators stress women's silence in these passages. Citing Paul's advice to women in 1 Timothy, the author of "On the Duties of Wives" asserts that a wife should remember that "silence indeed is for the most part apter to persuade than argument" and should "compl[y] with [her husband's] will."[62]

The requirement that women remain silent, antebellum commentators assert, extends beyond the private sphere. In an 1817 sermon to the Female Missionary Society for the Poor in New York, Matthew La Rue Perrine explains, "In [1 Tim. 2.11–14], the apostle refers to the original design and order of creation, as exhibiting the proper station and duties of women under the gospel. . . . It is very evident that women are not required to perform the office of public teachers . . . or to dictate in matters of faith and discipline. These, [Paul] clearly teaches." Disavowing public authority, the Christian woman was to avoid rhetorical activity. In his 1857 advice manual, *The True Woman,* Jesse Peck advises, "Woman is not the legislator, the business officer, the preacher, the pastor, the leader of the Church. There are, doubtless, questions in relation to which she is to 'keep silence in the Churches.'" This silence is not confined to religious settings, Peck maintains, but extends to all of the public sphere: "We grant that she can overcome [her instincts], that she can unsex and uncreate herself; that she can adjust her outward mien, her stern volitions, and even her feelings, to the rude indecorum of a public assembly, and affect the orator. . . . She can, but she should not."[63]

Traditional antebellum notions of gender, then, conflicted with women's organized reform activity and limited women's influence for societal reform to their homes. In particular, "True Women" should avoid public persuasion. Sarah Jane Hale maintains in her essay "Ought Ladies to Form Peace Societies?" in *Godey's Lady's Book,* "We deem it better that woman should study the things which make for peace at home, rather than devote her thoughts to the dissemination of peace principles abroad."[64] A woman might have antislavery sentiments—after all, the "Cult of True Womanhood" suggested that women's "moral superiority" would cause her to sympathize with the plight of others and wish to take a position on moral issues—but public abolitionist activity was not acceptable. If an antislavery woman was a "True Woman," she would confine her efforts to the private domestic sphere.

This position was championed by Catharine Beecher in her *Essay on Slavery and Abolitionism*. Writing in response to Angelina Grimké's *Appeal to the Christian Women of the South* and Grimké's plans to lecture in the North, Beecher applies her notions of the appropriate female role to the subject of abolitionist activity. She argues that a proper conception of womanhood is "entirely opposed to the plan of arraying females in any Abolition movement" for a variety of reasons: "because it enlists them in an effort to coerce the South . . . because it brings them forward as partisans in a conflict that has been begun and carried forward by measures that are any thing rather than peaceful in their tendencies . . . because it leads them into the arena of political collision, not as peaceful mediators to hush the opposing elements, but as combatants to cheer up and carry forward the measures of strife."[65]

Counseling women to remain in the private sphere, Beecher proposes that they can indirectly affect antislavery efforts in the public realm through their influence on male family members. If a woman wishes to be "a suppliant for a portion of her sex who are bound in cruel bondage," she must try to induce the men in her domestic sphere to "urge forward a public measure." Even this effort, however, should not be directly argumentative: "Woman is to win every thing by peace and love; by making herself so much respected, esteemed and loved, that to yield to her opinions and to gratify her wishes, will be the free-will offering of the heart. But this is to be all accomplished in the domestic and social circle. There let every woman become so cultivated and refined in intellect, that her taste and judgment will be respected . . . then, the fathers, the husbands, and the sons, will find an influence thrown around them, to which they will yield not only willingly but proudly." A woman may "quietly [hold] her own opinions," Beecher acknowledges, even "calmly avowing them, when conscience and integrity make the duty imperative"; but she must not assume "the attitude of a partisan." Instead, as a "mediator," setting an example of "candour, forbearance, charity, and peace" and bringing particular "topics" to "the attention of [her] friends," a woman could "exert a wise and appropriate influence, and one which will most certainly tend to bring to an end, not only slavery, but unnumbered other evils." Similarly, the Congregational Ministers of the General Association of Massachusetts responded to the Grimké sisters' 1837 New England lecture tour by issuing a "Pastoral Letter"—which was read in churches and published in the July 12, 1837, issue of the *New England Spectator*—condemning women's public persuasion as antithetical to Christianity. "The appropriate duties and influence of women are clearly stated in the New Testament," the letter advises, remarking that if a woman becomes a "public reformer," she disregards the dependent role God has assigned her and "her character becomes unnatural."[66]

Naturally, many white female abolitionists wished to work in a larger realm than Beecher and male religious authorities sanctioned. Yet assumptions about women's public activism and persuasion affected not only the audiences to which they would speak.[67] Most white male abolitionist leaders in the 1830s—whether they supported Garrison or the opposing platform—were also influenced by traditional notions that separated men's and women's proper realms. Although women attended AASS meetings from its inception, they were not officially members of the society until 1839, and their role in the male-dominated movement was limited. Beginning in 1832, women formed female antislavery groups—usually as "auxiliaries" to male antislavery organizations—in some parts of the West and throughout the Northeast, particularly in such major cities as Boston, Philadelphia, and New York. Female antislavery societies sponsored lectures by prominent abolitionist men; organized schools and homes for African American children; circulated petitions; published Sunday-school tracts, gift books, and tracts for children; and created crafts that would be sold at antislavery fairs or bazaars.[68] These efforts conformed to traditional notions of "women's sphere," favoring activities that were associated with children, religion, and domestic skills. Even petitioning, although an activity with political overtones, was not considered "unfeminine" when used by female abolitionists in the early 1830s. Deborah Bingham Van Broekhoven explains that women had been petitioning since colonial times; and, because it was considered "a humble prayer of an inferior . . . to a superior with power to grant the request," it did not violate traditional norms of femininity.[69]

Female antislavery societies justified their existence by the notions of female moral authority endorsed by Beecher, while extending the realm in which this influence should be practiced to include all-female organizations. The 1834 *Address of the Female Anti-Slavery Society of Chatham-Street Chapel* offers such a rationale for women's antislavery work: "Are we called . . . to keep down every thing like natural compassion or Christian sympathy, which might stir within us? . . . We have fathers, brothers, husbands, sons. *Are we not something in, and something to, our country?* Can the nation bleed, and we be free from pain?" Organized female activity, supporters argued, would have a particular moral influence on men. In an 1836 address to the Philadelphia Female Anti-Slavery Society, African American abolitionist James Forten Jr. assures his female colleagues, "Your efforts will stimulate the men to renewed exertion . . . for, in general, the pride of man's heart is such, that . . . [he] feels an innate disposition to check the modest ardour of [woman's] zeal and ambition, and revolts at the idea of her managing the reigns of improvement."[70]

Other aspects of "True Womanhood" also were used to support female organizations. The AASS's justification for auxiliary female societies draws on the ideals of domesticity: "The heart of woman can understand, that no political advantages, nor considerations of expediency can, for a moment, justify a system which desolates the *homes* of 460,000 families; which tears the tender babe from the arms of its mother; which makes a million of her own sex the mere property of the highest bidder; which lashes the mother to the toil of a brute, in the presence of, and perhaps by the very hands of her own sons! The ardor with which our fair countrywomen enter into this holy work, is already evidenced by many efficient auxiliaries." As the particular reference to slave women suggests, supporters of women's organizations called upon the traditional notion of the sympathetic bonds between women. Although antebellum rhetorical theory proposed that sympathy was a natural principle of human nature, the self-denying and emotional "True Woman" was assumed to be particularly susceptible to this feeling. Furthermore, the essentialist rhetoric of domesticity suggested that women of different classes were universally linked by gender. Because slave women were held in bondage, the supporters of female organizations argued, free women were called to work to liberate them. An announcement in the *Liberator* entitled "The Ladies of Boston and Providence" suggests such a foundation for women's efforts: "It is heart-cheering to know, that the females of our land are beginning to combine their energies and influence, for the rescue of more than a million of their sex who are held under the lash, in chains and servitude, at the south."[71]

As their status as "efficient auxiliaries" suggests, the role of these female societies was to assist and support the efforts of the male societies through fundraising and other supplemental activities. Because of the cultural taboo against women's public persuasion, however, rhetorical goals were problematic. Not surprisingly, when persuasion is included in the female societies' statements of their goals, it is mentioned self-consciously. A comparison of the stated objectives of various male and female antislavery societies demonstrates this apprehension. The Declaration of Sentiments of the male Ohio State Anti-Slavery Society proposes, "We shall seek to effect the destruction of slavery . . . by urging upon slaveholders, and the entire community, the flagrant enormity of slavery as a sin against God and man—by demonstrating the safety of immediate emancipation . . . by presenting facts, arguments and the results of experiment, establishing the superiority of free over slave labor." Traditional rhetoric, offering logical proof and empirical evidence, is central to these goals. Similarly, the Constitution of the New-York Young Men's Anti-Slavery Society states, "We shall address directly the understanding and conscience of the slave holder, and present such facts, arguments, and appeals, as we hope in the hands of God, may lead him to repentance."[72]

In contrast, women's societies did not explicitly endorse the use of persuasion—and often distanced their efforts from rhetorical appeals. The women of the Boston Female Anti-Slavery Society (BFASS) express their "motive" for offering publications as "the wish to promulgate TRUTH," claiming they "make no appeal to the public, as a body whose verdict they will abide; their purpose is to preserve a sketch of the times, as one from which valuable instruction may be drawn by their children." The Constitution of the Female Anti-Slavery Society of Chatham-Street Chapel, New York, similarly suggests that they will offer truth rather than argument to persuade audiences: "The objects of the Society shall be . . . [t]o aid in the diffusion of information on the subject of slavery; to portray its true character, to prove its utter indefensibleness, on any principle of religion, justice, expediency, or duty."[73] These statements suggest that any anti-slavery texts offered by these societies will focus not on creating arguments but on revealing objective "truth" and information, a process that ostensibly removes female society members from persuasion. The facts "speak for themselves," these women's organizations imply, and thus women need not assume rhetorical authority. The women of BFASS draw on the accepted female role of maternal teacher, framing their antislavery writing in terms of "instruction" of their children rather than persuasion of society.

Given this ambivalence over women's role in public rhetoric, it is not surprising that the abolitionist community often separated women's writing from men's and assumed women's texts would appeal to a primarily female audience. In the 1830s, articles by and for women appeared in a distinct section of the *Liberator* entitled the "Ladies' Department" and addressed subjects presumed to be of particular interest to women. In the "Ladies' Department" of 1832, for example, correspondents discussed the separation of women from their husbands and children on the auction block, the violation of female slaves' chastity, and the importance of thinking of and praying for slaves. Significantly, many essays in the "Ladies' Department" took the form of dialogues or of letters to the editor or to other women, allowing female writers to frame their contributions as private discourse. These texts, Garrison stresses in editorial commentary, were directed toward a female audience. In his introduction to an 1835 letter from Angelina Grimké, Garrison asserts that he "publish[ed] it, especially, that female abolitionists may derive support and comfort from its perusal."[74]

Yet not all white female abolitionists were satisfied with the restrictions placed on them by white male abolitionists, who seemed to expect them to work in all-female "auxiliary" organizations or to publish in separate women's forums. Although she joined BFASS in 1834, Lydia Maria Child explains in an 1839 letter to Lucretia Mott that the limitations of all-female societies made them seem "like half a pair of scissors." "For the freedom of women, they have probably done something," Child remarks, "but in every other point of view, I think their influence has been very slight." Speaking at an 1848 Woman's Rights Convention in Rochester, New York, abolitionist Lucretia Mott criticizes the "Ladies' Department," which was discontinued after 1837, as "sickly sentimentality" and approves the shift to "more substantial food" for women's minds.[75] Other women shared Child's and Mott's concern that the activities for women sanctioned by the abolitionist leadership were often too limited to allow them a meaningful role. These women opted to work publicly in the male-dominated movement, defying both the traditional hierarchies in the abolition movement and proscriptions against public persuasion. Most controversially, they dared to assume full membership in the

AASS and to persuade audiences of men and women—so-called "promiscuous audiences."

The reaction of male AASS members to the vote on women's membership at the 1839 meeting demonstrates the force of traditional proscriptions against women's public speaking and activism. The vote on the resolution granting women full membership was 180 to 140, with many prominent society members such as Lewis Tappan and Philadelphia convention president Beriah Green opposing the resolution, in spite of their previous encouragement of the "unofficial" participation of women at AASS meetings. Dissenters asserted that women's official participation offended the "moral sense" of many members. The opponents also feared the disapproval of the larger public whom they were trying to persuade; women's public activity, they argued, would bring "*unnecessary* reproach and embarrassment to the cause of the enslaved, inasmuch as that principle is at variance with the general usage and sentiment of this and all other nations."[76] Not only males opposed an expanded female role in the movement. Some female abolitionists, such as members of the Ladies' New York Anti-Slavery Societies, felt women should remain in a secondary role and avoid public speaking and leadership roles—or even full membership and voting rights—in male-dominated abolitionist organizations.[77] When Abby Kelley was elected to the business committee at the AASS convention in New York the following year, Lewis Tappan invited those who disagreed with the action to a separate meeting, at which they formed the AFASS. Needless to say, women were not voting members or eligible for office in the new organization.

After the split of the AASS, white women assumed an expanded, but still limited, role in the abolition movement. By the 1840s and 1850s, women gained a more prominent position in the Garrisonian wing of the movement than they had enjoyed in the 1830s. Those who had opposed Garrison were slower to accept female activism, but some members of this faction eventually adopted a more open stance toward women's public participation in the movement. Certain cultural factors influenced abolitionists' shifting views of women's public activity. The rise of mass democracy in the mid nineteenth century challenged traditional distinctions dictating the qualifications for speaking publicly.[78] With traditional standards for rhetorical authority in flux, women began to appear on the platform in increasing numbers. Women still faced considerable opposition to their public speaking, though, and male abolitionists did not always see them as equals. Lawrence Friedman notes that male abolitionists' tolerance of women's expanded roles was often based more on "expediency" than a true commitment to equality: women's contributions to the movement were needed. "Even the most enthusiastic new proponents of expanded female opportunities," Friedman remarks, "were not departing, in all significant respects," from a traditional conception of "Woman's Sphere."[79]

In addition to their public speaking, white female abolitionists persuaded in print by publishing tracts, writing to periodicals, and assuming editorships of antislavery newspapers. This form of persuasion was also controversial. Angelina

Grimké noted in correspondence with her sister Sarah that she found herself condemned for her 1835 letter to William Lloyd Garrison, which was published in the *Liberator* and constituted her first entrance into the public debate on abolition. Angelina was most distressed at the censure by Sarah herself. Sarah's displeasure is revealed in a diary entry, in which she confesses that she hopes Angelina "may learn obedience by the things that she suffers."[80] Sarah later supported Angelina's efforts, but others continued to criticize her writings. Lydia Maria Child incurred harsh criticism and ostracism from the Boston literary establishment for the 1833 publication of *An Appeal in Favor of That Class of Americans Called Africans,* a groundbreaking work that offered historical, legal, and economic analyses of slavery in various cultures; refuted claims that those of African descent are intellectually and morally inferior; and presented compelling arguments for immediate abolition.[81] When Child took over the editorship of the *National Anti-Slavery Standard* in 1841, she anticipated the criticisms of those who would assume that a man should edit the paper. "Had Mr. Child's business made it possible for him to remove to New-York," she explains in her first editorial, "his experience in editing, his close observation of public affairs, and the general character of his mind, would have made it far better for the cause to have him for a resident, and myself for an assistant editor."[82] This self-consciousness notwithstanding, Child and her white female colleagues would not be silenced, either in print or on the platform, in spite of the obstacles they faced.

White women often worked with African American women in the fight against slavery. Some female antislavery societies, such as BFASS, had African American as well as white members, although others excluded African American women from membership. Yet even in integrated groups, white women, influenced by biases and stereotypes, often limited the participation of their African American colleagues.[83] As we will see, this racism affected the antislavery work of African American women. Yet white women's abolitionist efforts were also shaped by norms and attitudes about race. Ruth Frankenberg argues that although white women do not perceive the influence of race on their lives, their consciousnesses are "racially structured." "Whiteness" may be an "invisible" racial category, Frankenberg maintains, but it nonetheless shapes white women's experiences, particularly because they experience the advantages of "white privilege" on a daily basis. In other words, since the "white/Western self" is perceived as the normative category and whiteness is the "point of reference for the measuring of others," white women "benefit" from the racism of American society. Frankenberg does not mean to imply that white women do not experience the oppression of sexism. Yet she notes that white women often are unaware of the way racial privilege influences their lives—or of the fact that racism and sexism cannot be separated in the lives of women of color.[84]

White privilege shaped the reform work of women abolitionists in various ways. Because femininity, like other culturally constructed categories, is defined in terms of the norm of whiteness, white women could use the assumption that they were "True Women" to their advantage. In other words, they could appeal to audiences to accept them based on their presumed femininity. A variety of material factors based on their whiteness—their access to public venues inaccessible to African American abolitionists, their close ties to white men in the leadership of the abolition movement, and their often relatively secure economic status—also affected their daily work for the cause. At the same time, white women abolitionists frequently ignored the way racism influenced their own experiences and shaped their lives and work, something their African American colleagues could never afford to forget.

"GREAT DIFFICULTIES" AND "GREATER EFFORTS": AFRICAN AMERICAN FEMALE ABOLITIONISTS

For African American women abolitionists, the intersection of racism and sexism influenced their experiences in unique ways, both within the white-dominated abolition movement and African American community organizations. Although they faced various obstacles—stereotypes based on the combined forces of racism and sexism, an "invisibility" in the abolition movement based on the frequent presumption that the struggle for freedom was to benefit African American *men,* often demeaning treatment from white female colleagues, and the expectation that they should adopt particular conventions of femininity—they also were able to assume agency through avenues that were unavailable to their white counterparts and to resist many aspects of traditional antebellum gender roles.[85]

In antebellum society and in the white-dominated antislavery movement, African American women confronted considerable obstacles. They were shackled by generalizations about African Americans that marginalized their male colleagues; they were represented as sexually promiscuous or driven by sexual desire and thus judged inherently inferior to "pure" and "modest" white women. In addition, because they often had to work outside the home to support their families, their experiences did not fit the antebellum rhetoric of the ideal domestic woman whose sphere of influence was her home. Thus although they were often judged in terms of the traditional standards of antebellum femininity, they were never considered "True Women"—an ideal based on the norm of white women's experiences.

Within the abolition movement, the needs and concerns of African American women were often ignored by reformers. bell hooks explains the underlying assumption that leads to this "invisibility": "[Black women] are rarely recognized as a group separate and distinct from black men, or as a present part of the larger group 'women.' . . . When black people are talked about the focus tends to be on black *men;* and when women are talked about the focus tends to be on *white* women." An example illustrates how this presumption affected antebellum African American women. Girls frequently could not attend schools established by reformers in various cities for African American children. To many abolitionists, it seems, the advancement of the race meant equal rights for African

American men, as a revealing 1831 announcement in the *Liberator* entitled "Advancing!" demonstrates: "At the Sabbath School Exhibition, held in Park-street Church on the Fourth of July, the colored boys were permitted to occupy pews one fourth of the way up the side aisle. The march of equality has certainly begun in Boston! The next stride, we trust, will carry them up to the pulpit. N. B. The colored girls took their seats near the door, as usual." The injustice, it would seem, was unnoticed by many white reformers.[86]

Even when not ignored, African American women were restricted from full participation in the abolition movement. White female abolitionists often had trouble accepting African American members in their organizations or seeing African American female abolitionists as their equals. Although various influential women's antislavery societies admitted African American members, others did not. In a letter to friend Jane Smith, Angelina Grimké sadly notes of a New York female antislavery society, "The Ladys [Anti-Slavery] S[ociet]y . . . is utterly inefficient & must continue so until our Sisters here are willing to giv up sinful prejudice. It is a canker worm among them. . . . No colord Sister has ever been in the board, & they hav hardly any colored members even & will not admit any such in the working S[ociet]y."[87] While they purported to support racial equality, many white women retained stereotypical perceptions of their African American female colleagues. The comments of Anne Warren Weston in a letter to her sister Deborah suggest this bias. Weston maintains that Susan Paul was chosen as a delegate to the First Anti-Slavery Convention of American Women in New York in 1837 because she was "a favorable specimen of the coloured race," while Julia Williams was selected "because the colored people regard her as one of themselves." In addition, Sarah Pugh's comment concerning a lunch provided for conventioneers by African American New Yorkers suggests a pattern of condescension by many white female abolitionists: "We should have been famished had not our thoughtful colored friends brought us baskets of refreshments. They are a race worth saving."[88]

Like their male counterparts, African American women noticed that their white colleagues' professed commitment to racial equality often remained abstract. In an essay in the *Charter Oak*, a Hartford reform periodical, an anonymous African American woman suggests that white women often did not put their principles into practice. Asking whether Connecticut free women have all supported antislavery petitions, she challenges, "Do you say you have so many family cares you cannot go? Thousands of your sisters may never hear the word *family* but to mock their desolation. But you must prepare your beloved children's *warm, winter clothing.* Look yonder. Do you not see that mother toiling with her *almost, or quite naked children, shivering in the keen blast?* Yet you cannot go, you must prepare the table for your family. The slave spends but little time in dressing her '*peck of corn per week.*' . . . Why do you delay, and take up a book to read?"[89]

Not surprisingly, then, African American women abolitionists seem to have felt that organizations dominated by white women were frequently unresponsive to their needs. Often, they did not participate in debates that seemed to have little to do with their particular concerns. Although at the First Anti-Slavery Convention of American Women, African Americans constituted 10 percent of the delegates, Dorothy Sterling remarks that they assumed a "low profile," speaking "only when resolutions touching on prejudice were under discussion."[90] Debra Gold Hansen notes that African American members of BFASS often remained "neutral" during debates among white members. Because the African American members had "different priorities and concerns," Hansen proposes, these arguments "may have seemed irrelevant to their own work for racial freedom and equality."[91]

These integrated organizations, though, were not the only avenues for African American women's antislavery activism. Like their male counterparts, they also worked in predominantly African American reform organizations. Within the African American community and its institutions, antebellum conceptions of femininity manifested themselves in unique ways and had particular implications for women's activism and their public speaking. On the surface, discussions of gender among antebellum African Americans appear similar to the rhetoric that defined femininity within the white community. Many "black male activists and political leaders" of the nineteenth century, bell hooks remarks, expected women to adopt traditional gender roles. This perception, she notes, was part of the sexism of American culture as a whole and of the elevated status given to men over women in nineteenth-century America. In addition, Shirley Yee maintains, African American men often expected African American women's activism to fit the limited "sphere" of all-female organizations or to be restricted to fundraising to support men's work.[92]

The pressures posed by antebellum stereotypes also influenced expectations of African American women. Yee explains that for many free African Americans, traditional gender roles were endorsed for particular reasons: "Constructing a life that truly reflected 'freedom' meant adopting many of the values of white society, in part symbolized by male dominance and female subordination. This model . . . became an important symbol of freedom to many black men and women, who were struggling for survival and acceptance within the dominant culture. By supporting sexual roles modeled after free society, they attempted to erase memories of enslavement and to prove false the assumption of many whites that blacks were incapable of creating stable family and community structures."[93] By following the tenets of "True Womanhood," many African Americans felt that negative stereotypes of African American women would also be disproved. Proslavery ideology proposed that African American women were fundamentally different from "pure" white women and therefore could be exploited and abused. If African American women could demonstrate that they, too, were "True Women," many assumed, they would discredit proslavery arguments and gain respect in antebellum society.

Yee does not imply, though, that African Americans' views of women were formulated merely in response to white America's expectations or simply to present an "acceptable" image to whites. African American women realized that "True

Womanhood" was based on white America's prejudices, was unrealistic for most women (including white women who were not middle class), and perpetuated both racial and sexual inequality.[94] They resisted traditional formulations of gender and critiqued the "True Womanhood" ideal, demonstrating that they had agency to define their own views of what their roles should be. Yet sexism still was an obstacle they often had to face, and its effects influenced their abolitionist work.

To understand how traditional notions of gender shaped the lives of African American women and how they defied these expectations and created alternative roles, consider various statements about women's roles published in the African American newspaper *Freedom's Journal.* Articles in the periodical often promoted traditional notions of femininity. In an 1828 letter to editor John Russwurm (at this time the sole editor of the journal), "Ophelia" highlights woman's self-effacing devotion to home and husband, affirming that "in adversity she is a ministering angel, whose kind and affectionate solicitude, breaks forth with all the grace and loveliness of female fondness; and whose inspiriting and consoling tenderness, wipes away the tear of misery, alleviates the pang of disease, assuages the agony of mental suffering, and smooths the ruffled brow of misfortune." In an essay entitled "Female Tenderness," contributor "S." draws a distinction between the male and female spheres, expressing the antebellum ideal of the selfless woman whose domestic influence was capable of negating even the harshest aspects of the public world: "When prejudice had barred the door of every honourable employment against me . . . when I wished . . . that I could retire from a world of wrongs, and end my days far from the white man's scorn; the kind attentions of a woman, were capable of conveying a secret charm, a silent consolation to my mind."[95] Significantly, "S." proposes that the "haven" the "True Woman" creates becomes, for the African American man, a refuge not only from the forces of competition and ambition but also from the debilitating effects of racial oppression. His comments suggest that the interplay of gender roles and racism for African Americans was complex, incorporating both the expectations of the larger society and the desire to resist American prejudices.

Following traditional antebellum advice, many contributors to *Freedom's Journal* counseled women to avoid controversy and to defer to male authority. The anonymous author of "Duties of Wives" cautions female readers to avoid this threat to domestic happiness: "Any well-disposed female can render the domestic fireside of a godly man more magnetic in its attractions than any other social circle whatever . . . but ill temper, or inattention, on the part of his wife, will assuredly wither his domestic feelings and affections. But how easily is all this avoided? It never can be a woman's interest to cross even the foibles of her husband, when they are harmless." Anticipating Catharine Beecher's advice about the limited role of women's opinion, the anonymous author of "Female Temper" remarks, "A woman who would attempt to thunder with her tongue, would not find her eloquence increase her domestic happiness. We do not wish that women should implicitly yield their better judgment to their fathers and husbands, but let them support the cause of reason with all the graces of female gentleness."[96]

Similarly, women's public activism was also debated in the columns of *Freedom's Journal*. Editor John Russwurm's comments on two African American female reform organizations illustrate these expectations. He praises the African Dorcas Association—a group formed in 1828 to supply clothing to children in New York's African schools—for their unassuming and modest ethos, declaring that "they have no annual processions; they have no blazing banners; pharisee-like to proclaim to the world the nature of their work." Yet he expresses disapproval of the Daughters of Israel, a mutual aid society he felt attracted too much public attention by organizing "such an uncommon sight as a female procession, dressed in the full costume of their order."[97]

At the same time, though, the pages of *Freedom's Journal* reveal that African American women did not merely accept these expectations or dictates. They challenged them, and, in doing so, opened up a larger sphere for women's activity than that circumscribed by the norms of "True Womanhood." In an 1827 letter to editors Cornish and Russwurm, "Matilda" asserts,

> I don't know that in any of your papers, you have said sufficient upon the education of females. I hope you are not to be classed with those, who think that our mathematical knowledge should be limited to "fathoming the dish-kettle," and that we have acquired enough of history, if we know that our grandfather's father lived and died. 'Tis true the time has been, when to darn a stocking, and cook a pudding well, was considered the end and aim of a woman's being. But those were days when ignorance blinded mens' [*sic*] eyes. The diffusion of knowledge has destroyed those degrading opinions, and men of the present age, allow, that we have minds that are capable and deserving of culture. There are difficulties, and great difficulties in the way of our advancement; but that should only stir us to greater efforts.[98]

Matilda suggests that African American women can and should define their own agendas; criticize perspectives of them that threaten to restrict them; and articulate their concerns and perspectives, even in a public forum like *Freedom's Journal*.

The fact that Matilda's critique was published in *Freedom's Journal* reveals that in spite of traditional assumptions about femininity held by some African American men and their ambivalence about whether women should assume public or assertive roles, their attitudes were often more progressive than those of their white male counterparts. Scholars have demonstrated that many African American male leaders were more supportive of women's rights than were white men. Men and women worked together in nineteenth-century African American reform organizations, Rosalyn Terborg-Penn notes, adding that "although some black male advocates of temperance, abolitionism, and moral reform resisted sharing equal status with black women, their antifemale prejudice was considerably milder than that of their white counterparts."[99] By the 1840s, many African American male abolitionists had accepted a more public role for women. In a speech at the 1844 New England Anti-Slavery Convention at Marlboro

Chapel in Boston, Charles Lenox Remond declares that he "belong[s] to that class of persons called women's rights men." In an 1848 editorial entitled "The Rights of Women," Douglass endorses complete equality for women, criticizing those who would restrict this freedom and claiming that "right is of no sex." These attitudes were not without conflict, as bell hooks and Cynthia Hamilton have shown; many African American male leaders, including Douglass and Remond, supported women's rights but frequently privileged male authority or ignored women's particular concerns.[100] Yet because assumptions about women's roles were often less rigid and more egalitarian among antebellum African Americans than among whites, African American women found avenues for their public work that were unavailable to white women.

Matilda's bold commentary demonstrates that, despite ambivalence among some male colleagues and the dual obstacles of racism and sexism, African American women asserted themselves, resisting limitations. "Collectively and individually," historian Darlene Clark Hine maintains, they "challenge[d] white and black patriarchal domination."[101] This self-determination is evident in the rhetoric of antebellum African American women who argued publicly and boldly, even criticizing male leaders. In an 1849 letter to Frederick Douglass published in the *North Star,* teacher Mary Ann Shadd boldly criticizes uneducated African American clergymen for assuming the role of educators and calls for education that would elevate the community. In an 1855 letter to Douglass that appeared in *Frederick Douglass' Paper,* teacher and abolitionist Barbara Ann Steward laments what she perceived to be the lack of interest in industrial education within the African American community. Responding specifically to the plan for the American Industrial School (an institution proposed by a committee of the National Council of the Colored People, which the committee passed by only two votes), Steward remarks that she was "mortified to find that men who were familiar with all the outlines of the proposed plan should oppose it."[102] Although their rhetorical endeavors remained controversial, African American female abolitionists continued to speak out throughout the antebellum period.

Paradoxically, then, the intersection of race and gender both presented unique restrictions for African American women and allowed them to resist traditional norms of gender that would limit them and to find avenues for activism that were unavailable to their white counterparts. Material considerations that prevented them from adopting the role of the ideal domestic woman, for example, gave them power in their communities and access to venues beyond the home. Economic necessity forced many African American women to work outside the home, diversifying their roles in their families. Thus African American women challenged the strict gender conventions of white society, breaking down the barrier between the domestic and public realms. In addition, antebellum African American women did not consider domesticity opposed to involvement in political concerns. Although African American women's role in the home and family was important, it was not considered women's only contribution to the community.

The daily struggle for civil rights, equality, education, and autonomy often demanded that women take economic or political action. In Maria Stewart's 1831 tract *Religion and the Pure Principles of Morality, the Sure Foundation on Which We Must Build,* the African American orator, author, and abolitionist exhorts female members of her audience to "excel in good housewifery," to "unite and build a store of [their] own," and to "sue for [their] rights and privileges." As Stewart's advice suggests, "good housewifery" did not require dependence upon a man— in fact, a responsible domestic woman might need to help support her family. "Possess the spirit of independence," Stewart recommends, adding, "The Americans do, and why should not you?" (*R,* 37–38).[103]

Through their devotion to education, self-help, and religion, in particular, African American women were able to voice their concerns and to assume responsibilities that gave them authority outside the home. Although even such a strict proponent of "True Womanhood" as Catharine Beecher applauded women's participation in education, she warned that intellectual advancement must not lead a woman to reject "her subordinate station." But African American women often had to fight to educate themselves and their children and could not afford the "dignified retirement and submission" Beecher endorsed for the privileged white female.[104] Thus, as Matilda asserts, the African American woman's "greater difficulties" in antebellum society led to "greater efforts" that often allowed them to assume authority beyond the domestic sphere.

Because of this expanded sphere for women's activity, African American women's organizations offered a more expansive range of activity than their white counterparts. Unlike many white women's benevolent organizations, African American female associations raised money for specific groups in the community rather than for distant recipients, combined benevolent activities with abolitionism, invited female as well as male speakers, and chose names that reflected a pride in their race and gender. Through their goals of self-help and community advancement, African American female benevolent societies gave women authority to improve their own lives and enrich their families and communities. In the Constitution of the Afric-American Female Intelligence Society of Boston, members declare that they "thought fit to associate for the diffusion of knowledge, the suppression of vice and immorality, and for cherishing such virtues as will render us happy and useful to society."[105] In *Religion and the Pure Principles of Morality,* Stewart challenges her female audience to form civic organizations to benefit the community: "Shall it any longer be said of the daughters of Africa, they have no ambition, they have no force? By no means. Let every female heart become united, and let us raise a fund ourselves; and at the end of one year and a half, we might be able to lay the corner stone for the building of a High School" (*R,* 37). Although white women's organizations also raised funds for charitable ends, these endeavors frequently provided financial assistance to struggling male benevolent societies. Stewart suggests that the efforts of the "daughters of Africa," by contrast, should be self-directed.

Religion, too, allowed African American women to resist traditional dictates that removed them from the public realm. Although many African American male religious leaders opposed women's preaching and leadership, women's participation in the religious community frequently allowed them to assume responsibilities outside the home. Because Christianity for African Americans represented resistance to oppression and the affirmation of the innate worth of all people, it allowed them to transform the ways in which antebellum society defined them.[106] Women could use this potential to resist traditional classifications and to speak publicly on behalf of moral causes—even, in some cases, assuming the role of preacher. In an 1832 speech, Sarah Douglass urges members of the Female Literary Society of Philadelphia, an African American women's organization, to fight against slavery and oppression. Douglass proposes that religious commitment gives them the right—and obligation—to do so, remarking that after she had experienced the effects of prejudice she felt called by God "to use every exertion in [her] power to elevate the character of [her] wronged and neglected race."[107]

Throughout the antebellum period, African American female abolitionists did not assume a secondary role, either to their African American male colleagues or to white women abolitionists. They spoke and wrote against slavery, edited newspapers, attended antislavery meetings, and worked for civil rights. It is noteworthy that a speech by an African American female abolitionist—Maria Stewart's September 1832 speech at Franklin Hall in Boston—constitutes the first recorded instance of an American-born woman of any race addressing a "promiscuous audience." Stewart's rhetorical efforts were met with opposition, but she asserts in *Religion and the Pure Principles of Morality* that she must speak: "I am sensible of exposing myself to calumny and reproach; but shall I, for fear of feeble man who shall die, hold my peace? Shall I for fear of scoffs and frowns, refrain my tongue? Ah, no!" (*R,* 30). Nor would those who followed her remain silent.

3

Too Long Have Others Spoken for Us

The Antislavery Rhetoric of African American Men

In their opening editorial "To Our Patrons" in the first issue of *Freedom's Journal,* Samuel Cornish and John Russwurm emphasize the "real necessity" for their periodical: "There are FIVE HUNDRED THOUSAND free persons of colour, one half of whom might peruse, and the whole be benefitted by the publication of the Journal; [and] no publication, as yet, has been devoted exclusively to their improvement." They stress that *Freedom's Journal* will not only educate African Americans, but will also provide their "friends" with information about their "actual condition" and their "efforts and feelings." It is particularly important, they maintain, that African Americans speak for themselves. "Too long have others spoken for us," they assert, adding, "From the press and the pulpit we have suffered much by being incorrectly represented."[1]

Freedom's Journal, then, set a standard for antebellum African Americans. On issues that concerned them, they wished to assert themselves and to craft arguments that brought their concerns both to other African Americans and into mainstream American discourse. Asserting that white reformers often allowed their prejudices to compromise their relationships with African Americans— "our friends . . . [are] actually living in the practice of prejudice, while they abjure it in theory"—Cornish and Russwurm opened their columns to a discussion of issues that affected African Americans. The periodical would also allow African Americans to respond to arguments that misrepresented them, the editors declare: "We believe that the time has now arrived, when the calumnies of our enemies should be refuted by forcible arguments."[2]

Many activists took up Cornish and Russwurm's call during the period from the late 1820s to the beginning of the Civil War, particularly to argue against slavery and the related issues of colonization, prejudice, segregation, and institutionalized oppression.[3] Among them was David Walker, a leader in the MGCA, a Boston agent for *Freedom's Journal,* and an influential voice of the late 1820s. Born free in Wilmington, North Carolina, Walker traveled in the South, eventually moving to Boston and establishing a clothing store. He was propelled into the public spotlight in 1829 with the publication of his controversial *Appeal to the Coloured Citizens of the World,* a militant condemnation of the evils of slavery and a prophetic call for a potentially violent end to the institution. Southern authorities were alarmed when copies of the pamphlet made their way into southern states, and they tried to prevent its circulation there. Many northern whites were also shocked by Walker's text; even those who opposed slavery were concerned about his militancy.[4] Nonetheless, Walker persisted, publishing two more editions of the pamphlet. Walker's abolitionist career was cut short by his mysterious death in 1830. Many presumed he was murdered.[5]

Other African American abolitionists who wrote and lectured in the late 1820s and 1830s took a less militant—but no less activist—approach. William Whipper, a free-born Pennsylvania businessman and one of the most affluent antebellum African Americans, was active in the Underground Railroad and was a strong proponent of moral reform and self-help. He helped create a national African American reform organization, the American Moral Reform Society (AMRS), founded in 1835 to promote self-help goals such as education and temperance, and edited the organization's periodical, the *National Reformer.*[6] William Watkins, born free in Baltimore, ran a school for African American youth and was a charter member of the AMRS. Watkins had been an early spokesman against colonization, writing many essays in the 1820s and 1830s for *Freedom's Journal,* the *Genius of Universal Emancipation*—an antislavery newspaper edited by colonization supporter Benjamin Lundy—and Garrison's *Liberator,* under the pseudonym "A Colored Baltimorean." By the late 1830s, both Whipper and Watkins came to question the efficacy of moral reform as a tactic to fight slavery but continued their antislavery activism.

The reformers of the 1820s and 1830s often spoke to African American organizations, and their speeches and writing were frequently published for wider audiences in newspapers such as *Freedom's Journal* and the *Liberator.* By the 1840s, African American orators were speaking publicly at biracial gatherings of whites and African Americans sponsored by organizations such as the AASS as they continued to work with African American organizations. Charles Lenox Remond and Frederick Douglass were two such speakers. Remond was born free, the son of Curaçaon immigrant John Remond, who was a member of the Massachusetts Anti-Slavery Society. Charles Lenox Remond became an agent for the *Liberator* in 1832 and was a founding member of the AASS. In 1838 he was hired as a lecturer by the AASS.

Douglass, born a slave in Maryland, escaped in 1838 to New York, and subsequently moved to New Bedford, Mass. There he became a subscriber to the *Liberator* and attended African American antislavery meetings. After he spoke in 1841 at a meeting of the Bristol County Anti-Slavery Society in New Bedford attended by Garrison and John Collins, the latter asked him to lecture for the Massachusetts Anti-Slavery Society. During the 1840s and 1850s, he became one of the most famous abolitionist orators as well as the author of two autobiographies and the editor of three antislavery periodicals, the *North Star, Frederick Douglass' Paper,* and *Douglass' Monthly.*[7] One of Douglass's associate editors at *Frederick Douglass' Paper* was William J. Watkins, the son of William Watkins, who followed in his father's footsteps, lecturing and writing against slavery. Although Remond, Douglass, and William J. Watkins were associated with the Garrisonian wing of the abolition movement at the beginning of their antislavery careers, each eventually came to doubt the efficacy of Garrison's approach and sought alternatives.

These activists did not all suscribe to the same philosophical approaches to reform and abolition, nor did they always agree on strategies and tactics. But they shared a marginalized status both within the abolition movement and in the larger society, and they all overcame the obstacles facing them to create forceful antislavery rhetoric. Through the variety of ways in which they negotiated the tensions of their unique position in antislavery organizations and in antebellum society, they assumed the agency to persuade effectively and to challenge societal assumptions and expectations.

SELF-HELP RHETORIC AS ANTISLAVERY PERSUASION

Although its import has often been misunderstood by scholars, self-help rhetoric served important functions for African American abolitionists.[8] They advocated powerful antislavery arguments through this form of discourse, often creating radical, even militant demands for societal change. Their rhetoric also challenges us to reexamine and expand theoretical frameworks. Muted group theorists suggest that those rhetors who occupy a marginalized position in society, outside of the dominant group that defines pervasive models of discourse, must often "encode" or present their ideas in forms that the dominant group will find "acceptable." These scholars note that, although this method of persuasion may seem to reinforce the ideology that keeps the dominant in power, muted rhetors may find ways to challenge the ideological bases of the dominant group from within these received models of discourse.[9] This perspective explains, in part, both the use of self-help rhetoric by African American abolitionists and scholarly misconceptions about this discourse. Through the rhetoric of moral reform, African Americans could draw on dominant values of their society—temperance, education, industry—and, by connecting their abolitionist concerns to these issues, "encode" their antislavery concerns in a pervasive form of antebellum discourse. Indeed, within this apparently traditional model, African American abolitionists could strongly critique antebellum society. Scholars have frequently overlooked the strong abolitionist messages in this rhetoric and its implicit condemnations of white America, characterizing it only in terms of the dominant form on which it draws rather than on the ways this mode of discourse is redefined by African American abolitionists.

Yet the self-help rhetoric of African American abolitionists also reveals a significant limitation of the muted group model. Most often, this discourse was directed toward an African American audience, not the members of the dominant group that muted group theorists assume will judge marginalized rhetors' discourse. The premises of muted group theory, then, are challenged by this aspect of African American self-help rhetoric and require revision. Consider, for example, William Whipper's 1828 address to the Colored Reading Society of Philadelphia, an organization created to promote intellectual advancement and to establish a lending library. Whipper connects the behavior and morals of his free African American audience to slavery. "There is an indifference in ourselves relative to emancipating our brethren from universal thralldom," he asserts, declaring that the remedy to this apathy is "a strict attention to education" by free African Americans. Whipper calls upon not only those African Americans who are uneducated or disadvantaged, but any who ignore the antislavery cause: "Those who enjoy liberty, and have accumulated considerable property are satisfied with their situation, and will not meddle with the cause; while the middle class are too busy in procuring the necessaries of life to alter their course. And the lower class remain regardless of themselves or their brethren, who are existing in a state of ignorance and under the debasing influence of slavery and wicked men.—Their only object is to become votaries to the cup of intemperance, and reflect disgrace on those who enjoy a more retired life and civil society."[10] Whipper builds on the values of "moral uplift" that antebellum society would endorse to create a sense of solidarity among all African Americans—not just those who live in "ignorance" or "disgrace"—and suggests that they have not only the right but the responsibility to fight slavery. Whipper, then, demonstrates that muted rhetors may draw on the assumptions of the dominant group not because they want to "encode" their messages in forms that will be perceived as "acceptable" by those in authority. Marginalized rhetors may feature these assumptions in rhetoric that functions within the muted group itself, transforming them significantly and making them their own. In this instance, Whipper marshals white Americans' judgment of all African Americans in terms of the few who behave immorally as a mandate for community solidarity rather than merely individual improvement. White America's generalizations about African Americans as a group become, in Whipper's speech, the bulwark of group consciousness.

This development of group consciousness through the creation of strong identification between slave and free, the already elevated and the still "ignorant," suggests an important rhetorical function for a seemingly problematic feature of African American self-help rhetoric. African American abolitionists often appear to endorse the assumption, supported by many white reformers, that once the free African American population had gained the respect of white Americans, prejudices would be countered and proslavery arguments would be disproved. Speaking before the AMRS in 1836, for example, William Watkins maintains that education will give African Americans a "moral power that will enable them to storm and batter down that great citadel of pride and prejudice, that great Babel of oppression that impiously lifts itself to the clouds." Yet

African American self-help rhetoric, by creating a strong identification between free African Americans and slaves, offers activist arguments that go far beyond—and challenge—the perspectives of white reformers. This approach to ending slavery constitutes not merely individual attention to self-improvement, but an organized effort among free African Americans to uplift their communities. Outlining the AMRS's objectives in 1835, William Whipper, Alfred Niger and Augustus Price propose, "We shall advocate the cause of peace. . . . We shall advocate a system of *economy*. . . . We shall endeavour to strengthen public sentiment against slavery, so long as a slave treads the soil of these United States."[11] Their language demonstrates that their antislavery efforts are not passive—waiting for change to result from white Americans' acceptance of "virtuous" African Americans—but active, firmly placing African Americans in control of their destiny.

This direct call for solidarity—and, by implication, community activism—reveals another limitation of muted group theory. If, as these theorists suggest, the language of the muted African American rhetor must be "acceptable" to white society, this rhetoric would primarily react to the larger societal context. Yet African American self-help rhetoric does not merely support community uplift to appease white Americans or to substitute for fundamental societal change, but because it contributes to activism. In fact, abolitionists assume agency through self-help rhetoric to sharply critique white America and its institutions—a notable feature of self-help rhetoric that is often overlooked. The critique of racism in self-help rhetoric is frequently misunderstood because of the tensions within self-help rhetoric that link societal racism and the behavior of African Americans. Because their self-help rhetoric often exhorts audiences to overturn the racist assumptions used to justify slavery, they seem to place the burden of proof in disproving stereotypes on African Americans. At the same time, though, they argue that African Americans should not have to shoulder this responsibility, and they condemn the racist society that demands that they are responsible for the prejudices of whites. In other words, although they assume that for practical reasons African Americans must disprove societal stereotypes, they challenge this inherent societal bias. In addition, they call attention to the hypocrisy of a nation that unjustly oppresses a group of people and then demands that they prove their oppression should end.

This critique of racism within self-help discourse is illustrated in Whipper, Niger, and Price's discussion of the goals of the AMRS. They suggest that moral reform will "aid in effecting the total abolition of slavery" by "remov[ing] many of the objections to immediate emancipation." Yet even as they exhort their audience to consider that the slaves' fate depends upon whites' judgments of the behavior of the free, they harshly attack the notion that they are responsible for disproving racist beliefs and the hypocrisy of a society that asks them to do so. African Americans have been denied privileges, they note, and yet are "tauntingly required to prove the dignity of [their] human nature, by disrobing [them]selves of inferiority, and exhibiting to the world [their] profound Scholars, distinguished Philosophers, learned Jurists, and distinguished Statesmen." This "expectation," they maintain, "to say the least, is unreasonable, for it is only when the seed is sown that we can justly hope to reap. . . . The general assertion that superiority of mind is the natural offspring of a fair complexion, arrays itself against the experience of the past and present age, and both natural and physiological science. The ignorance that exists on this subject we are not accountable for."[12] Although Whipper, Niger, and Price advocate moral improvement, they do not hesitate to criticize those who simultaneously deny African Americans opportunities and condemn them for a perceived lack of advancement. African Americans have to "disprove" white America's beliefs not because these assumptions hold any validity, they assert, but because this strategy is necessary to end slavery.

Similarly, in an 1834 speech before the Colored Temperance Society of Philadelphia, Whipper declares that if the "three hundred thousand free colored people" were to give up their intemperance—which he hyperbolically suggests is a greater evil than slavery—the "moral force" of their action "would disperse slavery" from the country by "reorganiz[ing] public opinion, dissolv[ing] the calumnies of [their] enemies, and remov[ing] all the prejudices against [their] complexion." Yet despite this overstated connection of temperance to ending prejudice, Whipper does not oversimplify the complexities of American racism itself. Although he suggests that African Americans must assume the responsibility of disproving common assumptions about them, Whipper explicitly states that these perceptions are inaccurate and based on irrational racial prejudices: "I wish not to be understood to insinuate, that we are more intemperate than the whites, for I do not believe it; but that we must be more pure than they, before we can be duly respected, becomes self-evident from the situation we at present occupy in our country." Nor does Whipper suggest that racism against any individual will end if he or she adopts even the highest moral character. Although he asserts that "the man of color in this country who possesses an unquestionable character for piety, morality and probity" is "a truly noble being," he notes that this exemplar is far from immune to prejudice: "He stands alone on his own merits . . . without the title of citizenship—without the enjoyment of a participation in the affairs of his government—without any share in the administration of its laws—without the hope of earthly reward or future fame."[13]

But what are we to make of the seeming contradiction between Whipper's statements that temperance reform can obliterate negative perceptions about African Americans—even overthrow slavery—and that the virtuous African American is still the victim of whites' racism? And what of the harsh or extreme language African American abolitionists often employ in their self-help rhetoric—such as in Whipper's condemnation of the "lower class" or his suggestion that intemperance is more harmful than slavery—that seem to judge the victims of the prejudice they condemn or to downplay the force of oppression? Again, these tendencies in African American self-help rhetoric often lead to mischaracterizations, particularly the notions that this discourse is elitist and that it too optimistically declares that moral reform can erase racism from the United States. To understand the tendencies in self-help rhetoric to harshly critique African Americans and to closely connect their behavior to oppression and slavery, we must examine the rhetorical functions of these appeals.

In their discussion of the "rhetoric of agitation," rhetoricians John Waite Bower and Donovan Ochs maintain that appeals to solidarity create a sense of cohesiveness within groups that are excluded from society's decision-making processes.[14] Stressing, even in an overly simplistic way, the direct consequences of free African American individuals on the perceptions and treatment of the group, rhetors create a feeling among audience members that they can assume the agency to effect change even though they are excluded from influence in society. In the case of the antislavery struggle, this strategy assigns African Americans a fundamental role in the antislavery crusade, one that is self-directed and independent of white reformers' leadership. In such empowerment lies the key to the apparent paradox between Whipper's seeming oversimplification of prejudice and his elucidation of the complexities of American racism. To create solidarity and to empower his audience in the antislavery struggle, Whipper must place them in a fundamental role in their community and persuade them that their individual behavior has communal implications. Yet Whipper also critiques the larger society that requires African Americans to assume the role of fighting the misconceptions of others, a society that hypocritically creates the very racist structures for which it holds African Americans responsible.

African American abolitionists' use of harsh language that seems to judge audience members or to overemphasize their ostensibly "degraded behavior" can also be seen in terms of strategies related to the "rhetoric of agitation." Bower and Ochs maintain that rhetors who persuade within a marginalized group often use strategies of "polarization"—dividing individuals into the committed and the uncommitted—to force allegiance to a cause, again creating and strengthening a sense of solidarity. Harsh language is often requisite to effect this bifurcation, as is the identification of various representative issues—which Bower and Ochs call "*flag issues*"—that symbolize the choice between commitment and disregard. In other words, agitators endeavor to create a strong negative emotional response on token issues that force a choice between "us" and "them."[15] The harsh portrayal of the intemperate or the "ignorant," then, suggests to audience members that to ignore their elevation is to choose the side of the oppressor. By contrast, supporting temperance or educational uplift serves to demonstrate one's allegiance to the antislavery cause.

The self-help rhetoric of David Walker often features this use of harsh language challenging the audience to make an either/or choice. In his *Appeal,* Walker declares to his African American readers, "You have to prove to the Americans and the world, that we are MEN, and not *brutes,* as we have been represented" (*DWA,* 30). For Walker, as for Whipper and Watkins, moral elevation is not an end in

itself, but a tool with which to fight against slavery. Walker explicitly links the elevation of the African American community to antislavery agitation:

> *Go to work and enlighten your brethren!* . . . Do any of you say that you and
> your family are free and happy, and what have you to do with the
> wretched slaves and other people? . . . If any of you wish to know how
> FREE you are, let one of you start and go through the southern and western
> States of this country, and unless you travel as a slave to a white man . . .
> or have your free papers, (which if you are not careful they will get from
> you) if they do not take you up and put you in jail, and if you cannot give
> good evidence of your freedom, sell you into eternal slavery, I am not a
> living man. . . . And yet some of you have the hardihood to say that you
> are free and happy! . . . [Y]our full glory and happiness . . . shall never be
> fully consummated, but with the *entire emancipation of your enslaved
> brethren all over the world.* You may therefore, go to work and do what you
> can to rescue, or join in with tyrants to oppress them and yourselves.
> (*DWA,* 28–29)

Walker's advocacy of moral improvement, Peter Hinks notes, has often been overlooked by scholars, who frequently "[identify] him and his *Appeal* exclusively with
a call for violent resistance and some form of racial separatism" and suggest that
Walker's thought was atypical of most African American leaders of his time.[16] A
closer analysis of the self-help rhetoric of Walker and other African American abolitionists, though, undermines this either/or choice between radicalism and the
advocacy of moral elevation. Both are significant features of their rhetoric, and they
are intertwined.

In Walker's advocacy of education, in particular, self-help becomes not only
a radical tool to fight slavery, but a form of militant resistance to oppression. In
an 1828 speech before the MGCA, Walker reveals this militant potential of self-
improvement through a forceful image: "Those who delight in our degradation
. . . glory in keeping us ignorant and miserable, that we might be the better and
the longer slaves. I was credibly informed by a gentleman of unquestionable
veracity, that a slaveholder upon finding one of his young slaves with a small
spelling book in his hand (not opened) fell upon and beat him almost to death,
exclaiming, at the same time, to the child, you will acquire better learning than
I or any of my family."[17] If the oppressor wishes African Americans to remain
ignorant, Walker implies, education represents defiance, resistance, and self-
assertion. In his *Appeal,* Walker proposes a more explicitly militant formulation
of this argument: "For coloured people to acquire learning in this country, makes
tyrants quake and tremble on their sandy foundation. . . . Do you suppose one
man of good sense and learning would submit himself, his father, mother, wife
and children, to be slaves. . . ? No! no! he would cut his devilish throat from ear
to ear, and well do slave-holders know it. The bare name of educating the
coloured people, scares our cruel oppressors almost to death" (31–32). To seek

intellectual advancement is a militant antislavery act, Walker implies, and violent resistance to oppression—even slave rebellion—is a natural consequence of education. Clearly, then, the articulation of self-help principles is neither accommodationist, as scholars often assume, nor merely reactive to white society, as muted group theory alone would imply. Self-help rhetoric can be part of a radical, militant, and offensive strategy for social change.

This alternative perspective on African American self-help rhetoric also elucidates the evolution of this form of discourse in the 1840s and 1850s. By the late 1830s, many African American abolitionists began to doubt that self-help would help counter racism or that it could help to directly end slavery. In a speech to the AASS in 1839, Andrew Harris reverses this notion, arguing that slavery had to be ended to truly end racial prejudice. Speaking the same year to the African Clarkson Association, a mutual aid society in New York City, Peter Paul Simons remarks that although African Americans are "a moral people," the continual focus on messages of "moral elevation" hampered true collective activity for freedom and civil rights. And not only did moral reform not necessarily alleviate prejudices, African American abolitionists noted, it often invoked white hostility. "The higher our aspirations," Remond maintains, "the loftier our purposes and pursuits, does this iniquitous principle of prejudice fasten upon us, and especial pains are taken to irritate, obstruct and injure."[18]

Although African American abolitionists began to reject the notion that elevation could directly affect societal prejudices, they continued to incorporate self-help principles—particularly those with radical and militant potential—into their rhetoric. The focus of this self-help rhetoric differs from but builds on earlier arguments, reflecting African American abolitionists' desire for increasing independence from white abolitionists in the 1840s. Arguing not that moral elevation would result in an end to oppression in and of itself but that it would lead to increased empowerment of—and solidarity among—African Americans, the self-help rhetoric of the 1820s and 1830s crystallized into a mandate for decisive, independent, and forceful antislavery action among free African Americans by the 1840s and 1850s.

In an 1849 speech at the Abyssinian Baptist Church in New York, Douglass exhorts African Americans to fight oppression through moral improvement, which would allow them to rise to positions of authority. After describing the prejudices and restrictions he and his audience face in schools, public accommodations, employment, and the political process, he laments, "The worst part of all is, that we are contented under these circumstances! He was ashamed! ashamed! ashamed of his identity with those who were thus indifferent—with oppressed cowards!" (*FDP*, 2:168). Douglass notes that "equality and respectability can only be attained by our own exertions" (*FDP*, 2:168), but the key to this enfranchisement is self-directed action, regardless of how whites will respond to their conduct. And for Douglass, as for his predecessor Walker, this elevation represents resistance to oppression. "We have no right to respect," Douglass remarks, "if, being under the hoof of oppression, we are not manly enough to rise in our own cause, and do something to elevate ourselves from our degraded position" (*FDP,* 2:168). Significantly, Douglass connects this empowerment to the ability to speak publicly: "Colored people are now beginning to exercise their gifts. They are now in a position to be heard. . . . We must elevate ourselves by our own efforts" (*FDP,* 2:170). For African Americans to speak for themselves is a consequence of their elevation and a tool of the antislavery struggle.

"I AM, HOWEVER, DIGRESSING":
"FACTS" AND "TRUTHS" AS PERSUASION

For African American abolitionists, creating self-directed rhetoric could pose certain challenges, particularly when their rhetoric was sponsored by white abolitionists, who were influenced by their own prejudices. Douglass's recollection of the expectation that he would provide only "facts" and not "philosophy" (*MB,* 367) is a case in point. Although John Blassingame identifies evidence to suggest that Douglass exaggerated the extent to which white leaders imposed this restriction,[19] his speeches indicate that, in part, the expectation that he should "narrate" rather than "persuade" influenced his rhetoric. Douglass frames many of his early speeches in terms that suggest he is emphasizing personal experiences. Speaking in 1841 in Lynn, Massachusetts, Douglass asserts, "I have come to tell you something about slavery—what I *know* of it, as I have *felt* it. . . . [T]hough [abolitionists] can depict its horrors, they cannot speak as I can from *experience*" (*FDP,* 1:3). And in an 1845 speech in New York, Douglass relates that since he began as an abolitionist lecturer, he has been "engaged . . . in telling the people what [he] know[s] of [slavery]" (*FDP,* 1:29). Yet Douglass's rhetoric goes beyond personal testimony, and he often presents strong arguments against slavery within the narrative form. As muted group theory would suggest, Douglass's announced emphasis on "facts" rather than "philosophy" and his framing of persuasion as narration can be seen as a reaction to the perspectives of antebellum society.

Yet this theoretical perspective on Douglass's narration has significant limitations. First, Douglass's use of storytelling may have had its roots not merely in the expectations of whites, but also in what Blassingame notes was one source for "[Douglass's] first rhetorical theories"—the "slave story teller." And narration itself can be seen as an effective rhetorical strategy that is not unique to those who are muted in society. Walter Fisher argues that rhetors in a variety of contexts feature narration as persuasion, recognizing the rhetorical power of stories, "metaphors, myths, gestures, and other means of creating communicative relationships."[20] Thus Douglass's self-described narration is more than merely a response to white expectations; it is a powerful strategy that allows him to assume a unique authority in the antislavery debate.

Further, Douglass's use of personal testimony does not force him to shape his discourse passively within narrow parameters. The expectation that he provide "facts" rather than "philosophy" is in actuality more flexible than white leaders and audiences might assume. Maintaining his ostensible emphasis on narration, Douglass marshals two strategies that allow him to assume a unique agency in his antislavery oratory. First, within ostensible presentation of "facts" or testimony, he offers forceful antislavery arguments, either explicitly or implicitly, demonstrating that the boundaries between narration and persuasion shift. By so doing, Douglass demonstrates how the discourse of marginalized rhetors challenges narrow conceptions of the public sphere. Narration, as Bruce Weal argues, relies on the "interrelationship" of the "personal, technical, and public spheres."[21] Second, highlighting his shifts from narration to persuasion in rhetoric that features his personal experiences, Douglass subtly calls attention to his command of both the "facts" and the "philosophy" of slavery. These strategies allow him to simultaneously negotiate his audiences' preconceptions, challenge the assumptions on which these expectations are based, and create effective antislavery arguments that expand the boundaries of the narrative form.

In his 1845 *Narrative of the Life of Frederick Douglass, An American Slave,* Douglass self-consciously underscores shifts from ostensibly objective presentation of "facts" to explicit persuasion. Discussing his creation of a Sabbath school to teach his fellow slaves to read, Douglass describes to the reader the necessary secrecy associated with the endeavor:

> It was necessary to keep our religious masters . . . unacquainted with the fact, that, instead of spending the Sabbath in wrestling, boxing, and drinking whisky, we were trying to learn how to read the will of God; for they had much rather see us engaged in those degrading sports, than to see us behaving like intellectual, moral, and accountable beings. My blood boils as I think of the bloody manner in which Messrs. Wright Fairbanks and Garrison West, both [religious] class-leaders . . . rushed in upon us with sticks and stones, and broke up our virtuous little Sabbath school . . . all calling themselves Christians! humble followers of the Lord Jesus Christ! But I am again digressing.
>
> . . . These dear souls came not to Sabbath school because it was popular to do so. . . . Every moment they spent in that school, they were liable to be taken up, and given thirty-nine lashes. They came because they wished to learn. Their minds had been starved by their cruel masters. (*N,* 71)

Douglass suggests that his "digression" into "philosophy" in this passage is anomalous, a singular persuasive effort in his narrative of facts. Yet the narration that precedes and follows his "digression" itself contains implicit antislavery arguments. Douglass's description of the opposition to his Sabbath school refutes the proslavery claims that masters "improve" or "Christianize" their slaves. Through his description of the slaves that attend the school, Douglass counters the stereotypical views of slaves as submissive, lazy, incapable of learning, and satisfied with their lot. This refutation of proslavery propaganda through storytelling has clear public policy implications, suggesting the potential conflict brewing in the nation as slaves resist their masters' tyranny. When issues of public argumentation involve "human action," Weal maintains, "argumentation in narrative form" powerfully illuminates the "processes" that underlie human behavior.[22]

In addition, Douglass's apparent minimization of his "digression" functions on two levels, creating a text that resonates deeply. Suggesting that his explicit opinion about the hypocrisy of so-called Christian slaveholders diverges from his narrative purpose, Douglass seemingly downplays its role in his narrative. At the same time, however, he brackets off his opinion of slaveholders that profess to be Christian by marking it as a "digression," thus emphasizing it within the passage and suggesting that he is more than capable of offering philosophical statements about slavery. Douglass's dual language resonates at both a surface and an implicit level, subtly appearing to conform to and reversing his audience's expectations in the same passage. The former slave's unique authority to argue against slavery, Douglass demonstrates, goes beyond the one-dimensional discourse anticipated by his audience.

In his 1855 *My Bondage and My Freedom,* Douglass expands this story of the Sabbath school, elaborating on various events and adding descriptions absent from the 1845 *Narrative.* Although he was at this time more independent of white abolitionist mentors, Douglass continues to exploit the expectation that he provide only the facts, to craft effective antislavery arguments through this narrative frame, and to call attention to overt expressions of his opinion. Describing the school's destruction, Douglass further develops his antislavery arguments and continues to bracket off his explicit persuasion from the rest of his narrative:

> The plea for this outrage [the school's destruction] was . . . the danger to good order. If the slaves learnt to read, they would learn something else, and something worse. The peace of slavery would be disturbed; slave rule would be endangered. I leave the reader to characterize a system which is endangered by such causes. . . . [The slaveholders] were Protestant, and held to the great Protestant right of every man to "*search the scriptures*" for himself; but, then, to all general rules, there are *exceptions.* How convenient! what crimes, may not be committed under the doctrine of the last remark. . . . I am, however, digressing. (*MB,* 299–300)

As in his 1845 *Narrative,* Douglass suggests that his explicit condemnation of the slaveholders' hypocrisy diverges from his main purpose of relating the mere facts of his experience. Again, though, his ostensible narration of the objections of the slaveholders reveals a central abolitionist argument—that slavery is maintained through dehumanization. Challenging the boundaries between narration and persuasion, Douglass strategically negotiates his desire to persuade and the expectation that he should offer only "facts." His highlighting of his "digression," as in the analogous passage from his 1845 *Narrative,* calls attention to his sharp criticism of slaveholders who profess Christianity and personalizes a nation's hypocrisy, adding particular emphasis to his explicit argument.

In his oratory, Douglass similarly blurs the boundaries between "facts" and "persuasion," again turning the seeming limitation of audiences' and white abolitionists leaders' expectations into a rhetorical strength. Even in early speeches, Douglass offered more than just eyewitness testimony, but he did so subtly and creatively. In an address to the Plymouth Church Anti-Slavery Society in December 1841, Douglass's "storytelling" of his experiences with prejudice demonstrate the flexibility of the narrative form. Douglass appears to begin without *exordium*—the report of his speech notes that he "rose, and gave an account of the effects of . . . prejudice, as he had experienced them in his own person" (*FDP,* 1:9). His language and his imagery, though, persuade more powerfully than would be possible in a philosophical account. "He alluded to his being dragged out of the cars lately," the report of the speech relates, "on the Eastern Railroad, after paying full fare, where the *dogs* of his fellow passengers were suffered to remain" (*FDP,* 1:9–10). Although identified as narration, the force of this image is powerfully persuasive. Similarly, Douglass epitomizes the hypocrisy of so-called Christian slaveholders in an unforgettable personal image: "My master . . . would talk most sanctimoniously about the dear Redeemer . . . yet he could lash up my poor cousin by his two thumbs, and inflict stripes and blows upon his bare back . . . all the time quoting scripture for his authority. . . . Such was the amount of this good Methodist's piety!" (*FDP,* 1:13). The rhetorical power of storytelling, which Douglass was exposed to as a slave, provides a model in which narration is a particularly potent form of argument—a model whose force depends not upon white audiences' perceptions of African American orators but upon the rhetorical traditions of African Americans.

Discussing the racism of white northern churches, Douglass draws on another African American rhetorical tradition in which narration functions persuasively: preaching.[23] Noting that he was a member of the Methodist Church in the South, Douglass recalls, "When I came North, I thought one Sunday I would attend communion" (*FDP,* 1:10). Describing religious practices in New Bedford, Douglass features Christian imagery in a unique parable: "It seems, the kingdom of Heaven is like a net; at least so it was according to the practice of these pious Christians; and when the net was drawn ashore, they had to sit down and cull out the fish; well, it happened now that some of the fish had rather black scales; so these were sorted out and packed by themselves" (*FDP,* 1:11). Douglass refers to Christ's advice to the disciples to be "fishers of men" (Matt. 4: 19, Mark 1: 17), but he revises this image to create a startling statement. Drawing on the influence of a story that would connect to his audience, but recreating the image so that it resonates at a new level, Douglass aptly demonstrates the depths of Northern prejudice.

As his speaking career progressed, Douglass placed less emphasis on his personal experiences as a slave. He continued, however, to suggest frequently that he was relating facts rather than his own opinions or beliefs. Although it might seem that this strategy was shaped in response to whites' continuing expectations that African Americans should—and indeed could, according to racist stereotypes—

relate only "facts," this perspective is incomplete. In this later oratory, Douglass does not simply accept the stereotypical notion that African Americans must relate "truths"; he exploits it. By frequently couching his central arguments against slavery in terms of accepted facts, Douglass assumes authority by turning this racist principle on its head and using it to his advantage. As Kenneth Burke maintains, this strategy—which he calls the use of "tonalities"—features suggestive terms through which a rhetor offers a controversial statement as if it were an accepted conclusion. In this manner, Burke suggests, the rhetor can advocate a particular position without drawing attention to his or her persuasive intent.[24] The position of the African American rhetor adds a new dimension to Burke's theoretical principle. Playing on the stereotypical assumption that he is capable only of providing facts, Douglass's "tonalities" exploit his audience's prejudices by framing his arguments as self-evident.

Two examples demonstrate the effectiveness of this strategy. Speaking in 1850 in Rochester, Douglass asserts that some will consider his lecture "far too tame," merely reinforcing "those truths . . . which they have so long cherished" (*FDP*, 2:260). However, he notes, he must offer the basic truths of slavery—what he calls "the anti-slavery alphabet"—to those who "have that simple lesson yet to learn" (*FDP*, 2:260). He will not, however, offer "new truths," he maintains, paraphrasing Ecclesiastes 1:9 that "there is, indeed, nothing new under the sun" (*FDP*, 2:260–61). Antislavery sentiments are self-evident, he suggests: "Man's right to liberty . . . existed in the very idea of man's creation. It was *his* even before he comprehended it. . . . The existence of this right is self-evident. It is written upon all the powers and faculties of man. . . . To assert it, is to call forth a sympathetic response from every human heart" (*FDP*, 2:261). Douglass indeed presents arguments, yet his "tonalities" give them the status of established facts. Ironically highlighting the "simple" truths that he is telling—at the basic level of an "alphabet"— Douglass exploits the stereotype that would deny him the ability to go beyond this elementary level.

In his famous oration "What to the Slave is the Fourth of July?" delivered in Rochester in 1852, Douglass similarly expresses his opinions as previously established conclusions. After fiercely denouncing slavery, he acknowledges that some might criticize his forceful tone, suggesting that he should "argue more, and denounce less . . . persuade more, and rebuke less" (*FDP*, 2:369). He asserts, however, that such persuasion would be unnecessary:

> Where all is plain there is nothing to be argued. What point in the anti-slavery creed would you have me argue? . . . Must I undertake to prove that the slave is a man? That point is conceded already. Nobody doubts it. The slaveholders themselves acknowledge it . . . when they punish disobedience on the part of the slave. . . . What is this but the acknowledgment that the slave is a moral, intellectual and responsible being? The manhood of the slave is conceded. . . .
>
> Would you have me argue that man is entitled to liberty? . . . You have already declared it. Must I argue the wrongfulness of slavery? Is that

a question for Republicans? . . . How should I look to-day, in the presence of Americans, dividing, and subdividing a discourse, to show that men have a natural right to freedom? (*FDP,* 2:369–70)

Presenting antislavery beliefs as self-evident conclusions—so obvious that even the opposition endorses them—Douglass again establishes antislavery claims through his ironic exploitation of a pervasive stereotype. Appropriating and recasting racist assumptions, Douglass is not passively reacting to white society, but actively assuming agency as a rhetor.[25]

"THE HUMBLEST MAY STAND FORTH": THE RHETORIC OF THE HIERARCHY

As his powerful arguments demonstrate, Douglass was a masterful orator. Yet he often opens his speeches by downplaying his ability, a commonplace also featured in the rhetoric of his colleagues Charles Lenox Remond and William J. Watkins. In a speech delivered at the tenth anniversary meeting of the AASS in New York in 1843, Douglass begins, "I have myself been a slave, and I do not expect to awaken such an interest in the minds of this intelligent assembly, as those have done who spoke before me" (*FDP,* 1:21). Speaking at the fourteenth anniversary meeting of the organization, he commences, "It is with great hesitation that I consent to rise here to speak. . . . I had far rather remain a listener to others. . . . I do not hope to be able, in the few remarks I have to make, to say anything new or eloquent" (*FDP,* 2:118).

This seeming "nonchalance" or self-deprecation, John Blassingame remarks, was a "nineteenth-century oratorical convention" that Douglass used "to establish rapport with his audiences."[26] However, this technique takes on additional significance for African American abolitionists. Because African American rhetors constantly negotiated the assumption that they were inferior to whites in both intellectual and oratorical skill, their deployment of this nineteenth-century commonplace appropriates audiences' expectations and recreates them in ways that grant them rhetorical authority. By exploiting the audience's expectations of their inadequacy, they take control of the terms of the antebellum hierarchy that would elevate whites over blacks. This strategy is elucidated by Kenneth Burke, who suggests that the force of societal hierarchies (such as those based on race) can be strategically marshaled in discourse for persuasive ends, turning the ostensible weakness of those who are "inferior" in the hierarchy into a rhetorical strength. Because division is based on the social stratification of individuals, Burke explains, it produces a hierarchical arrangement in which a "rhetoric of courtship" or "obeisance" is used by those lower in the hierarchy to address those at a higher level. This appeal to difference activates a corresponding desire for identification—which Burke calls "mystery"—because it evokes the desire of those who are divided by the hierarchical order to transcend their differences. Thus this "mystery" is a source of rhetorical power that can be used strategically through the highlighting of difference.[27] For antebellum African American abolitionists, invoking the hierarchy that divided antebellum Americans allows them to undermine racial stratification, establishing their authority to persuade.

For rhetors such as Douglass, Remond, and William J. Watkins, then, self-deprecatory remarks and professions of rhetorical inadequacy represent not just the use of a nineteenth-century commonplace; they constitute a particular strategy that authorizes the African American rhetor.

Speaking at the thirteenth annual meeting of the AASS in 1847, Douglass marshals a rhetorical form akin to Burke's "rhetoric of courtship": "I do not doubt but that a large portion of this audience will be disappointed . . . by . . . what I shall this day set forth. The extraordinary and unmerited eulogies which have been showered upon me . . . have done much to create expectations which, I am well aware, I can never hope to gratify. . . . I am not here to please you with an eloquent speech . . . but to speak to you . . . sober truths" (*FDP,* 2:58). Using the rhetoric of an "inferior" addressing "superiors," Douglass relies upon what Burke calls "the mimetics of inferiority," social forms in which "humility" is used to invoke "the magic of the hierarchic order itself, which imposes itself on superior and inferior both, and leads them both to aim at a dialectic transcending their discordancy of status."[28] This rhetorical strategy allows marginalized rhetors in particular to negotiate the obstacles imposed by their ostensible inferiority. Simultaneously deferring to those above him in the conventional racial hierarchy and challenging his audience to look beyond this power structure, Douglass presses his audience to temporarily forget their divisions and grant him authority to persuade.

Douglass's words, though, also have a force that transcends Burke's paradigm. Although Burke suggests that the language of any hierarchy implies its own reversal, his description implies that this reversal is inherent in hierarchical structures themselves and not in a rhetor's exploitation of hierarchical language: "The principle of *any* hierarchy involves the possibility of reversing highest and lowest."[29] Yet Douglass does not rely passively on the inherent influence of the hierarchy to invoke this reversal—he *actively* effects it through striking language that simultaneously evokes the antebellum hierarchy based on race and under-mines it. Douglass's use of irony and the multiple resonances of language cast himself as both the "inferior" and the "superior," revealing a flexibility within the "rhetoric of courtship" which can enable a marginalized rhetor to assume power. Douglass's self-deprecating remarks to the AASS' thirteenth annual meeting ironically call attention to his unique oratorical skill. As Douglass strategically minimizes his abilities, remarking to his audience that he cannot hope to live up to the praise that others have given him, he highlights the force of his discourse by referring to the "eulogies" of others and the high "expectations" his audience must hold for him. Thus, even as he seemingly disparages his rhetorical ability, Douglass authorizes his discourse by referring to the complimentary words and judgments of others.

This dual nature of Douglass's "rhetoric of courtship" is also illustrated in a striking passage from an 1850 lecture in Rochester. Douglass begins with an apparent disclaimer:

I come before you this evening to deliver the first lecture of a course which I purpose to give in this city . . .

I make this announcement with no feelings of self-sufficiency. If I do not mistake my own emotions, they are such as result from a profound sense of my incompetency to do justice to the task which I have just announced. . . .

There are times in the experience of almost every community, when even the humblest member thereof may properly presume to teach— when . . . the humblest may stand forth and be excused for opposing even his weakness to the torrent of evil. (*FDP,* 2:250)

On one level, Douglass seemingly defers to the hierarchy, adopting the rhetorical forms of the "inferior" addressing "superiors." At the same time, however, his language connotes a reversal of the hierarchy, suggesting that in fact he may be in the superior position. For Douglass, the significance of the key phrase "the humblest may stand forth" depends upon its ambiguity, which both depends upon the terms of the social order and implies its reversal. His ostensibly apologetic tone suggests one meaning: the "humblest" may be allowed, under these circumstances, to address apparent superiors on the subject of slavery. Another interpretation, however, is possible: the hierarchy may be reversed and "the humblest" may emerge in a superior role—"stand forth." Douglass's ambiguous disclaimer implies not only that he should be permitted to lecture, but that he has the right to "presume to teach" his audience. Thus he creates a particular authority that reverses usual societal relations and grants him the agency of a leader.

The dual connotations of Douglass's reference to his "humble" status are reinforced in this lecture by his use of Christlike imagery to justify his fierce antislavery rhetoric: "I grew up . . . as A SLAVE, eating the bread and drinking the cup of slavery with the most degraded of my brother bondmen. . . . In consideration of these facts, I feel that I have a right to speak, and to speak *strongly*" (*FDP,* 2:253). The force of Christian terminology, Burke indicates, lies in its merging of opposites. The figure of Christ, in particular, is simultaneously "victimized and victorious."[30] For the antebellum African American rhetor, to assume the power of this image defies white Christians' use of Christ's example to counsel submission to the oppressed. For African Americans, particularly for the slave or former slave, an alternate interpretation allowed them to assume agency through Christ's example. For slaves and other oppressed people, Christ's life not only promised vindication for the oppressed but demonstrated that the lowly in society could be granted a militant power that can free the oppressed and reverse human relations.[31] By using Christlike terminology to describe his experience, Douglass suggests this alternate—and empowering—interpretation of his role. Like Christ, he is both an oppressed member of society and a leader who has a right to persuade others and critique societal institutions. There is, Douglass implies, a powerful religious precedent for his assertion that "the humblest may stand forth."

Other African American abolitionists draw on the dual tendencies within Christ's teachings—which refer to both submission and liberation—to invoke a reversal of conventional social roles even as they appear to defer to those in authority. In an 1853 letter to the *Boston Herald,* William J. Watkins features Christ's parable of the unjust judge (Luke 18:1–8) to imply that, in fighting for equality and civil rights, African Americans recognize the societal dominance of those of superior social rank, but they will not yield under its weight. Watkins argues that Boston African Americans should be given the right to form their own militia company, a request for which they had petitioned the state legislature. The Committee on the Militia had refused to consider the petition. Watkins remarks,

> When we wish to demonstrate our capacity . . . our Committee on the Militia beg leave to "withdraw" from the field. . . .
>
> Well, *they* may take leave to withdraw, but *we* never. We recommend to their especial and pious consideration the parable of the unjust judge which they will find recorded in the 18th chapter of Luke. We intend, God willing, by our "continual" praying, to weary the "unjust judge," and possibly, he will "avenge" him of his "adversary." We have colored lawyers, physicians, and teachers; why not colored soldiers?[32]

The language of the parable allows Watkins to critique his purported "superiors" and even to suggest that their authority is unfounded. Even if those who would restrict African Americans' rights dominate society, Watkins undermines their power by casting them as "unjust judges" whose influence has no basis. And Watkins grants great agency to African Americans, who, like the widow in the parable who "troubles" the judge until he is "wearied" and grants her request, will not cease their petitions until the legislature will consider their demands—effectively overturning the conventional power dynamic.

These religious teachings that overturn traditional notions of status had a parallel in the antebellum secular realm. By the mid nineteenth century, mass democracy began to influence oratory, challenging traditional notions of rhetorical influence in ways that undermined traditional definitions of rhetorical "superiority" and "inferiority." As democratic principles gained hold, Americans began to apprehend that a person of "low" status might be more authoritative in many situations than those of "higher" rank. Kenneth Cmiel demonstrates that not only did many orators, grammarians, and Romantic philosophers assume that "coarse" or "informal" speech was necessary to reach the public; they also suggested that such linguistic forms were more trustworthy and "vital" than "refined" discourse, which they saw as "artificial." Even middle-class people who were traditionally educated often adopted what Cmiel calls a "middling rhetoric" that "married the high and the low," incorporating both the "folksy" and the "erudite." This rejection of conventional distinctions undermined norms dictating who should and who should not speak in public, challenging traditional notions of credibility. The authority of the pulpit and platform were no longer the exclusive property of elite orators.[33] This linguistic flux allowed African American men to turn the assumptions of audiences that their speech would be unsophisticated into a rhetorical advantage, creating a form of the "rhetoric of courtship" that exploited the influence of these particular societal factors.

In a letter to the West Newbury Anti-Slavery Society published in the *Liberator,* Charles Lenox Remond builds on this upheaval over traditional forms, suggesting that those rhetors who are considered "inferior" in the social hierarchy are actually more credible than elite orators. Remond "rejoic[es]" that antislavery meetings no longer merely feature the rhetoric of "particular individuals," and he calls for increasing participation of common people: "I long to see the trader from the market, the shoemaker with his apron, the farmer with his homespun frock . . . standing forward, eager with feeling, thought and voice, to be heard in behalf of a common origin and a common liberty. From such sources, eloquence emanates spontaneously. Men, women and children, who never spent the better half of their best days in learning to speak, cannot fail in interest." Such rhetors, Remond notes, will not only be popular with audiences. He also draws upon the notion that "refined" forms are "artificial" and less trustworthy than an untutored style: "[Common people] speak from the heart, and the natural heart seldom, if ever, when left free, proves traitor to its God, Liberty, or the Truth. I once loved to hang upon the lips of a favorite minister, the popular orator, and the prized student; but my taste, like their eloquence, was empty, heartless, and selfish; and painful experience tells me, it is all a trade with them. Education and usage, together with the applause of aristocrats and oppressors, has well nigh rid them of their natural hearts."[34] Remond draws upon the cultural flux concerning "high" and "low" eloquence in order to challenge traditional notions about rhetorical authority and to suggest the particular agency of those who are marginalized.

THE "MYSTERY" OF RACE

As the power of the "rhetoric of courtship" demonstrates, the force of a hierarchy is such that even when suggesting its reversal, a rhetor exploits its pervasive societal influence. And even cultural factors that seem to undermine hierarchies—like the "rhetoric of the common man" evoked by Remond—do not erase the power of entrenched societal distinctions. In spite of the force of democracy in antebellum America, most thinkers separated democratic tendencies from the leveling of racial distinctions.[35] Because antebellum racial prejudices were bolstered by "scientific" and religious justifications, they were influential cultural forces that could not be ignored by African American male rhetors or their audiences. The essentialist rhetoric of biological or divinely ordained racial differences, in particular, made physical characteristics salient markers of distinction. African American male rhetors would automatically evoke for antebellum audiences the pervasive racial stereotypes based on physical characteristics and related cultural expectations. And their discourse was judged in terms of standards based on racial difference, as the comments of white abolitionists and audiences demonstrate. In order to persuade effectively in spite of these obstacles, the antebellum African American male orator had to appropriate assumptions about race to empower his discourse.

These rhetors often relied upon what Burke calls "mystery"—the ineffable cultural force of differences—to turn the influence of racial distinctions and white-supremacist arguments into a rhetorical advantage. Emphasizing the "mystery" of racial difference, African American male abolitionists highlight the very aspects of racial difference that are used against them. As Burke's theory suggests, this strategy depends upon appealing to the "fascination" that those who are divided by a "social gulf" have for one another. As with the "rhetoric of courtship," appeals to "mystery" invite a transcendence of difference at the same time that they exploit the power of societal distinctions.[36]

Yet an examination of the use of the "mystery" of race by African American male abolitionists suggests that Burke's theory needs expansion and revision to account for the particular power of their discourse. Discussing "mystery" in somewhat static terms, Burke suggests that its influence resides in cultural definitions of difference themselves. Yet the invocation of "mystery" is very different for those rhetors who hold cultural authority than for those who are marginalized by societal definitions of difference. Whites, for example, who themselves control the terms that define what distinctions are consequential, emphasize those differences that they consider "safe" or "manageable." By bounding diversity in ways that do not disturb their hegemony, whites attempt to manage cultural difference and control racial classifications. In contrast, for people of color the act of naming, highlighting, defining, and redefining the racial differences that are assumed by society can represent resistance to cultural assumptions, an act of redefinition that undermines white control. Ruth Frankenberg, in her discussion of white women's perceptions of people of color, elucidates this point: "People of color are 'good' only insofar as their 'coloredness' can be bracketed and ignored, and this bracketing is contingent on the ability or the decision . . . of a 'noncolored'—or white—self."[37] Conversely, then, when African American rhetors take control of the terms that define the "mystery" of race, they actively assume authority. Unlike whites who discuss racial differences in a "safe" way that maintains white control, African American rhetors undermine whites' domination when they manage the terms of the debate, appropriating, challenging, and redefining racial categories; articulating their own definitions of themselves; and assuming the power inherent in racial difference to gain agency.

In his *Appeal,* Walker emphasizes the physical differences of African Americans and whites not only to establish a common ground beyond these distinctions but to challenge whites' perceptions of race and to gain control of the way racial difference is defined. Discussing historical instances of God's punishment of oppressors, Walker proposes that current political unrest and civil conflict in Spain are a result of the "judgments of God" for the existence of slavery in the Spanish empire (*DWA,* 4–5). He suggests that this conclusion is obvious to those who can put aside prejudice: "All persons who are acquainted with history, and particularly the Bible . . . and who can dispense with prejudice long enough to admit that we are *men*, notwithstanding our *improminent noses* and *woolly heads*, and believe that we feel for our fathers, mothers, wives and children, as well as the whites do for theirs . . . can easily recognize the judgments of God among the Spaniards" (*DWA*, 4–5). In this passage, Walker ironically highlights distinct physical characteristics to demonstrate the absurdity of using these differences to justify slavery. Sarcastically emphasizing the derisive language of whites— "*improminent noses*" and "*woolly heads*"—Walker ridicules these portrayals of African Americans. Revealing the insignificance and absurdity of whites' artic-ulations of difference, Walker offers a definition proving these physical distinc-tions are meaningless—to be human resides in feelings and attachments, not in the variations of hair and skin that preoccupy whites. Further, Walker's sugges-tion that God recognizes the fundamental humanity of those who are enslaved challenges the common antebellum assumption that God's ordination of essential biological differences grants whites superiority. In Walker's articulation, the idea that God would support whites' petty definitions of inferiority appears ridiculous.

Furthermore, Walker's explicit invocation of difference in conjunction with God's vengeance for oppression does not merely imply the possibility of reversal that Burke notes is inherent in any hierarchy. By juxtaposing physical distinc-tions with a potentially violent reversal of the hierarchy, Walker upsets the "safe" definitions of racial difference proposed by whites—definitions that do not dis-turb whites' hegemony. Distinct physical characteristics, in Walker's revised def-inition, may be markers of a potential superiority that can empower African Americans in ways that whites should fear. Although Walker maintains that the reversal of the hierarchy will be effected by God, the references to civil turmoil in Spain connote a situation that assigns African Americans an active rather than a passive role. God may empower African Americans to fight their oppression, but their role in this struggle will clearly be dynamic.

When Walker comments on Jefferson's description in his *Notes on the State of Virginia* of the "unfortunate difference of colour" that "is a powerful obstacle to the emancipation" of American slaves,[38] he similarly defines racial characteristics in ways that empower African Americans. Rather than maintaining that distinctions of skin color are irrelevant, Walker highlights them:

> Millions of [whites], are this day, so ignorant and avaricious, that they can-not conceive how God can have an attribute of justice, and show mercy to us because it pleased Him to make us black—which colour, Mr. Jefferson calls unfortunate! ! ! ! ! ! As though we are not as thankful to our God, for having made us as it pleased himself, as they, (the whites,) are for having made them white. . . . [W]e wish to be just as it pleased our Creator to have made us, and no avaricious and unmerciful wretches, have any business to . . . hold us in slavery. How would they like for us to make slaves of . . . and murder them as they do us? . . . The world will have an opportunity

to see whether it is unfortunate for us, that our Creator *has made us* darker than the *whites*. (*DWA*, 12)

Walker emphasizes physical differences, drawing on the influence of their "mysterious" nature. He exploits the "fascination" Burke notes results from racial difference, but he goes a step further, actively controlling the terms in which these distinctions are defined. He reinterprets the conventional notion of racial characteristics as divinely ordained, for example. Demonstrating that African Americans do not share whites' perspective about God's intentions in creating physical distinctions—revealing that they, in fact, are "pleased" to have been created as they are—Walker suggests the subjectivity inherent in notions of racial inferiority. Societal dominance, then, which is dependent on whites' definitions of racial difference, is arbitrary, and roles can be reversed.

As in his passage about Spain, Walker implies in his commentary on Jefferson that God has the power to effect such a reversal, but his reference to divine vengeance does not diminish the influence of African Americans. The agents of vengeance that Walker refers to are African Americans themselves, who will have a chance to prove that their color is anything but "unfortunate"—or that, in a clever dual meaning, their color may give them a strength that will prove to be unfortunate to whites. As with his use of jeremiadic rhetoric, which will be discussed in detail in the next section, Walker's references to God do not deny African Americans agency. God may sanction and ordain their actions, but they will play an indispensable role in their vindication.

Walker also explicitly redefines biblical "evidence" of racial inferiority, exploiting the influence of this antebellum discourse of race as he undermines its conventional interpretations. After describing whites as the "natural enemies" of African Americans, Walker defines this phrase:

Shem, Ham and Japheth, together with their father Noah and wives, I believe were not natural enemies to each other. . . . [A]fter the flood . . . there were no other living men in all the earth, notwithstanding some ignorant creatures hesitate not to tell us that we, (the blacks) are the seed of Cain the murderer of his brother Abel. . . . [I] have never seen a [biblical] verse which testifies whether we are the seed of Cain or of Abel. Yet those men tell us that we are the seed of Cain, and that God put a dark stain upon us, that we might be known as their slaves!!! Now, I ask those avaricious and ignorant wretches, who act more like the seed of Cain, by murdering[,] the whites or the blacks? . . . How many thousand souls have the blacks murdered in cold blood, to make them work in wretchedness and ignorance, to support them and their families? (*DWA*, 60–61)

Walker cleverly uses one biblical text often cited as evidence of the inferiority of those of African descent—the story of Noah and his sons—to refute the racist interpretation of another biblical passage—the curse on Cain. Building on the antebellum premise that the Bible is literally true, he argues that Africans cannot be

ing in 1842 before a legislative committee of the Massachusetts State
vened to consider a petition calling for an end to segregated public
ion, Remond explicitly expresses confidence that his audience will
cial distinctions. But at the outset he demonstrates that this erasure of
rence is not possible—and that he intends to use the salience of racial
to his advantage:

g at this time, and on this occasion, being the first person of color
s ever addressed either of the bodies assembling in this building . . .
. . . be subject to . . . misconceptions from the moment I open my
ehalf of the prayer of the petitioners for whom I appear, and there-
l I have the right at least to ask, at the hands of this intelligent
ittee, an impartial hearing; and that whatever prejudices they may
nbibed, be eradicated from their minds, if such exist. I have, how-
o much confidence in their intelligence, and too much faith in their
ination to do their duty as the representatives of this Common-
, to presume they can be actuated by partial motives. Trusting, as I
t the day is not distant, when, on all questions touching the rights
ens of this State, men shall be considered *great* only as they are
and not that it shall be told, and painfully experienced, that . . .the
privileges and immunities of [Massachusetts's] citizens are meas-
complexion.[42]

tention to his position as the first person of color to address the Massa-
islature, Remond highlights the "misconceptions" and "prejudices"
tion provokes. His opening overshadows his claim that his audience is
ed by prejudice; if this assertion were true, clearly he would not have to
e at all. Remond draws attention to his audience's discomfort with his
he asks them to overlook it. As he appears to defer to a "colorless" society
offer rights regardless of "complexion," Remond draws on the "mys-
al distinctions to control and redefine the terms of racial difference.
rategy becomes clear in a passage in which Remond exploits the
reoccupation with racial difference to offer a reversal of racial power
disconcert his audience. "Complexion" should not, Remond asserts,
y made the criterion of rights. Should the people of color, through a
f Providence, become a majority, to the last I would oppose it upon
rinciple; for, in either case, it would be equally reprehensible and
—alike to be condemned and repudiated."[43] This passage suggests
n principle that hierarchies imply their own reversal; but, like
mond does not passively allude to societal upheaval. He actively
mmon antebellum fear—that the increasing African American pop-
atened the safety of the white population[44]—and articulates a poten-
of oppressor and oppressed. His "opposition" to a reversed hierarchy
e notwithstanding, Remond indicates that white dominance is arbi-
nsitory.

Cain's descendents because all races descend
Shem, and Japheth were not "natural enemies,"
between the races—the brothers' descendents—

However, even as he denies that there is a
races and questions whether the story of Cain
he draws on the racial significance of the topos of
"seed of Cain." Questioning his audience abo
rates the races by their actions, rewriting the
whites act like Cain's descendents, he propose
are "marked." Walker's interpretation clever
normative status. Scholars have noted that w
that this invisibility is a result of white heg
words, "color" is associated with those wh
becomes the norm against which people of co
hegemony requires that whiteness be made "
is shown to be an arbitrary cultural construct r
terpretation of the Cain and Abel story can be
project. Walker disturbs conventional racial
mulations of race are arbitrary, and makes wh
the mark of Cain may be white skin. He dem
color can marshal when they question the n
undermine whites' arbitrary definitions of o
suggests that there was precedent for Walker
of the Cain and Abel story. Lawrence Levine
can slaves and Africans exposed to the teachin
racist formulation of this biblical narrative. In
nally gave all people dark skin, but Cain an
white as a result of his sin. In an 1831 *Liberat*
at a "public exhibition" by a pupil at a "scho
this reversed myth appears. The student note:
the first white man, through fear"—presuma
of killing Abel.[40]

For African American orators who spol
biracial audiences, this process of claiming tl
ence took on an added significance. Their pre:
for antebellum audiences the connotations of
claims that such distinctions were proof of inl
lectures, for example, frequently refer to his
Robert Fanuzzi notes, that white audiences
black orator" a "public spectacle."[41] Rather th:
ing to make their audiences "comfortable" v
Douglass point out racial distinctions and h
and presuppositions about race in their speecl

Spe
House c
transpor
overlook
racial dif
distinctic

In ri
who
I ma
lips i
fore
Con
have
ever,
dete
weal
do, t
of ci
good-
right
ured

Drawing
chusetts
such a sit
not influe
mention
race even
that wou
tery" of ra

This
America
that wou
"be right
revolutio
the same
unjustifia
the Burk
Walker,
exploits a
ulation th
tial revers
based on
trary and

In an 1853 speech before the AFASS in New York City, Douglass draws even greater attention to his race to challenge his audience's preoccupation with racial divisions, to reveal their arbitrary nature, and to undermine white hegemony. A "peculiar relation" exists between him and his audience, Douglass notes at the beginning of his speech, immediately establishing that he will not ignore race or leave it to others to define his position as an African American orator. He continues,

> I am a colored man, and this is a white audience. No colored man, with
> any nervous sensibility, can stand before an American audience without
> an intense and painful sense of the immense disadvantage under which he
> labors. . . . The ground which a colored man occupies in this country is
> every inch of it sternly disputed . . . by a cold, flinty-hearted, unreasoning
> and unreasonable prejudice. . . . [W]ere I a white man, speaking before
> and for white men, I should in this country have a smooth sea. . . . The
> Hungarian, the Italian, the Irishman, the Jew, and the Gentile, all find in
> this land a home, and . . . willing ears, warm hearts and open hands. . . .
> But for my poor people enslaved—blasted and ruined—it would appear,
> that America had neither justice, mercy nor religion. (*FDP,* 2:424–25)

Through repetition of the "colored-white" dichotomy, Douglass reveals that he can assume the agency to name racial difference and to draw on the authority inherent in this act. Rather than using difference to evoke identification, as Burke's model would suggest, for Douglass the "mystery" of racial difference prevents his audience from establishing a complete identification with him. The whites among his abolitionist audience, then, are faced both with their own prejudices that Douglass will not allow them to forget and with the usurpation of their societal authority.[45] If whites' hegemony resides in their ability to classify racial difference in ways that make them comfortable, then Douglass has undermined this power and speaks to them from a position of influence that they cannot manage.

Douglass also comments in this passage on the social construction of "whiteness," revealing the arbitrariness of racial categories. If, as he notes, the category "white" gathers together people with great differences from a variety of ethnic and religious backgrounds while the "colored-white" opposition divides those who live in the same country, these classifications are merely cultural constructs that serve the traditional power structure. Rather than assuming the normative status of whiteness, Douglass shows that it can be interrogated and challenged. Questioning white authority, he suggests that African Americans can assume the agency to articulate definitions of race that do not marginalize them. He also challenges white Americans by revealing the way that race structures their daily lives. For whites, Frankenberg notes, discourse on race focuses on the oppression experienced by others rather than on the privileges they enjoy.[46] Douglass, though, draws attention to the results of white privilege, the "smooth sea" that white immigrants find in America and the "willing ears, warm hearts and open hands" that are extended to them. Race is redefined in Douglass's articulation, becoming not just a part of the lives of people of color, but a defining principle for all Americans. Douglass demands that whites do not turn away from the implications of race in their lives or assume that they are removed from the system of racial privilege and oppression.

By highlighting how race influences the lives of all Americans, Douglass suggests that the African American rhetor must emphasize race to assert authority. He reiterates this point later in the speech in a comment on the evasion of racial difference. A discourse that purports to shun racial distinctions, Frankenberg maintains, avoids engaging the realities of white hegemony. Thus even when this "color-evasive" discourse seems to "assert the idea of crossracial common humanity," it does so on "white-centered terms" and does not challenge "the harsh realities of power imbalance."[47] Douglass suggests this limitation of "color-evasive" language when he harshly criticizes the comments of Remond before a Cincinnati audience the previous month. In this speech, Remond remarked, "He would not speak as a colored man, but as *a man*. The Anti-Slavery movement had grown to that extent, that its interests were the interests of the whole country. When the nature, claims and inevitable tendencies of human slavery were fully considered, the colored man would be lost sight of."[48] Implying that Remond's words demonstrated "cowardly meanness," Douglass asserts, "As a colored man I do speak—as a colored man I was invited here to speak—and as a colored man there are peculiar reasons for my speaking. The man struck is the man to cry out. I would place myself—nay, I am placed—among the victims of American oppression" (*FDP*, 2:427–28). Douglass implies that to evade racial terms is to ignore the way race contributes to victimization and to avoid assuming the agency to critique the racism of American society.

Yet, as we have seen, not all of Remond's oratory downplays the salience of race. Like Douglass, Remond adopts a variety of strategies through which he exploits American preoccupation with race and appropriates racial terms. Both men feature humor and irony to challenge traditional racial distinctions. Speaking before the AASS in 1858, Remond features a pun to make an ironic double commentary about his racial status. He compares his position before the AASS to another occasion at which he spoke, remarking, "Not long since, I happened to attend a public demonstration in Massachusetts, where I believe I chanced to be the only person of color present. I did not expect, by any means, to be called upon to say a word . . . and I cannot well understand why I was called upon to speak, unless it was to give *color* to the occasion. (Laughter and applause.) I am here this morning . . . not only to give color to this occasion—and a pretty deep one at that—but to give my most hearty approval of the resolutions to which we have listened."[49] Remond's words resonate at two levels. Demonstrating that abolitionists and audiences often treat him differently because of his color, he exposes their preoccupation with his race, not with his arguments. By voicing this implicit assumption, Remond criticizes this concern with race that constrains African American abolitionists and dictates that they remain in certain limited positions within the movement. But Remond's remarks about his color also make another point, one that shows that he controls his own presence on the platform and will not merely play a role assigned him. Calling attention to his dark complexion, Remond assumes the authority to describe his racial difference, exposing his audience's fascination with race by appropriating its terms. The often unspoken discussions of racial difference that focus on "darkness" or on particular physical characteristics are brought out into the open in Remond's commentary and rendered open to critique.

Douglass also features irony to reveal the arbitrariness and absurdity of traditional ideas about race. Speaking in Rochester on August 1, 1848, the tenth anniversary of West Indian emancipation, he ironically reverses antebellum conventions that exclude African American rhetors from the platform:

> I rejoice to see before me white as well as colored persons. . . . [T]he great truth to which we have met to do honor, belongs to the whole human family. From this meeting, therefore, no member of the human family is excluded. We have this day a free platform, to which, without respect to class, color, or condition, all are invited. Let no man here feel that he is a mere spectator—that he has no share in the proceedings of this day, because his face is of a paler hue than mine. The occasion is not one of color, but of universal man—from the purest black to the clearest white, welcome! welcome! In the name of liberty and justice, I extend to each and to all, of every complexion . . . a heartfelt welcome. (*FDP,* 2:134)

Douglass's "welcoming" of white rhetors reverses the usual condescending invitations to African American rhetors to "share in the proceedings" of abolitionist gatherings. Overturning the usual discourse of race in which "whiteness" is normative and color is highlighted, Douglass calls attention to the physical characteristics of whites—their faces that are of "a paler hue" than his own. Demonstrating that authority resides in the ability to define racial classifications, Douglass demonstrates that his race can place him in the dominant role. In what can be seen as an ironic reformulation of Burke's "rhetoric of courtship," Douglass is the superior patronizing his "paler" colleagues. As Douglass redefines race and challenges the normative status of whiteness, he reveals that although whites may define what racial characteristics are significant, they cannot control the interpretation of these distinctions. African American rhetors can appropriate and recontextualize the discourse of race in antebellum America in ways that authorize their persuasion and undermine white hegemony.

"I AM IN THE HAND OF GOD": JEREMIADIC STRATEGIES

As we have seen, Walker frequently alludes to God's vengeance in his *Appeal* as he condemns whites' racism and oppression of African Americans. These references are linked to the rhetorical form of the jeremiad, a genre that has particular resonance for American rhetors and audiences.[50] Jeremiadic rhetoric, named for the Old Testament prophet who sought to call Israel back to piety and righteousness, depends upon the notion that a particular group of people who are "chosen" by God have strayed from the right path. Jeremiadic or prophetic speakers warn audiences that they have sinned and exhort them to change their ways to avoid punishment for their transgressions. Thus, although the prophet's message may create anger or even hostility in an audience that is being rebuked, the jeremiad in its traditional form ultimately depends upon and reinforces the shared beliefs of the community in their special mission and principles.

A jeremiadic ethos can enable marginalized rhetors in particular to establish credibility before skeptical audiences because prophetic speakers are inherently on the margins of society, removed from those they criticize. The rhetor's difference from the audience is in fact a central motivating force in a jeremiad, allowing the rhetor to stand apart from the mainstream society, which has gone astray. The prophetic ethos can also offer marginalized rhetors the authority to harshly condemn their society and to call for change while simultaneously deflecting attention from themselves. The prophetic figure is frequently self-effacing, claiming to be a vessel through which divine wisdom is given to the audience. This strategy both authorizes his or her discourse and removes conventional restrictions on those who are not in traditionally authoritative positions in society. Distancing themselves from the force of their words or the success of their persuasive efforts, rhetors can present boldly critical arguments through the genre of the jeremiad.

This general theoretical perspective on the jeremiad requires some adjustment to account for the particular prophetic rhetoric of African American rhetors. David Howard-Pitney and Wilson Jeremiah Moses propose that African American rhetors have developed a particular form of the American jeremiad. The African American jeremiad shares significant features with the broader genre of the American jeremiad, but also contains distinct elements of its own. In particular, it is based on fundamental paradoxes—or, put another way, defining tensions. Because African Americans are both part of American culture and excluded socially from it, the African American jeremiadic speaker demonstrates both a hostility toward American culture and a loyalty to fundamental American values. Although African American jeremiadic rhetors rely on the notion that America is a "chosen" nation with a divine purpose, they also feature African Americans in particular as a "chosen" people. Relying on the strong parallels between the biblical plight of the Israelites and American slavery, African American jeremiadic rhetors call vividly upon Old Testament examples and language in order to argue that, like the long-suffering Old Testament Jews, African Americans will eventually be vindicated by God.[51] The plight of African Americans, then, assumes messianic significance, embodying God's promise to redeem American society. Thus the African American jeremiadic rhetor simultaneously offers a radical critique of society and draws on dominant cultural topoi.[52]

Moses and Howard-Pitney suggest that the deployment of these dominant myths can be problematic, seeming to uphold some of the values about which African Americans were ambivalent. A loyalty to America's special mission, for example, might connote an ultimate faith in the authority of white leaders to eventually fulfill America's promise. Similarly, the acceptance of the role of "redeemer" of America may imply that African Americans' suffering is necessary or even justified and that they should submit to oppression. On the other hand, these scholars argue that the African American jeremiad has the potential to further an agenda of "black nationalism," an assertion of African Americans' authority to articulate and define their future in America.[53] In the prophetic rhetoric of Walker, William Watkins, and Frederick Douglass, I will demonstrate, the latter tendency toward militancy and self-assertion is predominant. Although they draw on traditional American assumptions, these rhetors redefine conventional perspectives in ways that grant themselves agency in particular and empower African Americans in general. Their formulation of America's divine mission challenges the perception that white Americans have spiritual authority and gives African Americans a central role in America's redemption. Although they stress a religious mission and an adherence to God's plan, their articulations of divine judgments do not deny agency to African Americans, whose assertive and even militant actions they authorize. The particular form of the jeremiad employed by these abolitionists suggests that prophetic rhetoric can be a genre that evokes revolutionary power and refashions seemingly conservative ideals for radical ends.

Even before he published his strongly jeremiadic *Appeal,* Walker relied on prophetic themes in his abolitionist oratory. In his 1828 speech before the MGCA, Walker exploits the influence of a fundamental topos of the African American jeremiad—the idea that African Americans are a "chosen people" whom God will ultimately vindicate. At the outset of the speech, Walker remarks, "When I reflect upon the many impediments through which we have had to conduct [the MGCA's] affairs . . . I cannot . . . but be of the opinion, that an invisible arm must have been stretched out in our behalf." Similarly, he ends by affirming that God's plan includes the ultimate vindication of African Americans: "Though this, and perhaps another, generation may not experience the promised blessings of Heaven, yet, the dejected, degraded, and now enslaved children of Africa will have, in spite of all their enemies, to take their stand among the nations of the earth. . . . I verily believe that God has something in reserve for us, which, when he shall have poured it out upon us, will repay us for all our suffering and miseries."[54] Walker's reference to the divine plan for God's "chosen people" invokes hope and optimism, demonstrating that they must remain true to their ideals in spite of suffering. At the same time, Walker suggests the promise of God's ultimate justice, implying God's vengeance upon those "enemies" who oppress African Americans.

Notably, though, Walker's references to divine authority and God's ultimate plan do not deny African Americans agency. In contrast, Walker argues that it is imperative that they take an active role in furthering the divine mission, suggesting that their participation is instrumental to their eventual vindication. Walker proposes, for example, that African Americans are called upon by God to take decisive action, particularly organized efforts such as those undertaken by the MGCA:

> Do not two hundred and eight years [of] very intolerable sufferings teach us the actual necessity of a general union among us? . . . Shall we keep slumbering on, with our arms completely folded up, exclaiming every now and then, against our miseries, yet never do the least thing to ameliorate our condition, or that of posterity? . . .
>
> Yes . . . it is indispensibly our duty to try every scheme that we think will have a tendency to facilitate our salvation, and leave the final result to that God . . . who ever has, and will, repay every nation according to its works.[55]

Walker may defer to God's ultimate authority, but he also maintains that African Americans have a fundamental role in furthering God's plan. Walker's jeremiadic rhetoric does not counsel that his audience submit to oppression or acquiesce to the racist status quo with the passive hope that it will eventually be overturned. Divinely empowered, he suggests, African Americans have a responsibility to take decisive, even radical or militant, action.

The dual authority Walker grants to African Americans in this speech—as agents of God and as self-determining actors—is a foundation of his *Appeal*. Walker creates a prophetic ethos that simultaneously invokes God's plan and empowers him as a strong and assertive earthly agent of God's purpose. Even if, he asserts in his "Preamble," his audience does not "profit by" his arguments, his text represents the fulfillment of his duty to them, to "[his] country and [his] God" (*DWA*, 3). Traditional theories of the jeremiad suggest that such professions remove the rhetor from his or her words, deflecting authority solely to God. Yet Walker turns the role of the vessel for God's words into a position of great rhetorical strength by invoking his potential status as martyr. Explicitly denying concern for his life or safety, he claims that he writes "without the fear of man," fearing only God (*DWA*, 54). Echoing Paul's words to the Ephesian elders before he goes to Jerusalem (Acts 20:24), Walker assures his audience, "I am in the hand of God, and at your disposal. I count my life not dear unto me, but I am ready to be offered at any moment" (*DWA*, 71–72). Instead of removing authority from himself, Walker's position as a potential martyr allows him to argue fearlessly and impassively. One who is in the "hand of God" and ready to be sacrificed will not compromise his principles or his rhetoric. Walker activates the forceful symbolism of Christian sacrifice, in which, Burke remarks, the martyr is paradoxically both victim and victor.[56] Thus Walker transforms the stereotype of the selfless and suffering African American—the "romantic racialism" of many condescending white reformers—into a more complex and powerful ethos, encompassing the authority and insistence of the righteous martyr as well as the inspired follower of God's will.

Relying on this righteous and authoritative ethos, Walker's *Appeal* refers explicitly to the punishment of white Americans for their sins against African Americans. Walker remarks that God will determine the form this retribution will take and that African Americans may not be the agents of vengeance. This deference to God's plan, though, does not remove authority from Walker as a prophetic messenger. From the beginning of the text, Walker assumes the agency to assert in confident and vivid terms a radical vision of the future. In his "Preamble," he maintains, "[God] will at one day appear fully in behalf of the oppressed, and arrest the progress of the avaricious oppressors; for although the destruction of the oppressors God may not effect by the oppressed, yet the Lord our God will bring other destructions upon them. . . . Will [God] let the oppressors rest comfortably and happy always? Will he not cause the very children of the oppressors to rise up against them, and oftimes put them to death?" (*DWA*, 3). Walker does not leave the answer to this question abstract, recalling (via an *occultatio*) a vivid example that implies the extent of the violence he predicts: "I will not here speak of the destructions which the Lord brought upon Egypt, in consequence of the oppression and consequent groans of the oppressed—of the hundreds and thousands of Egyptians whom God hurled into the Red Sea for afflicting his people in their land. . . . I am aware that you know too well, that God is just, as well as merciful!" (*DWA*, 3–4). Walker's graphic message to white America relies on a central topos of the American jeremiad. Sacvan Bercovitch explains that the function of the jeremiad to effect social change depends upon the notion that "the future, though divinely assured, [is] never quite there" and thus the jeremiadic speaker must "provide the sense of insecurity that [will] ensure the outcome."[57] In Walker's formulation, this "insecurity" has militant overtones, giving his rhetoric urgency. Walker may defer to God's plan, but it is in Walker's vivid rhetoric that the plan becomes concrete rather than abstract. Walker's radical vision empowers the earthly author of the *Appeal* with a distinctive authority.

Through his references to divine vengeance, Walker creates a dual rhetoric of retribution. He invokes—and thus, indirectly, calls for—a divinely inspired punishment for white Americans for their sins against African Americans. At the same time, he professes a concern for white Americans' welfare that is consonant with his role as a prophet who must try to bring about a peaceful transformation. These seemingly paradoxical tendencies in his jeremiadic rhetoric draw on the tensions within Christianity, which simultaneously evokes images of submission and of militant empowerment. These aspects of Christianity are fundamental to its force, allowing the oppressed to marshal its influence and turn the position of apparent weakness into one of divine authority. Walker features this complex dynamic within his jeremiadic rhetoric. Discussing the complicity of American religious authorities with slavery, for example, he warns Americans of God's impending judgment. "Know this," he apostrophizes American ministers, "that although you treat us and our children now, as you do your domestic beast—yet the final result of all future events are known but to God Almighty alone . . . who dethrones one earthly king and sits up another, as it seemeth good in his holy sight" (*DWA*, 38). Walker's vision of the future depends upon God's will, but he suggests that earthly actors will be empowered—namely African Americans who will be given agency to end their oppression and possibly to punish their oppressors. Walker's message, then, is potentially militant, calling for radical action against slavery in the name of God.

At the same time, Walker alludes to Christianity's messages of peace and reconciliation, maintaining the ethos of the prophet who has the spiritual welfare of his audience at heart. Professions of charity often coexist with his visions of divine vengeance in rich passages that evoke the powerful tensions within Christianity. Quoting from Revelation (22:11), he notes that he does not wish for the punishment that he nonetheless believes is inevitable:

> Hear it Americans! ! "He that is unjust, let him be unjust still:—and he which is filthy, let him be filthy still: and he that is righteous, let him be righteous still: and he that is holy, let him be holy still." I hope that the Americans may hear, but I am afraid that they have done us so much injury . . . that their hearts will be hardened, so that their destruction may be sure.
>
>   . . . God suffers some to go on until they are ruined for ever! ! ! ! ! Will it be the case with the whites of the United States of America?—We hope not—we would not wish to see them destroyed notwithstanding, they have and do now treat us more cruel [*sic*] than any people have treated another. . . . The will of God must however, in spite of us, *be done*. (*DWA*, 39–41)

Walker's use of the Old Testament terminology of Pharaoh's refusal to free the Israelites because he "hardened his heart" suggests the precedent of God's punishment for those who persist in the sin of slavery. Although he professes concern for whites' welfare, these comments do not minimize his ultimate prediction of harsh punishment. In fact, they give it a greater urgency, suggesting that any personal motives are overshadowed by a divine plan. Seemingly offering white Americans goodwill, Walker predicts a future in which they must face retribution. As the spokesman for this militant vision, Walker assumes great power and authority. Simultaneously evoking apparently conflicting aspects of Christianity, Walker challenges the supremacy of white Americans and suggests a unique and influential mission for the African American prophetic rhetor.

This complexity inherent in the African American jeremiad allowed even those African American abolitionists who explicitly professed nonresistance to create forceful arguments that invoke retribution against white America for slavery. In an 1831 letter to Garrison published in the *Liberator,* William Watkins protests the efforts of colonizationists and remarks that he hopes that the fight to grant African Americans civil rights in America, their "native land," will be a peaceful one "accomplished in a way sanctioned by the gospel of peace: 'without confused noise, or garments rolled in blood.'" Watkins's reference to the prophet Isaiah's call for the reign of the Prince of Peace implies a complex relationship between peace and discord, based on the notion that divinely sanctioned violence may bring about eventual harmony. The full passage from which Watkins quotes—"every battle of the warrior is with confused noise, and garments rolled in blood, but this shall be with burning and fuel of fire" (Isa. 9:5)—implies that although this battle may not be traditional, it may involve force nonetheless. Later in his letter, Watkins reinforces this notion that God may use violence to punish oppressors, quoting from Psalms, "Our cause will yet triumph. . . . 'The rulers' of the land may 'take counsel together' . . . but 'He that sitteth in the heavens shall laugh: the Lord shall have them in derision.'"[58] His references to Pss. 2:2 and 2:4 are significant. In these biblical verses, "the rulers"—in Watkins's analogy, proslavery forces—try to conspire against the Lord's "Anointed," but God eventually overcomes them: "Then shall he speak unto them in his wrath, and vex them in his sore displeasure" (Ps. 2:5). Through the jeremiadic form and its evocation of the tensions within Christianity, even the nonresistant Watkins can assume the authority to call for a severe punishment for those who support slavery.

In "What to the Slave is the Fourth of July?" Douglass also features the language of the prophet Isaiah to blame American religious institutions harshly for their complicity with slavery.[59] The American church, he argues, "has made itself the bulwark of American slavery, and the shield of American slave-hunters" and "many of its most eloquent Divines . . . have shamelessly given the sanction of religion and the Bible to the whole slave system" (*FDP,* 2:377). Explicitly outlining the sins of American Christian authorities, Douglass boldly challenges the conventional religious assumptions of his society. In his reformulation, American Christianity is unchristian:

> These ministers make religion a cold and flinty-hearted thing . . . a religion which favors the rich against the poor; which exalts the proud above the humble . . . which says to the man in chains, *stay there;* and to the oppressor, *oppress on* . . . it makes God a respecter of persons, denies his fatherhood of the race, and tramples in the dust the great truth of the brotherhood of man. . . . In the language of Isaiah, the American church might well be addressed, "Bring no more vain oblations. . . . Yea! when ye make many prayers, I will not hear. YOUR HANDS ARE FULL OF BLOOD; cease to do evil, learn to do well; seek judgement; relieve the oppressed; judge for the fatherless, plead for the widow." (*FDP,* 2:378)

Douglass affirms Christian principles, but he challenges the traditional interpretation given them by white religious leaders who counsel submission and deny equality. Through the form of the jeremiad, he exploits the power of Christianity to liberate the oppressed and bring down the guilty. White religious leaders, Douglass demonstrates, cannot control the implications of Christ's teachings; rather, the African American prophet can assume an authority that undermines their traditional interpretations of Christianity and articulates a new vision of God's plan.

Like Walker and Watkins, Douglass's rhetoric is informed by the duality of Christian imagery that valorizes both mercy and militant liberation. In an 1849 address in New York, Douglass simultaneously appeals to God's ultimate punishment, even in terms that suggest powerful African American action, while strategically denying any personal interest in this vengeance. Slaves, Douglass remarks, "may yet imitate the example of our fathers of '76" (*FDP*, 2:151). In a passage reminiscent of Walker's rhetoric, Douglass explicitly maintains that he does not wish for this potential revolutionary action at the same time that he articulates a radical vision:

> I do not mean to say here, my friends, that this result is a desirable one . . . but I look to it as an inevitable one, if the nation shall persevere in the enslavement of the coloured people. . . . I do not say that I would hasten it, I do not say that I would advocate the result or aim to accomplish or bring it about . . . I only base myself upon the doctrine of the Scriptures, and upon human nature, and speaking out through all history. "Those that lead into captivity shall go into captivity." "Those that take the sword shall perish by the sword." Those who have trampled upon us for the last two hundred years . . . may expect that their turn will come one day. (*FDP*, 2:151–52)

Drawing on the authority of Scripture, Douglass implies the inevitability of the radical future he simultaneously regrets and endorses. His reference to the apocalyptic vision of Revelation (13:10) empowers his rhetoric with the millenialism of the Christian tradition. At the same time, Christ's words to the disciple who strikes the ear of an officer who arrests Jesus—"all they that take the sword shall perish with the sword" (Matt. 26:52)—embody the paradoxical tendencies within Christianity toward peace and retribution. Christ's words resonate with multiple meanings that Douglass features in this complex jeremiadic passage. The influence of American religious tradition, Douglass and other African American jeremiadic rhetors imply, cannot only be marshaled by those who are in power. The militant potential of Christianity is not controlled by white America and can be a persuasive force in the rhetoric of those who are marginalized.

"DO YOU UNDERSTAND YOUR OWN LANGUAGE?": REVOLUTIONARY RHETORIC

Douglass's reference to potential slave insurrection in terms of both "the example of our fathers of '76" and Christian principles demonstrates the strong connection in American culture between sacred traditions and the "secular religion" associated with the texts and symbolism of the founding of America. As the Bible was an authoritative text of American religious tradition, the Declaration of Independence was often elevated in nineteenth-century rhetoric to a religious significance in mythologizing the founding of America, idealizing the creation of a completely new nation dedicated to liberty and equality. This text was resonant for antebellum Americans, who debated its meaning and significance, often focusing particularly on its relevance to slavery and the rights of free African Americans.[60]

For supporters of slavery, the Declaration of Independence presented a particular theoretical and exegetical problem. To justify enslavement in an ostensible land of liberty, they engaged in complicated rhetorical gymnastics to support the ideals of the American Revolution as well as the nation's "peculiar institution." Many proslavery rhetors argued that, based on the Founding Fathers' intentions, the Declaration's promises of freedom and equality did not include African Americans. In "The Education, Labor, and Wealth of the South," Samuel Cartwright maintains, "Mr. Jefferson never meant to say that negroes were equal to white men; but that white men, whether born in England or America were equal to one another." Discussing the Declaration, Albert Taylor Bledsoe asserts that the ideal of equality could be consistent with denying rights to African Americans, explaining convolutedly, "If [a law] excluded some from a privilege or power which it conferred upon others, this is because they were not included within the condition on which alone it should be extended to any. Such is not an equality of rights and power . . . but it is an equality of justice." Some supporters of slavery even downplay the significance of the articulation of certain rights in the Declaration of Independence. Bledsoe proposes that because "the right of the individual" could be "held in subjection to the undoubted right of the community to protect itself and secure its own highest good," the Declaration's profession of the right to liberty was "a slight mistake." Congressman John Tyler argues more critically that because "distinctions will exist," the proposition "that all men are, by nature, equally free, sovereign, and independent," is clearly a "fallacy."[61]

Within this context, African American abolitionists who wished to feature the Declaration of Independence and the related themes of the American Revolution in their antislavery rhetoric could not rely on conventional interpretations. They needed to appropriate these topoi, redefining them in the service of abolition. Celeste Michelle Condit and John Louis Lucaites demonstrate that antebellum African American rhetors crafted a concept of equality that countered proslavery formulations, using "rhetorical revision" of the Declaration of Independence to "extend the scope" of terms such as equality, liberty, and human rights. Condit and Lucaites emphasize rhetoric that is, in Gary Woodward's terms, primarily "adaptory"—appealing to common ground with an audience and aiming to reduce dissonant messages that clash with their beliefs. In adaptory rhetoric, the "expectations of others" form the basis of a persuasive situation, and the rhetor attempts to adapt the message to avoid a clash with the audience's beliefs and attitudes. Shared values of rhetor and speaker, rather than conflict between them, are emphasized.[62] In the case of African American abolitionists arguing for equality, adaptory strategies include constructing inclusive ideals of equality, interpreting the Declaration of Independence to support African American freedom, and deploying the measured ethe of those asking for their rights and defending their inclusion in American society.

Yet Condit and Lucaites's analysis does not account for the full range of arguments of African American male abolitionists featuring the Declaration of Independence and topoi associated with the Revolution. African American rhetors do not rely solely on this adaptory tradition as they argue for equality; in fact, their most powerful persuasion often does not fit this paradigm. An alternative tradition of discourse involves rhetoric that Woodward calls "advisory." Advisory speakers resist "traditional conciliatory gestures," emphasize conflict and dissent between rhetor and audience, "challenge conventional attitudes," and judge audiences harshly. They specifically appeal to major premises listeners may not wish to hear or may not even endorse, perhaps even evoking shock as they attempt to reveal their audiences' hypocrisy. Rather than appealing to logical proof, advisory rhetors often marshal a rhetoric of "moral absolutism" to authorize their harsh messages.[63]

Although Woodward designates the categories of advisory and adaptory rhetoric as discrete, "competing" forms, it may be more accurate to see the two traditions as opposite ends of a continuum. Indeed, as Woodward notes, discourse may simultaneously feature adaptory and advisory strategies.[64] The advisory model, though, has particular features that elucidate the rhetoric of African American abolitionists. When they feature America's rhetoric of liberty and equality, African American abolitionists frequently highlight their *exclusion* from American society and their marginalized status, directly challenging America's commitment to principles expressed in the Declaration of Independence and emphasizing American hypocrisy. Instead of demonstrating that the rhetorical declarations of America's founders extend equality to African Americans— a task that assumes they are responsible for proving they are entitled to rights— they confidently appropriate the rhetoric of the American Revolution, assuming their rights as given and chastising Americans for violating them. These strategies allow African American men to create emphatic, harshly critical arguments, marshaling the dominant culture's texts and myths for both overt and subtle condemnation of America and for implication of radical action—even violent measures—to end slavery. Notably, these tactics grant the African American male abolitionist agency that is unavailable through adaptory rhetoric. Rather than shaping their rhetoric in response to the expectations of white Americans, they appropriate, exploit, and redefine the beliefs of their society in order to argue for radical change. Eschewing conciliatory tactics that may not directly challenge white hegemony, they confront Americans with their hypocrisy and even suggest militant action against those who hold authority in their society. Furthermore, exploiting the complexities of language and simultaneously invoking and recreating their society's dominant texts and topoi, they turn the language of those in power into a critique of their society. America's language is not a source of authority for white leaders alone, they demonstrate; it can be marshaled by the oppressed in contexts that empower them.

The militant, absolutist rhetoric these African American abolitionists deploy also elucidates a paradox inherent in the extra-logical discourse of moral certitude. Denying alternatives, the rhetoric of moral absolutism foreshadows the end of discourse, when only violence remains to bring about change. This implication that the fulfillment of argument may be violence would have resonance for audiences of abolitionist rhetoric. Eighteenth-century and antebellum Americans' attitudes toward rebellion, Kimberly Smith demonstrates, were fraught with tension, and "distinctions between violence and argument" were not always clear.[65] African American abolitionists draw on this source of cultural ambivalence as they comment not only on the use of language but on its limits, suggesting the potential for violence in all revolutionary rhetoric.

In his 1828 address to the Colored Reading Society of Philadelphia, Whipper demonstrates this advisory approach to the language and myths of America's founding. Whipper describes proslavery politicians who rejoice in the American Revolution:

> Yet these wise men, who hate the very idea, form, and name of slavery as respects themselves, are holding and dooming an innocent posterity . . . to slavery in their own country . . . in a bondage ten times as severe as the one already mentioned, that their fathers denounced as being too ignominious to be borne by man. . . .
>
> May the letter and spirit of the constitution of the United States stare them in their faces—May the unalienable rights of man stand as a mirror for them to view their words.[66]

Rather than prove African Americans should be included in America's promises of liberty, Whipper features the oppression of African Americans in order to highlight the hypocrisy of American leaders. In fact, he assumes the general application of the language of "unalienable rights," separating the famous aphorism from the Declaration from the motives of its slaveholder and colonizationist author and elevating it to the level of a universal principle—what Burke calls a "god-term," an ideal that is "pure," removed from its human context. His reference to the "letter and spirit" of the Constitution reinforces the perspective that the founding documents inherently invalidate slavery, even if their authors did not intend to do so. Avoiding particular textual controversies about the Constitution's connection to slavery, Whipper emphasizes more than its words.[67] It is also, he suggests, a repository of eternal principles—its "spirit"—that must guide American life.

In his *Appeal,* Walker also marshals the words of the Declaration of Independence to argue that America has not lived up to its ideals. After quoting from the document, Walker demands, "See your Declaration Americans! ! ! Do you understand your own language? . . . 'We hold these truths to be self evident— that ALL MEN ARE CREATED EQUAL! ! that they *are endowed by their Creator with certain unalienable rights;* that among these are life, *liberty,* and the pursuit of happiness! !' Compare your own language . . . with your cruelties and murders inflicted by your cruel and unmerciful fathers and yourselves . . . on us—men who have never given your fathers or you the least provocation! ! ! ! ! !" (*DWA*, 75). Walker strategically deploys white America's "own language" to condemn those who hold authority in society, aptly highlighting their hypocrisy. Like Whipper, Walker wastes no time on proslavery interpretations of the Declaration. His challenge—"Do you understand your own language?"—suggests, in fact, that America's own rhetoric is unequivocal. Those who do not see the injustice of denying equality to African Americans, Walker implies, misunderstand—deliberately or ignorantly—their own professed ideals.

Walker's question, itself exploiting the ambiguity of language, holds a second meaning. The discourse of the American Revolution has implications that are beyond the control of its authors and national leaders—and Walker, as we shall see, reveals that this discourse can be turned against white America to empower the oppressed, even to the point of violence. In light of the eventuality of a violent end to slavery, Walker's question to Americans resonates as an ominous prediction. Walker challenges Americans not only to examine the multiple meanings of their "own language," but to recognize that their own revolutionary proclamations ultimately herald the end of discourse.

In an 1831 letter to the newspaper the *Genius of Universal Emancipation,* William Watkins (under the pseudonym "A Colored Baltimorean") also features the language of the Declaration in order to argue against the oppression of African Americans. Writing on the Fourth of July, Watkins ironically asks to be excused from celebrating this "day peculiarly dear to the white inhabitants of the U. States," on which the Declaration is enshrined by white Americans, who "[proclaim] in tones of thunder, from centre to circumference of this wide-spread Union, the 'self-evident truths,' that *all men* are created *equal,* and endowed by their Creator with certain *inalienable* rights, &c." He must "retire from the exulting multitude," Watkins remarks, when he "feel[s] the injustice done [him] by the laws of [his] country."[68]

Yet white America's shallow references to the Declaration of Independence do not negate the document's importance for Watkins. He, too, honors it and suggests that although white Americans may mouth its words, the language is not theirs alone. The Declaration takes on a force that transcends its historical context, becoming a moral force that will vindicate African Americans:

> The Declaration of Independence, whose all-potent energies burst asunder
> the cords of British power . . . will never permit . . . the *perpetuation* of our
> degradation. This imperishable document, whose attributes are truth,
> justice, and benevolence, has declared to the world that *liberty,* in the full
> sense of the word, is the birth-right of "*all* men;" (consequently, of every
> colored man in the Union;) that we are not only "*born free,*" but have . . .
> "certain rights," which are emphatically termed "*inalienable.*"

> Now, as these are admitted to be *"self-evident truths,"* it may be asked, in the name of justice and consistency, who can wrest from us these our natural rights, without flying in the face of this sacred instrument— without a dereliction of its principles, and a contempt of its authority? The Declaration of Independence is our advocate.[69]

In Watkins's letter, the Declaration is not a text whose meaning must be debated, but a repository of unquestionable principles and a weapon against oppression. In a strategy reminiscent of Douglass's references to "facts" rather than opinions or interpretations in his oratory, Watkins presents his interpretations of the Declaration's words as inherent truths embodied in the document itself. Watkins does not need to explore the meanings of the text's words; they are "self-evident," the "moral absolutes" of the advisory rhetor. Watkins creates, then, an ethos of moral certainty that empowers his appropriation of the language of the Declaration.

Watkins's "retirement" from Fourth of July celebrations contrasts with Douglass's role as a principal speaker at a similar event twenty-one years later, the occasion for his speech "What to the Slave is the Fourth of July?" Yet Douglass preserves a sense of exclusion from the festivities, featuring his presence on the platform ironically throughout the oration.[70] As did Watkins, Douglass appropriates the Declaration of Independence and American Revolutionary principles as moral absolutes, featuring these topoi as standards against which his treatment in American society is judged. Douglass draws upon the epideictic language of America's glorious history and mission used by traditional Fourth of July orators, but subtly condemns his society for its failure to live up to its ideals:

> This, for the purpose of this celebration, is the 4th of July. It is the birthday of your National Independence, and of your political freedom. . . . This celebration also marks the beginning of another year of your national life. . . . I am glad, fellow-citizens, that your nation is so young. . . . [Y]ou are, even now, only in the beginning of your national career. . . . There is hope in the thought, and hope is much needed, under the dark clouds which lower above the horizon. The eye of the reformer is met with angry flashes . . . but his heart may well beat lighter at the thought that America is . . . still in the impressible stage of her existence. (*FDP*, 2:360)

Douglass's diction—particularly his use of "your" rather than "our" throughout the oration—positions him as the representative of America's failure. Douglass offers no direct argument for equal rights, instead drawing on the indirect power of language to highlight the exclusion of African Americans from America's promise of freedom and equality. Douglass's marginal status itself becomes his argument.[71]

Telling his audience that he "shall not presume to dwell at length on the associations that cluster about" the Fourth of July and that he shall present merely the "simple story" of the Revolution (*FDP*, 2:361), Douglass begins an ostensible history lesson. His summary, however, draws on American Revolutionary language to create implicit arguments against slavery, suggesting that antebellum

America has no allegiance to its founding rhetoric or principles. "Your fathers," Douglass declares, "pronounce[d] the measures of government unjust, unreasonable, and oppressive, and altogether such as ought not to be quietly submitted to. I scarcely need say, fellow-citizens, that my opinion of those measures fully accords with that of your fathers" (FDP, 2:361). After unsuccessfully trying peaceful means to redress their grievances, the nation's founders took decisive action: "Oppression makes a wise man mad. . . . With brave men there is always a remedy for oppression" (FDP, 2:362). Praising the courage of the Founding Fathers, who "preferred revolution to peaceful submission to bondage," Douglass draws an explicit contrast to current leaders: "[The Founding Fathers'] solid manhood stands out the more as we contrast it with these degenerate times" (FDP, 2:364–65). Avoiding the implications of the Founding Fathers' views of African Americans, Douglass recreates them by emphasizing their revolutionary struggle. Chaim Perelman and Lucie Olbrechts-Tyteca indicate that this strategy depends upon the "construction" of a particular perception of a person that distinguishes between aspects of his or her identity that are "important" and those that are "transitory."[72] Douglass's construction of the Founding Fathers implies that their resistance to oppression is their enduring legacy, not their prejudicial views or their tolerance of slavery.

After presenting this historical overview, Douglass again draws upon his marginal position as an antislavery argument—this time, though, confronting his audience directly. Douglass highlights his ironic presence at a celebration honoring the attainment of freedom, turning his anomalous position into a demonstration of America's shallow commitment to true liberty:

> Fellow-citizens, pardon me, allow me to ask, why am I called upon to speak here to-day? What have I, or those I represent, to do with your national independence? Are the great principles of political freedom and of natural justice, embodied in that Declaration of Independence, extended to us? and am I, therefore, called upon to . . . express devout gratitude for the blessings resulting from your independence to us?
>
> Would to God, both for your sakes and ours, that an affirmative answer could be truthfully returned to these questions! . . .
>
> But, such is not the state of the case. . . . I am not included within the pale of this glorious anniversary! Your high independence only reveals the immeasurable distance between us. . . . This Fourth [of] July is *yours,* not *mine. You* may rejoice, *I* must mourn. . . . Do you mean, citizens, to mock me, by asking me to speak to-day? (FDP, 2:367–68)

Douglass's withering comments feature irony and a dual discourse in which his surface meaning encodes an alternative message. His exaggerated politeness and tone of embarrassment at his awkward position pretend to connote deference to his audience—maintaining that he is not the "appropriate" rhetor for this "auspicious" occasion. Yet he highlights the irony of his incongruous presence to suggest a very different implicit meaning. Douglass's contrast with his audience disrupts and reverses the usual values associated with Fourth of July celebrations, casting his audience—and not him—as the ones who should be embarrassed at his exclusion from the liberties he praises.

The parallels these rhetors draw between African Americans and the heroes of the American Revolution are significant. Although in the aforementioned passages this connection is not used to advocate explicit resistance, in some cases African American antislavery rhetors take this analogy to a dramatic conclusion, asserting their right to take emphatic action to secure liberty. Marshaling the strategy Perelman and Olbrechts-Tyteca call the "rule of justice"—in which a rhetor argues for "giving identical treatment to beings or situations of the same kind," particularly when there is precedent to do so[73] —they defend their right to fight oppression based on the actions of their American Revolutionary counter-parts. The resulting arguments are not only insistent, but militant, supporting potentially violent action by African Americans to overthrow slavery, including slave insurrections. By appropriating white America's rhetoric and traditions—"your own language," as Walker reminds his audience—these rhetors push their antislavery rhetoric to the militant limits inherent in revolutionary language.

Walker borrows directly from the language of the Declaration of Independence to support African Americans' right to rebel. After repeating the passage from the Declaration claiming the "right" and "duty" of those oppressed by "absolute despotism" to "throw off such government" and "provide new guards for their future security," Walker applies this principle to the plight of African Americans: "Now, Americans! I ask you candidly, was your sufferings [sic] under Great Britain, one hundredth part as cruel and tyranical [sic] as you have rendered ours under you? Some of you, no doubt, believe that we will never throw off your murderous government and 'provide new guards for our future security.' . . . [W]ill not these very coloured people whom they now treat worse than brutes . . . humble them low down enough?" (DWA, 75–76). Walker appropriates America's "own language" of revolution to support militant antislavery action in a striking argument a fortiori that proposes that violent opposition to slavery is not only inevitable, but justified.

Remond similarly calls upon the precedent of the American Revolution to defend slave rebellion, demonstrating that all can access the influence of revolutionary language and that such discourse can authorize militant action. In a speech at the 1844 New England Anti-Slavery Convention at Marlboro Chapel in Boston, Remond endorses the controversial AASS principle that the political union between North and South should be dissolved. Although the official policy supporting disunion was based on nonresistance, Remond's argument against the union expresses his endorsement of militant action to end slavery—even the action taken by the most notorious leader of a slave revolt:

> What was [the Union] to [Nat] Turner of Southampton, than whom a nobler soul has never risen upon the human race in all the long line of its prophets and its heroes! The Union does not even preserve his name. . . . [H]ad he been a white man, Massachusetts and Virginia would have

united to glorify his name and to build his monument; and is it strange, seeing all these things, that I should [reject the Union] too, and act upon the feeling? Yet, when such thoughts as these get such imperfect utterance as I am able to give them, men say to me, "Remond! you're wild! Remond! you're mad! Remond! you're a revolutionist!" Sir, in view of all these things, ought not this whole assembly—this whole nation to be revolutionists too?[74]

Remond's question poses a significant challenge to his audience, who, because of their history, ostensibly perceive themselves as "revolutionists." Based on this self-image, it is hypocritical for them to condemn Nat Turner's actions. Just as those "revolutionists" who founded the country are treated with reverence, so should Turner's heroic, militant action be supported. Remond demonstrates that the power of revolution does not belong solely to white Americans. The influence of their own language, he reminds white America, can be beyond their control. And Remond, too, suggests that the end of discourse may be violence—that his language may be rejected as "wild," ultimately making the actions of a leader such as Turner the only means to end slavery.

Many African American (as well as white) abolitionists began to endorse or participate in resistance to slavery as the country moved toward war—and, notably, the rhetorical force of the precedent of the American Revolution was called upon to support righteous violence. In an 1854 editorial in *Frederick Douglass' Paper* entitled "Who are the Murderers?" William J. Watkins recounts an incident in which the Fugitive Slave Law was used in Massachusetts to arrest Anthony Burns, a fugitive slave from Virginia. A group of African American and white abolitionists unsuccessfully attempted to rescue Burns, fatally stabbing a deputy in the process. Watkins describes the fugitive, "living quietly in Boston, one mile from Bunker Hill Monument" when he is arrested to be returned to slavery. A deputy marshal is shot, Watkins relates, as he tries to "rob [Burns] of his God-given rights." Addressing the question that constitutes his title, Watkins draws an explicit comparison to the American Revolution. "Is that man a murderer who sent the well-directed bullet through [the deputy marshal's] stony heart?" Watkins asks. "He would not be so considered if the parties were white. If he be a murderer, then was Gen. Washington; then were all who wielded swords and bayonets under him, in defence of liberty, the most cold-blooded murderers."[75] The actions of America's mythical heroes, Watkins challenges his audience, set precedent that is not limited by race and that can be accessed against antebellum America's own institutions. Those who condemn militant antislavery action are hypocrites who ignore the fact that they thereby condemn their forefathers.

Douglass, too, refers to the precedent of the American Revolution in his 1855 autobiography *My Bondage and My Freedom* to suggest not only that America's founding validates slave rebellion, but also that violence may evolve from discourse. At the end of the chapter preceding his first escape attempt, Douglass offers a militant assertion: "The slaveholder, kind or cruel, is a slaveholder still—the every hour violator of the just and inalienable rights of man; and he is, therefore, every hour silently whetting the knife of vengeance for his own throat. He never lisps a syllable in commendation of the fathers of this republic . . . without inviting the knife to his own throat, and asserting the rights of rebellion for his own slaves" (*MB*, 301–2). Removing the language of the Declaration from its context, the phrase "inalienable rights" becomes a transcendent ideal that can be used to overthrow slavery. Paradoxically, it is the master's language itself that leads to the violence that will overthrow slavery. American discourse, narratives, and mythology do not belong solely to those in positions of influence in American society. The rhetoric that created America can be recreated by those who wish to bring about radical change.

ON BRITISH SOIL

The appropriation of the themes associated with the American Revolution would naturally evoke the American memory of rebellion against Britain. Drawing on the power of this historic association between the two nations, African American abolitionists feature Britain as a specific topos in their antislavery persuasion. In this discourse, Britain often functions rhetorically as an idealized realm in which they propose that—in contrast to American society—prejudice is minimal. This topos was readily available for African American abolitionists because of their travels to Britain. American abolitionists in the 1830s established connections with the British antislavery movement, adopting many of its ideals and organizational techniques. Various abolitionists visited the British Isles, meeting with their English counterparts and lecturing at antislavery gatherings. African American abolitionists played a significant role in these exchanges, touring Britain and speaking on the abolition of slavery, the evils of prejudice, and social reforms such as temperance. In the 1830s, African American abolitionists such as Nathaniel Paul, pastor of the Hamilton Street Baptist Church in Albany, and Moses Roper, a former slave, crossed the Atlantic to lecture and to meet with antislavery leaders, followed by Remond and Douglass in the 1840s.[76]

Inevitably, their rhetoric abroad found its way home. The speeches of African American abolitionists in Britain were featured in American antislavery periodicals such as the *Liberator* and *Frederick Douglass' Paper*. In addition, African American abolitionists frequently refer to England, Scotland, and Ireland in their speeches and writing to American audiences. Featuring Britain as an ideal, African American abolitionists maintain that although in America they experience prejudice based on supposed inferiority, Britain is a place beyond such distinctions, an "ultimate" domain where the racial hierarchy does not exist. Appeals to such an idealized realm, Burke suggests, have an inherent rhetorical force. Because humans both uphold hierarchies and desire transcendence of the divisions they impose, the evocation of an "ultimate" arena beyond such distinctions has forceful—even "mystical"—symbolic connotations.[77] Yet Burke's perspective on the power of "ultimate" realms alone does not elucidate the influence of African American male abolitionists' references to Britain in their persuasion. These rhetors also capitalize on the unique resonance of Britain as a cultural topos for American audiences. As the country from which America's ancestors rebelled to gain their freedom, Britain traditionally symbolizes that which America is defined against—a restrictive, oppressive, stratified society. In the rhetoric of African American abolitionists, this relationship is rewritten, often with specifically ironic connotations. Reversing the relationship of America to Britain, these rhetors undermine a traditional cornerstone of America's self-image and expose American hypocrisy.

An account in the *Liberator* of a speech given by Remond at an 1841 meeting of the British and Foreign Anti-Slavery Society at Exeter Hall in London demonstrates the force of this reversal. Beginning his speech, Remond succinctly and cleverly reverses the progression of white America's ancestors from oppression to freedom: "Mr. C. L. REMOND, of the United States, a man of color, came forward, and said he would offer no other apology for his appearance there than the simple fact that for the first time in his life he stood upon the soil which a slave had but to tread to become free—[Loud cheers]—that for the first time he now breathed the atmosphere that an American slave had but to breathe and his shackles fell. [Cheering.]"[78] Remond's statements serve not only to flatter his British listeners but also play an important function for the American audience of the *Liberator* account of his speech. Remond creates an ironic revision of the conventional topos of the journey of America's founders from tyranny to freedom—for the slave, it is a reversal of this traditional journey that ironically brings liberty. America's founding mythology is undermined through Remond's assertion, in which British soil becomes not the land of the oppressor but the province of freedom.

Douglass similarly describes his travel from America to England as a journey from slavery to freedom, ironically reversing America's founding mythology. In an 1859 speech in Halifax, England, an account of which was published in various British newspapers and for American audiences in *Frederick Douglass' Paper,* Douglass evokes the commonplace of American self-definition that humans have a fundamental right to liberty. Yet America does not fully implement this principle, he notes in a passage reminiscent of the appropriation of American Revolutionary ideals described in the previous section: "[Americans] had decreed, in the fundamental laws of the land, that they held this truth [of the right to liberty] to be self-evident. . . . And yet . . . in the face of their conceited boast of liberty, they held in that land four millions of the human family in the most abject, the most terrible bondage ever imposed on any portion of mankind" (*FDP,* 3:277–78). In contrast, Douglass achieves true liberation from the oppression associated with slavery on British soil: "When [Douglass] escaped from slavery . . . although free from the master who claimed his body and soul as his property, he was continually reminded of his slavery by the invariable bitterness and malignant prejudice that surrounded him. . . . Never till he set his foot on the soil of England did he feel relieved from this incubus. . . . He went back to America, almost forgetting that he was a black man, or that he had a woolly head" (*FDP,* 3:278–79). Like Remond, Douglass suggests that for African Americans, the traditional realms of freedom and oppression are reversed, drawing on the resonance of America's relationship to Britain in a context that undermines America's national mythology. It is significant, too, that Douglass articulates in this speech the connection between American slavery and prejudice. Although many white abolitionists did not focus their attention on the prejudice that permeated antebellum society, Douglass voices this central concern of African American abolitionists, assuming the agency to redefine the boundaries of abolitionist rhetoric and to connect slavery to related societal issues.

The symbolism of the relationship between America and England, as is suggested by Remond's and Douglass's meaningful descriptions of their arrivals on British soil, depends upon a variety of oppositional terms that can be reversed—freedom and oppression, monarchy and democracy, equality and aristocracy. In his speech before the thirteenth annual meeting of the AASS in New York in 1847, Frederick Douglass draws on the resonance of the latter opposition, inverting traditional connotations and thereby exposing American hypocrisy. Recalling his ethos before English audiences, Douglass remarks, "I never appealed to Englishmen in a manner calculated to awaken feelings of hatred or disgust, or to inflame their prejudices toward America as a nation. . . . I always appealed to their conscience—to [their] higher and nobler feelings. . . . I always appealed to their manhood, that which preceded their being Englishmen . . . I appealed to them as men, and I had a right to do so. They are men, and the Slave is a man, and we have a right to call upon all men to assist in breaking his bonds" (*FDP,* 2:61). By suggesting that British audiences can be appealed to in terms that emphasize humanity rather than prejudices, Douglass implicitly calls attention to America's failure to live up to this standard. Conventional associations with Britain are thus undermined; in Douglass's terms, it is not an aristocratic society, but a country where he is recognized as a man. By implication, America's failure to live up to this ideal reveals the shallowness of America's professions of equality.

Responding to the charge made upon his return from Britain that he had fostered "warlike feeling" against America in Britain, Douglass cleverly rewrites the story of the American Revolution, reversing another important oppositional pair in America's mythological past—Americans as the rebels from tyranny, the British as the oppressors. He notes, "I embraced every opportunity to propagate the principles of Peace while I was in Great Britain. I confess, honestly, that were I not a Peace man . . . I should have gone through England, saying to Englishmen, as Englishmen, 'There are 3,000,000 of men across the Atlantic who are whipped, scourged, robbed of themselves, denied every privilege . . . go to their rescue; shoulder your muskets, buckle on your knapsacks, and in the invincible cause of Human Rights and Universal Liberty, go forth" (*FDP* 2:68). In Douglass's reformulation, America's and Britain's roles in the Revolution are transposed—

America is the land of tyranny against which those across the Atlantic should struggle. As we have discovered, African American abolitionists' allusion to American Revolutionary ideals serve to redefine them and appropriate them to argue against American institutions, revealing that American Revolutionary themes and language are not solely the province of those in positions of authority. In Douglass's hypothetical scenario, revolutionary ideals ironically empower Britain to fight America to end slavery. The nation's historical narratives, Douglass implies, do not constitute a static heritage that only serves the status quo. Indeed, they can be appropriated by the oppressed and marshaled against the very society that endorses them.

In Remond's rhetoric, too, the traditional associations of the pairs monarchy and democracy, equality and hierarchy, are inverted in the discussions of America and Britain. Demonstrating that more freedom is available to the African American in Britain, he contrasts white Americans' prejudices with their professed ideology, exposing the hypocrisy of the American commitment to democratic principles. In an 1840 letter written to Thomas Cole from Edinburgh—subsequently published in the *Liberator*—Remond eulogizes England and Scotland, drawing an ironic contrast with his native land: "England and Scotland, now, are every thing to me that they have been represented to be; and could I forget the poor slave and our proscribed associates at home, I should lose sight entirely of my own color—only when I chance to meet an American, who only dares look or show his teeth; for bite he must not in this country. Monarchical governments don't allow it. They leave such blackguard work for *republicans.*"[79] Remond's valorization of England and Scotland suggests Burke's notion of the resonance of the "ultimate" realm beyond distinction, but his rhetoric draws additional force from his striking and ironic contrasts between two regions linked by a powerful history. Ironically evoking the conventional descriptions of the two countries—a monarchy versus a republic—with their actual commitments to equality, Remond demonstrates that America's self-identity is built upon hypocrisy.

Remond similarly transposes the conventional notions of America as a society of equality and Britain as a land of hierarchy in his descriptions of his travels in Britain. In his 1842 testimony before the committee of the Massachusetts State House, Remond contrasts his experience as a traveler in America and Britain:

> In the course of nineteen months' travelling in England, Ireland and Scotland, I was received, treated and recognized, in public and private society, without any regard to my complexion. . . . [A]ll that know anything of my usage in the American ship [on the voyage to England], will testify that it was unfit for a brute. . . . But how unlike that afforded in the British steamer *Columbia*! Owing to my limited resources, I took a steerage passage. On the first day out, the second officer came to inquire after my health; and finding me the only passenger in that part of the ship, ordered the steward to give me a berth in the second cabin; and from that hour

until my stepping on shore in Boston, every politeness was shown me by the officers, and every kindness and attention by the stewards.[80]

Remond's references to the treatment by the British second officer and steward are significant, showing that in England the hierarchy is not only erased but, in some cases, reversed. The contrast with his treatment in America—the professed realm of equality—undermines America's self-conception. Although it may not have always been the idealized realm they described, Britain becomes a source of rhetorical agency for African Americans. America's historical perspective of Britain makes it a resonant topos that African Americans can appropriate and marshal against American society.

TAKING LIBERTY, TAKING LITERACY:
STRATEGIES OF SIGNIFYING

Strategies of appropriation are connected to a particular African American rhetorical genre, based on the trope of signifying, which is elucidated by theorists such as Henry Louis Gates, Claudia Mitchell-Kernan, and Roger Abrahams. An understanding of signifying begins with the Signifying Monkey from African American folklore, a trickster figure who depends upon linguistic ambiguity—irony, indirection, and implication—to trump others. The monkey does not merely use speech, Gates explains; his verbal trickery comments on the multiple meanings and indeterminacy of language. Thus his linguistic techniques occur at a level of "meta-discourse" in which the trickster "reflect[s] on the use of formal language." Abrahams notes that signifying is informed by "indirect argument or persuasion," the use of a "language of implication" that relies on irony, ambiguity, and innuendo. Mitchell-Kernan explains the assumptions underlying these strategies and provides various examples: "The Black concept of *signifying* incorporates essentially a folk notion that dictionary entries for words are not always sufficient for interpreting meanings or messages, or that meaning goes beyond such interpretations. Complimentary remarks may be delivered in a left-handed fashion. A particular utterance may be an insult in one context and not another. What pretends to be informative may intend to be persuasive. The hearer is thus constrained to attend to all potential meaning carrying symbolic systems in speech events—the total universe of discourse." Signifying, Gates indicates, subsumes many particular tropes, all of which play on the ambiguities of language and the indeterminacy of meaning. Forms of signifying include aporia, a rhetorical form that deploys language to call attention to the inadequacies of language; repetition and revision of a received meaning, tradition, or trope from another text; exploitation of multiple linguistic meanings, including punning; irony and ironic reversal; intertextuality that parodies, revises, or comments on other texts; and apparent flattery that is at once praise and mockery.[81]

Many of the rhetorical strategies deployed by African American abolitionists are informed by signifying—including the use of irony, the exploitation of the ambiguities of language, and the revision of conventional linguistic forms. As

we have seen, these rhetorical forms are not exclusively identified with signifying and can be analyzed in terms of other rhetorical genres or tactics. In addition,
though, a theoretical paradigm based primarily on signifying can elucidate significant features of the rhetoric of African American abolitionists whose power is
not fully explained in terms of other genres. Furthermore, because signifying
"arises from within the black idiom exclusively," Gates notes, a theoretical framework based on this rhetorical genre informs analysis of African American rhetoric
that "allow[s] the black tradition to speak for itself."[82]

Walker and Douglass deploy three forms of signifying in their antislavery persuasion: they use irony, ambiguity, and the language of implication to reverse the
traditional hierarchy that allows the oppressor to dominate over the oppressed; they
put to advantage strategies of indirection that feature language whose surface
meaning encodes alternative confrontational messages; and they appropriate canonical texts of white America in language that parodies and revises this discourse,
challenging and undermining conventional interpretations. Consider Douglass's
1848 letter to his former master Thomas Auld, published in the *North Star.* Douglass
begins,

> The long and intimate, though by no means friendly, relation which
> unhappily subsisted between you and myself, leads me to hope that you
> will easily account for the great liberty which I now take in addressing
> you in this open and public manner. . . . I will frankly state the ground
> upon which I justify myself in this instance. . . . All will agree that a man
> guilty of theft, robbery or murder, has forfeited the right to concealment
> and private life; that the community have a right to subject such persons
> to the most complete exposure. . . . Sir, you will undoubtedly make the
> proper application of these generally-admitted principles, and will easily
> see the light in which you are regarded by me. I will not, therefore, mani-
> fest ill-temper, by calling you hard names. I know you to be a man of some
> intelligence, and can readily determine the precise estimate which I enter-
> tain of your character. I may therefore indulge in language which may
> seem to others indirect and ambiguous, and yet be quite well understood
> by yourself.[83]

Just as the Trickster of slave folklore bests the slaveholder through verbal wit, ironically reversing their roles,[84] Douglass relies on a "double-voiced" language in this
passage to turn the tables on his former master. Adopting a tone of exaggerated deference and apparent flattery toward Auld, Douglass harshly condemns the slaveholder and draws attention to the reversal of power in their relationship. In a phrase
that resonates with ironic double meaning, Douglass highlights the "great liberty"
he takes in publicly addressing Auld, the man who deprived him of liberty—and
from whom he literally took his liberty when he escaped from slavery. Douglass
similarly appropriates conventions of politeness as he mockingly compliments Auld,
noting that he has enough "intelligence" to ascertain Douglass's opinion of him.

Douglass's "left-handed compliment"—a strategy that Mitchell-Kernan explains is often a part of signifying[85]—ironically suggests deference to Auld while revealing that the master's command has been usurped. Douglass now has control of the situation and the authority to judge Auld and expose his sins to the world.

Later in the letter, Douglass pretends to defer to his former master by defending his escape from him: "I have often thought I should like to explain to you the grounds upon which I have justified myself in running away from you. I am almost ashamed to do so now, for by this time you may have discovered them yourself." The implications of this second sentence are revealed as Douglass explains that his escape is moral because he and Auld are both men, "two distinct person[s], equal persons" and neither "by nature bound to" the other. Douglass's suggestion that Auld "may have discovered" these facts is deeply ironic—if Auld has learned this lesson, it is Douglass who has taught it to him through his escape.[86]

Douglass mocks Auld further as he seemingly justifies the stealth involved in his escape: "In leaving you, I took nothing but what belonged to me, and in no way lessened your means of obtaining an *honest* living. . . . I therefore see no wrong in any part of the transaction. It is true, I went off secretly, but that was more your fault than mine. Had I let you into the secret, you would have defeated the enterprise entirely; but for this, I should have been really glad to have made you acquainted with my intention to leave."[87] Turning the tables on Auld, he blames his former master for forcing him to adopt secrecy, inverting the stereotype of the naturally guileful slave. This comment also pokes fun at Auld's loss of control over his former slave, both past and present. As a slave, Douglass easily hid his plans from the master, whose power was based on spurious authority. As a free man, Douglass controls the terms of debate between him and Auld. Deploying language to ostensibly justify his escape, he calls attention to his self-determination, demonstrating that he need neither defend nor apologize for his actions.

Douglass's use of irony to assume agency in this letter suggests not only the rhetorical force of signifying but also the connection between the genre of signifying and the particular rhetorical constraints faced by the African American rhetor. Douglass's self-determination can only be articulated ironically because of his ambiguous position in a society that denies him authority over his own actions and identity. The American notion of equality, Gates explains, demands that one "speak properly" in Western terms, but this assumption contains an inherent contradiction for Douglass and other African American rhetors: "The relation of the speaking black subject to the self figured in [Western] languages must by definition be an ironical relation, since . . . these languages encoded figuratively the idea that blackness itself is a negative essence, an absence."[88] Through irony, Douglass exploits conventions of "proper" speaking—apparent flattery, politeness, self-consciousness, and deference to purported superiors—to undermine the assumptions about power relations in antebellum society on which these forms are based.

Douglass also features a striking reversal of roles to emphasize specifically the relationship between the control of language and dominance. Reminding Auld of the fact that he is still "probably the guilty holder" of Douglass's brother and sisters, Douglass asks Auld to "write and let me know all about them." Again combining apparent politeness with insult, Douglass notes, "I would write to them, and learn all I want to know of them without disturbing you in any way, but that, through your unrighteous conduct, they have been entirely deprived of the power to read and write. . . . Your wickedness and cruelty committed in this respect on your own fellow-creatures, are greater than all the stripes you have laid upon my back, or theirs."[89] But Auld's control over the literacy of Douglass's siblings highlights by contrast his lack of control over Douglass's language. Auld could not prevent Douglass from gaining literacy, which the ex-slave now uses against his former master. Within the system that the master has created, in which language conveys power, Douglass now has the upper hand. Douglass's signifying, then, not only deploys language but comments on its influence, illustrating how signifying engages a level of "meta-discourse" that comments on language itself.

Douglass explicitly points to the influence of language by constructing a hypothetical scenario with which he confronts Auld. Douglass asks Auld how he would feel should his former slave, "in company with a band of hardened villains," seize and enslave Auld's daughter, subjecting her to brutality and sexual abuse and "denying her the right and privilege of learning to read and write." Douglass notes, "Oh! the vocabulary of the damned would not afford a word sufficiently infernal, to express your idea of my God-provoking wickedness. Yet sir, your treatment of my beloved sisters is in all essential points, precisely like the case I have now supposed."[90] Auld and other masters can manipulate language to defend oppression, Douglass reveals, but that language would be inadequate if their relationship with their slaves were reversed. Language does not convey inherent truth, Douglass suggests; its force depends upon who is in command. And Douglass, who can now claim the authority of language, demonstrates to Auld that any claims the slaveholder has to domination are invalid.

Douglass's ironic tone in his letter to Auld—as well as his comments at the beginning of the letter that he will "indulge in language which may seem to others indirect and ambiguous" but that will be "well understood" by his former master— suggests the indirection that is central to signifying. Douglass's use of the epistolary form can itself be seen as part of a strategy of indirection. Seemingly part of an interaction between two men, the letter appears to function dialogically, although Douglass controls the discourse. Indirect strategies, Mitchell-Kernan notes, are particularly effective in granting authority to a rhetor who attacks an opponent because the language of implication can often be more forceful than direct confrontation. A rhetor may thereby provoke conflict and simultaneously leave his or her intent ambiguous, gaining "control of the situation" at the "expense" of the adversary.[91]

Mitchell-Kernan describes a particular strategy that effects this result—the "proverbial *signifying*" of the Signifying Monkey in the famous tale, who stirs up trouble between a lion and an elephant by describing to the lion how the elephant has insulted the lion and his family. These allegations prompt the lion to challenge the elephant, who wins the ensuing fight. Analogously, Mitchell-Kernan explains, those who signify may promote "some kind of ill-will, aggression, or disturbance in the relationship between, not speaker and addressee, but addressee and some third party." The receiver of the message is provoked, but the rhetor maintains the appearance of goodwill.[92]

Douglass signifies in this manner in his speech before the thirteenth annual meeting of the AASS. To criticize Americans for their support for slavery, Douglass marshals the comments of the Reverend John Marsh, an American clergymen who, it was alleged, had defended slaveholders in 1846 in a speech in England. "Dr. Marsh went about saying, in so many words," Douglass summarizes, "that the unfortunate Slaveholders in America were so peculiarly situated . . . that they could not liberate their slaves; that if they were to emancipate them they would be, in many instances, cast into prison" (*FDP,* 2:67). Douglass signifies upon Marsh's implication that American society and its institutions support the institution of slavery: "The country is not, after all, so bad as Rev. Dr. Marsh represented it to be. . . . He said you were not only pro-Slavery, but that you actually aided the Slaveholder in holding his Slaves securely in his grasp; that, in fact, you compelled him to be a Slave-holder. This I deny. You are not so bad as that. You do not compel the Slaveholder to be a Slaveholder" (*FDP,* 2:67). Through the third party of Marsh, Douglass can criticize Americans for their complicity with the system of slavery while seeming merely to report Marsh's accusations and even to doubt them. In addition, Douglass's denial of Marsh's claim constitutes a clever left-handed compliment. Americans are not "so bad" as to "compel the Slaveholder to be a Slaveholder," Douglass insists, but his implication is clear—they are bad enough. Douglass implies that Marsh's other accusation—that Americans are "pro-Slavery"—is indeed apt.

The fact that Douglass's argumentation draws on the texts and assumptions of his opponents suggests the key paradox facing African American rhetors—they must often rely on discourse that is defined by their oppressors in order to challenge the assumptions of their society. As in their appropriation of the language of the American Revolution and Christian themes and language, the premises that African American rhetors must engage are frequently encoded in white America's canonical texts such as the writings of Western philosophers and legal thinkers. Thus, Gates explains, African American rhetoric is in a "dialectical" relationship with the discourse of the dominant culture—including in particular those texts that are used to oppress them—which forms "the frame against which each black text [is] read." To oppose dominant perceptions and articulate alternatives, African American rhetors may engage in strategic appropriation of the canonical texts used against them through strategies that rely on "repetition and revision," "repeating and reversing simultaneously . . . in one deft discursive act." Gates outlines the specific techniques that effect this revision: a repetition and an inversion of an original text that reinterprets its meaning; a "fairly exact repetition of a given narrative or rhetorical structure, filled incongruously with a ludicrous or incongruent content"; or a "formal parody" that uses "repetition and difference" to reverse traditional meanings.[93]

Walker and Douglass rely on these intertextual strategies to appropriate and revise particularly authoritative antebellum texts. Because of its resonance in antebellum thought on race, Jefferson's *Notes on the State of Virginia* was a text on which African Americans could productively signify to undermine conventional racial beliefs. Jefferson's pronouncements on the inferiority of those of African descent were well known. His claims that whites and free African Americans could never coexist peacefully were marshaled by proslavery forces and by those who advocated the colonization of free African Americans in Africa. Jefferson adopts an ostensibly objective tone in his assertions about race. Although he acknowledges that whites have insurmountable prejudices against African Americans, he distances himself from this inherent bias, creating the ethos of a dispassionate observer who views racial differences "with the eye of philosophy." Nonetheless, Jefferson posits that even after "mak[ing] great allowances" in his judgments for the barriers African Americans face in American society, he must conclude not only that African Americans are inferior, but that "their inferiority is not the effect merely of their condition of life"—that it is due to "nature." As "proof" of these claims, Jefferson offers a historical argument. Roman slavery, he argues, was more cruel than American slavery, yet "[Roman] slaves were often [the] rarest artists"—a talent he maintains African American slaves lack. The key, he argues, is race: "[The Roman slaves] were of the race of whites. It is not their condition then, but nature, which has produced the distinction." Yet after offering his judgments about those of African descent, Jefferson notes that he cannot be sure of them: "The opinion, that they are inferior in the faculties of reason and imagination, must be hazarded with great diffidence. . . . [T]he races of black and of red men . . . have never yet been viewed by us as subjects of natural history. I advance it therefore as a suspicion only, that the blacks . . . are inferior to the whites in the endowments both of body and mind."[94]

In his *Appeal,* Walker signifies on Jefferson's arguments about the inferiority of African Americans, parodying the language and structure of Jefferson's claims as he reverses their meaning. The history of white oppression, Walker proposes, shows that "the whites have always been an unjust, jealous, unmerciful, avaricious and blood-thirsty set of beings, always seeking after power and authority" (*DWA,* 16). Imitating Jefferson's form—the argument from history—Walker offers an alternative account that overturns Jefferson's assertions. Jefferson distinguishes between the oppression of the Romans and Americans; Walker's historical commentary undermines such distinctions to highlight the cruelty of white people throughout the ages. Jefferson's history lesson focuses on the inadequacies of the slaves; Walker emphasizes the moral deficiencies of the masters. Walker then marshals strikingly similar language to Jefferson's pronouncements about African American inferiority as he inverts Jefferson's conclusion: "I . . . in the name and fear of the Lord God of Heaven and of earth, divested of prejudice either on the side of my colour or that of the whites, advance my suspicion of them, whether they are *as good by nature* as we are or not. Their actions, since they were known as a people, have been the reverse, I do indeed suspect them, but this . . . is shut up with the Lord, we cannot exactly tell, it will be proved in succeeding generations" (*DWA*, 17). Walker not only adopts Jefferson's phrasing but also features an exaggerated sense of hesitancy—"we cannot exactly tell," "I do indeed suspect them, but"—that parodies Jefferson's tentative tone. Within the context of the rest of the treatise, in which Walker rarely minces words, these formulations are striking. Similarly, Walker imitates Jefferson's ethos of the unbiased observer, whose argument is based on evidence rather than prejudice. Repeating Jefferson's form and parodying his tone, Walker inverts Jefferson's conclusion, undermining and demystifying his seminal racist principles.[95]

His beliefs about the inferiority of those of African descent notwithstanding, Jefferson's view of slavery was fraught with tension—as was his personal relationship to the "peculiar institution." A slaveholder, Jefferson nonetheless expresses great anxiety in *Notes on the State of Virginia* about slavery, predicting God's ultimate judgment for this national sin. In perhaps the most famous passage of the text, one well known in antebellum America, Jefferson alludes to the possibility of divine punishment as well as to slave rebellion:

> Can the liberties of a nation be thought secure when we have removed their only firm basis, a conviction in the minds of the people that these liberties are of the gift of God? . . . Indeed I tremble for my country when I reflect that God is just: that his justice cannot sleep for ever: that considering numbers, nature and natural means only, a revolution of the wheel of fortune, an exchange of situation, is among possible events: that it may become probable by supernatural interference! The Almighty has no attribute which can take side with us in such a contest.[96]

In his *Appeal*, Walker signifies masterfully on this famous Jeffersonian pronouncement. After discussing Jefferson's well-known question about the slaves—"What further is to be done with these people?"—Walker laments that many African Americans submit to slavery or even help their oppressors, thereby seeming to prove Jefferson's claims of their inferiority (*DWA*, 27–28). The "ignorant deceptions and consequent wretchedness of [his] brethren" dishearten him, Walker remarks, leading him to ask, "Lord didst thou make us to be slaves to our brethren, the whites?" (*DWA*, 28). In his response, however, Walker's tone shifts: "But when I reflect that God is just, and that millions of my wretched brethren would meet death with glory—yea, more, would plunge into the very mouths of cannons and be torn into particles as minute as the atoms which compose the elements of the

earth, in preference to a mean submission to the lash of tyrants, I am with stream-
ing eyes, compelled to shrink back into nothingness before my Maker, and exclaim
again, thy will be done, O Lord God Almighty" (*DWA,* 28). Walker repeats the language of Jefferson's famous prophecy and similarly foretells divine intervention in
America's institutions, but ironically inverts the significance of Jefferson's remarks.
Jefferson "trembles" at the prospect of rebellion; Walker welcomes it. Jefferson is
vague about how God's vengeance will be effected, mentioning "supernatural interference"; Walker is concrete, describing vividly how his "wretched brethren"
would fight for their freedom. In Walker's revision of the prediction, Jefferson's
influential ideas about race are inverted. If the present situation of the slaves seems
to justify Jefferson's claims, Walker implies, the outcome of Jefferson's prophecy
will overturn these notions.

Douglass, too, signifies on Jefferson's words, repeating the latter's warning
to America, but with a significant alteration. In an 1850 lecture in Rochester,
Douglass notes, "It was the sage of the Old Dominion that said, (while speaking
of the possibility of a conflict between the slaves and the slaveholders), 'God has
no attribute that could take sides with the oppressor in such a contest. I tremble
for my country when I reflect that *God* is *just,* and that his justice cannot sleep
for ever'" (*FDP,* 2:272). Douglass replaces Jefferson's word "us" with "the oppressor,"
shifting the tone of Jefferson's pronouncement to more severely condemn America.
As did Walker, Douglass presents Jefferson's remark in a context that shifts the
significance of his prediction. Douglass, like Walker, discusses the possibility of
rebellion not in Jefferson's vague terms that suggest "supernatural interference,"
but through concrete images. In a statement that contrasts strikingly with the
Jeffersonian pronouncement, in which the agency of the slave does not seem to
play a prominent role in rebellion, Douglass remarks, "Those sable arms that
have, for the last two centuries, been engaged in cultivating and adorning the fair
fields of our country, may yet become the instruments of terror, desolation, and
death, throughout our borders" (*FDP,* 2:271). Douglass marshals Jefferson's
influential words, but recreates their meaning. Douglass's revision implies that
all of Jefferson's literary tools—including his influential arguments about racial
inferiority and colonization—can be appropriated by the slave and used to
undermine the master's command.

Another literal and metaphorical master in antebellum society was Kentucky politician and slaveholder Henry Clay. Clay presided at the first meeting
of the ACS, was its president from 1836 to 1852, and often spoke on its behalf.
His well-publicized speeches were particularly harsh in their descriptions of free
African Americans and demonstrate that many ACS supporters had no intention of interfering with slavery. He describes free African Americans as a "corrupt,
depraved, and abandoned" population; deems them a "disease" in the "body
politic" of America, a "different caste, of a different physical, if not moral constitution, who can never amalgamate with the great body of our population"; and
insists that the ACS not take an antislavery position. It would be "unwise" to

emancipate slaves, he maintains, without the "removal" from the country of those who are freed.[97]

Given Clay's influence and the publicity afforded his speeches, it is not surprising that both Walker and Douglass found it particularly useful to use Clay's own assertions against his positions. Through signifying, they parody, revise, and reinterpret Clay's own rhetoric in order to undermine it. In his *Appeal,* Walker refutes Clay's arguments by appropriating his opponent's words and using them against him. Walker claims that before he "giv[es] [his] sentiments, either for or against [colonization]," he will present the arguments of colonization supporters (*DWA,* 45). Yet Walker's discourse belies his stated intent. Turning to Clay's 1816 speech at the inaugural meeting of the ACS, Walker forsakes an objective presentation of Clay's words. Instead Walker inserts his arguments against colonization in his ostensible summaries of his opponent's speech, thus rewriting Clay's arguments. This presentation of Clay's words and assumptions in an altered context renders Clay's defenses of colonization ridiculous. Walker's discussion of Clay's choice for a colony's location illustrates his strategy: "'For his part, Mr. C. said, he had a decided preference for some part of the Coast of Africa. There . . . [the colony] might be rendered instrumental to the introduction into that extensive quarter of the globe, of the arts, civilization, and Christianity.' [Here I ask Mr. Clay, what kind of Christianity? Did he mean such as they have among the Americans—distinction, whip, blood and oppression? I pray the Lord Jesus Christ to forbid it]" (*DWA,* 46).[98] Brackets notwithstanding, Walker's mocking questions challenge his opponent's argument and demolish Clay's credibility, ironically juxtaposing Clay's invocation of Christianity with the actions of self-professed Christian slaveholders. Walker's paradoxical call for Christ to "forbid" such "Christianity" highlights white America's disingenuous defense of oppression.

Walker similarly challenges Clay's remarks about the oppression of African Americans, repeating Clay's words in order to reveal their sinister intent. Walker cites Clay's allegation that there would be a "moral fitness" in sending African Americans to Africa, where, Clay asserts, "instead of the evils and sufferings which we had been the innocent cause of inflicting upon the inhabitants of Africa, we can transmit to her the blessings of our arts, our civilization, and our religion."[99] Apparently confused about Clay's meaning, Walker reveals that Clay's apology for America's enslavement of Africans has no foundation:

> I solicit your notice, brethren, to the foregoing part of Mr. Clay's speech, in which he says . . . "and if, instead of the evils and sufferings, which we had been the innocent cause of inflicting," &c.—What this very learned statesman could have been thinking about, when he said in his speech, "we had been the innocent cause of inflicting," &c., I have never been able to conceive. Are Mr. Clay and the rest of the Americans, innocent of the blood and groans of our fathers and us, their children?—Every individual may plead innocence . . . but God will . . . separate the innocent from the guilty. (*DWA,* 46–47)

Walker's specious tone of respect for Clay enhances his indirect refutation of this prominent Southern statesman. Purporting that he has tried unsuccessfully to understand Clay's arguments that absolve white America of guilt, Walker undermines Clay's defense. Walker's rebuttal is underscored by his assertion that God knows who is truly innocent, a statement that on the surface appears general, but that implicitly condemns Clay. Walker's apparent deference to Clay allows him not only to attack his opponent's arguments indirectly, but also to dismantle the assumptions upon which they are based.

In a letter to Clay published in the *North Star* almost twenty years after the publication of Walker's *Appeal,* Douglass signifies on an 1847 speech delivered by Clay in Lexington, Kentucky. Noting that he has just read Clay's oration, he asserts that he would like to "say a few words to [Clay] on one or two subjects which form a considerable part of that speech." He then signifies on Clay's own words, undermining them through revision. Because he features Clay's words—as did Walker—Douglass, too, creates a "double-voiced" text that recreates Clay's arguments, exposes his hypocrisy, and ironically marshals his discourse in order to overturn it. As in his letter to Auld, Douglass begins by adopting a tone of apparent deference: "You will, I am sure, pardon the liberty I take in thus publicly addressing you, when you are acquainted with the fact, that I am one of those 'UNFORTUNATE VICTIMS' whose case you seem to commiserate, and have experienced the cruel wrongs of Slavery in my own person." Since Clay represents himself as sympathetic to those who endure slavery—whom he calls in his speech "unfortunate victims"—Douglass maintains, surely he will not mind hearing from one of the oppressed.[100] For readers of the *North Star,* however, these words would resonate beyond this literal interpretation. Douglass's request that the slaveholder Clay "pardon" him for "taking liberty" implies, as in his letter to Auld, a deeper—and deeply ironic—meaning.

Maintaining his tone of ironic deference, Douglass undermines Clay's claim that he "disavow[s] . . . any desire . . . to acquire any foreign territory whatever, for the purpose of introducing slavery into it." Douglass comments, "As one of the oppressed, I give you the full expression of sincere gratitude for this declaration, and the pledge which it implies, and earnestly hope that you may be able to keep your vow unsullied by compromises, (which, pardon me,) have too often marred and defaced the beauty and consistency of your humane declarations and pledges on former occasions." Douglass's "left-handed compliment" puts Clay's words in a new context that reveals the contrast between his former declarations and his subsequent "compromises." Purporting to give the statesman the benefit of the doubt, Douglass ironically attacks Clay's credibility.[101]

Addressing Clay's claims that slavery is a "great evil," and a "wrong," and that he "should rejoice if not a single slave breathed the air or was within the limits of our country," Douglass again recontextualizes Clay's words:

> These are noble sentiments, and would seem to flow from a heart over-borne with a sense of the flagrant injustice and enormous cruelty of slavery, and of one earnestly and anxiously longing for a remedy. . . .

But what are the facts? You are yourself a Slaveholder at this moment, and your words on this point had scarcely reached the outer circle of the vast multitude by which you were surrounded, before you poured forth one of the most helpless, illogical, and cowardly apologies for this same wrong, and "*great evil*" which I ever remember to have read. Is this consistency, and uniformity? if so, the oppressed may well pray the Most High that you may be soon delivered from it.

Beginning with seeming praise for Clay's words, Douglass exposes their contrast with the orator's other statements and with his status as a slaveholder. Douglass thus not only undermines Clay's apparent concern for the slaves but also mocks Clay's earlier professions in his speech that his "opinions on the subject of slavery . . . have the merit . . . of consistency, uniformity, and long duration."[102]

Adopting an ironic tone of goodwill toward Clay, Douglass examines his opponent's proposed response to the institution of slavery. Clay proposes that African Americans can be "dealt with" in the United States "with a due consideration of all circumstances affecting the security, safety and happiness of both races." Douglass asks,

What do you mean by the security, safety and happiness of both races? do you mean that the happiness of the slave is augmented by his being a slave, and if so, why call him an "unfortunate victim." Can it be that this is mere cant, by which to seduce the North into your support, on the ground of your sympathy for the slave. I cannot believe you capable of such infatuation. I do not wish to believe that you are capable of either the low cunning, or the vanity which your language on this subject would seem to imply, but will set it down to an uncontrollable conviction of the innate wickedness of slavery, which forces itself out, and defies even your vast powers of concealment.[103]

By outlining the base motives that propel Clay's arguments while pretending to acquit him of these intentions, Douglass ironically and indirectly denounces his opponent's proslavery position. Furthermore, the ambiguous term "conviction" resonates on two levels. On the surface, Douglass remarks that although Clay does not mean to "cunningly" support slavery through his apologies for the system, his argument is inadvertently tainted by the wickedness of the system. At a deeper level, "conviction" connotes Clay's complicity in the system, a guilt that is clear in spite of his attempts to "conceal" it in ostensibly benevolent rhetoric.

When Douglass turns to the passage he describes as "one of the most helpless, illogical, and cowardly apologies" for slavery, he simultaneously professes that language is insufficient to counter Clay's arguments and features striking terms that attack his opponent. In response to Clay's remark that "the moral and physical condition of the African race in the United States, even in a state of slavery, is far better than it would have been if their ancestors had never been brought from their native land," Douglass marshals aporia. "I can scarce repress the flame of rising indignation, as I read this cold blooded and cruel sentence," he remarks; "there is so much of Satan dressed in the livery of Heaven, as well as taking consolation from crime, that I scarcely know how to reply to it." Language is not to be completely trusted, Douglass suggests—particularly since Clay uses language to subvert morality—and thus it cannot appropriately counter Clay's remarks. At the same time, though, Douglass's strong accusation indicts Clay more powerfully than a direct attack. In addition, Douglass does not leave Clay's argument unanswered, but offers a dialogic response: "Let me ask you what has been the cause of the present unsettled condition of Africa? . . . Because of this very desolating traffic from which you seem to draw consolation. For three hundred years Christian nations . . . have looked to Africa only as a place for the gratification of their lust and love of power."[104] Using language dialogically to speak what he suggests cannot be completely conveyed, Douglass overturns his opponent's purported message, demonstrates his hypocrisy, and reveals his true motives.

Signifying highlights a tension implicit in the rhetoric of African American abolitionists—the paradoxical connection between literacy and liberty. Literacy meant proficiency with the language of society's literal and figurative masters, often deployed as a tool of enslavement. Yet as their persuasion demonstrates, literacy also allowed African Americans, slave and free, to fight oppression. And literacy, like liberty, could not simply be acquired; both had to be taken. "I owe my liberty and my learning all to stealth," Douglass asserts in a speech to a Scottish audience (FDP, 1:198). Speaking in England the same year, he remarks, "All the education I possess, I may say, I have stolen while a slave. . . . I am now in the eyes of American law considered a thief and a robber, since I have not only stolen a little knowledge of literature, but have stolen my body also" (FDP, 1:372–73). Douglass aptly suggests the paradox inherent in the rhetoric of African American antislavery rhetors—to use the tools of the master, gained through deceptive means, to fight the master is an inherently ironic act.[105] It is also an act of empowerment— a continual demonstration that African American abolitionists' rhetoric is not just about liberty; it is itself fundamental to freedom.

4

If I Was a Man, How I Would Lecture!
White Women Rhetors in the Abolition Movement

In an 1837 letter, Angelina Grimké hypothesizes that her feelings about speaking to "promiscuous audiences" are similar to those experienced by her African American male colleagues. "Tho' *my principles* were all in favor of [speaking to men and women]," she notes, "I felt a timidity about it, similar to that which I suppose our colored brethren felt when they first began to address *white* as well as colored persons. I am sure I know from experience just what their feelings are." Similarly, Abby Kelley opines in an 1839 letter to the *Liberator* that the oppression felt by white women is similar to that experienced by African American men: "If you can imagine a colored man's feelings, when kept at bay and held in contempt by his white brother, then can you have some faint conception of a woman's heart, when she awakes to a realizing sense of her true position, as a responsible being, and sees herself . . . debarred from appearing in that position."[1] As marginalized members of antebellum society, white women and African American men shared the need to negotiate societal constraints, yet Grimké's and Kelley's analogies have significant limitations. In particular, the obstacles faced by white women and African American men differed in significant ways. White women abolitionists may have shared their exclusion from societal institutions with their African American male colleagues, but they did not face the threat of a literal return to slavery endured by escaped slaves such as Frederick Douglass. And white privilege shaped their daily lives in ways that granted them opportunities unavailable to African American men. On the other hand, although African American male abolitionists were often patronized and given little authority in antislavery organizations, they were allowed to hold office and did not have to respond to biblical sanctions against their speaking publicly. White women may naturally have felt allied with their African American male colleagues, but the challenges each group faced were unique.

The paradoxical position of the white women who attended AASS meetings during the organization's early years illustrates the general difficulties facing white female abolitionists, particularly those who wished to argue publicly.

In his eyewitness account of the antislavery movement, Oliver Johnson maintains that from the society's formation in 1833, women played an active and vocal role in meetings and debates. The Reverend Samuel J. May, another prominent AASS member, recalls in his memoir that at the Philadelphia convention at which the society was formed, Lucretia Mott delivered "a more impressive and effective speech than any other that was made in the Convention, excepting only [convention president Beriah Green's] closing address." Yet women were not granted membership in the AASS until 1839. Johnson notes that women attended the 1833 meeting "not as members, but as spectators," and thus they did not have an official right to speak or vote. His further comments reveal the precariousness of their rhetorical authority: "If the propriety of woman's speaking in public had been introduced in that body as an abstract question, how many of the members would have been quick to cite the authority of Paul against the practice. But when the women themselves were actually present, and seeking an opportunity to speak for the enslaved, no one even thought of objecting."[2] These rhetors' position, then, was fraught with tension. Accepted for their aid to the antislavery cause, they were not seen as equals by male abolitionists. Allowed to speak (albeit unofficially), their right to persuade was always open to question.

Various white women abolitionists negotiated these tensions and assumed the authority to speak and write publicly, both under the auspices of societies such as the AASS and in other forums.[3] Prior to Lucretia Mott's involvement with the AASS in the 1830s, she was no stranger to public speaking and activism. She had been preaching as a Quaker minister since the early 1820s[4] and was involved in the 1820s with efforts to boycott products of slave labor. By the 1830s, this antislavery work linked her with prominent activists such as William Lloyd Garrison. She continued to speak against slavery before religious and secular gatherings until it was abolished.

Also in the 1830s, Lydia Maria Child publicly entered the antislavery crusade. Already a prominent Boston writer of children's books and domestic manuals, Child had taken up the subject of slavery in her literature for children in the 1820s, but she did not yet express the radical perspective she advocated after meeting Garrison in the early 1830s. Garrison inspired her to move toward a more militant position and to write explicitly antislavery texts for a general audience. "He got hold of the strings of my conscience," she recalls in an 1879 letter, "and pulled me into Reforms. It is of no use to imagine what might have been, if I had never met him." In 1833, Child published *An Appeal in Favor of That Class of Americans Called Africans,* a groundbreaking work that offered historical, legal, and economic analyses of slavery in various cultures; refuted claims that those of African descent are intellectually and morally inferior; and presented compelling arguments for immediate abolition. Child supported and admired female lecturers, and she seemed to enjoy oral argument. In an 1837 letter to Louisa Loring, she describes a victory in an argument with a male opponent about abolition, exulting, "The poor man winced. . . . I burnt him up like a stroke of the sun, and swept his ashes up after him." This success notwithstanding, she appeared to feel she must limit herself to written persuasion. She laments to Loring, "Oh, if I was a man, how I *would* lecture! But I am a woman, and so I sit in the corner and knit socks."[5] In fact, Child did much more than mind her needles, writing numerous antislavery tracts and editing the *National Anti-Slavery Standard* for two years. Nor did she avoid controversy by confining herself to written antislavery persuasion, incurring harsh criticism and ostracism from the Boston literary establishment for her *Appeal*.

Like Child, Angelina Grimké, the daughter of a South Carolina slaveholder, expressed nascent abolitionist sentiments in the 1820s. In her diary, she wrote of her concern with the oppression she witnessed daily. Yet before she began speaking publicly against slavery, Grimké shared Child's belief that her sex excluded her from the public platform. Writing to Jane Smith in 1837, she declares, in terms strikingly similar to Child's, "How little! how *very little* I supposed, when I used to say, 'I wish I was a *man,* that I might go out and lecture,' that *I* would ever do such a thing." After moving to Philadelphia in 1829 and becoming a Quaker, Grimké began reading abolitionist literature. In response to two editorials in the *Liberator,* she felt compelled to write a letter to Garrison. In an epistle to her older sister Sarah, she remarks, "It seemed to me I *must* write to him." The letter, published in the *Liberator* on September 19, 1835, was Angelina's first public rhetorical act on behalf of abolition, and it inspired Elizur Wright Jr., the corresponding secretary of the AASS, to suggest that she come to New York under the auspices of the executive committee of the AASS to speak to groups of women in private parlors about abolition. Unable to decide how to respond, she continued her written efforts, publishing the *Appeal to the Christian Women* of the South in 1836. It was, as she notes in a letter to Sarah, "a pretty bold step."[6]

But Sarah, also a devoted Quaker, at first found Angelina's efforts *too* bold. Like Angelina, she had rejected the slaveholding culture into which she was born and had moved to Philadelphia eight years prior to her sister. Yet although she had tried to enter the ministry (an effort stymied by her shyness and the opposition of orthodox male Quaker leaders), supported the Free Produce movement to boycott the products of slave labor, and opposed the segregated seating at Quaker meetings, Sarah noted in her diary her feelings of discomfort at Angelina's involvement in abolition societies and her public exposure through the published letter to Garrison.[7] By 1836, however, Sarah had changed her position and had become active in the antislavery movement. When Angelina was invited to a convention that year to train agents, Sarah accompanied her. At the end of 1836, Angelina and Sarah began lecturing throughout New England under the auspices of the AASS. At first they spoke to groups of women in private parlors, as Elizur Wright had proposed, but the size of their audiences soon required that they speak in more public spaces, such as churches. Soon their lectures were attended by both men and women—but not without opposition.

Catharine Beecher's objection to Angelina's lecturing in her 1837 *Essay on Slavery and Abolitionism, with Reference to the Duty of American Females* was not the only negative response to the sisters' efforts. The Congregational ministers of the General Association of Massachusetts responded to the Grimkés' lecture tour by issuing a "Pastoral Letter"—which was read in churches and published in the July 12, 1837, issue of the *New England Spectator*—condemning women's public persuasion. The sisters retired from lecturing in 1838 after Angelina married abolitionist Theodore Dwight Weld.

But clerical and societal opposition could not curb the influence of the precedent set by the female rhetors of the early 1830s. Abby Kelley—who began her work as an abolitionist in the mid-1830s—met Mott, Child, and the Grimkés at the first Anti-Slavery Convention of American Women in 1837. She spoke at this convention as well as at the second Anti-Slavery Convention of American Women in 1838. In 1839, she decided to become an antislavery lecturer, beginning her career speaking in Connecticut. She encountered opposition from ministers as well as from male abolitionist leaders for her public speaking and her outspoken advocacy of women's rights as well as of abolition, but she persisted, also writing letters and articles for the *Liberator* and other periodicals. In 1845, she married abolitionist Stephen Foster, but did not retire to domesticity as the Grimkés had. Even after the birth of a daughter in 1847, she continued her antislavery work and her lecturing. Kelley and the women she met at the 1837 Anti-Slavery Convention of American Women negotiated the obstacles against their public persuasion, assuming the authority to speak and to offer powerful antislavery arguments. As they did so, they both explicitly argued for women's right to speak publicly and demonstrated that women could be capable and influential rhetors.

ANTISLAVERY RHETORS AS "TRUE WOMEN"

The antebellum ideal of "True Womanhood," which posited that a woman should be self-effacing, noncompetitive, unassuming, and modest, seemed to dictate that women eschew public persuasion. If a woman was to assume any role in an argument, it should be as a "mediator," and her persuasion should be restricted to the domestic sphere. Traditional rhetorical authority, by contrast, requires creating a credible ethos, engaging a conflict, and establishing expertise. How could a woman appear virtuous—in traditional feminine terms—and rhetorically authoritative? White female abolitionists often negotiated these seemingly contradictory requirements by strategically deploying traditional notions associated with "True Womanhood" in ways that allowed them to create ethe that were both apparently feminine and credible.[8] In this way, they marshaled antebellum society's terms and representations of womanhood in order to challenge and expand traditional assumptions of their society about gender.

Muted group theory provides some insight into this rhetorical strategy. As muted rhetors in the white-dominated abolition movement and in antebellum society, white female abolitionists needed to authorize their discourse in terms of the dominant group's norms and assumptions. Because white femininity was defined by the male-dominated antebellum society, muted group theory suggests that they had to "encode" their concerns in a linguistic form that would be "acceptable" to their audiences.[9] This framework elucidates in part the reliance of white women abolitionists on the traditional premises of antebellum femininity. Speaking before audiences skeptical of women's right to persuade, they could appear to uphold their society's expectations of women—even those that might paradoxically seem to counter their authority—thus creating feminine ethe that could help defuse critics' judgments of their public rhetoric.

But muted group theory also has limitations as a framework for analysis of the rhetoric of white women abolitionists. The assumption that muted groups' rhetoric is primarily shaped in response to an oppressive society tends to deny agency to muted rhetors and to suggest that their rhetoric is often conservative.[10] Yet as we have discovered through the rhetoric of African American male abolitionists, muted rhetors may feature premises that seem to oppress them in contexts that demand fundamental, even radical change in society. The appropriation of traditional ideals of womanhood by white women abolitionists can similarly advocate fundamental change in antebellum society. In particular, they strategically deploy conventions of gender to articulate a public and rhetorical role for women, thus featuring the premises of "True Womanhood" in contexts that challenge and expand the boundaries of this ideal.[11] Although they need to attend to antebellum conventions, they need not be fettered by them—and they can, in many cases, refashion traditional notions to assume rhetorical authority.

In addition, muted group theory does not account for an important aspect of the position of white women abolitionists. Although oppressed by sexism, their whiteness granted them privileges unavailable to their African American counterparts, male or female. The complex ways in which both oppression and privilege may shape the experiences of a rhetor are not fully explored by muted group theorists. Although scholars such as Shirley Ardener note that various structures may threaten to silence a subgroup within a muted group,[12] the muted group framework does not explore the converse—that muted members of society may also enjoy certain privileges that shape their rhetoric. For white women abolitionists, the implications of their whiteness shape their rhetoric in general and their deployment of gendered ideals in particular. Since masculinity and femininity are constructed racially, scholars note, femininity is constructed in terms of white women's experiences.[13] Antebellum "True Womanhood" was implicitly *white* womanhood. Although African American women were often judged by similar standards, they were not automatically assumed to be "True Women." White women, however, could take advantage of ideal gender roles. For white female abolitionists, thier privileged position meant that their essential femininity was already assumed by their audiences, even if critics might argue that they were denying their natural womanhood by taking a public role. They could strategically exploit this presumption, drawing on their "natural" femininity as they deployed traditional notions of antebellum femininity in their rhetoric.

Yet the deployment of traditional and presumably "natural" ideals does not necessarily leave societal assumptions about gender unchallenged. Appropriating the conventions that were associated with their race and gender, white women abolitionists reshaped these notions and redefined the ways in which women could assume rhetorical agency. Their engagement with controversy is a case in point. In traditional terms, an ideal woman would avoid any controversy, and disagreement with men would be particularly taboo. Yet white female abolitionists exploit traditionally feminine qualities to create the authority to oppose arguments offered by men. Abby Kelley's rhetoric demonstrates that this strategy allowed female abolitionists to offer even biting criticism of the opinions of prominent antebellum men. In an 1841 letter to Garrison describing a "row" between abolitionists and supporters of slavery that took place at a Quaker meeting in Millbury, Mass, Kelley implies that her text is not a part of the disagreement, but is instead a report of the disputes of others that "the cause of humanity" requires her to make public. Even as she purports that she is removed from the controversy, Kelley, turning traditionally feminine qualities to her advantage, engages the dispute with particular authority. "I am sorrowful," she maintains, "not that it devolves upon me to give these facts to the press, thereby warning others to escape the pollutions of slavery, but that there has been cause for the existence of these facts—that such deep moral corruption is found to have had a place among us."[14] The "moral duty" of ideal women to "redeem" their society from evil becomes a position of rhetorical authority for Kelley, who is particularly empowered to reveal slavery's corrupting influence.

Kelley's appropriation of the notions of women's moral duty becomes a license for bold criticism and even direct confrontation. She notes, for instance, that presumably noble motives justify her naming of names in her summary: "In what may follow, it will be necessary to be somewhat personal. I do not love personalities, and would avoid them, did the cause of truth permit; but the fact that some of whom I may speak were once my personal friends, (and perhaps they are so still, I am theirs, certainly,) constrains me more strongly to hold up the mirror to them than if they were strangers." If the ideal woman has benevolent intentions, she can expose the faults of her opponents for purely charitable reasons—for their own good. The traditional woman, then, who purportedly dislikes confrontation, is empowered nonetheless by her gender to offer sharp criticism. And Kelley's diction demonstrates that the exploitation of a feminine ethos does not demand conciliatory rhetoric or concessions to a woman's opponents. Her report of the Millbury "row" sharply criticizes the supporters of slavery in damning terms, noting the "ferocious manner" of one man toward Stephen Foster and describing another as a "champion of the baby-stealing institution."[15]

A report of Kelley's brief remarks to the New England Anti-Slavery Convention in 1854 similarly demonstrates that she frames sharp criticism in terms that play on traditional stereotypes of women's dislike of controversy. Addressing Henry Wilson, a leader of the Free Soil Party who was soliciting abolitionist support, Kelley—now Abby Kelley Foster—was blunt in her criticism of George Boutwell, a Democratic candidate for Massachusetts governor supported by Massachusetts Free Soilers, and Benjamin Hallett, the antiabolitionist editor of the *Boston Times:*

> Mrs. ABBY KELLEY FOSTER wished to ask Gen. Wilson one question. What security has any one, said Mrs. F., in giving his vote to the Free Soil party, that we shall not be helping the worst pro-slavery men into office? Heretofore we have seen the Free Soil party coalescing with the Democratic party, electing George S. Boutwell, a timid doughface [white supporter of slavery], to the Governor's chair. . . . Who can assure us that we shall not, by and by, see them putting that wretched tool of slavery, Benjamin F. Hallet, into office? Mrs. F. said she asked these questions in good faith, and not from any wish to cavil.[16]

Kelley inserts her opinions boldly into the debate among male leaders, strategically ending with professions of traditional goodwill that connect to women's ostensibly pure motives. Thus Kelley defuses criticism of her confrontational remarks, but she does not detract from their significance. By anticipating her opposition and marshaling conventional assumptions to check their censure, she bolsters her authority.

When directly confronting those men who vehemently oppose her public participation in abolition, Kelley strategically deploys the conventions of femininity to expand the expectations of women's role in society and to create a specific mandate for women's public persuasion. Consider, for example, her 1839 letter to Elizur Wright—who was an opponent of women's public participation in the antislavery movement, although he supported abolitionist women's speaking at private female gatherings—which was published in the *Liberator.* Kelley appropriates the commonplaces of "True Womanhood" to argue that men and woman should assume the same responsibilities and participate as equals in moral causes. Kelley maintains that she has "charity" toward those men in the antislavery movement who oppose women's public speaking "for their blindness in relation to this matter of the *true equality of human rights.*" She is not surprised, she maintains, "that those who have not yet learned to value God's image, for *its own sake,*" judge women unfairly; she does not find it unexpected "that those who have not yet received the spirit of full christian liberty, are incapable of appreciating it."[17] Kelley's hyperbolic charity becomes ironic—entering the traditionally masculine rhetorical realm of wit and sarcasm by exploiting a tenet of antebellum womanhood. Pushing the conventional feminine qualities of charity, forgiveness, and patience to their limit, Kelley takes up the masculine weapon of irony and turns it on her critics. Her ostensibly feminine virtues give her access to a vision of women's equality that is denied to her male colleagues and that empowers women as activists and public speakers.

By invoking feminine commonplaces—even in subtly ironic ways—white female abolitionists appeal to white male leaders from their subordinate social position. In Burkeian terms, they marshal the power inherent in the antebellum "hierarchy" based on gender and feature terms reminiscent of the Burkeian "rhetoric of courtship." Their appeals, though, complicate this rhetorical model as well. Although Burke maintains that the "rhetoric of courtship" invokes the ideal of an "ultimate" reversal of the hierarchy, its force depends upon the traditional relations of superior and inferior in society. Even when stratification is "masked," it is always an underlying structural principle that informs the relationship between humans.[18] But the complex—and inherently contradictory— antebellum view of women's "natural" moral nature complicates divisions between superior and inferior. The notion that women are "morally" elevated over men paradoxically both classifies women condescendingly and affords them the opportunity to exert influence based on their moral authority. The tensions inherent in women's assumed moral superiority are embodied in the often contradictory rhetoric of the proponents of "True Womanhood." Catharine Beecher, for example, proposes that men will "condescend" to the moral advice of their wives, daughters, mothers, and sisters if these women assume a deferential ethos: "A man is never ashamed to own such influences, but feels dignified and ennobled in acknowledging them. . . . [A]ll the generous promptings of chivalry, all the poetry of romantic gallantry, depend upon woman's retaining her place as dependent and defenceless." The woman who is the most powerless, then, paradoxically has the most influence. Similarly, John Putnam, pastor of the Congregational Church in Dunbarton, maintains in an address to the Female Anti-Slavery Society of Concord, New Hampshire, "[Women] have a mighty influence in controlling public opinion; an influence . . . operating on the secret springs of society, and controlling unperceived its destinies. They have an influence which all the men in the world cannot resist. . . . [Slavery] will *die* beneath their frown."[19] Women's control over public opinion, Putnam implies, depends upon its "invisibility."

White female abolitionists draw on these tensions within antebellum definitions of femininity. In their persuasion, the "rhetoric of courtship" becomes a complex form that simultaneously allows women to exploit their presumed inferiority and assert a particular superiority. The move by women reformers to draw on their moral authority as a basis for activism, Lori Ginzburg explains, is simultaneously "radical" and "conservative," featuring a tension between conformity to stereotypes of women's roles and defiance of women's restriction to a narrowly defined domestic sphere.[20] Consider, for example, an 1837 letter published by Sarah and Angelina Grimké in the antislavery newspaper the *Friend of Man*. This letter responds to "Clarkson," the author of a letter to the New Haven *Religious Intelligencer*, who suggests that the Grimkés do not need to expose northerners to the horrors of slavery and challenges them to offer practical ways in which northerners could effect abolition. Clarkson's condescending tone suggests that his invitation to the Grimkés is less a true request than a critique of the impractical nature of their antislavery rhetoric: "As you are so ready to instruct us in facts, you will confer a particular favor on the people of the *north* by presenting the *definite, practicable means,* by which they can put an end to slavery in the *south.*"[21]

Exploiting a stereotypical female tendency to attribute good motives to others, the Grimkés take Clarkson at his word. From his denunciation of their rhetoric, they create an argument that both appears to defer to him (and, by implication, other critics of their rhetoric) and asserts the authority to counsel northerners on their antislavery responsibilities. The sisters describe their response not as an argument *per se,* but rather as their obedience to the appeal from Clarkson: "We cheerfully embrace the earliest opportunity to comply with the request of our unknown correspondent." Their response to a request, a seeming act of deference, allows them to act as moral superiors who can outline the "*sins of the North*" and exhort the guilty to repent. Ending their epistle with an apology for "trespass[ing]" on Clarkson's "patience," they maintain the tension in their letter between their roles as inferior and superior. Telling Clarkson that they hope that he "wilt immediately begin to carry into operation" the principles they have outlined, they simultaneously defer to his higher status and presume to advise him on his duties, expressing a confidence that he cannot reject their advice.[22]

In Sarah Grimké's 1836 *Epistle to the Clergy of the Southern States,* the influence of women's presumed "moral superiority"—and the complex "rhetoric of courtship" which arises out of this stereotype—has an explicitly religious component.[23] Because a "True Woman" was naturally pious, traditional religious principles could be marshaled to offer strong arguments against slavery and to chastise opponents while appearing respectful. In these arguments, the paradoxes inherent in women's moral status are amplified by the tensions within Christianity itself. As we have discovered through the rhetoric of African American male abolitionists, marginalized rhetors can draw on Christianity's opposing tendencies toward submission and power, deference and authority. Grimké marshals the force of these defining tensions when she asserts her authority to address male religious authorities: "It is because I feel a portion of that love glowing in my heart towards you, which is infused into every bosom by the cordial reception of the Gospel of Jesus Christ, that I am induced to address you as fellow professors of this holy religion" (*E,* 90). In Grimké's pious ethos, women's religious nature is a position of empowerment, allowing her to criticize southern clergymen and directly engage their biblical defenses of slavery, including the argument based on the curse on Canaan.[24] Female moral superiority allows Grimké, too, to sharply expose hypocrisy by seemingly offering moral advice. Discussing southern clergymen's pride in their distribution of Bibles abroad, Grimké condemns their efforts to keep slaves illiterate: "Oh, my brethren! when you are telling to an admiring audience that through your instrumentality nearly two millions of

Bibles and Testaments have been disseminated throughout the world, does not the voice of the slave vibrate on your ear . . . 'Hast thou but one blessing my father? *bless me, even me also,* O my father!'" (*E,* 107). Evoking the language of the wronged Esau, who is tricked out of his birthright (Gen. 27:34), Grimké demonstrates that the Bible is not solely the province of male rhetors. Grimké uses the complexities of a female Christian ethos to meet her opponents on their own ground, debating proslavery interpretations of biblical passages and deploying biblical language to intensify her antislavery arguments.

White female abolitionists' evocation of a religious basis for their authority reveals another limitation of Burke's rhetorical theory. References to God and divine principles, Burke suggests—what he calls "god-terms"—allow rhetors to overcome the limitations of social status inherent in human life. Because these terms evoke an "ultimate ground" beyond the vagaries of social hierarchies, "god-terms" deflect attention from a rhetor's individual influence and imply "impersonal motive[s]."[25] In their assertions of religious authority, though, white female abolitionists need not keep their authority impersonal. In her 1836 *Appeal to the Christian Women of the South,* Angelina Grimké explains God's role in her persuasion, implying that although her rhetoric has divine sanction and is part of a larger plan, it is based on her particular persuasive efforts and her personal identification with the cause: "As a Southerner, I have felt it was my duty to address you. . . . I have attempted . . . to plead the cause of the poor and oppressed. . . . I have sowed the seeds of truth, but I well know . . . '*God only* can give the increase'" (*ACW,* 78–79).[26] Grimké is not removed from her rhetoric; it is compelling precisely because of her response to her personal duty and her commitment to abolition.

Balancing the demands of the personal and the divine, Grimké's *Appeal to the Christian Women of the South* challenges rigid formulations of a public sphere of argument removed from the private and personal. Grimké's voice in the text "resonates between private conviction and public appeal," Stephen Browne asserts, and "speaks to the universal in unmistakably personal ways." Grimké, Browne demonstrates, addresses issues of the bonds connecting humans to one another and to society as well as the ways rhetoric constructs relationships "between self and community."[27] Her rhetoric demonstrates that powerful public persuasion need not avoid questions often deemed personal—indeed, that rhetoric may be central to mediating between the private and the public.

Yet Angelina Grimké and other white female abolitionists were not always liberated from the traditional bifurcation of the public and the personal. Willing to challenge notions that certain subjects should not intrude into public argument, they were limited by conventions of femininity from fully articulating other concerns that were considered private. This restraint compromised their criticism of certain aspects of slavery in ways that minimized the force of their rhetoric. In particular, the sexual abuse of female slaves, although a powerful antislavery theme, was problematic for the white antebellum woman constrained

by traditional definitions of modesty. In discussing such issues, white female abolitionists create a feminine ethos that attempts to balance the need to portray the
horrors of slavery with appropriate female modesty. But because their overly deli-
cate engagement with the issue of sexual abuse does not deal with the particulars
of this form of oppression, white women abolitionists leave their arguments
abstract and thereby weaken them. As John Arthos argues, "rhetoric benefits by
the transgression of the public stage" with "personal meanings." Conversely,
attempts to sever the private—particularly concerns about the body—from public
rhetoric compromise its integrity.[28]

In *Appeal to the Christian Women of the South,* Angelina Grimké creates an
emotional but seemingly proper ethos when she refers obliquely to the issue of
the sexual oppression of slave women, demonstrating the shock appropriate to
the antebellum woman on such a topic while avoiding immodest discussion. "Do
the *fathers of the South ever sell their daughters?*" Grimké challenges her readers.
"My heart beats, and my hand trembles, as I write the awful affirmative, Yes! . . .
Is it not so, my friends? I leave it to your own candor to corroborate my assertion"
(*ACW,* 41–42). Yet to leave this topic to southern women's "own candor" merely
perpetuates the avoidance of the subject that—as Grimké had no doubt experienced firsthand as a southerner—characterized discussions of slavery in the
South. Furthermore, Grimké deflects attention from the primary victims of this
form of oppression—the slave women abused by their masters—focusing
instead on the children produced by this abuse. The demands of modesty compromise Grimké's critique, preventing a direct and powerful confrontation of
her audience.

Similarly, discussing the vulnerability of female slaves in *An Appeal in Favor of
That Class of Americans Called Africans,* Child's self-consciousness shifts attention
from female slaves to herself. She defends her introduction of the topic of sexual
abuse even as she tells her readers she has restricted her discussion: "There is
another view of [slavery], which I cannot unveil so completely as it ought to be. I
shall be called bold for saying so much; but the facts are so important, that it is a
matter of conscience not to be fastidious" (*A,* 23).[29] Drawing attention to the traditions of femininity that she challenges and the criticism she may receive, Child
highlights the sacrifice she makes by discussing sexual abuse. This self-conscious
declaration shifts attention from the particulars of her criticism to her personal
negotiation of conventions of decorum and the demands of her subject. Child's persona overshadows that of the slave woman, whose abuse is described discreetly and
through innuendo:

> The negro woman is unprotected. . . . She is the property of her master,
> and her daughters are his property. They are allowed to have no consci-
> entious scruples, no sense of shame, no regard for the feelings of husband,
> or parent; they must be entirely subservient to the will of their owner. . . .
>
> Those who know human nature would be able to conjecture the
> unavoidable result, even if it were not betrayed by the amount of mixed

population. Think for a moment, what a degrading effect must be produced on the morals of both blacks and whites by customs like these!

Considering we live in the nineteenth century, it is indeed a strange
state of society where the father sells his child, and the brother puts his
sister up at auction! (*A,* 23)

In Child's oblique description, sexual abuse is a "custom"; instead of calling the slave
woman a victim, her relationship to her master is implied in the generic term
"property." As in Angelina Grimké's *Appeal to the Christian Women of the South,*
Child's most ardent criticism renders the direct victims of abuse invisible, focusing
instead on the slave children of masters and slave women. Significantly, too, by suggesting that both whites and African Americans are "victimized" by the moral
degradation that results from slave women's sexual oppression, Child defuses the
force of the abuse itself. Child may treat the topic of sexual abuse, but her engagement is selective and does not directly challenge her audience.

Child's and Angelina Grimké's comments reveal that more than modesty
limits their discussions of slave women. Their ability to remain fastidious about
the topic is a measure of their distance from African American women—in
other words, their privileged position in society due to their race allows them to
avoid the realities of slave women's sexual abuse. If it is traditionally "feminine"
to be modest about sexual abuse, it is also a luxury that African American
women, vulnerable to both physical and verbal attacks because of their race and
gender, could not afford. White women abolitionists may claim to argue on
behalf of African American women and articulate their needs, but their privileged position often shapes their rhetoric in ways that erase the experiences of
African American women and preserve the normative status of white womanhood. Indeed, just as race influences the rhetoric of their African American colleagues, white privilege shapes white women's arguments about female slaves
and about the institution of slavery itself.

"I DO FEEL AND DO PRAY FOR YOU":
THE RHETORIC OF SYMPATHY

The notion of sympathy between women constituted a powerful theme in white
women abolitionists' rhetoric. Because of the essentialist rhetoric of domesticity,
antebellum women were presumed to have instinctive sympathy toward other
women, particularly based on their shared status as mothers. This feature of "True
Womanhood" could be a particular advantage for white women abolitionists
appealing to skeptical audiences. Ostensibly, the bonds of womanhood transcended
race, linking white female abolitionists to African American women as well as to
other white women. Yet, like their discussion of the sexual abuse of female slaves,
white female abolitionists' apparently "color-blind" appeals to sympathy are shaped
by whiteness in significant ways.

White women abolitionists rely on two strategies as they invoke the ideal of
sympathy between women. First, they use this commonplace to justify persuasion

ostensibly aimed at other white women but which actually would reach a larger "promiscuous audience." Considered naturally linked to other women, white female abolitionists suggest that they are authorized to appeal to them in terms of their shared femininity, even those who oppose their views. Within this woman-to-woman frame, female abolitionists take the authority to offer strong arguments against slavery in terms that emphasize concerns assumed to be natural and universal to women. White women abolitionists also marshal the notion of inherent sympathy between women to argue that—connected to them by bonds of femininity—they have particular authority to speak for female slaves.

The title of Angelina Grimké's *Appeal to the Christian Women of the South* suggests the attitude of a supplicant to women of the region where she once lived, an attitude that she deploys strategically to persuade her audience of the sinfulness of slavery. Opening with a quote from the book of Esther (4:14), she implies that silence on the subject of slavery constitutes a culpable complicity: "For if thou altogether holdest thy peace at this time . . . thou and thy father's house shall be destroyed: and who knoweth whether thou art come to the kingdom for such a time as this" (*ACW,* 36). Her sympathetic concern for white southern women, Grimké implies, motivates her text. Having established that they will be divinely judged, Angelina Grimké asserts that her sympathy for them—not a selfish desire to take authority—drives her to exhort them:

> It is because I feel a deep and tender interest in your present and eternal welfare that I am willing thus publicly to address you. . . .
>
> . . . Sisters in Christ I feel an interest in *you,* and often has the secret prayer arisen on your behalf, Lord "open thou their eyes that they may see wondrous things out of thy Law"—It is then, because I *do feel* and *do pray* for you, that I thus address you upon a subject about which of all others, perhaps you would rather not hear any thing. . . . It is true, I am going to tell you unwelcome truths, but I mean to speak those *truths in love.* (*ACW,* 36–37)

Even if her audience would be predisposed against antislavery arguments, Grimké suggests, her sympathetic intentions authorize her appeals. And, she argues, her persuasion itself is based on her sympathy for southern white women. Slavery threatens them, and thus she has the right, based on her natural connection to them, to warn them of its dangers. It is notable that Grimké frames her text not in terms of an appeal on behalf of all the women of the South—slave and free. Her title notwithstanding, her argument is an appeal to *white* women, presumably those with some influence in slaveholding families. Although her professions of sympathy may mask the racial overtones in her text, Grimké's *Appeal* creates an authority for herself and other well-to-do white women while erasing the influence of other women.

The text's epistolary frame also draws power from notions of sympathy, deferring to inherent connections between women at the same time as it reveals the limitations of white women's sympathetic ethe. Although Grimké desired a general audience for the *Appeal*—she submitted it to the AASS publishing committee, which brought out the text as part of its *Anti-Slavery Examiner* series—her strategic use of the epistolary form allows her to discuss political questions for a wider audience within a sanctioned form of a discourse between women. Personal appeals among women were considered acceptable even by the strictest guardians of "True Womanhood." Catharine Beecher endorsed such communication—if properly motivated: "A woman may seek the aid of co-operation and combination among her own sex, to assist her in her appropriate offices of piety, charity, maternal and domestic duty."[30] By invoking such values and explicitly appealing to white southern women, Grimké strategically uses traditional feminine qualities to authorize her text. And the epistolary form allows Grimké to use the ostensible bonds between women to effectively negotiate between the private and the public. The letter form, Browne notes, was "a way of asserting herself into public consciousness, even as she retained its posture of privacy."[31]

Yet as she defers to presumably inherent connections between women, Grimké reveals the limitations of this sympathetic ethos. Writing to a narrow group of well-to-do white women, Grimké reveals that the "natural" feminine qualities she assumes will win out over slavery—the "piety, charity, maternal and domestic duty" referred to by Beecher—are not based on universal women's experiences. These qualities are defined in terms of the lives of privileged southern women, who can afford to lead lives that embody traditional domestic values. As Grimké's text reveals, sympathy between women, while purporting to valorize universal feminine qualities, often normalizes the experiences of particular women, marginalizing those of women who are less privileged.

Although Angelina Grimké's rhetoric of sympathy is informed by a relatively narrow view of femininity, its potential power should not be ignored. In her *Letters to Catherine* [sic] *E. Beecher, in Reply to An Essay on Slavery and Abolitionism, Addressed to A. E. Grimké*—which first appeared as a series of letters in the *Liberator* in 1837 and was subsequently published in book form[32]—Grimké features a rhetoric of sympathy in a scathing refutation of Catharine Beecher's *Essay on Slavery and Abolitionism*. In her private correspondence, Grimké acknowledges her "indignation at the view [Beecher] takes [of] the *woman's* character & duty."[33] A public refutation of Beecher, however, required a strategic deployment of feminine sympathy in order to establish the authority to criticize her opponent. Creating the ethos of a concerned friend, Grimké attacks Beecher's lack of true antislavery sentiment: "Oh, my very soul is grieved to find a northern woman thus . . . fitting soft excuses for the slaveholder's conscience, whilst with the same pen she is *professing* to regard slavery as a sin" (*LCB,* 152). In the concluding letter, Grimké presents a series of questions apparently designed to provoke Beecher to self-examination and repentance for her antiabolition sentiments:

> Hast thou ever asked thyself, what the slave would think of thy book, if he could read it? Dost thou know that, from the beginning to the end, not

a word of compassion for *him* has fallen from thy pen? Recall, I pray, the memory of the hours which thou spent in writing it! Was the paper once moistened by the tear of pity? . . . Oh, listen and weep, and let thy repentings be kindled together, and speedily bring forth, I beseech thee, fruits meet for repentance, and henceforth show thyself faithful to Christ and his bleeding representative the slave.

I greatly fear that thy book might have been written just as well, hadst thou not the heart of a woman. It bespeaks a superior intellect, but paralyzed and spell-bound by the sorcery of a worldly-minded expediency. (*LCB,* 202–3)

Within this ostensible appeal to Beecher's spiritual welfare, Grimké presents a withering critique of Beecher's arguments against organized abolition. Grimké insightfully turns Beecher's criticism of abolitionist women against her, revealing that women who support slavery are the truly unfeminine ones. In Grimké's critique, Beecher lacks the "heart of a woman," the fundamental qualities of "True Womanhood" that would enable her to feel sympathy for the oppressed.

Grimké's tactics are related to a larger strategy of abolitionists, particularly those followers of Garrison who asserted that women had a right to speak publicly. Because of their endorsement of women's public speaking, these abolitionists were often accused of undermining "natural" gender roles. Kristin Hoganson demonstrates that Garrisonian abolitionists "shifted the tables" on these opponents by representing supporters of slavery as "the true threat to gender order." This strategy has both "radical and conservative implications," Hoganson notes, simultaneously defusing the criticism against women public speakers and leaving unchallenged the notion that female authority was based on a "traditional gendered framework."[34] Similarly, appropriating conventional gendered ideals of sympathy to argue against Beecher's formulation of women's sphere, Grimké both upholds traditional formulations of gender and expands the roles this ideology endorses for women.

Child also deploys sympathy between women, the presumably feminine epistolary form, and a traditional gendered ideology to attack female supporters of slavery and to portray them as "unfeminine" in one of her most influential works. *Correspondence Between Lydia Maria Child and Governor Wise and Mrs. Mason, of Virginia* was the record of a famous exchange inspired by John Brown's attack on Harpers Ferry, his arrest, and his imprisonment to await execution. Child wrote a letter to Brown in prison indicating a desire to "nurse" him and to express her "sisterly words of sympathy and consolation" (*C,* 14). She included a letter to Governor Wise of Virginia with the letter to Brown, asking permission to visit him in prison for these purposes. Wise sent the correspondence to the press, presuming, Carolyn Karcher explains, that "he had scored a propaganda victory from which the northern public might benefit." Child used this opening to her advantage, publishing a response to Wise in the *New-York Tribune.* The publication of these letters prompted a vituperative response to Child by Margaretta Mason, the wife of a Virginia senator, published in the Virginia press, to which Child responded in the *Tribune*. The entire series of letters was published by the AASS as *Correspondence Between Lydia Maria Child and Governor Wise and Mrs. Mason, of Virginia,* selling a record three hundred thousand copies.[35]

Child's ethos in her letter to Mason is particularly compelling, strategically marshaling a traditionally feminine style and the notion of womanly sympathy to attack her opponent. Ostensibly showing concern for Mason, she is able to condemn the South's irrational defense of slavery and to underscore Mason's angry—and thus presumably "unfeminine"—tone. "Can you not believe that we may hate the system, and yet be truly your friends?" she asks. "I make allowance for the excited state of your mind, and for the prejudices induced by education. I do not care to change your opinion of me; but I do wish you could be persuaded to examine this subject dispassionately, for the sake of the prosperity of Virginia, and the welfare of unborn generations, both white and colored" (*C,* 25). Traditionally feminine qualities are turned into striking condemnations of Mason. Child's assertion that she is not concerned with Mason's judgment of her, for example, not only plays on the commonplace of feminine self-denial, but also allows her to disparage her opponent's moral character and rhetorical talent. Child subtly uses the guise of selflessness to discount the effectiveness of Mason's arguments, noting to Mason that her letter "fell harmless upon me" (*C,* 18). Stereotypes of feminine behavior, Child demonstrates, can be exploited for purposes usually only reserved for men—to judge and argue against opponents' arguments. Indeed, despite Mason's attempts to portray Child as "unfeminine," it is Mason and not Child who appears to violate "True Womanhood." From the opening of her letter, Mason criticizes Child in blunt terms and warns her to "keep away from Charlestown," while Child begins her response with a womanly declaration of sympathy: "I sincerely wish you well, both in this world and the next" (*C,* 17–18).

White female abolitionists do not only profess their sympathy with other white women. As their discussion of the sexual abuse of female slaves suggests, they express concern for enslaved women and appeal to their shared womanhood. Through this strategy, they authorize their persuasion against slavery by maintaining that, as women, they are called to argue for their "slave sisters." Yet their construction of an ideal of sympathy that links women of different races at an essential level is problematic. Rhetoric that professes to be "color-blind" actually relies on whiteness as a norm, ignoring the particular experiences of people of color. In particular, bell hooks argues, white women abolitionists' professions of an essentialist sympathy with slaves does not challenge the white power structure. And, as hooks notes, asserting the similarities between their situation and that of female slaves, white women minimize the experiences of slave women, "appropriating the horror of the slave experience" in contexts that empower white female reformers but efface African American women's particular concerns.[36]

A few examples will illustrate these tensions in white women abolitionists' rhetoric of sympathy. In her *Letters to Catherine* [sic] *Beecher,* Angelina Grimké refutes Beecher's arguments against female antislavery work with rhetorical questions basing women's right to agitate on sympathy for slave women. Responding to Beecher's insinuation that it is improper to condemn others' racial prejudices, she asks, "Couldst thou think so, if thou really loved thy colored sisters *as thyself?"* (*LCB,* 169). Similarly, Sarah Grimké suggests in her 1838 *Letters on the Equality of the Sexes and the Condition of Women*[37] not only that sympathy with slave women gives white women the right to argue against slavery, but that they deny their true nature if they do not: "Female slaves suffer every species of degradation and cruelty, which the most wanton barbarity can inflict; they are indecently divested of their clothing, sometimes tied up and severely whipped, sometimes prostrated on the earth, while their naked bodies are torn by the scorpion lash. . . . Can any American woman look at these scenes of shocking licentiousness and cruelty, and fold her hands in apathy and say, 'I have nothing to do with slavery'? *She cannot and be guiltless"* (*LES,* 225). The Grimké sisters grant agency to women through their activation of sympathy, but this empowerment clearly depends upon the privilege available only to white women. Asserting a universal bond between women, they nonetheless assume that it is white women who will be authorized through their concern for the powerless slave woman.

Appropriating slave women's experiences of sexual abuse, white female abolitionists reveal another limitation of their rhetoric of sympathy. They focus on the sexual oppression of female slaves not for the purpose of revealing the particular horrors of these experiences but to illustrate the extent of white women's proper feminine sensibilities. The story of a "Miss G." in Child's 1835 *Authentic Anecdotes of American Slavery* illustrates how this focus on white women's sympathy prevents a true exploration of slave women's oppression. "Miss G.," Child notes, claims that she has "always been accustomed to the blacks, and [that she] really like[s] them" (*AA,* 1:5). But Miss G.'s narrative of a beautiful female slave she owned reveals her true feelings. After a male friend of Miss G. makes advances toward her, the slave tells Miss G. that she is "troubled" by his attentions and wants to "get rid of him" (*AA,* 1:5). Miss G. at first tries to honor this request, but explains that eventually she had to give in to the slave's admirer: "For a few weeks he desisted; but at the end of that time, he came to me and said, 'Miss G., I must have that girl! I cannot live without her!' He offered me a very high price. *I pitied the poor fellow, and so I sold her to him"* (*AA,* 1:5–6). Child does not leave Miss G.'s hypocrisy implicit, remarking, "Miss G. . . . would have considered herself insulted, if any one had doubted her modesty and sense of propriety. Yet she told this story with perfect *unconsciousness* that there was any thing disgusting or shocking, or even wrong, in one woman's trafficking away another, under such circumstances!" (*AA,* 1:6). Miss G. is clearly complicit in the degradation induced by slavery, yet it is notable that she is the central focus of Child's story rather than the slave she sells. Although the slave woman's plight is briefly described, it serves to reveal not the horrors of slavery for African American women but the damage to white women's natural feminine sensibilities.

In both Sarah Grimké's graphic description of the cruelties inflicted on slave women and Child's detailed story of Miss G., the emphasis on white women reveals that the rhetoric of sympathy maintains rather than challenges white privilege. Sympathy, Burke indicates, operates by invoking a "vicarious sharing" of another's "pleasures and pains," inviting a person to identify "imaginatively" with the thoughts and feelings of another. A "vicarious sharing," though, inevitably calls attention to the power imbalance between the person experiencing actual oppression and the sympathetic advocate, highlighting the divisions which give rhetorical force to the imaginative identification with another's experiences.[38] Ultimately, although readers may feel a certain degree of sympathy for the slave women in Sarah Grimké's and Child's texts, the focus of their commentaries are the white women who, looking on, should be called to action.

The potential of white women's rhetoric of sympathy to grant themselves agency while marginalizing the experiences of African American women is illustrated strikingly in Kelley's comments at an 1853 meeting of the AASS. Significantly, Kelley features sympathy for slave women as a rhetorical parallel to the firsthand experience of African American male orators who had been slaves. Kelley speaks after Frederick Douglass, drawing on her connection to two particular slave women to assert her right to persuade: "She said that she rose to second the resolution which had been offered by Frederick Douglass; that he had been a slave: that he was now free, and could speak for himself: but that his mother and sister were still in the hands of the outragers, and that it was therefore fit that she, a woman, should stand there by his side, and bear her testimony in favor of the cause, which had made him, and which, under God, would make them, free!"[39] Kelley suggests that her connection to Douglass's mother and sister places her, like Douglass, in a close connection to slavery that authorizes her persuasion. Yet Kelley's professions that her gender identifies her with these particular slave women erase the unique concerns of female slaves. Her implication that gender overrides race minimizes the realities of slavery that Douglass's mother and sister experience. And Kelley's suggestion that she, as a woman, is authorized to voice the concerns of slave woman deflects attention from the consequences of slave women's imposed silence. Speaking for them, Kelley denies agency to African American women. For a white woman to speak for slave women, however sympathetically, appropriates female slaves' experiences to authorize the rhetoric of white women, further silencing the enslaved.[40]

These tensions inherent in the rhetoric of sympathy assume tangible form in the emblem of the kneeling female slave, a figure that was featured in antislavery periodicals, particularly above the "Ladies' Department" of the *Liberator;* printed on stationery and the frontispieces of tracts; embroidered on work-bags; and even imprinted on metal tokens. The motto "Am I Not a Woman and a Sister?" appeared below or above the figure, who was shown as a chained supplicant.

Although a male form of this kneeling figure was also an emblem of the abolition movement—featuring the motto "Am I Not a Man and a Brother?"—Jean Fagan Yellin aptly notes that while the male figure appears "powerful and athletic" as if he can rise from his supplicant position, the female appears "weak," able only to "plead." Significantly, too, the female slave's chains bind her to the ground; the male slave's do not.[41] A variant of the figure, featured on the cover of Child's 1838 edition of *Authentic Anecdotes of American Slavery,* also included the popular antislavery verse: "Remember them that are in bonds as bound with them. Heb. 13:3."[42] In this emblem of the kneeling female slave, the sympathy of the white woman for the slave woman does not mitigate the differences in their status. The image appeals to free women to identify with the slave, Yellin maintains, and to feel her chains as if she is "bound with her"; simultaneously, the slave's position as supplicant and her assertion of her womanhood in a question rather than a statement suggest the sharp division between slave and free—and the superior position of the white female abolitionist.[43] In this image, then, the limitations of white female abolitionists' sympathy take a visual form. The rhetoric of sympathy may suggest a connection between women beyond the racial hierarchy, but the hierarchy's power is preserved. The female slave remains kneeling, and without the acknowledgment of the white female abolitionist, her question—"Am I not a woman and a sister?"—remains unanswered. The rhetoric of sympathy, while claiming a connection across racial lines, preserves white privilege and often renders African American women invisible.

ABOLITION, SLAVERY, AND THE
RHETORIC OF DOMESTICITY

As we have seen, white female abolitionists' deployment of traits associated with the ideal of "True Womanhood" cannot be easily classified as conservative or radical. Leaving various antebellum assumptions unchallenged, these women build on conventional premises to argue against slavery and for a public role for women activists. Similarly, they feature in their antislavery persuasion a rhetoric of domesticity, which assumes traditional aspects of an antebellum woman's appropriate role to argue for change in the very society that endorses these ideals. Two strategies are evident: They frame their arguments in terms of domestic commonplaces while expanding the implications of traditional roles to incorporate antislavery reform. They also marshal conventions of domesticity in their particular arguments about slavery, maintaining that the institution of slavery interferes with the proper domestic roles of both slave and free women. Purportedly based on a domestic ideology that was "universal," the rhetoric of domesticity featured by white women abolitionists is nonetheless based on the experiences of white females, often minimizing the experiences of slave women even when it claims to advocate for them.

Deploying the rhetoric of domesticity in contexts that expand the scope of women's activism beyond traditional boundaries, white female abolitionists authorize their public persuasion and activism. This strategy was not exclusive

to women abolitionists; Catherine Clinton describes a general trend among antebellum women reformers to "extend female jurisdiction into the public and hitherto
exclusively male realm by using their 'domestic' role as a lever—wedging themselves into positions of power, however limited, through exploitation of their
domesticity." These rhetorical tactics, Clinton and other scholars note, should
not be perceived as exclusively conservative or radical. Rather, this rhetoric
simultaneously endorses various traditional societal assumptions—that women
are naturally suited for particular domestic duties and that women's primary
roles are as wives and mothers—while extending the scope of women's domestic
concerns to include public reform, such as abolition.[44] A few examples will
demonstrate how these tensions shape white female abolitionists' defenses of
women's reform work.

In her *Letters on the Equality of the Sexes,* Sarah Grimké establishes a moral
equality between man and woman. Neither husband nor wife must be submissive
to the other, she argues; and the moral responsibilities of men and women are the
same. A woman who works for "moral reform" in society, she maintains, "goes as
the dignified messenger of Jehovah, and all she does and says must be done and said
irrespective of sex" (*LES,* 218). Yet even as she argues for this egalitarian sense of
duty, Grimké does not challenge the notion that women are particularly suited for
domestic roles. In fact, she defends her claim that women have the right and the
authority to publicly "communicate with all" as they work for societal reform by
establishing that this work is fundamentally connected to women's domestic duties:

> While laboring to cleanse the minds of others from the malaria of moral
> pollution, [woman's] own heart becomes purified. . . . Such a woman is
> infinitely better qualified to fulfil the duties of a wife and a mother, than
> the woman whose *false delicacy* leads her to . . . shrink from *naming those*
> *sins* which she knows exist. . . . . Such a woman comes to the important
> task of training her children in the nurture and admonition of the Lord,
> with a soul filled with the greatness of the beings committed to her
> charge. . . . [S]he instils into her children that genuine religion which
> induces them to keep the commandments of God. (*LES,* 218–19)

Far from violating her domestic duties, the woman who is a public reformer,
Grimké suggests, is *more* qualified for her particular obligations as wife and mother
than the retiring woman who avoids public activism. Upholding the importance of
woman's domestic responsibilities, Grimké links them to public work for reform.

Similarly, Lucretia Mott, speaking in 1849 on women's reform work, endorses
the antebellum assumptions that women have unique and separate responsibilities
from men and that these obligations are based on women's domestic nature. While
maintaining that woman's province is unique from man's, Mott argues for expansion of the "narrow sphere" that many men assign her to (*LM,* 147).[45] In her formulation, true femininity actually depends upon woman's using her natural talents,
particularly on behalf of reform: "So far from her 'ambition leading her to attempt

to act the man,' she needs all the encouragement she can receive, by the removal of obstacles from her path, in order that she may become a 'true woman.' . . . Let her cultivate all the graces and proper accomplishments of her sex. . . . [I]f cultivated and refined woman would bring all her powers into use, she might engage in pursuits which she now shrinks from as beneath her proper vocation" (*LM*, 148–49). Like Sarah Grimké, Mott maintains that women's domestic talents will actually be increased by their participation in reform work, illustrating her point through the example of British prison reformer Elizabeth Fry:

> Nor will woman fulfill less her domestic relations, as the faithful companion of her chosen husband, and the fitting mother of her children, because she has a right estimate of her position and her responsibilities. . . . Did Elizabeth Fry lose any of her feminine qualities by the public walk into which she was called? Having performed the duties of a mother to a large family . . . she was empowered by Him who sent her forth, to go to kings and crowned heads of the earth. . . . Did she lose the delicacy of woman by her acts? No. (*LM*, 150–51)

White women abolitionists argue not only that public reform will enhance women's domestic work, but that the traditional roles of wife and mother can inform women's reform efforts. In her *Correspondence Between Lydia Maria Child and Governor Wise and Mrs. Mason,* Child frames her request to minister to John Brown in terms of such feminine roles: "He needs a mother or sister to dress his wounds, and speak soothingly to him. Will you allow me to perform that mission of humanity?" (*C,* 3). In this initial letter—intended only for Governor Wise, although Wise had it published—Child asks merely to care for Brown and not for an explicitly public role in Brown's defense. Yet her request is controversial, aligning her with one of the most well-known militant abolitionists of the period and endorsing his strong abolitionist principles although she repudiates his violent actions (*C,* 14). And Child's role as advocate for Brown becomes explicitly public when, after Wise's publication of her initial letter, their correspondence is featured in popular newspapers. In an explanatory letter to the *New-York Tribune,* Child again connects her advocacy of Brown to women's domestic duties: "I heard his friends inquiring, 'Has he no wife, or sister, that can go to nurse him? We are trying to ascertain, for he needs some one'" (*C,* 13). Child's domestic qualities become a springboard for her not only to ask to minister to Brown, but to create a public argument that endorses Brown's antislavery sentiments and reveals the hypocrisy of the Virginia officials who imprison him.

As the preceding examples reveal, white female abolitionists often leave unchallenged particular premises of the ideology of domesticity even as they question antebellum assumptions that these duties should be confined to a limited sphere. At times, though, they extend their critique of societal conventions to include the assumptions on which antebellum domestic ideology is based, revealing the potentially radical implications of their redefined rhetoric of domesticity.

Child, in the preface to her *Appeal in Favor of That Class of Americans Called-Africans,* uses domesticity ironically to buttress her public argument, implicitly undermining society's expectations of women. "READER, I beseech you not to throw down this volume as soon as you have glanced at the title," Child begins. "Read it, if your prejudices will allow, for the very truth's sake. . . . Read it, from sheer curiosity to see what a woman (who had much better attend to her household concerns) will say upon such a subject:—Read it, on any terms, and my purpose will be gained" (*A,* iv). Her audience's assumption that her domestic role should prevent her from arguing against slavery becomes, ironically, an inducement for them to read her text and satisfy their "curiosity." She exploits the gap between her actions and her audience's stereotypical expectations to create an ironic authority for a female antislavery author. At the same time, she challenges her audience's limited premises. Because other motives will prompt them to read her text, their conventional principles become irrelevant. In spite of their possible skepticism, she can gain a persuasive victory.

White female rhetors also create particular arguments about slavery's deleterious effect on domesticity, arguments they can make because of their presumed interest in domestic concerns. Yet, as with their rhetoric of sympathy, these strategies validate white women's rhetoric of domesticity while minimizing the experiences of slave women themselves. Because conventions of domesticity are based on the experiences of upper-class white women, their arguments elevate white women's concerns and portray female slaves in terms that do not fully account for their particular experiences. Often they present white southern women as the "victims" of slavery's corrupting influence on proper feminine roles, eliminating slave women from consideration and shifting the focus of antislavery argument away from the realities of slavery. When female slaves are present in their persuasion, they are judged in terms based on whiteness, and their particular experiences are effaced. Representing slave women as "True Women," white female abolitionists argue against the slave system that interferes with their proper domestic duties, and they call attention to the hypocrisy of their society, which purports to valorize womanhood while denying slave women the opportunity to be truly feminine. Although they argue generally against slavery, then, they minimize the true horrors of slavery by framing slave women's particular concerns in terms of the domestic experiences of privileged white women. Their arguments also deny agency to female slaves, suggesting that it is only through the norms of "True Womanhood" that they can achieve their full potential and gain meaningful freedom.

White women abolitionists often argue that slavery disrupts the home's status as a refuge in which order reigned and women preserved stability. In the presence of slavery, white women did not assume their proper domestic roles, and the integrity of their homes suffered.[46] In *An Appeal in Favor of That Class of Americans Called Africans,* Child anticipates Harriet Beecher Stowe's 1854 comment that the worst "abuse" perpetuated by slavery is its "outrage upon the family."[47]

After quoting a Mr. Faulkner, a Virginia legislator who comments that slavery produces "indolence" and "weakness" in the white population, Child suggests how these qualities manifest themselves in white women. She quotes Robert Sutcliff's 1811 *Travels in Some Parts of North America:* "A person . . . would naturally think that where families employ a number of slaves, every thing about their houses, gardens, and plantations, would be kept in the best order. But the reverse of this is generally the case. I was sometimes tempted to think that the more slaves there were employed, the more disorder appeared. I am persuaded that one or two hired servants, in a well-regulated family, would preserve more neatness, order, and comfort" (*A*, 81). Slavery's danger to the home is revealed—order and regulation slip as white women become lazy and renounce the duties of "True Women." Notably, the threats slavery poses to slave women are not explored in this passage. It is white women's experiences that are normative, and slave women are, for the most part, invisible.

In Child's ironically titled tract *The Patriarchal Institution, as Described by Members of Its Own Family,* she reveals that slavery's damage extends beyond the orderliness of white southern women's households. The sanctity of their domestic relations, too, is violated by slavery. Child cites the observations of a Mrs. Margaret Douglass, a woman who has lived in various southern towns: "The female slave . . . knows that she is a *slave.* . . . If [her master] casts upon her a desiring eye, she knows that she *must* submit. . . . Still, she *feels* her degradation, and so do others with whom she is connected. She has parents, brothers, sisters, a lover, perhaps, who all suffer through her and with her. White mothers and daughters of the South have suffered under this custom for years; they have seen their dearest affections trampled on, their hopes of domestic happiness destroyed" (*PI*, 28–29). It is significant that Child mentions the slave woman's plight and reveals that she "suffers" as do the white women of the South. Yet this articulation of a shared oppression of slave and free women of the South detracts from the particular abuses faced by female slaves. When white reformers make such comparisons between the situation of white women and that of female slaves, bell hooks explains, they are "not revealing an awareness of or sensitivity to the slave's lot; they [are] simply appropriating the horror of the slave experience to enhance their own cause."[48] In the case of Child's remarks, hooks's observation may overstate the case—Child does, after all, reveal a true concern for slave women and their families. Yet hooks's comments aptly elucidate the limitations of Child's rhetoric, which, by equating the abuse of female slaves with white women's "sufferings," detracts from slave women's particular victimization.

In her *Letters on the Equality of the Sexes,* Sarah Grimké similarly highlights the effects of female slaves' sexual abuse on white women. In particular, she argues that this form of oppression compromises white women's respect for proper domestic ties. "The moral purity of the white woman" in the South, Grimké maintains, "is deeply contaminated. In the daily habit of seeing the virtue of her enslaved sister sacrificed without hesitancy or remorse, she looks upon the crimes of seduction and illicit intercourse without horror, and . . . she loses that value for innocence in her own, as well as the other sex, which is one of the strongest safeguards to virtue. She lives in habitual intercourse with men, whom she knows to be polluted by licentiousness" (*LES*, 224–25). Slavery is dangerous, Grimké suggests, primarily because of its effect on white women. Although she mentions slave women's plight and describes them as having inherent "virtue," she focuses her primary concern on the daily lives of white women. She features the word "horror" not to describe the oppression the female slave faces, but to characterize the appropriate response of the white woman to the "contamination" of her family.

White women, though, are not merely innocent victims of slavery's deleterious influence on the domestic realm. Marshaling the strategy associated with the rhetoric of sympathy, in which supporters of slavery are represented as violating conventions of gender, white female abolitionists portray women who support the slave system as both unfeminine and hypocritical, claiming to have respect for domesticity that their support for slavery belies. This argument is illustrated in Child's striking response to Margaretta Mason in her *Correspondence Between Lydia Maria Child and Governor Wise and Mrs. Mason*. In her letter to Child, Mason accuses northern women of lacking the "charity" toward the poor that southern women have toward the slaves. In particular, Mason demands, "Do *you* soften the pangs of maternity in those around you by all the care and comfort you can give? . . . *We* do [this] and more for our servants" (*C*, 17). Child's response reveals the extent of southern women's respect for slaves' domestic ties: "I have never known an instance where the 'pangs of maternity' did not meet with requisite assistance; and here at the North, after we have helped the mothers, *we do not sell the babies*" (*C*, 26). Although they refer to female slaves, white women are clearly the focus of the exchange between Mason and Child. Slave women's experiences are important only insofar as they reveal white southern women's lack of commitment to fundamental domestic principles. Like the rhetoric of sympathy, the rhetoric of domesticity focuses on white women, preserving their position of power over the female slave.

Yet white female abolitionists do not ignore female slaves in their arguments about slavery and domesticity. Child also asserts that slavery leads to disorder in slave quarters, allowing her both to argue against slavery based on its effects on women's homes and to expose the hypocrisy of antebellum society's presumed respect for women's conventional roles. The description of an elderly slave named Judy in *Authentic Anecdotes of American Slavery* exemplifies this claim: "Her bed (which was but an apology for one) was so filthy, that it required some resolution to approach it. She used to mourn because she could not keep things more tidy. She would say, 'Missa, the dirt makes me sick; but I can't help it'" (*AA*, 1:2). By demonstrating that slavery keeps Judy from the order and cleanliness she desires, Child implicitly criticizes antebellum society's ostensible commitment to domestic ideology. The patriarchy's endorsement of "True Womanhood" is shallow and hypocritical in light of its support for a system that subverts the domestic sentiments of slave women. From within the ideology of domesticity, Child critiques those who profess to support it, demonstrating their hypocrisy and, by implication, suggesting the weak foundation of contemporary domestic conventions. Yet, again, the ideology of femininity upon which Child builds is defined by the experiences of privileged women. Judy's experience of slavery is characterized by her longing for a clean home, a desire presumably universal but clearly of lesser importance than other more traumatic aspects of slavery. The female slave's oppression is framed in terms of privileged women's concerns, allowing antebellum society to ignore the unique realities of slavery.

Lest her antebellum audience counter her arguments about slave women's domestic concerns with the suggestion that female slaves would be incapable of properly managing domestic affairs if free—a stock argument of proslavery rhetors[49]—Child calls upon historical evidence in *The Right Way the Safe Way, Proved by Emancipation in the British West Indies and Elsewhere,* published in 1860. As the title promises, Child offers copious documentation of the benefits of emancipation. She discusses, for example, the changes in domestic life in post-emancipation Jamaica: "In the days of slavery, laborers generally lived in thatched hovels, with mud walls, thrown together without any order or arrange-ment. . . . As the women were driven into the fields to toil early and late, they had no time for household cleanliness. . . . Now, the laborers live in Free Villages, regularly laid out. . . . Most of [the houses] are neatly thatched, and generally plastered and white-washed outside and in. They now have looking-glasses, chairs, and side-boards decorated with pretty articles of glass and crockery" (*RW,* 79–80). Again, antebellum society's hypocrisy is revealed—slavery is antithetical to the domestic values that it professes to support. Slave women wish to be "True Women," Child proposes, revealing that female slaves deserve to be treated with the respect society gives to white women. Yet as she defends freed female slaves' domestic abilities, Child portrays liberty in rather narrow terms. Freedom means tidy houses and the time for domestic affairs rather than field work. These goals might resonate for white readers, but they diminish the true value of freedom. The antislavery cause, in Child's description, is not characterized as a fight for African American self-determination but as the effort to allow African Ameri-can women to live like privileged white women.

Because women's roles as wives and mothers were central in antebellum America, arguments that feature the slave woman's relationship to her husband and children were particularly salient. These arguments were based upon an acceptance of the existence of strong bonds between slave women and their husbands and children, a premise that necessitated refuting claims of proslavery rhetors, who dehumanized persons of African descent and suggested that they did not feel familial affections—particularly that African mothers were not emotionally attached to their children.[50] Child negates these proslavery assertions in her *Appeal* by calling upon the evidence from Mungo Park's famous *Travels in the*

Interior Districts of Africa of Africans' "strong affections" and "domestic tenderness" (*A,* 177). Child cites Park's particular observations: "Maternal affection, neither suppressed by the restraints, nor diverted by the solicitudes of civilized life, is every where conspicuous among them" (*A,* 184).[51] Park's commentary, in fact, suggests not only that Africans are capable of maternal devotion but that—because of their "uncivilized" culture—they are more "naturally" susceptible to such feelings. This formulation of African character, however stereotypical and paternalistic, activates in the audience an acute sense of slavery's unnatural interference with maternal instincts.

Arguing that slave women are more naturally devoted to husbands and children than white women, white female abolitionists espouse views akin to the "romantic racialism" that portrays people of African descent as particularly emotional, innocent, and "childlike." Slave women's more instinctual devotion to their families, white female abolitionists suggest, leads them to act on their feelings rather than on rational decision-making. This description clearly has racist implications; yet, paradoxically, by articulating a unique form of domesticity that is distinct from white women's feelings, white female abolitionists grant to slave women a form of agency that can even lead to militant antislavery resistance. Consider, for example, the story in Child's *Authentic Anecdotes of American Slavery* of a woman in a coffle of slaves passing through Washington, D.C., en route to Georgia. Not allowed to see her husband, she jumps out of a window. She is subsequently sold and separated from her children (*AA,* 2:3–4). The body of the woman becomes concrete evidence of her strong familial attachments, Child suggests: "Slave-owners would fain convince us that the colored wife and mother has no feeling;—but the shattered limbs and bleeding wounds of this poor woman, tell too plain a story of her frantic agony!" (*AA,* 2:4). Unlike in other descriptions of slave women, the victimization of this wife and mother is described vividly rather than subjugated or compared to white women's oppression. Indeed, the extremity of the slave woman's act calls attention to the uniqueness of her oppression and suggests that she is empowered to even self-destructive acts of resistance.

Similarly, in an installment of her "A, B, C, of Abolition" column in the *National Anti-Slavery Standard,* Child relates an even more disturbing incident in which a slave mother kills her children and herself the night before they are to be sold. Such evidence, she remarks, demonstrates that slaves have a deeper maternal devotion than others: "I believe the attachments of slaves are even stronger than ours. . . . Hundreds of instances might be told, were [*sic*] they have preferred death to separation."[52] The slave woman in this narrative may be a victim, but she is not passive. Nor is she to be judged by the standards of white femininity. Slave mothers, she implies, are separated from their white counterparts by their more extreme maternal feelings, and in their particular devotion lies a great power. Preferring death to losing her children, the slave woman assumes a unique agency and determines her own destiny.

In white women abolitionists' deployment of the rhetoric of domesticity—as in their appropriation of "True Womanhood" and their rhetoric of sympathy—they underscore the essentialism that is inherent in constructions of gender. The category of "womanhood," it is presumed, fundamentally defines women, even those of different races. Although racial categories were also defined by antebellum society as rooted in biology, essentialist conceptions of race and gender have very different implications for white women and African Americans, both male and female. As white women abolitionists' allusions to slave women demonstrate, the essentialist category of "womanhood" pushes aside African American women while privileging the experiences of white women. Thus essentialism for white women is a construct that both limits them by defining them in narrow terms and places them in a position of power. Essentialist definitions of African Americans, on the other hand, systematically limit their power by portraying them as innately inferior to white men and women. Thus the deployment of essentialist notions of gender by white women abolitionists differs notably from the responses of both African American male and female abolitionists to essentialist constructions of race. African American male abolitionists such as David Walker ironically challenge white Americans' racial perceptions and disrupt the assumptions that define racial categories. And, as we shall see, African American women also call attention to the inadequacies of essentialist racial categories when they highlight the unique ways race and gender structure their lives. The relationship of white women to essentialist definitions of womanhood, as the gendered rhetoric of the white women abolitionists illustrates, is more conflicted. While they challenge and expand narrow articulations of women's roles, white women abolitionists draw power from various conventional premises about gender. Thus, unlike their African American colleagues, they do not thoroughly challenge their audiences' assumptions.

THE "RHETORIC OF COURTSHIP" AND THE "MYSTERY" OF GENDER

Although white female abolitionists asserted their particular right to speak through their appropriation of the conventions of "True Womanhood" and domesticity, they could not eliminate the particular obstacles they faced due to their position in antebellum society. Like their African American male colleagues, white female abolitionists were, to use Burke's terms, in an "inferior" position in an antebellum "hierarchy"—in their case, a hierarchy based on gender. And, as with African American male abolitionists, attention was often called to their bodies when they spoke publicly.[53] Yet white women abolitionists faced a unique paradox. On the one hand, because their status as women was continually used to question their authority, they had to negotiate expectations based on gender in their rhetoric. On the other hand, unlike their African American male abolitionists, who could argue for racial equality as they advocated for their enslaved brethren, female orators who highlighted questions of women's rights were often accused by critics of placing the rights of women before those of the slave. Even men who supported women's right to persuade were uncomfortable with female rhetors who emphasized their gender. Although John Greenleaf Whittier and Theodore Dwight Weld supported women's right to speak publicly, they counseled the Grimké sisters to exclude considerations of gender from their persuasion and to focus solely on abolition. Yet the sisters realized that it was impossible for audiences to "forget" or ignore their status as women. As Angelina remarks in a letter to Weld, "They look at me in utter amazement. I am not at all surprized they are afraid lest such a woman should usurp authority over the men." "In every place that we lectured the subject of our speaking in public was up for discussion," Sarah informs Weld.[54] In effect, white female antislavery rhetors were constantly reminded that they were arguing as women and yet advised to "forget" this aspect of their identity.

The very advice of those male abolitionists who counseled women to "forget" their gender when speaking for the slave often demonstrated that such an approach was unfeasible. Editor Nathaniel Rogers's comments in the *National Anti-Slavery Standard* about his successor Lydia Maria Child reveal her paradoxical position: "We greatly rejoice . . . not merely that we have her extraordinary ability and faithfulness enlisted, and her reputation *invested* in the cause—but that they come to our aid in the form of *woman*. . . . We trust our distinguished friend will forget on the occasion and in the warfare before her, every circumstance and every incident to her existence, except her *humanity;* that she will remember her womanhood, as such, as little as the maid of Orleans did when she led France to the rout and expulsion of England from her native shores." Child's brief but apt response exposes the contradictory nature of Rogers's request: "In answer to his wish, that I should, on this occasion, 'forget every incident of my existence, except my humanity,' I merely reply that I would *he*, too, had forgotten all else."[55]

These paradoxical expectations created for female abolitionists a complex rhetorical situation. Because their gender would continually be in their audiences' minds, their antislavery rhetoric could not be successful if they did not address audiences' preconceptions based on their gender. Yet they had to do so in ways that would simultaneously turn the expectations of their audiences into a rhetorical advantage and avoid the criticism that they were pushing the agenda of women's rights. They address these conflicting constraints by marshaling the rhetorical forms that Burke notes arise from any hierarchy—the "rhetoric of courtship" and appeals to the "mystery" of gender—upon which their African American male colleagues also draw.

Because of the specific rhetorical demands on them, though, their deployment of these rhetorical forms differs significantly from the strategies marshaled by African American men. In particular, as we have discovered, the "rhetoric of courtship" employed by African American male abolitionists depends upon ambiguity, upon the multiple resonances of language that can be exploited to simultaneously offer differing interpretations. As in Douglass's inherently ambiguous remarks that the "humblest may stand forth," they feature an enigmatic "rhetoric of courtship" that simultaneously places them in the position of "inferior" and "superior." The "rhetoric of courtship" of white women abolitionists, by contrast, does not draw on this ambiguity. The implication that they could be "superior" might be seen as an advocacy of the cause of women's rights in their rhetoric, making them vulnerable to the accusation that they were elevating the concerns of women over those of the slave. Unlike their African American male colleagues, then, white women create a "rhetoric of courtship" that does not exploit multiple levels of meaning. Their discourse negotiates the paradoxical demands that they downplay the very gender difference that is central to their restricted position as rhetors by relying on a traditional "rhetoric of obeisance" that features difference in a circumscribed way that does not challenge women's purportedly "inferior" role.

White women abolitionists rely on this "rhetoric of courtship" most strongly when they address white male leaders directly. Although no text of Lucretia Mott's remarks at the 1833 Philadelphia convention at which the AASS was formed was preserved, eyewitness testimony suggests that she strategically marshaled this rhetorical form when addressing the white male leaders of the gathering. In his memoir of the antislavery movement, Oliver Johnson notes that Mott did not immediately assume the authority to speak at the meeting, but "seemed to be hesitating" when she rose and waited to be "welcomed" before beginning her remarks. Samuel May recalls that Mott's speech was "made all the more engaging by the emotion of deference to the supposed prejudices of her auditors, with which it was suffused." Angelina Grimké's 1835 letter to William Lloyd Garrison provides a concrete example of this construction of a deferential ethos. Grimké responds to two editorials by Garrison that preached faithfulness to the antislavery cause even as abolitionists faced increasing mob violence against them. "It seems as if I was compelled at this time to address thee," Grimké begins, "notwithstanding all of my reasonings against intruding on thy valuable time, and the uselessness of so insignificant a person as myself offering thee the sentiments of sympathy at this alarming crisis."[56]

This self-deprecation notwithstanding, white female abolitionists could create strong antislavery appeals by appearing deferential. The "rhetoric of courtship," as Burke explains, draws rhetorical power from the hierarchy even as it preserves its influence. Although they appear to accept the dominance of male leaders, Mott and Grimké also activate in their listeners a desire to identify with them, to temporarily transcend their differences in status. In Burke's words, the "magic of the hierarchic order itself . . . imposes itself upon superior and inferior both, and leads them both to aim at a dialectic transcending their discordancy of status." Thus, by relying on a rhetorical form based on the hierarchy of gender, white female abolitionists dispose their audiences to attend to their arguments, creating a powerful sense of rhetorical exigency.[57] Even though they do not question the hierarchy of gender as their African American male colleagues challenge the hierarchy of race, they nonetheless take authority by evoking its influence.

The power inherent in this strategy is revealed in an 1843 sermon given by Mott in the Unitarian Church in Washington, D.C., in which the abolition of slavery is one aspect of the "righteousness" she discusses. Mott makes note of her inferior social status while invoking a higher spiritual calling to build her authority: "I come before you this evening, my friends, with all the disadvantages of a woman breaking through the proscribed customs of the times, to endeavor to elevate the standard of righteousness . . . and I desire to be received in that spirit which has induced me thus to appear before you" (*LM,* 43). Mott's comments do not feature the ambiguity of Douglass's prediction that "the humblest may stand forth." She suggests that the humblest may be allowed to take authority in spite of social inferiority, but she does not allude to a potential superiority that may be the special province of an ostensible "inferior." Yet she does ask her audience both to make allowances for her gender and to look beyond gender differences as she persuades. Although she defers to the influence of the social hierarchy of gender, she alludes to the "spirit" of "righteousness" that authorizes her to speak, suggesting that she can create an authority that both acknowledges her "inferiority" and transcends it.

The related strategy of emphasizing particular aspects of gender difference— thus activating the force of the "mystery" of gender—also allows white women abolitionists to negotiate the tensions between the need to respond to constraints posed by their gender and the demand that they do not emphasize the rights of women. Angelina Grimké's influential 1838 speech before a committee of men from the Massachusetts legislature illustrates the power of this emphasis on the mystery of gender difference. She begins with an explicit identification of herself with the biblical heroine Esther: "MR. CHAIRMAN—More than 2000 years have rolled their dark and bloody waters down the rocky, winding channel of Time into the broad ocean of Eternity, since woman's voice was heard in the palace of an eastern monarch, and woman's petition achieved the salvation of millions of her race from the edge of the sword." Grimké asserts, however, that there are key distinctions between her position and that of this Old Testament figure. Esther, having studied King Ahasuerus, knew that he could only be reached "through the medium of his sensual appetites." In great detail, Grimké describes Esther's strategies for preparing the "voluptuous" king for her request: "We find her arrayed in royal apparel . . . hoping by her personal charms to win the favor of her lord. . . . She *felt* that if her mission of mercy was to be successful, *his* animal propensities must be still more powerfully wrought upon—the luxurious feast must be prepared, the banquet of wine must be served up, and the favorable moment must be seized when, gorged with gluttony and intoxication, the king's heart was fit to be operated on."[58]

After this detailed description, Grimké argues that her identification with Esther excludes these "sensual" strategies:

> Mr. Chairman, it is my privilege to stand before you on a similar mission
> of life and love; but I thank God that we live in an age of the world too

enlightened and too moral to admit of the adoption of the same *means* to obtain as holy an end. I feel that it would be an insult to this Committee, were I to attempt to win their favor by arraying my person . . . or by inviting them to partake of the luxurious feast. . . . I understand the spirit of the age too well to believe that *you* could be moved by such sensual means—means . . . unworthy of you. . . . Yes, I feel that if you are reached at all, it will not be by me, but by the truths I shall endeavor to present to your understandings and your hearts.[59]

Grimké protests too much; she has prepared the committee for her petition by appealing to elements of their "sensual" nature just as Esther did. Activating the "mystery" of gender roles, she creates, in Burkeian terms, a dual "rhetoric of obeisance" to those higher in the gender "hierarchy" that simultaneously caters to their appetites and flatters them that they are "above" such a strategy. Employing difference as an element of "mystery," Grimké draws on women's "sensual" power even as she claims that she will be judged by standards that transcend these base considerations.

And Grimké, while arguing for a rhetorical authority for women based on intellectual worth, highlights the possibility of another type of influence. "It is often said that women rule the world, through their influence over men," she maintains. "If so, then may we well hide our faces in the dust, and cover ourselves with sackcloth and ashes. It has not been by moral power and intellectual, but through the baser passions of man.—*This* dominion of women *must* be resigned—the sooner the better."[60] Grimké may purport to aspire to an authority not based on women's sensual power over men, but she emphasizes the mystery of women's sexuality as an influential force. As she aspires to influence a group of male legislators, her command over her male auditors—however "base"—is a potential form of authority. Although Grimké purports to shun a sexual basis for her appeal to men, her emphasis on this form of rhetorical agency implicitly draws on this source of influence.

Grimké's appropriation of a traditional formulation of women's sexuality in her appeal to the Massachusetts legislators points to important differences between white female abolitionists' use of the "rhetoric of courtship" and the "mystery" of gender and the reliance on similar rhetorical forms by their African American male counterparts. As African American male abolitionists create a "rhetoric of courtship" and deploy the "mystery" of race, they appropriate traditional societal stereotypes and assumptions about race in ways that continually challenge and undermine these premises. Using ambiguity, they complicate the "rhetoric of courtship," marshaling the force of this rhetorical form while resisting a fixed position in the hierarchy of race. For white female abolitionists, the "rhetoric of courtship" is a source of persuasive power, but they do not fundamentally challenge the premises on which the hierarchy of gender is based. Deferring to traditional conceptions of gender, they formulate appeals that draw authority from these notions but do not explicitly question their society's essentialist definitions of womanhood and of male-female relationships.

This difference from the rhetoric of African American male abolitionists stems from the ways in which, as we have seen, essentialist definitions of gender can be a basis for white women's authority, albeit restricted, while essentialist definitions of race inherently minimize African Americans' agency. Thus the "rhetoric of courtship" and appeals to the "mystery" of difference, forms which depend upon essentialism, have different implications for white women and for African American men. Because whites attempt to classify racial difference in ways that preserve their hegemony, for people of color to name and define aspects of race gives them a power that inherently disrupts white domination. For African American male abolitionists, taking control of the terms of racial distinction is an act of defiance to restrictive definitions, which allows them to redefine racial categories in ways that challenge white hegemony. They can undermine societal assumptions, then, by marshaling the premises that underlie the "rhetoric of courtship" and the mystery of racial difference.

White women, though, have a different relationship to conventional definitions of gender. White women's femininity is constructed in terms that valorize whiteness and represent white women's experiences as normative. Traditional formulations of gender, then, can be a source of power for white women. This relationship of white women to conventional notions of gender should not be interpreted as minimizing the ways in which male domination is encoded in traditional assumptions about femininity. Yet it is important to acknowledge that white women are simultaneously privileged and restricted by conceptions of gender. When they marshal the "rhetoric of courtship" or the "mystery" of gender difference, they do not need to challenge the premises on which these forms are based to gain legitimacy from their authority. Yet their agency is often precarious, leaving unchallenged hegemonic definitions of womanhood that limit white women and restrict their roles in society.

BIBLICAL AUTHORITY AND PAULINE PROSCRIPTIONS

Because one component of essentialist antebellum definitions of femininity was the assumption that the ideal woman was naturally pious, white women abolitionists could potentially draw on their religious commitments to authorize their antislavery persuasion. Indeed, many women abolitionists assert that they feel called by God to argue publicly against slavery. Angelina Grimké, for example, defends her 1835 letter to Garrison in terms of her spiritual vocation. In her diary, she notes, "I believd I had done right, that tho' condemnd by human judges, I was acquitted by him whom I believ qualifyd me to write [the letter]. . . . I felt my great unworthiness of being used in such a work but rememberd that 'God hath chosen the *weak things* of this world to confound the wise' & so was comforted." Similarly, Child describes her editorship of the *National Anti-Slavery Standard* as a religious calling: "Such as I am, I am here—ready to work . . . ready to pass away whenever a fitter instrument of God's will offers to take my place."[61]

Yet traditional interpretations of the Bible—particularly of the roles dictated to women in Genesis and the proscriptions against women's public speaking articulated by Paul—presented female antislavery rhetors with a dilemma. They wished to speak publicly and to exhort other women to follow their lead, but they could not dismiss or ignore these scriptural injunctions for reasons both pious and practical. White women abolitionists' descriptions of their vocation in terms of Christian principles suggest that they were unwilling to reject deeply held Christian beliefs; and, because of the connection of "True Womanhood" to Christianity, their credibility depended upon audiences' perceptions of their piety. In addition, because most members of antebellum audiences would naturally grant the authority of Scripture, appeals to logos built upon biblical authority were potentially very persuasive.

It was necessary, then, for female Christian abolitionists to engage biblical authority directly in their defenses of women's public speaking. Beginning from the premise that Scripture—including the Pauline letters—is authoritative and directive, female Christian abolitionists create alternatives to traditional interpretations, particularly of those passages appearing to forbid women's public speaking, thus demonstrating that women's public speaking against slavery is not inherently incompatible with Christian principles. They feature precedent from the Old and New Testaments supporting women in the public sphere, create exegetical responses to Genesis that counter traditional arguments for women's subordination, and formulate empowering alternative interpretations of the Pauline passages often cited against women's public speaking.

Although muted group theory suggests that white women abolitionists must ground their argumentation on the assumptions of their audiences—even those that threaten to marginalize them—it does not provide specific tools for analyzing the ways in which they engage traditional biblical interpretations. And muted group theory, by suggesting that marginalized rhetors respond primarily to the beliefs and opinions of the dominant group, does not account for the complexity inherent in these rhetors' relationships to Christianity. Although antebellum religious leaders often dictated particular interpretations of Scripture, white women abolitionists shared with them many fundamental beliefs, including a commitment to the Bible as a sacred guide. It is too simple to assume that the religious principles to which white women abolitionists responded were solely dictated by those who sought to oppress them or that they rejected all of the dominant religious assumptions of antebellum society. Instead, we need to examine the strategies they used to redefine and shape the implications of many conventional religious beliefs and interpretations.

Chaim Perelman and Lucie Olbrechts-Tyteca contend that rhetors seek not to prove abstract truths but to translate audiences' "adherence" to premises and categories into acceptance for desired conclusions. Their model suggests methods of analysis that augment the general premises of muted group theory. Although they focus on how audiences' assumptions shape rhetoric, they do not assume that these premises are necessarily imposed on rhetors by others. Furthermore, their emphasis on particular rhetorical strategies frequently deployed by those arguing in the realm of values and interpretation is a useful tool for textual analysis. In addition, David Frank establishes that their New Rhetoric is influenced by the "pluralism" of the Talmudic tradition, in which "competing values" and opposing voices all contribute to the "search for truth," a foundation that elucidates the complexities of exegesis, particularly that which advocates alternative scriptural interpretations.[62]

Steven Mailloux's concept of "rhetorical hermeneutics" is also germane to the arguments of white women abolitionists that engage particular biblical passages. Mailloux examines the ways in which rhetors on opposite sides of a debate may be equally committed to a text although they offer differing interpretations of specific textual evidence. He addresses how "texts are established as meaningful through rhetorical exchanges" that take place "against an ever-changing background of shared and disputed assumptions, questions, assertions, and so forth." The use of textual evidence in persuasion, Mailloux suggests, must not be judged in terms of "correctness" or abstract logic. What "counts" for the rhetor and audience as "relevant" or "significant" is how meaning is created through an act of persuasion that is dependent upon the beliefs and assumptions of the audience and upon the larger historical and cultural context. In Mailloux's model, rhetors do not merely appropriate terms defined by others, as muted group theory suggests; they create meaning actively through interpretation that engages the shared assumptions of rhetors and audiences.[63]

In their defenses of women's persuasion, white women abolitionists often seek, in Perelman and Olbrechts-Tyteca's terms, to establish "adherence" to their conclusions about women's public speaking through appeals to biblical precedent. Their strategies can be analyzed in terms of what Perelman and Olbrechts-Tyteca call the "rule of justice," which exhorts audiences to "giv[e] identical treatment to beings or situations of the same kind." Arguing from scriptural precedent, they rely on antebellum audiences' acceptance of biblical authority to advocate conclusions that empower women as rhetors. In addition, Perelman and Olbrechts-Tyteca explain that the "rule of justice" makes arguments appear "undeniably rational."[64] Because white women abolitionists' very credibility is at stake in their defenses of women's public speaking, they cannot ask audiences to grant them authority because of personal credentials. Instead, they must establish an ostensibly rational basis for their credibility.

In her *Appeal to the Christian Women of the South,* Angelina Grimké invokes biblical precedent to authorize women's public involvement in abolition. Anticipating her audience's objection that women are incapable of public antislavery work because they cannot—as she puts it—"endure persecution," she offers scriptural evidence that women can and should be leaders for reform:

> Have not *women* stood up in all the dignity and strength of moral courage to be the leaders of the people, and to bear a faithful testimony for the truth whenever the providence of God has called them to do so? . . . Who led out the women of Israel from the house of bondage. . . ? It was a

woman; Miriam, the prophetess. . . . Who went up with Barek to Kadesh to fight against Jabin. . . ? It was a *woman!* Deborah the wife of Lapidoth. . . . Who dared to *speak the truth* concerning those judgments which were coming upon Judea. . . ? It was a *woman.* Huldah the prophetess . . . Who was chosen to deliver the whole Jewish nation from that murderous decree of Persia's King. . . ? It was a *woman;* Esther the Queen; yes, weak and trembling *woman* was the instrument appointed by God. (*ACW,* 60–61)

Emphasizing the term "woman," Grimké stresses femininity as a fundamental connection linking women of all historical periods, strategically relying upon her audience's essentialist notions of gender to suggest that the innate and timeless qualities of womanhood connect her to her biblical foremothers. Thus she suggests that contemporary women should be treated as "identical" to women speakers and leaders in the Bible, establishing the foundation of the "rule of justice." From this premise and from her audience's acceptance of the authority of Scripture, Grimké argues that women in the antislavery movement should be granted the authority given to influential women in the Bible.

Similarly, Angelina Grimké relies on biblical precedent in *Letters to Catherine* [sic] *E. Beecher.* Calling upon the examples of Miriam, Deborah, Huldah, Anna, Phoebe, and Philip's daughters, she demonstrates that women's influence need not be confined—as Beecher argues—to the "domestic circle." In particular, she proposes that biblical heroines were called upon to *"prophesy"* (*LCB,* 189–90). From these scriptural examples, she argues that if God chose and appointed women as leaders in biblical times and gave them voice, contemporary women must not assume that they cannot be similarly called.

Not all female biblical figures, though, would have positive connotations for antebellum audiences. In particular, Eve presented a potentially problematic precedent. Because arguments about Eve were often cited by opponents of women's authority, female abolitionists had to respond to the book of Genesis to defend women's public activism. In particular, they feature exegesis of two passages, Gen. 1:26–27 and Gen. 2:18–3:24, to offer alternative interpretations of Eve's creation, transgression, and role in relation to Adam. Gen. 1:26–27 suggests that man and woman are created simultaneously by God: "And God said, Let us make man in our image. . . . So God created man in his own image, in the image of God created he him; male and female created he them." Sarah and Angelina Grimké marshal this more egalitarian account of creation to counter traditional interpretations of women's subordinate role. These arguments can be productively analyzed in terms of Mailloux's rhetorical hermeneutics. The Grimkés' arguments about the simultaneous creation story illustrate Mailloux's assertion that in disputes about biblical exegesis, disputants construct what is "relevant" or "significant" to the text.[65] For the Grimké sisters, the account of Gen. 1:26–27 is meaningful to discussions about women's place in society.

In the first letter of her *Letters on the Equality of the Sexes and the Condition of Women*—significantly titled "The Original Equality of Women"—Sarah Grimké cites Gen. 1:26–27. She notes, "In all this sublime description of the creation of man (which is a generic term including man and woman) there is not one particle of difference intimated as existing between them. They were both made in the image of God; dominion was given to both over every other creature, but not over each other" (*LES*, 205). For Grimké, Gen. 1:26–27 is relevant to the debate about women's role, demonstrating that man and woman were "created in perfect equality" and expected by God to rule jointly over other beings (*LES*, 205).

In *Letters to Catherine* [sic] *Beecher*, Angelina Grimké similarly references this scriptural passage to suggest that Beecher's view of women as dependent upon men is not divinely ordained. "[Woman] was created, like [man], in the image of God," she maintains, "not, as is almost universally assumed, a little lower than man; on her brow, as well as on his, was placed the 'diadem of beauty,' and in her hand the sceptre of universal dominion. Gen: i. 27, 28" (*LCB*, 195–96). Grimké adds to Gen. 1:27 the language of Isa. 28:5—"In that day shall the Lord of hosts be for a crown of glory, and for a diadem of beauty, unto the residue of his people"—suggesting that scriptural references to God's followers apply equally to both men and women.

The Grimké sisters also respond to the better-known account of the creation and the fall from grace in Gen. 2:18–3:24, traditionally cited as a divine mandate for women's subordination, which describes Eve's creation after Adam from one of his ribs; her status as "help-meet"; and her temptation, sin, and punishment. Using rhetorical hermeneutics, they create alternative interpretations, asserting that the meaningful parts of the passage suggest women's equality with men. These arguments also require that they create a particular account of Eve that grants her equality with Adam. As Perelman and Olbrechts-Tyteca explain, rhetors construct a particular "concept of [a] person" by highlighting certain aspects of his or her identity and de-emphasizing others.[66] The "rule of justice," too, is deployed in their interpretations of Gen. 2:18–3:24. In contrast to antebellum commentators, who suggest that Eve's transgression relegates all women to a subordinate role, the Grimkés argue that, based on their reinterpretations, Eve sets a precedent for women's authority.

For the Grimkés, the significance of the account of creation in Gen. 2:18–25 is Adam and Eve's relationship rather than Eve's creation after Adam. This relationship, they argue, puts man and woman on an equal footing. Sarah Grimké maintains in *Letters on the Equality of the Sexes* that woman was created as man's "companion, *in all respects* his equal; one who was like himself *a free agent*, gifted with intellect . . . a moral and responsible being." "If this had not been the case," she asks, "how could she have been a help meet for him?" (*LES*, 205). Significantly, she equates the word "help meet"—a term that traditionally connotes women's subordinate role—with the more egalitarian term "companion." This expanded meaning makes her assertion that "God designed woman to be a help meet for man in every good and perfect work" a mandate for women's public activism rather than a traditional articulation of women's secondary status (*LES,* 205).

Angelina Grimké creates a slightly different interpretation of the relationship between Adam and Eve as related in Gen. 2:22–23. In *Letters to Catherine* [sic] *E. Beecher,* she features scriptural evidence more literally than her sister but similarly offers an alternative to traditional interpretations: "'And the rib which the Lord God had taken from man, made he a woman, and brought her unto the man.' . . . Adam immediately recognized her *as part of himself*—('this is now bone of my bone, and flesh of my flesh')—a companion and equal . . . not placed under his authority as a *subject,* but by his side . . . under the government of God only" (*LCB,* 196). She boldly suggests that those who argue that Scripture requires women to be subordinate disregard God's command that both sexes are under divine authority alone: "Instead of *Jehovah* being *her* king, *her* lawgiver, and *her* judge, she has been taken out of the exalted scale of existence in which He placed her, and subjected to the despotic control of man" (*LCB,* 196).

The sisters also address the issue of Eve's transgression (Gen. 3:1–24). Although both concur that Eve succumbed to temptation, neither allows that her sin justifies her subordination or her exclusion from the public sphere. In Perelman and Olbrechts-Tyteca's terms, they distinguish between aspects of Eve's identity that are "important" and those that are "transitory."[67] For Angelina Grimké, Eve's sin not only fits the latter category but also serves as evidence that women must be given authority over their own destiny. In *Letters to Catherine* [sic] *E. Beecher,* she argues, "Woman was the first transgressor, and the first victim of power. . . . I believe it is woman's right to have a voice in all the laws and regulations by which she is to be *governed.*" (*LCB,* 197). In this spirit, Eve's sin is secondary to her "victimization," which demonstrates that women must codetermine societal regulations.

For Sarah Grimké, too, Eve is a victim whose fault is "transitory," a consequence of satanic power. Significantly, though, she does not spare Adam in her *Letters on the Equality of the Sexes:*

Woman was exposed to temptation from a being with whom she was unacquainted. . . . [O]f satanic intelligence, she was in all probability entirely ignorant. Through the subtlety of the serpent, she was beguiled. . . .

We next find Adam involved in the same sin, not through the instrumentality of a super-natural agent, but through that of his equal, a being whom he must have known was liable to transgress the divine command, because he must have felt that he was himself a free agent. . . . Had Adam tenderly reproved his wife, and endeavored to lead her to repentance instead of sharing in her guilt, I should be much more ready to accord to man that superiority which he claims; but as the facts stand . . . it appears to me that to say the least, there was as much weakness exhibited by

Adam as by Eve. They both fell from innocence . . . *but not from equality.*
(*LES,* 206)

Implicitly, Grimké asserts that Adam is *more* guilty than Eve. Tempted by another
human rather than by powerful satanic forces, he should have known better.
Grimké's argument both constructs a perception of Eve that mitigates her transgression and evokes the "rule of justice" to argue that Eve's postlapsarian status
should be equivalent to Adam's because she is no more guilty than he.

Because it was most explicitly connected to women's silence and often cited by
antebellum clerics, Paul's advice to women—the admonitions of 1 Cor. 14:34–35
and 1 Tim. 2:11–14 against women's public speaking—presented perhaps the
most daunting challenge to white women abolitionists. To maintain their authority as religious women before their antebellum audiences, they could not reject
Paul's instructions. Instead, they reinterpret Paul's counsel, asserting that the
apostle's advice to women does not prohibit their speaking publicly against slavery. Two principal strategies of interpretation underlie female Christian abolitionists' commentary on Paul's letters: focusing on Pauline passages that provide
an alternative to 1 Cor. 14:34–35 and 1 Tim. 2:11–14 and that can be interpreted
as empowering women leaders and speakers; and separating the spirit from the
letter and the general from the particular in Paul's commentary on women's
silence.

As in their arguments about creation that cite Gen. 1:27, the Grimké sisters
use rhetorical hermeneutics to suggest that alternative Pauline passages to those
cited by critics challenge the interpretation that women must remain silent.
Expanding traditional views of what advice to women is significant in Paul's
epistles, they suggest that often-overlooked comments about women's ministry
and preaching are relevant to the work of contemporary women. In *Letters to
Catherine* [sic] *E. Beecher,* Angelina Grimké refers to 1 Cor. 11:5, in which Paul
advises "every woman that prayeth or prophesieth" to cover her head, and Phil.
4:3, in which the apostle asks his followers to "help those women which labored
with [him] in the gospel." Arguing that women's speaking and public action are
significant components of these passages, she challenges Beecher's restriction of
women to the domestic sphere: "I read in [1 Cor. 11], some particular directions
from the Apostle Paul, as to *how* women were to pray and prophesy in the assem-
blies of the people—*not* in the domestic circle. . . . And what, I ask, does the Apostle mean when he says in Phillipians iv. 3.—'Help those women who labored
with me in the gospel'? Did these holy women of old perform all their gospel
labors in 'the domestic and social circle'? I trow not" (*LCB,* 190).

Similarly focusing on alternative passages from Paul's epistles that are
potentially empowering to women, Sarah Grimké marshals rhetorical hermeneutics
to challenge the basis of critics' arguments. Paul's reference to female ministers is
significant, she suggests, but opponents of women's leadership have tried to conceal
this biblical evidence. In *Letters on the Equality of the Sexes,* she points out the
arbitrariness of a translation of a passage relevant to debates about women's

authority: "The same word, which, in our common translation, is now rendered a servant of the church, in speaking of Phebe, Rom. 16:1, is rendered minister, Eph. 6:21, when applied to Tychicus" (*LES,* 252). Translators, Grimké implies, have undermined a part of Paul's letters that is truly relevant to women's leadership by a misleading translation—in effect, a rhetorical hermeneutics of their own that has minimized a precedent for women's authority.

In an 1841 sermon delivered in Boston and reprinted in the *Liberator,* Lucretia Mott similarly notes that translators have called Phoebe a "servant" even though the Greek word used to describe her is translated "minister" when applied to men. Rendering Sarah Grimké's implicit criticism of translators explicit, Mott challenges her audience: "Has not conscious evidence been afforded by this translation, of the priest-craft and monopoly of the pulpit, which have so long held women bound?" (*LM,* 28). Engaging in rhetorical hermeneutics as well as demystifying the interpretive choices of their opponents, Mott and the Grimké sisters treat the Bible not as an abstract document to which they must react but as a text with which they and other Christians must interact to create meaning in their lives.

When white female abolitionists respond to the specific Pauline passages traditionally interpreted to prohibit women's public speaking, they adopt a rhetorical strategy that allows them to address and reinterpret Scripture while remaining true to antebellum assumptions that the Bible should guide human behavior. This strategy is based on what Perelman and Olbrechts-Tyteca describe as the dissociation of concepts into "philosophical pairs," or ideas that are conceptually connected, such as "letter and spirit" or "appearance and reality." Effecting such a dissociation, the rhetor suggests that one element of the pair is of higher value than the other and that the more valued term should guide judgments while aspects of the devalued term are unimportant. Dissociation is a particularly salient strategy for women abolitionists who address Paul's proscriptions against women. As Perelman and Olbrechts-Tyteca note, if "conceptual data"—in other words, information that already guides an audience's beliefs—are a "basis of argument," this strategy can create a "profound change" in the way the data are perceived.[68] Strategies based on this dissociation allow white women abolitionists to reframe Paul's injunctions to advocate new interpretations for their audiences.

In her defense of the public speaking of the Grimkés in particular and women antislavery orators in general, Lydia Maria Child distinguishes the letter and the spirit of Paul's advice about women's public activity. In an 1841 editorial in the *National Anti-Slavery Standard,* Child proposes that two camps ultimately emerge in any discussion of social change: "The 'conservative' and the 'reform,' the 'stop there,' and the 'go ahead' spirit straightway manifests itself." She identifies the latter with the spirit of "Christian reform." Arguing that Paul was a member of "the 'go-ahead' school," she cites his disagreement with Peter over the "custom of not eating with the Gentiles" and "the custom of circumcision" as evidence of his commitment to reform principles (Gal. 2:3–14). She then restates Paul's position in "modern phrase" for her readers: "The Idea which binds Peter and [Paul] together in one discipleship, appears to [Paul], in its full application, to overturn customs and prejudices, which [Peter] continues to hold sacred." Thus she defines Paul as an advocate of spirit over letter. This strategy allows Child to disclaim aspects of the letter of Paul's laws without appearing to reject the essential spirit of his message. In particular, literal injunctions against women's public speaking become unimportant compared with the spirit of "Christian reform" embodied in the Epistles. Child remarks, "Curiosity, combined with better motives, brought crowds to hear the [Grimké] sisters; and it became necessary to ask the use of churches to accommodate them. . . . 'Stop there'! minds looked back anxiously to St. Paul to arrest the progress of this innovation. . . . [A] class of minds more entirely of the 'go-ahead' cast . . . boldly asked, 'What if I do differ from St. Paul? So he differed from Peter on some points.'"[69] The spirit of Paul's "go-ahead" message, Child implies, justifies the Grimkés' work, even if his literal advice does not.

In another 1841 editorial in the *Standard* entitled "Speaking in the Church," Child features the spirit/letter dichotomy to criticize clerics who reference Paul's advice to women to exclude them from speaking against slavery. Child subtly discloses how their elevation of letter over spirit leads to thoughtless—and ultimately meaningless—application of the letter of Paul's injunctions. She relates the story of her conversation with a minister whose parish, with his blessing, is to hear Angelina Grimké speak on abolition. However, when he discovers that she will speak in the "meeting-house" of the church rather than the "school-house," he is troubled, telling her, "If there were only a suitable place provided, there would be no difficulty. . . . I consider the injunction of Scripture binding upon us in all particulars; and you know St. Paul says, 'I suffer not a woman to speak in the Church.'" Child's response exposes the shallow nature of such letter-based exegesis: "You told me, did you not, that all your people would go to hear her? If the Church are assembled in the school-house, will she not, to all intents and purposes, speak in the Church? I presume you do not consider the plank and boards, which compose a building, the Church?" The minister, having no answer to these questions, cannot defend his lockstep interpretation; and his hypocrisy is exposed further when he agrees that Grimké should speak in another church, thus avoiding a true resolution of his "difficulty."[70]

Abby Kelley marshals a similar example in an essay entitled "The Woman Question," in which she demonstrates how a strict adherence to the letter of Pauline law concerning women's participation in public discussion is not only ridiculous, but interferes with true religious duty. Kelley explains that in a recent conversation with "an eminent D. D.," she asked if a woman could participate in a discussion of religious principles in a parlor containing "fifty gentlemen and as many ladies." When he answers in the affirmative, she asks if the case would differ if the gathering were a formal meeting with an appointed chairman and secretary held in a "public hall, or a meeting-house." The preacher maintains that although women's speaking would not be "sinful" in this case, "public opinion is against it." Kelley has already gained a fundamental point—the minister concedes that it is society and not Christian principles that forbid women's official participation in religious discussion. She does not overlook the opportunity, however, to marshal the spirit/letter dichotomy to demonstrate the absurdity of this prejudice:

> Let us listen a little to this omnipotent PUBLIC OPINION, and hear what it says. Women may talk in congregations, large or small, in public or in private . . . if the formalities that are adopted in meetings for instruction or for business are laid aside: but when these formalities are adopted, they must be silent. . . .
>
> . . . Will SIR PUBLIC OPINION have the kindness to . . . show how it becomes sinful to speak in orderly meetings, when at the same time it is no sin to speak in disorderly ones? He must do this, or we shall not be able to act understandingly, and shall be in constant danger of getting out of HIS sphere.[71]

For Sarah Grimké, dissociation into another philosophical pair, the particular and the general, suggests that certain aspects of Paul's letters are a product of his historical context and thus are not relevant to the lives of contemporary Christians. In *Letters on the Equality of the Sexes,* she argues that Paul's injunctions suggesting women's inferiority must be interpreted as historical particulars: "I believe his mind was under the influence of Jewish prejudices respecting women, just as Peter's and the apostles were about the uncleanness of the Gentiles" (*LES,* 242). One can reject these principles without denying Paul's divine authority, Grimké argues, noting other aspects of Paul's advice and behavior that are similarly bound to his historical context and Jewish tradition: "When I see Paul shaving his head for a vow, and offering sacrifices, and circumcising Timothy, to accommodate himself to the prepossessions of his countrymen, I do not conceive that I derogate in the least from his character as an inspired apostle, to suppose that he may have been imbued with the prevalent prejudices against women" (*LES,* 242). Just as her audience would dismiss head shaving or sacrifices as customs specific to Paul's time and irrelevant to contemporary Christian behavior, they should similarly disregard Paul's professions of women's inferiority.

Lucretia Mott also relies on dissociation into the particular and the general to negotiate with Paul, preserving his authority—even in a literal sense—while disagreeing with traditional interpretations of his words. In her 1841 sermon delivered in Boston, Mott defers to Paul's authority in his advice to women in 1 Corinthians, but suggests that his counsel has been extended inaccurately beyond his specific intention:

> I am aware that the apostle Paul recommended to the women of Corinth, when they wanted information, to "ask their husbands at home." I am not disposed to deny, that under the circumstances of the case, he did it wisely. But do we find him saying, that they were not to preach or prophecy? So

far from it, that he has expressly given them directions how to preach and prophecy [1 Cor. 11:5–15]. . . . Anyone will, I think, see that to make a standing rule of the apostle's directions to the ignorant Corinthian women, is to make him inconsistent with himself. (*LM*, 26–27)

Mott effectively argues her conclusion from the antebellum premise that Scripture must be taken literally and that Paul therefore cannot contradict himself. From this foundation, she proves that Paul's mandate against women's public speaking must be particular rather than general.

"AM I THEN YOUR ENEMY BECAUSE I TELL YOU THE TRUTH?": THE WHITE FEMALE ABOLITIONIST AS PROPHET

As their arguments reconciling women's public speaking with their Christian commitments demonstrate, religious tradition could be a source of empowerment for the white female abolitionist rhetor. Like their African American male colleagues, they draw on the power of the traditional form of the jeremiad in their antislavery persuasion, building on their difference from the audience to create critical, even harsh appeals for change. In addition, their articulation of a prophetic vision allows them to assume agency to call for societal transformation while deflecting attention from themselves. Through prophetic rhetoric, they can articulate radical, even militant, arguments that may potentially threaten their audiences and can negotiate societal expectations that are often used to limit their rhetorical authority. Simultaneously drawing on their society's fundamental self-definition as a "chosen people" and condemning their audiences' lack of commitment to their mission, white female prophetic rhetors both reinforce and challenge societal beliefs. This combination of conservatism and radicalism allows them, like their African American male colleagues, both to draw on and to question societal assumptions, even about their own rhetorical authority. Yet, as we shall see, although similar general premises underlie the prophetic rhetoric of both white female abolitionists and African American male abolitionists, there are important differences as well.

In Sarah Grimké's *Epistle to the Clergy of the Southern States,* her prophetic ethos deflects attention from her particular authority as she offers strong antislavery arguments. Grimké begins her appeal by invoking Jesus' lamentation over Jerusalem in the gospel of Luke: "And when he was come near, he beheld the city and wept over it, saying—if thou had'st known, even thou, at least in this thy day, the things which belong unto thy peace. Luke, xix, 41–42" (*E,* 90). The citation is significant, preparing the audience for Grimké's adoption of a prophetic voice and her call to her audience to turn from the sin of slavery. Grimké does not include Jesus' subsequent words in the passage, although they would be implied for her Christian readers: "For the days shall come upon thee, that thine enemies shall cast a trench about thee, and compass thee round, and keep thee in on every side, and shall lay thee even with the ground, and thy children within thee; and they shall not leave in thee one stone upon another" (Luke 19:43–44). The implications of this ominous prophecy—that violent destruction eventually comes to those who do not uphold Christian principles—sets the stage for Grimké's harsh and urgent argument against slavery. Yet by leaving Christ's radical prediction implied, she avoids beginning with a severe tone that might be judged overly antagonistic or unfeminine.

In an 1843 sermon in the Unitarian Church in Washington, D.C., Mott similarly demonstrates how a prophetic female rhetor, whose ethos is that of a vessel for God's words, can establish credibility that seems to efface her own authority and maintain an ostensibly feminine tone. Claiming to speak God's truth, she declares, "I come before you to preach no other righteousness, no other gospel, but the righteousness of God, that which is a spiritual righteousness . . . and I believe it will meet conviction in every breast" (*LM,* 39). Mott uses this prophetic ethos to challenge the acquiescent attitudes of many Christians toward slavery. Notably, she avoids an overly confrontational tone by featuring questions rather than accusations: "As a community of christians, are we . . . striving to promote that righteousness which exalteth a nation? are we endeavoring to remove the great evils which beset us as a nation? If this were the case would these great sins which blight this country be suffered to remain? . . . [W]ould slavery be crushing its millions? . . . [V]ice and wrong are suffered to remain unrebuked, and teachers of religion may glide along in the popular current with a faith without works" (*LM,* 42). Even this last statement, framed in the passive voice, does not accuse her listeners directly. Like Sarah Grimké, Mott assumes an authority that is divine rather than worldly, but she nonetheless defers to earthly considerations as she avoids overt challenges to the audience.

Unlike African American male abolitionists such as Walker or Douglass, Sarah Grimké and Mott imply but do not explicitly articulate the radical notions that their audiences are directly implicated in the sin of slavery, that they will suffer divine punishment if slavery persists, and that antislavery violence is not only possible but likely. Whereas African American male abolitionists judge their audiences and evoke concrete images of destruction, white women rhetors maintain a more traditionally feminine tone that is not directly threatening to their audiences. Mott's use of "we" rather than the "you" favored by Walker and Douglass is also significant, revealing not only that she is, unlike African American men, a member of the white society that she criticizes but also that she wishes to avoid an overly combative stance toward her audience. These distinctions point to a fundamental difference between the position of the African American jeremiadic rhetor and the white woman prophet. The African American jeremiad depends upon the fundamental paradox that African American rhetors are both part of the American society that they condemn and removed from it. This contradictory position informs their stance toward their audience, to whom they are simultaneously connected through their devotion to America's ultimate mission and opposed through their distance from white society. White women, on the other hand, are inextricably connected to the white society that they rebuke. Although they can exploit the tensions inherent in the position of prophet, who is both within and without, they must create a critical rhetoric that nonetheless acknowledges their link to those they chastise.

One resource of the jeremiadic form that allows white women abolitionists to balance these demands is the status of the prophet as a vessel for a divine message. Speaking in 1848 at the fourteenth annual meeting of the AASS, Mott features impersonal terms that emphasize her position as medium for God's authority. Rewriting Christ's Sermon on the Mount, Mott suggests that many who oppose slavery—even those who are part of the abolitionist community—do not actively pursue God's will:

> Let the Abolitionist, who should be as the Jesus of the present age on the Mount Zion of Freedom, continue to say: "Ye have heard that it was said by them of old, thou shalt treat thy slaves kindly, thou shalt prepare them for freedom at a *future* day; but I say unto you hold no slaves at all, proclaim liberty now throughout the land to all the inhabitants thereof." . . . [L]et there be increasing activity on the part [of] Abolitionists; they must not cease their labours and fold their hands, thinking their work done, because they have effected so much: they must not be satisfied with coming to these anniversary meetings, they must continue to work at home. (*LM*, 76–77)

Mott's use of impersonal terms here—"Let the Abolitionist . . . say . . ."; "Let there be . . ."—suggests that her authority arises not from her individual credentials but from her status as a vessel through which the divine message is delivered.[72] She presents her forceful message through self-denial, suggesting that the power of her divine words comes from beyond her own authority. Thus she can remain connected to the society she condemns although her message distances her from her audience. Mott's agency, then, is predicated on a paradox—her rhetorical power comes from beyond her rather than arising from her own authority. From this rhetorical position, she can offer strong antislavery arguments; yet she appears removed from them, merely the medium for the message rather than fundamentally connected to it. Unlike in the prophetic rhetoric of African American men, her voice is sublimated to an impersonal authority.

Yet we should not be too quick to assume that that this ambiguous position entirely diminishes Mott's agency. Margaret Zulick asserts that effective jeremiadic speakers highlight the tensions between their connection to society and their distance from their audience, creating an ethos that is not monolithic but that allows "divergent authorial identities" to "appear dialogically as voices in the ongoing argument."[73] The tension between disputing factions thus becomes a motivating force in the prophetic persona. Through her shift from the prophetic "I" to the communitarian "we," Mott draws on the resources of this interplay between "divergent authorial identities" to suggest that she upholds antebellum society and its traditions even as she criticizes them. Her prophetic rhetoric, then, gains legitimacy simultaneously from opposing forces, transforming tensions inherent in the prophet's position into rhetorical strengths.

Another fundamental distinction separates white women abolitionists' prophetic rhetoric from that of their African American colleagues. As we have seen, African American male abolitionists create in their jeremiads a complex tone that balances an ostensible goodwill for the audience with demands for harsh retribution. Drawing on the fundamental tensions of Christianity, they exploit the paradoxes of Christian rhetoric, which both advises charity and promises divine justice. White female abolitionists, on the other hand, often emphasize the former quality and leave the latter implicit. Maintaining the stance of mercy and forgiveness, they defer to antebellum tradition that counseled women to reconcile disputing factions rather than to promote controversy. Questioning her audience about the "fear" of "examin[ing]" the "question of slavery," for example, Mott assures them, "I ask the question, not in the spirit of reproach; I do not wish to injure the feelings of a single individual. If we could come together in a christian spirit, and with a right estimate of the true dignity of man, we would calmly and profitably discuss our best interests. . . . When we come to understand thoroughly our duties as christians, we will not judge a brother, though we may warn one another" (*LM,* 42–43). Mott does not explicitly articulate the divine punishment that is described in the rhetoric of her African American colleagues, but she does suggest—through her remark that Christians may "warn one another"—the possibility of retribution. The white female prophetic rhetor may not embrace the vivid images of punishment evoked by rhetors such as Walker, but within her ostensibly feminine style she can allude to these threatening possibilities without appearing to embrace conflict.

Similarly, Sarah Grimké often overtly emphasizes the compassion inherent in a Christlike ethos while implying the theme of divine vengeance. At the beginning of her *Epistle to the Clergy of the Southern States,* she explicitly adopts Christ's stance toward Jerusalem (as recorded in Matt. 23:37), asserting that she feels toward her "dear native land" of the South "such feelings, may I presume to say, as brought the gushing tears of compassion from the Redeemer of the world, when he wept over the city which he loved . . . 'O Jerusalem! Jerusalem! thou that killest the prophets, and stonest them which are sent unto thee, how often would I have gathered my children together, even as a hen gathereth her chickens under her wings, and ye would not'" (*E,* 90). Grimké appeals explicitly to the power of Christ's compassion for his sinful people. But her remarks are also informed by Christ's ultimate predictions of Jerusalem's destruction for their sins and his denunciation of the Scribes and Pharisees, which provide the context for the words she cites (Matt. 23). Casting her message in biblical terms, she both maintains a compassionate tone and suggests divine predictions of violence and destruction. It is notable, too, that in the passage Grimké features, Christ's metaphor suggests maternal impulses, making it particularly appropriate for a female rhetor. In this image, Christ's authority is inherently feminine, authorizing the female prophet to marshal the force of Christ's words.

Yet white female abolitionists do not always leave the prophetic theme of divine judgment implicit. Although Sarah Grimké emphasizes the compassionate aspects of Christianity at the outset of her *Epistle to the Clergy of the Southern States,* merely suggesting vengeance, her tone shifts later in the text. Still adopting a Christlike ethos, Grimké revisits the biblical chapter featured at the beginning of her text—Matt. 23—as a vehicle for God's message to antebellum society. This time, though, she emphasizes not Christ's compassion for Jerusalem but his judgment of the Pharisees:

> Repent! Repent! God, if I so may speak, is waiting to see whether we will harken unto his voice. . . .
>
> What an appalling spectacle do we now present! With one hand we clasp the cross of Christ and with the other grasp the neck of the downtrodden slave! . . . My Christian brethren, if there is any truth in the Bible, and in the God of the Bible, *our hearts bear us witness* that he can no more acknowledge us as his disciples, if we willfully persist in this sin, than he did the Pharisees formerly. . . . Does not the rebuke of Christ to the Pharisees apply to some of those who are exercising the office of Gospel ministers, "wo unto you, Scribes and Pharisees, hypocrites! for ye devour widow's [*sic*] houses, and for a pretence make long prayers, therefore ye shall receive the greater damnation." (*E,* 101)

Like Frederick Douglass in his predictions of slave insurrection, Grimké maintains that these ominous predictions do not arise from her own authority, but from the word of God as proclaimed in the Scriptures. Through this seemingly impersonal power, she, like Douglass, assumes the agency to articulate a radical vision that has militant implications. Her identification with the oppressors rather than the oppressed—the "we" that is absent in Douglass's predictions—reveals that, unlike African American male abolitionists, white female rhetors cannot escape their complicity in white America's guilt. Yet they still can draw on the militancy inherent in the jeremiadic tradition that informs the rhetoric of their African American male colleagues. And the topos of divine vengeance gives the rhetoric of white women, like that of African American male abolitionists, force and urgency. Grimké, for example, refers to the enigmatic nature of God's possible retribution to call for immediate and radical change: "How long the space now granted for repentance may continue, is among the secret things which belong unto God, and my soul ardently desires that those who are enlisted in the ranks of abolition may regard every day as possibly the last, and may pray without ceasing to God, to grant this nation repentance and forgiveness of the sin of slavery" (*E,* 101–2).

Through the theme of divine vengeance, white women abolitionists offer other potentially militant arguments reminiscent of the jeremiadic persuasion of African American men. In her *Appeal to the Christian Women of the South,* Angelina

Grimké takes a particularly radical stance. Like both Douglass and Walker, she suggests the inevitability—and thus the implicit justification—of slave violence should audience members fail to renounce their sinful ways:

> Slavery always has, and always will produce insurrections wherever it exists. . . . The opposers of abolitionists fully believe this; one of them remarked to me not long since, there is no doubt there will be a most terrible overturning at the South in a few years, [because] such cruelty and wrong, must be visited with Divine vengeance soon. Abolitionists believe, too, that this must inevitably be the case if you do not repent, and they are not willing to leave you to perish without entreating you, to save yourselves from destruction; well may they say with the apostle, "am I then your enemy because I tell you the truth," and warn you to flee from impending judgments. (ACW, 64)

Grimké's apocalyptic warning allows her not only to chastise her audience for their sins, but to introduce a subject usually considered taboo for women: the righteousness of violence in the antislavery cause. Grimké articulates this thesis in terms every bit as forceful as her male counterparts Walker and Douglass, suggesting the inevitability of God's punishment and endorsing militant antislavery action. Yet a particular feature of Grimké's warning separates it from that of her male counterparts. Grimké appropriates a strong prophetic voice—Paul's challenge to the Galatians, "Am I therefore become your enemy, because I tell you the truth?" (Gal. 4:16)—yet she does not make it completely her own. The words are those of "abolitionists" and not exclusively of Grimké herself, and thus she distances herself in part from the force of her militant prediction. It would seem that although prophetic rhetoric has the potential to offer white women abolitionists authority that transcends some traditional gender constraints, they often exhibit caution when espousing particularly militant themes.

Yet, as Angelina Grimké's 1838 speech at Pennsylvania Hall demonstrates, white female abolitionists did not always have the luxury to be cautious in their condemnation of slavery. Actual—and not implied—threats of violence become part of her rhetoric on this occasion, not the potential for slave violence but an angry mob outside the building that threatens those inside throughout Grimké's oration. Grimké incorporates the mob violence into her insistent and relentless antislavery message, creating a prophetic ethos using the language and imagery of the Old and New Testaments that eschews conciliation and explicitly features the mob's actions as illustrations of her prophetic pronouncements. Shunning the professions of goodwill offered by other female prophetic speakers, Grimké immediately adopts a severe tone, demanding that her audience examine the motives that brought them to the gathering: "Men, brethren and fathers—mothers, daughters and sisters, what came ye out to see? A reed shaken with the wind? Is it curiosity merely, or a deep sympathy with the perishing slave, that has brought this large audience together?" Her allusion to Christ's question about John the

Baptist (Matt. 11:7) not only compels her audience to examine their spiritual motives, but also positions her in the prophetic tradition. Just as Christ admonishes his audience because they expected a more socially prestigious messenger than John the Baptist (Matt. 11:8), Grimké utilizes her marginal position as a source of authority, implicitly warning her audience of the consequences of rejecting her words. Grimké also confidently appropriates the words of God's instructions to Isaiah (58:1) as a prophetic foundation for her persuasion: "Animated with hope . . . I will lift up my voice like a trumpet, and show this people their transgression."[74] Grimké does not distance herself from her prophetic pronouncements; she makes them her own.

Like her sister, Angelina Grimké cites Christ's warnings—but the admonition she chooses is not the loving profession of the "mother hen" who wishes to "gather her chickens under her wings." Instead, she adopts Christ's militant warning to the uncommitted (Matt. 12:30): "We may talk of occupying neutral ground, but on this subject . . . there is no such thing as neutral ground. He that is not for us is against us, and he that gathereth not with us, scattereth abroad. . . . God swept Egypt with the besom of destruction, and punished Judea also with a sore punishment, because of slavery. And have we any reason to believe that he is less just now?" Unlike other Christlike pronouncements, which draw power from a paradoxical interplay of submission and authority, Grimké's bifurcation is rigid and commanding, demanding an either/or choice.[75]

The urgency of Grimké's demands that her audience choose a side is underscored by the mob outside Pennsylvania Hall. As they threaten, shout, and throw rocks at the windows, Grimké strategically refers to their actions in her speech to demonstrate the immediacy of the threat that slavery poses. The mob's anger becomes an illustration of Grimké's pronouncements that northerners cannot remain neutral on the question of slavery. After a yell is heard from the mob, Grimké notes, "Do you ask, 'what has the North to do with slavery?' Hear it—hear it. Those voices without tell us that the spirit of slavery is *here*. . . . This opposition shows that slavery has done its deadliest work in the hearts of our citizens." The mob also demands an immediate choice from the audience as to their commitment: "What if the mob should now burst in upon us . . . and commit violence upon our persons—would this be anything compared with what the slaves endure? No, no: and we do not remember them 'as bound with them,' if we shrink in the time of peril, or feel unwilling to sacrifice ourselves, if need be, for their sake." The mob's threats allow Grimké to make the role of potential martyr real rather than theoretical. Anticipating her subsequent charge that audience members cannot occupy "neutral ground," she refers to the mob's threats as concrete evidence that her militant call to action cannot be ignored.[76]

In fact, the mob's interjections assume significance beyond the immediate rhetorical situation. The speech was published in the 1838 *History of Pennsylvania Hall, Which Was Destroyed by a Mob, on the 17th of May, 1838,* with bracketed notes about the mob's conduct interjected in the text. Gary Woodward notes that persuasive encounters often do not "just 'happen'"; they are frequently also "depicted" in accounts of a speech. The edited text of Grimké's address also features the mob as a rhetorical device that accentuates Grimké's rhetoric and gives it an urgency for the audience of her printed as well as spoken words. Depictions of "persuasive encounters," Woodward argues, may feature hostile audiences that, because they demonstrate the immediacy of the problem the rhetor addresses, serve to "define" the rhetor's "place in a controversy."[77] The reactions to Grimké's prophetic speech give an urgency to her socially marginal—but spiritually powerful—role as prophet and potential martyr, serving as a concrete warning of the dangers she predicts. In both Grimké's speech itself and the mediated text that includes the mob's threats, the female prophet is unconditionally fearless, militant, and authoritative.

"A TROOP OF HORSE SHOD WITH FELT": STRATEGIES OF INDIRECTION

Although white women abolitionists could create influential antislavery arguments by building on commonplaces of antebellum femininity and featuring concerns presumably natural to women, not all topics could be framed in these terms. The antebellum woman was ostensibly barred from any direct discussion of political concerns, and she was expected to refrain from debating national policy. In order to negotiate such restrictions on their antislavery persuasion, female rhetors had to find strategies that allowed them to argue indirectly, to engage topics considered "unfeminine" without explicitly appearing to do so. The potential power of indirect rhetorical strategies is aptly described in terms of a metaphor marshaled by Child. In a letter to Samuel May about her tract *The Right Way the Safe Way,* Child suggests that the work should be sent to politicians and to southern readers *"quietly,"* without any "sounding of the trumpet *before* it." "My plan," she remarks, "is to attack them with a 'troop of horse shod with felt.'"[78] This image captures not only the plan for distribution of Child's text, but a multitude of strategies used by abolitionist women to engage political and economic aspects of slavery.

Cheris Kramarae notes that such indirection is characteristic of members of muted groups, particularly when discussing issues considered to be beyond their limited sphere of influence.[79] And we have discovered the power of African American male abolitionists' use of signifying, which often relies on strategies based on indirection. Yet significant differences distinguish signifying—a form arising from within the African American tradition and reflecting the unique position of African American rhetors—from the various forms of indirect argumentation featured in the texts of white women rhetors. White female abolitionists deflect attention from their own authority in their indirect persuasion, while rhetors who signify draw attention to their control of the processes of interpretation. In their indirect persuasion, white women rhetors do not rely on irony or the inherent ambiguity of language, fundamental components of strategies of signifying. And while white women rhetors may adopt other voices in their rhetoric to shift the focus from their role as rhetor, African American men appropriate the texts and arguments of others in order to highlight their control and revision of white America's language. Thus even when white female abolitionists marshal similar rhetorical strategies to those of their African American male colleagues—such as *occultatio* (in which a rhetor surreptitiously discusses an issue in the process of declaring that he or she does not intend to talk about it)—these fundamental underlying differences distinguish their indirect persuasion from their African American colleagues' deployment of signifying.

In addition, gender also shapes the indirect strategies white women abolitionists marshal. Since antebellum women's education was usually centered in the domestic realm, Karlyn Kohrs Campbell maintains, certain aspects of "the process of craft-learning" influenced their rhetoric. In particular, she notes that their discourse was often "personal," soliciting "audience participation, including the process of testing generalizations or principles against the experiences of the audience."[80] Instead of directly arguing her point, the female rhetor might offer the requisite preconditions for the desired conclusion, shifting the direct responsibility for persuasion onto the audience.

Sarah Grimké deploys this indirect tactic in her *Epistle to the Clergy of the Southern States*. She couches her criticism of southern ministers for their sanction of slavery in terms that suggest not that she directly condemns them, but that she prods them to examine their own conduct and draw their own conclusions. Telling them that their great responsibility is to teach Christians "not to trust in man," she asks, "Oh my brethren, is this duty faithfully performed? Is not the idea inculcated that to you they must look for the right understanding of the sacred volume, and has not your interpretation of the Word of God induced thousands and tens of thousands to receive as truth, sanctioned by the authority of Heaven, the oft repeated declaration that slavery, American slavery, stamped as it is with all its infinity of horrors, bears upon it the signet of that God whose name is LOVE?" (*E,* 91). Although her questions condemn them, Grimké's indirection appears to grant her audience authority and avert attention from herself. In her 1841 sermon delivered in Boston, Mott frames her argument that northerners are complicit in the slave system in similar terms. Implying that the proper deductions must come from the auditors' scrutiny of their own experiences and consciences rather than from her influence, she urges, "Let us examine our own clothing—the furniture of our houses—the conducting of trade—the affairs of commerce—and then ask ourselves, whether we have not each, as individuals, a duty which, in some way or another, we are bound to perform" (*LM,* 31–32).

Placing the audience in the position of judge allows the white female abolitionist to offer strong arguments while deflecting attention from her own authority. Child concludes *The Right Way the Safe Way* with an apparent request to readers to draw their own conclusions: "I appeal to candid readers whether I have not, in the preceding pages, fairly made out a case in favor of immediate emancipation. . . . I ask whether experience has not proved [immediate emancipation] to be a measure of plain, practical good sense, and sound policy" (*RW,* 93). Even when she explicitly proves a point to her audience, Child suggests that the conclusion is the reader's rather than her own. She deploys this indirect strategy in her *Appeal* when demonstrating the fallacy of a stock proslavery argument: "The planter tells us that the slave is very happy. . . . How far the slave laws are conducive to the enjoyment of those they govern, each individual can judge for himself. In the Southern papers, we continually see pictures of runaway negroes, and sometimes the advertisements identify them by scars. . . . Is it natural for men to run away from comfort and happiness, especially when any one who meets them may shoot them, like a dog! and when whipping nearly unto death is authorized as the punishment?" (*A,* 140–41).

Although they purport to give their audiences the power to infer conclusions, Grimké, Mott, and Child clearly present implicit theses. Their strategies, though, suggest that they do not control the interpretive process and that their audiences have the authority to create meaning from their texts. In the signifying of African American male abolitionists, by contrast, the rhetor always has control of interpretation, and he highlights this power. He may, in fact, pretend to deny that he manipulates the terms of interpretation, but this denial is ironic, actually calling attention to his linguistic command. Frederick Douglass may claim, for example, that he will let his former master Auld draw his own inferences about Douglass's opinion of him, and David Walker may purport that he cannot understand Henry Clay's racist rhetoric and must leave it to his audience to construe it; but their ironic tone and their ambiguous language call attention to their ability to manipulate the process of interpretation. White women rhetors, by contrast, downplay their position as interpreters of language. In contrast to African American men's emphasis on linguistic ambiguity, they suggest that language is clear and that the audience can draw unambiguous conclusions from the information they provide without the rhetor's interference.

The differences in the use of questions in the antislavery persuasion of white women and African American men similarly call attention to these rhetors' varying relationships to the process of interpretation. In her *Appeal to the Christian Women of the South,* Angelina Grimké presents many of her most powerful points as queries to her audience. Her refutation of scriptural support for slavery illustrates this strategy: "But it has been urged that the patriarchs held slaves, and therefore, slavery is right. Do you really believe that patriarchal servitude was like American slavery? Can you believe it? If so, read the history of these primitive fathers of the church and be undeceived. Look at Abraham . . . it appears that one of his *servants* was to inherit his immense estate. Is this like Southern slavery? I leave it to your own good sense and candor to decide" (*ACW,* 39–40). Although answers are clearly implied, Grimké appears to empower her audience to take authority themselves rather than relying on her own arguments.

Child similarly features questions to engage the subject of politics. In her *Appeal,* for example, she refutes a political proslavery argument interrogatively:

"It is a favorite argument that we are not to blame for slavery, because the British engrafted it upon us, while we were colonies. But did we not take the liberty to *change* English laws and customs, when they did not suit us? Why not put away *this,* as well as other evils of much less consequence? . . . Have not other nations been making alterations for the better, on this very subject, since we became independent? Is not England trying with all her might to atone for the wrong she has done?" (*A, 75*). By appealing to the audience's judgment, Perelman and Olbrechts-Tyteca point out, questions suggest an "implicit agreement" on a particular issue.[81] The negative form of Child's questions—"But did we not . . . ?"; "Have not . . . ?"—strengthens this sense of implicit agreement, suggesting that her queries are not open-ended.

Although Grimké and Child imply answers to their questions, their tone indicates that they respect their audiences' ability to form their own conclusions. African American male rhetors, although they use questions in their signifying, do not suggest that they trust their audiences to judge their rhetoric. Nor do they rely on the implicit agreement of their audiences. Their use of the question form, by contrast, challenges their audiences, featuring loaded language that forces their opponents to reveal their hypocrisy. When Walker asks Clay what "kind of Christianity" colonization will bring to Africa or Douglass confronts Clay as to whether he has demonstrated "consistency" in his wavering arguments on slavery, their questions themselves function as indictments. Their queries resonate ironically at two linguistic levels—appearing to be questions, they are also accusations. When white women rely on questioning, they do so very differently. These variations suggest a limitation of the general premises of muted group theory. Members of muted groups, Kramarae maintains, frequently rely on strategic questioning to offer opinions without seeming to assume the power inherent in a direct statement.[82] Yet, as my analysis demonstrates, this general premise of muted group theory fails to explain the widely varying forms of questioning deployed by white women abolitionists and African American male abolitionists.

White female rhetors could also feature *occultatio* to argue about topics while purporting to avoid them. In *American Slavery As It Is: Testimony of A Thousand Witnesses,* an 1839 AASS publication that records the personal testimony of various observers on the subject of slavery, Angelina Grimké effectively deploys this strategy. At the beginning of her remarks, she impresses upon her audience the horrors of plantation slavery even as she claims she will not testify on this subject: "I think it important to premise, that I have seen almost nothing of slavery on *plantations.* My testimony will have respect exclusively to the treatment of '*house-servants.*' . . . I never visited the *fields* [on her family's plantation] *where the slaves were at work,* and knew almost nothing of their condition; but this I do know, that the overseers who had charge of them, were generally unprincipled and intemperate men." Grimké's strategy allows her to imply criticism of an aspect of slavery about which she cannot give eyewitness testimony even as she proposes that she will not do so. She similarly uses *occultatio* to offer her judgment on the moral condition of slaves, a subject that falls outside of the request for her eyewitness evidence only. Noting that she has been asked "to testify respecting the *physical condition* of the slaves merely," she declares, "I say nothing of the neglect of their *minds* and *souls* and the systematic effort to imbrute them. A wrong and an impiety, in comparison with which all the other unutterable wrongs of slavery are but as the dust of the balance."[83]

Sarah Grimké also uses *occultatio* in her *Epistle to the Clergy of the Southern States* to refute the common proslavery argument that slavery was sanctioned by God through the Old Testament precedent of Jewish servitude.[84] Grimké proposes that she will not prove the very subject that she proceeds to argue:

> I need not enter into an elaborate proof that Jewish servitude, as permitted by God, was as different from American slavery, as Christianity is from heathenism. The limitation laws respecting strangers and servants, entirely prohibited cruelty and oppression, whereas in our slave states, "THE MASTER MAY, AT HIS DISCRETION, INFLICT ANY SPECIES OF PUNISHMENT UPON THE PERSON OF HIS SLAVE". . . . The same word in the Septuagint which is translated servant, is also translated child, and as the Hebrew language is remarkable for its minute shades of distinction in things, had there been as is asserted, slaves in Judea, there would undoubtedly have been some term to designate such a condition. . . . The want of any term therefore in the Hebrew, to mark the distinction between a slave in the proper sense of the term and other servants, is proof presumptive to say the least, that no such condition as that of slaves was known among the Jews of that day. (*E*, 96–97)

Grimké's proof is nothing if not "elaborate," and she engages the traditionally masculine subjects of legal history and biblical translation. Yet her disclaimer makes the force of her arguments indirect, deflecting attention from her logical appeals on subjects presumably outside "women's sphere."

When discussing political issues in various editorials for the *National Anti-Slavery Standard*, Child similarly engages an "unfeminine" topic while professing to avoid it. In her 1841 editorial "The Third Political Party," she declares that politics corrupts antislavery discussion and destroys its moral base. Framing her argument in terms of this nonpolitical stance, she presents opinions on important political questions facing abolitionists, such as the formation of a third political party: "No step could possibly have been taken, so likely to diminish our zeal, to undermine our faith in principles, to create distrust of our motives, and in every way to shear us of our strength." Her commentary on this issue demonstrates that within this seemingly "nonpolitical" stance lies a strong political argument against a third party: "If abolitionists remain true to their first position, trusting in God . . . they will be a continually disturbing power, feared by both parties [the Whigs and Democrats], and able at all times to hold the balance between them." Child's claim to be uninterested in political questions aptly illustrates Burke's contention that rhetors often identify with a cause through suggesting its "antithesis." "Whenever you find a doctrine of 'nonpolitical' esthetics affirmed with fervor," Burke aptly remarks, "look for its politics."[85]

These strategies share, on the surface, some features with the signifying of African American rhetors such as Douglass. When Douglass tells Auld, for example, that he will not call his former master "hard names" or professes that he cannot believe Clay capable of the "cunning" and "vanity" the statesman's rhetoric suggests, he employs a form of *occultatio*, emphasizing precisely what he appears to deny. Again, though, Douglass adopts an explicitly ironic tone in these professions, in contrast to the seemingly respectful tone of Child or the Grimké sisters. While Child and the Grimkés purport to conform to what is expected or asked of them in their rhetoric, Douglass ironically features conventions of politeness in an exaggerated manner that undermines them. Unlike the white woman rhetor, the African American male rhetor, in an inherently ironic relationship with white society and its language and traditions, appropriates conventional forms in ways that parody, satirize, and undermine them. The traditional rhetorical strategy of *occultatio* that allows white women rhetors to negotiate audiences' expectations becomes for African American men way to challenge societal conventions.

Notably, it is in those cases in which white women rhetors appear to remove themselves entirely from their persuasion, adopting other voices or personae to present arguments, that they can employ strategies such as irony and attack opponents forcefully although indirectly. In various editorials for the *National Anti-Slavery Standard* that engage political topics, Child features a dialogic form, placing her antislavery arguments in debate with the opposing view. In "A Slaveholder's Argument," Child asserts that the dialogue she presents is based on "conversations [she has] actually had with slaveholders"—with the proviso "that all the remarks were not made by one individual." However, by designating her comments in the exchange as those of a "Northerner" debating a "Southerner," she suggests that her views are not particular to her, rendering the antislavery voice less personal. Within this form, Child is able to engage many political aspects of the debate over slavery. For example, when the southerner claims that the North is "violating the laws and the Constitution" by interfering in the business of another state, the northerner offers an interpretation of the Constitution advantageous to abolitionists: "I am glad you construe the Constitution so strictly. I suppose you are aware that honored instrument declares, that 'Congress shall make no law, abridging the freedom of speech, or of the press?' . . . We at the North like this feature of the Constitution so well, that if Governor McDuffie chooses to come here and lecture in favor of slavery, we will all bid him welcome to overthrow our free institutions by as much discussion as he pleases."[86] It is significant that Child, through the voice of the northerner, deploys irony here —a presumably "masculine" form and one marshaled frequently by African American men. It would seem that by adopting the voice of a generic northerner rather than inserting her own voice into the dialogue, Child can deploy this powerful rhetorical tool she often seems to shun in her other antislavery persuasion.

Adopting the voice of both the southerner and the northerner in the dialogue, Child assumes the authority to define, control, and ultimately destroy her opposition's arguments. Through the southerner's voice in the exchange, in fact, she best demonstrates the weaknesses of the proslavery position. When the two parties discuss violence against abolitionists, Child strategically reveals through the southerner's own words the violent, irrational, and vicious impulses that underlie the South's support for slavery:

> *Southerner.* . . . We dislike to resort to [violent] measures, as much as you do. But . . . [t]here is no *law* to reach you, and so we are compelled to lynch, in self-defense.
>
> *Northerner.* I thought you said just now, that we violated the Constitution and laws, every day of our lives! It is an odd corollary to this, that there is no law to reach our continual offenses.
>
> *Southerner, (red in the face.)* If an abolitionist comes on my plantation, I shall make no more of shooting him than I would a rattlesnake.
>
> *Northerner.* I thank you for the warning. . . . When you choose to come among us, I promise that you shall be shot with nothing except fair arguments.[87]

The southerner expresses the South's faults even more directly than does the northerner. Child's voice may disappear in this argument, but her strategic appropriation of her opponents' arguments is nonetheless very effective.

Similarly, Child's "A, B, C, of Abolition" series in the *National Anti-Slavery Standard* allows her to offer strong political arguments in a unique—and seemingly impersonal—question-and-answer format. Both the series' title and subtitle—"Anti-Slavery Catechism"—suggest that the column's questions and answers are universal truths rather than statements of Child's opinion. Although Child's voice is sublimated in this seemingly impersonal format, the form allows her, as in her "Slaveholder's Argument," to control the articulation of her opponents' position, revealing its flaws. Consider, for example, an installment of this column in which Child offers incisive commentary on proslavery legal arguments. Responding to the question of why a slaveholder who professed to dislike slavery would not emancipate his slaves, the catechist remarks, "He would tell you that he could not do it, because the laws of the State in which he lives impose such heavy penalties, that the process of emancipation is extremely difficult and expensive." In the subsequent question and answer, Child reveals her strong opinion of this apologetic stance:

> *Q.* Who make the laws of the Southern States?
>
> *A.* The slave-holders themselves. When I hear a man say that he would gladly emancipate his slaves, if the *laws* would allow it, it makes me think of an anecdote. . . . A little girl had been ordered to perform some household work in the absence of her mother. When the parent returned,

and saw that her orders had not been obeyed, she said, "My child, why have you not done as I bid you?" The little girl replied, "I should have been glad to do it, mother; but I could not. Don't you see I am tied?" "And pray who tied you?" inquired the mother. "I tied myself," was the reply. Now this is plainly the case with the slave-holders. They make oppressive laws, and persist in upholding those laws, and then say, "I would do my duty if I could; but the *laws* will not permit it."[88]

As a woman, Child may shun direct commentary on legal issues, but in her "Anti-Slavery Catechism" she assumes an alternate voice that enables her to create strong arguments and refute her opposition.

In some respects Child's appropriation of others' claims connects to strategies employed by her African American male colleagues. Signifying, as we have seen, often involves the appropriation of other voices, particularly the ironic repetition and reversal of canonical texts of white America. Walker and Douglass, for example, adopt the language and arguments of Clay and Jefferson in contexts that redefine them. Child also assumes the agency to appropriate the arguments of others; however, unlike her African American male counterparts, she does not call attention to her manipulation of their language. While Walker and Douglass highlight, through parody and ironic revision, their strategic manipulation of the terms of white America and their assumption of control over the language that defines them, Child deflects attention from her own role in her indirect rhetoric. Yet this persuasion is nonetheless effective. As with other strategies marshaled by Child and her white female colleagues, her influence simultaneously depends upon responding to stereotypical expectations restricting women's public argumentation and challenging those limitations, often obliquely. Their power, like that of the "troop of horse shod with felt," is forceful although often unnoticeable.

5

What If I Am a Woman?
The Rhetoric of African American Female Abolitionists

The dual forces of racism and sexism constituted unique constraints for African American female abolitionists. They were frequently ignored in discussions of the concerns of African Americans; expected to conform to traditional gender roles by antebellum society, including white women and African American men; and marginalized by white women abolitionists. Two incidents suggest the influence of both the biases of white female abolitionists and the ambivalence of African American male abolitionists about African American women's antislavery work. In England in 1859, Sarah Remond—the sister of Charles Lenox Remond and an active antislavery lecturer in the 1850s—indirectly described her marginalization by her white female colleagues in the American abolition movement. After speaking to a group of women at the Red Lion Hotel in Warrington, Remond was presented with a watch inscribed, "Presented to S. P. Remond by Englishwomen, her sisters, in Warrington. February 2nd, 1850." A reporter for the *Warrington Times* relates her reaction: "MISS REMOND was so taken by surprise at this manifestation of feeling towards her that her utterance was for some moments prevented by her emotions. At length she said, I do not need this testimonial. I have been received here as a sister by white women for the first time in my life."[1] Although white women abolitionists often called their African American female colleagues their "sisters," Remond's comments reveal that she and other African American women abolitionists felt they were rarely granted the respect or equality the term connotes.

At the Convention of the Colored Citizens of the State of New York in 1855, although delegates passed resolutions pertaining to equal rights, suffrage, and political representation, the participation of Barbara Ann Steward was not recognized by the assembly. The minutes indicate, "The roll was then read. The name of Miss Barbara Ann Stewart [*sic*] was stricken out from the roll, several gentlemen objecting to it on the ground that this is not a Women's Rights Convention."[2] Not all African American men shared the perspective of those objecting to Steward's recognition at the convention. African American male abolitionists' views of—and reactions to—the public abolitionist work of African American women varied; and many believed that women should have equal rights in the movement, including the right to speak publicly. On the other hand, other African American male abolitionists did not endorse women's public role in abolition, and some who favored women's rights in general felt that the issue should not be a part of the abolitionist agenda. The support of some of their male colleagues notwithstanding, women abolitionists such as Steward often faced obstacles to working as equals in African American groups.

African American women abolitionists, then, were in a position unlike that of their white female and African American male colleagues. Their unique concerns were frequently overlooked and their participation in the abolition movement was often challenged, restricted, or ignored. Yet although they faced particular obstacles to their participation in the abolition movement, they also found avenues for their antislavery work that were unavailable to white female abolitionists. Although they were often judged in terms of traditional antebellum gender roles, they found ways to resist these definitions and to expand the range of activities considered acceptable to women. In their antislavery writing and oratory, African American women created rhetorical authority through unique strategies that were shaped by their particular concerns and experiences in antebellum society.

African American women from a variety of backgrounds, former slaves and women born free, participated in the abolition movement.[3] Maria Stewart was born in 1803 in Hartford, Conn., orphaned at the age of five, and "bound out" as a servant to a northern clergyman's family, performing duties in exchange for room, board, and education. She left servitude to marry, and, after settling in Boston, began writing and lecturing in the 1830s. Stewart was influenced by the work of David Walker and developed a strong friendship with Garrison after she began her writing career in 1831. Her September 1832 speech at Franklin Hall in Boston is the first recorded instance of an American-born woman of any race addressing a "promiscuous audience." In 1833, Stewart left Boston for New York, giving up her speaking career for teaching, discouraged by criticism she had received for her bold rhetoric. She continued to be politically active, joining women's organizations and attending the Women's Anti-Slavery Convention in 1837.

While Stewart lectured and wrote in Boston, Sarah Douglass joined the antislavery crusade in Philadelphia. Douglass was born in 1806, the daughter of abolitionists Robert and Grace Bustil Douglass. Although the particulars of her education are unknown, she was tutored as a child. She participated in various literary and reform organizations in the early 1830s, including the Female Literary Association of Philadelphia and the Philadelphia Female Anti-Slavery Society, which she helped found. She attended the three Anti-Slavery Conventions of American Women in 1837, 1838, and 1839, and she wrote many articles for the *Liberator*'s "Ladies' Department" and "Juvenile Department" under the pseudonym "Zillah." A tireless educator, Douglass opened a school in Philadelphia and lectured on hygiene and physiology after studying in the 1850s at the Female Medical College of Pennsylvania and Pennsylvania Medical University.

Other women with family ties to the abolition movement also joined the antislavery crusade in the decades that followed. Frances Ellen Watkins was raised by her aunt and uncle, abolitionist William Watkins, at whose school she was educated. During the 1840s, she wrote poetry—often with abolitionist themes—publishing her first collection of poems, *Forest Leaves,* in 1846. Teaching in Pennsylvania in the early 1850s, she came into contact with abolitionists such as William Still, the son of a former slave, who was active in the Underground Railroad. She began lecturing in 1854 for the Maine Anti-Slavery Society, travelling throughout the North and Canada. She also wrote articles and short stories for periodicals such as the *Anglo-African Magazine.* In 1860 she married Fenton Harper, and is often known by her married name, under which she published her 1892 novel *Iola Leroy,* thought to be the third novel written by an African American woman. Charles Lenox Remond's sister Sarah also began her career as an antislavery lecturer in the 1850s. She became an agent for the AASS in 1856, and lectured throughout the North from 1856 to 1858. In 1859 and 1860, she lectured throughout Britain, where she remained throughout the Civil War. After the war, she studied medicine in Florence, Italy, and became a physician.

Women who had been slaves also took up the pen and ascended the platform on behalf of the antislavery cause. The powerful orator Sojourner Truth was born Isabella, a slave in upstate New York, probably in 1797. In 1826, after her master broke his promise to free her a year before her legal emancipation according to New York law, she ran away. She traveled first as an evangelist and preacher, taking on the name Sojourner Truth, and began working in the 1850s for abolition, women's rights, and women's suffrage. Also in the 1850s and early 1860s, the written texts of former slave Harriet Jacobs presented antislavery arguments from the perspective of an eyewitness. Born a slave in North Carolina around 1813, Jacobs hid from her master in her grandmother's house for almost seven years before escaping to the North in 1842. Pursued by her master, she left her hiding place for Boston in 1844 and traveled to England in 1845. After moving to Rochester in 1849, she began reading antislavery literature and meeting with abolitionists. She developed a strong friendship with white Quaker abolitionist Amy Post, who encouraged her to write her life story as an abolitionist text. She published anonymous letters about her experiences as a slave in the *New-York Daily Tribune* in 1853 before writing the extended narrative *Incidents in the Life of a Slave Girl, Written by Herself,* in which she assumed the pseudonym Linda Brent. Although the manuscript was completed in 1858, it was three years before she could get it published, with the help and endorsement of Lydia Maria Child, who edited it and wrote an introduction. An English edition was published in 1862 under the title *The Deeper Wrong.*

These rhetors deployed a variety of strategies to assume the agency to persuade publicly. In some cases, their persuasion shares certain features with that of white female or African American male abolitionists. Yet they also marshal unique strategies, both in terms of the theoretical concerns that underlie their rhetoric and the practical manifestations that distinguish their discourse from those of other abolitionists.

"UNLOOSE THOSE FETTERS!":
SELF-HELP AND ABOLITION

Like their male colleagues, African American women abolitionists rely on self-help rhetoric as part of their antislavery persuasion. As we have discovered by examining the discourse of African American men, this rhetorical form need not be conciliatory to white society, conservative, or individualistic. Indeed, self-help rhetoric serves important functions, revising and critiquing white America's beliefs, advocating group solidarity for African Americans, placing individual actions in a larger communal context, and forcing commitment to abolition among free African Americans through often harsh either/or choices. The self-help rhetoric of African American female abolitionists shares many features with that of their male counterparts. Yet there are also unique implications of African American women's arguments for moral reform and community uplift.

Self-help rhetoric allowed African American women to negotiate restrictions based on gender and to expand the range of roles available to them. Two important features of African American women's experiences—their need to fight for fundamental rights for themselves and their families and their belief that domesticity and activism were not incompatible—enabled them to assume authority outside the home. Persuasion based on devotion to moral improvement balanced their dedication to home and family with their work in the larger community. Because self-help rhetoric links the traditionally "domestic" issues of education of children, morality, and religion with more "public" concerns such as prejudice, abolition, and societal change, African American women could use this genre to draw on their simultaneous commitments to family and community. Indeed, as Patricia Hill Collins argues, African American women's community work challenges traditional gendered notions of a male public sphere that does not encompass ostensibly personal interests.[4]

In the works of African American women, Collins maintains, there is an "interdependence" of "experience and consciousness" and "thought and action." Everyday experiences are central to African American women's worldview, fostering a "collective standpoint" that gives them agency and self-definition.[5] As we will see, these defining features of African American women's rhetoric affect their antislavery persuasion in a variety of ways. For self-help rhetoric, in particular, the focus on experience as a defining component of consciousness links individual concerns and communal reform, suggesting that a personal commitment to moral regeneration necessarily leads to activism.

Sarah Douglass's 1832 speech before the Female Literary Society of Philadelphia, an organization of African American women who met to read and discuss essays written by members, illustrates how the "interdependence of experience and consciousness" structures African American women abolitionists' self-help rhetoric.

Douglass explicitly connects her own personal self-improvement to antislavery activism, featuring her own concerns as a basis for an activist perspective:

> One short year ago, how different were my feelings on the subject of slavery! It is true, the wail of the captive sometimes came to my ear in the midst of my happiness, and caused my heart to bleed for his wrongs; but, alas! the impression was as evanescent as the early cloud and morning dew. I had formed a little world of my own, and cared not to move beyond its precincts. But how was the scene changed when I beheld the oppressor lurking on the border of my own peaceful home! I saw his iron hand stretched forth to seize me as his prey, and the cause of the slave became my own. I started up, and with one mighty effort threw from me the lethargy which had covered me as a mantle for years; and determined, by the help of the Almighty, to use every exertion in my power to elevate the character of my wronged and neglected race.[6]

Douglass proposes an activist message—that she and her audience must identify with slaves, fight their oppression, and work to "elevate the character of" all African Americans—framed in terms of her own moral transformation. Douglass's shift in consciousness is a result of concrete circumstances—she realizes the dangers she and all free African Americans face as a result of slavery. Indeed, kidnappers posed a very real threat to fugitive slaves as well as to free African Americans, whom they sought to sell into slavery.[7]

Yet self-help is not an individualistic endeavor for Douglass; although it begins with personal change, its implications extend into the community. In Collins's terms, her "altered experiences . . . stimulate a changed consciousness."[8] Drawing on her personal concerns, Douglass calls attention to American society's oppression of African Americans and implies that self-help is a form of resistance. Douglass's realization of the threats posed to her by a racist white society transcends the abstract realm, suggesting to her audience that self-help does not merely encompass theoretical moral principles but also leads to concrete action for survival.

Like Douglass, Maria Stewart uses her own experience to authorize her larger vision of self-help as a part of antislavery activism. In an 1832 speech before the Afric-American Female Intelligence Society of America, Stewart uses personal terms to explain her advocacy of moral reform: "The only motive that has prompted me to raise my voice in your behalf, my friends, is because I have discovered that religion is held in low repute among some of us; and purely to promote the cause of Christ, and the good of souls, in the hope that others more experienced, more able and talented than myself, might go forward and do likewise" (*MWS*, 50). Stewart's own experiences demonstrate the necessity of self-help, giving her a framework for advocating moral uplift among African Americans. It is also significant that Stewart refers to her religious commitments in authorizing her self-help persuasion. Stewart draws on the traditionally "feminine" devotion to religion, but she expands the purview of women's work beyond the home. A commitment to self-help connects women's concerns to the larger sphere of community action. Her deferential tone also balances conventions of femininity with activism. Her speech, she modestly claims, will serve to empower others.

Yet Stewart's self-help rhetoric also demonstrates that this genre can empower African American women to assume agency that resists the norms of traditional femininity. In contrast to Douglass's gentle prompt to her audience to connect moral improvement to the slaves' emancipation, Stewart harshly chastises African Americans in this speech, condemning their moral failings. Stewart maintains that the moral weakness of free African Americans perpetuates prejudice against them:

> It appears to me that there are no people under the heavens so unkind and so unfeeling towards their own, as are the descendents of fallen Africa. I have been something of a traveller in my day; and the general cry among the people is, "Our own color are our greatest opposers;" and even the whites say that we are greater enemies towards each other, than they are towards us. . . .
>
> And why is it, my friends, that we are despised above all the nations upon the earth? Is it merely because our skins are tinged with a sable hue? No . . . it is because that we and our fathers have dealt treacherously with one another, and because many of us now possess that envious and malicious disposition, that we had rather die than see each other rise an inch above a beggar. No gentle methods are used to promote love and friendship among us, but much is done to destroy it. (*MWS*, 53–54)

Stewart's harsh rhetoric recalls William Whipper's severe condemnations of free African Americans. Rhetors who are excluded from society's decision-making processes, we have discovered, may use harsh language to create the sense of solidarity necessary to evoke a strong group consciousness. Seen in terms of this rhetorical function, condemnatory language may actually empower those who are marginalized in society by giving their individual actions wide-ranging effect. For Stewart, the "malicious dispositions" and destructive attitudes of free African Americans are not just personal problems; they further societal oppression. Stewart's assertion that it is not skin color but behavior that leads to prejudice is somewhat problematic, oversimplifying the complexities of prejudice. But her wider point—that African Americans must realize the activist potential of their individual moral perspectives—gives agency to her audience to effect societal change.

Significantly, Stewart's language here does not conform to a stereotypical nineteenth-century "feminine" tone. Although she, like Douglass, begins with her personal experience—her travels have given her the context from which she speaks—she assumes the authority to produce a wide-ranging critique. Through the genre of self-help rhetoric, various limitations on women's speech can be lifted. Appealing to the urgency that links self-help to the end of oppression,

Stewart discards the deferential tone that characterizes her discussion of her motives and assumes the agency to challenge her audience.

We have seen that even when African American male abolitionists suggest that moral reform can aid in eradicating whites' prejudices, they do not contend that African Americans are responsible for the racism that affects their lives. Even while implying that African Americans need to help "disprove" whites' misconceptions, they harshly critique white America's racism in their self-help rhetoric, demonstrating that this form of discourse need not be conservative or conciliatory. Stewart's oratory reveals that for African American women, too, a discourse of moral reform can be harshly critical of white prejudices. Although she connects prejudice somewhat simplistically to appropriate behavior rather than race, she nonetheless refutes white America's stereotypical preconceptions. "We might become a highly respectable people," Stewart notes, "a highly distinguished and intelligent people. And how? In convincing the world, by our own efforts, however feeble, that nothing is wanting on our part but opportunity" (*MWS*, 53). Stewart's assertion counters traditional conceptions of African Americans as "naturally" inferior to whites; they are capable, Stewart suggests, of disproving this assumption. Furthermore, her remark that African Americans can demonstrate that "nothing is wanting on our part but opportunity" indirectly criticizes white Americans for restricting the advancement of African Americans. Just as William Whipper, Alfred Niger and Augustus Price suggest in their outline of the AMRS's goals three years later, Stewart implies that African Americans should counter white America's prejudices not so they will be accepted by whites, but so that they will be able to realize their potential, advance, and assert themselves as members of American society. Significantly, this message, although presented to a woman's organization (and reprinted in the "Ladies' Department" of the *Liberator*), is not confined by traditional assumptions about women's sphere or stereotypes about women's particular responsibilities. African American women, Stewart suggests, have a responsibility to work for the advancement of their community.

In her 1832 speech at Franklin Hall, Stewart again presents a somewhat simplistic view of how moral reform can help end slavery. She declares, "Methinks were the American free people of color to turn their attention more assiduously to moral worth and intellectual improvement, this would be the result: prejudice would gradually diminish, and the whites would be compelled to say, unloose those fetters!" (*MWS*, 46). Stewart appears to suggest that African Americans should emulate the values of white Americans, a perspective that is underscored by the lines of poetry that follow: "Though black their skins as shades of night / Their hearts are pure, their souls are white" (*MWS*, 46). Yet when Stewart describes how African Americans should improve their moral condition, she reveals a more complex perspective of how their "fetters" will be "unloosed." "Few white persons of either sex," Stewart notes, "who are calculated for anything else, are willing to spend their lives and bury their talents in performing mean, servile labor. . . . O, horrible idea, indeed! to possess noble souls aspiring after high and honorable acquirements, yet confined by the chains of ignorance and poverty to lives of continual drudgery and toil. Neither do I know any who have enriched themselves by spending their lives as house-domestics, washing windows, shaking carpets, brushing boots, or tending upon gentlemen's tables" (*MWS*, 46). Stewart's self-help message may assume that African Americans should emulate whites in their moral and intellectual strivings, but not because it will lead to deference to whites. Indeed, she suggests the opposite—if African Americans aspire to the same accomplishments as whites, they will free themselves from positions of service to whites in society. Implicit in this argument is a radical critique of African Americans' exploitation in the work force. If whites will not demean themselves in debasing jobs, Stewart maintains, neither should African Americans. Moral improvement, in her argument, becomes not a means of adopting white values, but of gaining equal power in society.

Stewart's implicit criticism of white society for keeping African Americans in demeaning jobs is also made explicit in the speech. Responding to a claim made by colonizationists that African Americans are "lazy and idle," Stewart asserts, "I confute them on that point. Take us generally as a people, we are neither lazy nor idle; and considering how little we have to excite or stimulate us, I am almost astonished that there are so many industrious and ambitious ones to be found; although I acknowledge, with extreme sorrow, that there are some who never were and never will be serviceable to society. And have you not a similar class among yourselves?" (*MWS*, 46–47). Stewart implicitly reveals the hypocrisy of white society, which condemns African Americans for their lack of advancement while denying them opportunities to progress. Stewart's pointed question to her audience about a "similar class" of unambitious whites demonstrates, too, the injustice of racism, which judges an entire race by a few individuals. In Stewart's self-help rhetoric, the limitations of gender do not keep her from mounting a wide-ranging critique of white society for its racism and criticizing the societal and institutional factors that perpetuate oppression. Like her male colleagues, she assumes the agency to challenge white Americans strongly and directly.

Stewart explains that she does not condemn service occupations for elitist reasons, but because such jobs have a negative effect on workers. "I do not consider it derogatory, my friends," she maintains, "for persons to live out to service. . . . I would highly commend the performance of almost anything for an honest livelihood; but where constitutional strength is wanting, labor . . . is painful. . . . And what literary acquirement can be made, or useful knowledge derived, from either maps, books, or charts, by those who continually drudge from Monday morning until Sunday noon?" (*MWS*, 47–48). Her mention of education here is notable, highlighting the connection between educational opportunity and African American women's activism. Because education was a fundamental component of racial uplift for African Americans, Rosalyn Terborg-Penn notes, women's education was endorsed. Both women's and men's education was seen not as merely individual advancement, but as an effort on behalf of the community.[9] Thus through advocating education, African American women could assume agency to argue for community change.

Stewart frequently features education as a theme in her self-help rhetoric, allowing her to make radical arguments. Speaking in 1833 at the Masonic Hall in Boston, she draws on the impressive history of Africa to articulate the power that resides in education. Africa, she remarks, once "one of the most learned nations of the whole earth . . . the seat, if not the parent, of science," has fallen from this position (*MWS,* 58). Stewart's attribution of Africa's downfall to her people's "sins and abominations" harshly blames those of African descent (*MWS,* 58). As we have found in African American men's self-help rhetoric, though, this form of condemnation can be intended to spur activism within a disenfranchised community, evoking a sense of group solidarity by exhorting audience members to reject their subordinate position.

Stewart's exhortation to African Americans to rise above their current position appeals to this sense of community consciousness:

> Our condition as a people . . . will continue to be [low], unless by true piety and virtue, we strive to regain that which we have lost. White Americans, by their prudence, economy, and exertions, have sprung up and become one of the most flourishing nations in the world. . . . While our minds are vacant and starve for want of knowledge, theirs are filled to overflowing. Most of our color have been taught to stand in fear of the white man from their earliest infancy, to work as soon as they could walk, and to call "master" before they could scarce lisp the name of mother. . . . But give the man of color an equal opportunity with the white from the cradle to manhood, and from manhood to the grave, and you would discover the dignified statesman, the man of science, and the philosopher. (*MWS,* 58–59)

As in her speech at Franklin Hall, here she suggests that African Americans should follow whites' example and elevate themselves not because they will be accepted by white society, but because they will be able to assert themselves, avoid subservience to whites, and determine their own futures. Indeed, as her references to Africa suggest, African Americans do not need to look to white Americans for positive models of intellectual greatness, but to their own cultural heritage. Far from "rejecting African origins," Shirley Logan asserts, Stewart and other antebellum African American orators draw on Africa's "proud past" to emphasize community and empower their audiences.[10]

Like her mentor David Walker, Stewart also draws on the militant potential of educational advancement. Stewart may not go quite so far as Walker, who explicitly maintains a connection between violent resistance and education, but she implies that education can empower African Americans to assert themselves and to take radical action. Arguing in her speech at the Masonic Hall that African

Americans should spend their money on "schools and seminaries of learning for our children and youth," she notes, "We ought to follow the example of the whites in this respect. . . . The rays of light and knowledge have been hid from our view; we have been taught to consider ourselves as scarce superior to the brute creation; and have performed the most laborious part of American drudgery. Had we as a people received one-half the early advantages the whites have received, I would defy the government of these United States to deprive us any longer of our rights" (*MWS*, 60–61). This last statement articulates, although somewhat obliquely, a militant view. The elevation of African Americans can lead to their self-assertion and their radical "defiance" of their oppression. As a woman, Stewart may avoid the explicitly violent terms of Walker, but in her vision—as in his—education and self-improvement lead to resistance. And she demonstrates that "following the example" of white America is not a conciliatory effort, but can in fact be an act of defiance. White America's values can be appropriated by African Americans in their struggle against oppressive American institutions.

The perspective of African American female abolitionists on the subject of self-help—like that of their male counterparts—shifted after the 1830s, replacing the assumption that African Americans are responsible for ending prejudice with the notion that elevation would empower them to fight societal restrictions. At a meeting in January 1849 to organize the Women's Association of Philadelphia, African American women pledged their support to an agenda of moral uplift that would foster strong activism to end oppression. Their constitution—presented by the African American male abolitionist Martin Delany, who helped organize several African American self-help organizations—expresses this modified position: "Whereas, Believing Self-Elevation to be the only true issue upon which to base our efforts as an oppressed portion of the American people; and believing that the success of our cause depends mainly upon Self-Exertion . . . Therefore, we do Agree to form ourselves into an Association . . . the object of which shall be, to . . . support the Press and Public Lecturers, devoted to the Elevation of the Colored People in the United States by Self-Exertion."[11] As in the rhetoric of African American male abolitionists, "elevation" no longer connotes a way to counter whites' prejudice but rather a means to fight barriers to African Americans' advancement both individually and collectively.

Thus, as with their male colleagues, the modified self-help message of African American women abolitionists in the 1840s and 1850s redefined the values and standards by which moral improvement should be judged, more explicitly connecting elevation to leadership and activism. African American women as well as men continued to assume agency through the self-help genre, particularly to articulate a vision of African American leadership that would lead to self-direction and independence from whites. In an 1859 essay for the *Anglo-African Magazine* entitled "Our Greatest Want," Frances Ellen Watkins rejects earlier notions of respectability as defined by economic success. Arguing against those who elevate material wealth and believe that money will bring "the rights which power and prejudice now deny us," Watkins offers an alternative: "We want more soul, a higher cultivation of all our spiritual faculties. We need more unselfishness, earnestness and integrity." This vision of self-help must have as its ultimate goal the creation of community leaders with a far-reaching vision: "Our greatest need is not gold or silver, talent or genius, but true men and true women. We have millions of our race in the prison house of slavery, but have we yet a single Moses in freedom. And if we had who among us would be led by him?"[12] Self-help in Watkins's essay has radical implications for leadership among free African Americans and for the abolition of slavery. And her vision involves the concerted efforts of both male and female leaders on behalf of the community. She may hope for the overarching authority of a male figure—a Moses—but she assigns central roles in directing the future of the race to "true men and true women."

"OUTSIDERS WITHIN": REINVENTING "TRUE WOMANHOOD"

Watkins's call for both men's and women's leadership notwithstanding, African American women abolitionists' particular experiences necessitated unique strategies for asserting authority. Antebellum society's constructions of gender as well as African American women's challenges to these formulations shaped their antislavery rhetoric. African American women were often judged in terms of "True Womanhood" although neither their lives nor their beliefs conformed neatly to this ideal, which was defined in terms of white women's experiences. In their antislavery rhetoric, African American women often appropriate the terms and assumptions of the ideal of "True Womanhood," but they do so very differently from their white female counterparts. White women, we will recall, feature conventional antebellum notions of gender in ways that both uphold and seek to expand these assumptions in order to give women a larger sphere for their "feminine" concerns. African American women abolitionists also draw on the resonance of conventional notions of gender for their audiences, but they challenge the very assumptions on which "True Womanhood" is based and redefine this paradigm in significant ways.

Muted group theory provides some insight into African American women abolitionists' redefinition of the ideals of "True Womanhood." Shirley Ardener notes that muted rhetors may inscribe the values and standards of the dominant group within "a muted counterpart system," an alternative model that more fully represents their needs and perspectives. Yet this premise does not explain how a rhetor may in fact directly challenge the dominant group's assumptions and draw on conventional beliefs in ways that undermine and redefine them. Muted rhetors, Ardener explains, may appear to be conservative in their appropriation of the dominant group's values, "even clinging to models which seem to disadvantage them." But although African American women abolitionists appropriate societal assumptions about gender in their rhetoric, they do not leave these premises unquestioned. Nor do they leave their reformulations of antebellum society's views—their "muted counterpart system," in Ardener's terms—implicit.[13] They draw on their society's assumptions to challenge their audiences directly, to create an explicit alternative to "True Womanhood" that incorporates their particular experiences and concerns, and to assume the agency to articulate their alternate models directly.

The work of Patricia Hill Collins provides insight into aspects of African American female abolitionists' redefinitions of "True Womanhood" unaccounted for by the muted group model. Discussing the ways in which African American women, through their domestic work in white families, have been historically both connected to and excluded from the dominant culture, Collins notes that "the result was a curious outsider-within stance, a peculiar marginality that stimulated a special Black women's perspective." This "outsider-within" viewpoint gives them "a distinct view of the contradictions between the dominant group's actions and ideologies" and provides "a new angle of vision" that leads to "alternative interpretations" of hegemonic ideas about womanhood. These alternatives, Collins explains, are a foundation for African American women's resistance and their "self-definitions." The "outsider-within" perspective is also based on "intersectionality," informed by the multiple influences of "intersecting systems of race, class, gender, sexual, and national oppression."[14]

From their "outsider-within" perspective, African American female abolitionists reshape "True Womanhood" in two significant ways. First, because their work and their involvement in community affairs blurred the distinctions between "public" concerns that affected community life and "private" or domestic considerations, African American female abolitionists problematize the notion that women have to choose between traditional femininity and public activism. In other words, they challenge a central tenet of antebellum femininity and of traditional conceptions of the public sphere—that women's work and concerns should be relegated to the "private" realm—and assume the agency to define important public roles for African American women. In addition, they appropriate traditional notions of gender in order to question them, demonstrating the ways in which these ideals are formulated exclusively in terms of white women's experiences. By exposing how "True Womanhood" is based on whiteness, they demystify its power and presumed "universality" and suggest a broader conception of women's experiences that grants them agency.

In her speech to the Afric-American Female Intelligence Society of America, Maria Stewart appropriates traditional feminine ideals in a context that suggests that her influence is not restricted to the private realm—and that, indeed, the private and the public are necessarily intertwined for African American women. In a rhetorical move reminiscent of the self-deprecating statements of African American men about their oratorical abilities, she downplays her authority and suggests that she is merely a catalyst, speaking "in the hope that others more experienced, more able and talented than myself, might go forward and do likewise" (*MWS*, 50). She wishes that her audience would allow her "to express [her] sentiments but this once . . . and then hereafter let [her] sink into oblivion, and let [her] name die in forgetfulness" (*MWS*, 52). On the surface, Stewart's professions seem to conform both to the oratorical convention of "self-deprecation" and to a traditional self-denying femininity. But Stewart articulates in her speech a form of female influence that challenges traditional definitions of womanhood and that enhances rather than diminishes women's public authority. Woman's agency is not limited to the private sphere, she maintains, demonstrating that the private and public worlds are connected for the African American woman and implying that her influence must resonate within both realms. Stewart appeals to African American women: "O woman, woman! Upon you I call; for upon your exertions almost entirely depends whether the rising generation shall be any thing more than we have been or not. O woman, woman! Your example is powerful, your influence great; it extends over your husbands and your children, and throughout the circle of your acquaintance. . . . And, O, my God, I beseech thee to grant that the nations of the earth may hiss at us no longer! O suffer them not to laugh us to scorn forever!" (*MWS*, 55). In Stewart's formulation, women's leadership in the African American community links her roles in the home and in the community, suggesting that women's work has even global implications.

In an 1833 speech at the African Masonic Hall in Boston, Stewart further challenges the traditional limitation of women's work to the private sphere. She features irony to show that, for African American women, the abstract ideals of women's appropriate role are inadequate. Stewart appears to concede that she may be inferior to African American men, but she points out that because these presumably superior men are often silent, she is compelled to speak: "I am sensible that there are many highly intelligent men of color in these United States, in the force of whose arguments, doubtless, I should discover my inferiority; but if they are blessed with wit and talent, friends and fortune, why have they not made themselves men of eminence, by striving to take all the reproach that is cast upon the people of color, and in endeavoring to alleviate the woes of their brethren in bondage?" (*MWS*, 57–58). In fact, Stewart remarks, she would prefer a more private role: "Had those men among us who had an opportunity, turned their attention as assiduously to mental and moral improvement as they have to gambling and dancing, I might have remained quietly at home and they stood contending in my place" (*MWS*, 60). Traditional male and female positions become ironic here. Women's conventional role, Stewart suggests, is a luxury that the African American woman cannot afford. African American women's work is necessary, and theoretical notions of inferiority and superiority, the "public" and the "private," become meaningless. Stewart offers a powerful basis for African American women to assume agency, contrasting abstract ideals with the urgent needs of the African American community that empower women as activists.

Stewart's articulation of a public role for African American women depends upon the interdependence for African American women of thought and experience, beliefs and action. African American female abolitionists feature their experiences to directly confront the abstract and white-centered notions of "True Womanhood," revealing the limitations of this ideal and the hypocrisy of American society, which professes theoretical beliefs that it does not honor in practice. In her speech at Franklin Hall, Maria Stewart draws on her own experience to suggest the limitations of "True Womanhood." Her comment early in the oration that she has not "received the advantages of an early education" (*MWS,* 45) may appear, on its own, to be merely a conventional self-deprecating remark. But in the context of Stewart's speech, this remark is part of a larger challenge to traditional standards of femininity that are based on the narrow experiences of white women. Stewart reveals that, in fact, it is not necessarily virtuous and even traditionally "feminine" qualities that comprise a "True Woman," but whiteness. "Let our girls possess whatever amiable qualities of soul they may," Stewart laments, "let their characters be fair and spotless as innocence itself . . . it is impossible for scarce an individual of them to rise above the condition of servants. Ah! why is this cruel and unfeeling distinction? Is it merely because God has made our complexion to vary?" (*MWS,* 46). Stewart exposes the precariousness of antebellum ideals of gender and demystifies their basis, showing that such formulations of femininity are based on racist presumptions.

Furthermore, Stewart's comment about her own limited education takes on a larger significance when she confronts her audience with their hypocrisy in holding African American women to standards of femininity that are based on white women's narrow experiences:

> O, ye fairer sisters, whose hands are never soiled, whose nerves and muscles are never strained, go learn by experience! Had we had the opportunity that you have had, to improve our moral and mental faculties, what would have hindered our intellects from being as bright, and our manners from being as dignified as yours? Had it been our lot to have been nursed in the lap of affluence and ease, and to have basked beneath the smiles and sunshine of fortune, should we not have naturally supposed that we were never made to toil? And why are not our forms as delicate, and our constitutions as slender, as yours? Is not the workmanship as curious and complete? (*MWS,* 48)

Confronting antebellum society with its inconsistencies and revealing its racist formulations of gender, Stewart argues for an ideal that will include African American women and will address their needs and concerns. Race and class intersect with gender, Stewart reveals, to dictate what is considered natural and acceptable for women.

In the rhetoric of Sarah Douglass, too, the ideal woman operates beyond the private sphere. Under particular circumstances such as those faced by African Americans, Douglass asserts, women have a mandate for public action. In her 1832 essay "To a Friend," published in the *Liberator,* Douglass remarks, "I am aware that it will be our lot to suffer much persecution, and I have endeavored, for the last year, to fortify my mind against approaching trials, by reading what others have suffered." This reading has introduced her to a female exemplar:

> In perusing Sewell's History of the people called the Quakers, I was particularly struck with the account of Barbara Blaugdon, a young and timid woman, who, by the help of the Almighty, was enabled to endure cruel persecution, not only with patience but with joy. On one occasion, being severely whipped, even until the blood streamed down her back, she sang the praises of her God aloud, rejoicing that she was counted worthy to suffer for his name . . . and afterwards declared if she had been whipped to death, she should not have been dismayed. Earnestly have I prayed, my friend, that a double portion of her humility and fortitude may be ours.[15]

Qualities usually associated with conventional notions of feminine virtue—self-sacrifice, piety, patience, humility—are translated from the private sphere into the public realm, becoming fundamental components of Blaugdon's activism. Like Stewart, Douglass connects particular circumstances to abstract ideals to redefine the roles that are available to women. She also reveals that women need not look only to conventional men or women to find role models for their activism. Strong women throughout history have challenged the boundaries of "True Womanhood," Douglas suggests, diminishing the presumably "natural" and "universal" force of this ideal.

Although Sojourner Truth's often ironic tone contrasts with Stewart's and Douglass's straightforward styles, she challenges traditional definitions of femininity, expanding women's proper role and confronting her audiences with the limitations of "True Womanhood." In an 1853 lecture given in New York to an African American audience (a third-person account of which was published for a wider audience in Horace Greeley's *New-York Daily Tribune*), Truth insightfully deploys conventional notions of men's and women's appropriate duties in order to argue for women's right to speak publicly. Male preachers, she remarks, oppose women's desire to preach for a particular reason: "[They] had been befogging the world, and getting its affairs into the most terrible snarl and confusion, and then when women came in to their assistance, cried 'shame on the women!' They liked the fat and easy work of preaching and entangling too well, not to feel alarmed when woman attempted to set matters aright. . . . [W]omen were peculiarly adapted to fill the talking professions, and men should no longer unsex themselves by leaving the plow and the plane, for the pulpit and the platform."[16] Truth exploits traditional notions that men should do physical labor and leave "leisurely" activities to women in order to propose that preaching—an intellectual and rhetorical activity—is properly a feminine profession. At the same time, she overturns the notion that women are inferior rhetors, suggesting that they can be logical and effective. Women, she implies, are in fact superior rhetors; male preaching is merely "entangling" while women's preaching serves to "set matters aright."

Truth's boldness challenged antebellum audiences to confront the racist foundations of their assumptions about femininity. She thwarted those who tried to silence her because of her gender, transforming their attempts into a foundation of her authority, revealing the limitations of their assumptions, and creating an alternative view of womanhood. In a letter to Garrison published in the *Liberator,* William Hayward describes an 1858 interchange in Indiana between Truth and hostile members of her audience. Although Hayward does not record Truth's speech, he states that her audience questioned her credibility—and, in particular, her femininity:

> At the close of the meeting, Dr. T. W. Strain, the mouthpiece of the slave Democracy . . . stated that a doubt existed in the minds of many persons present respecting the sex of the speaker, and that it was his impression that a majority of them believed the speaker to be a man. . . . [H]e now demanded that Sojourner submit her breast to the inspection of some of the ladies present, that the doubt might be removed by their testimony. . . . Sojourner . . . immediately rising, asked them why they suspected her to be a man. [Strain] answered, "Your voice is not the voice of a woman, it is the voice of a man, and we believe you are a man."[17]

In charging that Truth's voice sounded like a man's, Strain also implies that Truth's bold words are not feminine. Suggesting that she bare her breast, he attempts to humiliate her; even if this evidence proves his accusation wrong, he will have undermined her credibility by compelling her to violate norms of gender.

Truth, however, uses Strain's confrontation to turn the tables on those who would question her:

> Sojourner told them that her breasts had suckled many a white babe, to the exclusion of her own offspring; that some of those white babies had grown to man's estate; that, although they had sucked her colored breasts, they were, in her estimation, far more manly than they (her persecutors) appeared to be; and she quietly asked them, as she disrobed her bosom, if they, too, wished to suck! In vindication of her truthfulness, she told them that she would show her breast to the whole congregation; that it was not to her shame that she uncovered her breast before them, but to their shame.[18]

Truth demonstrates that her bold words do not detract from her womanhood while exposing her audience's hypocrisy and the racist foundations of their beliefs about gender. She ironically reveals how her status as a woman has been the basis for exploitation by the very society that accuses her of being unfeminine. Traditional notions of femininity are meaningless, Truth suggests, at the same time ironically proposing that the doubt of the men in her audience undermines their masculinity.

Truth affirms her womanhood while refusing to be rendered submissive, silent, or merely sexual.

In fact, by defying the request that she show her breast only to the ladies in deference to traditional modesty, Truth takes control of the power of the stereotypes that are used against African American women. For African American women, Collins asserts, self-definition is a form of resistance to victimization and a way to reject "externally defined, controlling images of Black womanhood." Truth's baring of her breast is such an act, a reclaiming of her body from racist stereotypes that would render her entirely sexual. She confronts her audience with the fact that their appropriation of her body for their own purposes is their "shame," not hers, revealing that she is not limited by their definitions of her femininity and questioning her audience's presumptions about the intersections of womanhood, sexuality, and race. In addition, Truth interweaves the presumably private act of nursing children with her authority, demonstrating how, as John Arthos argues, the "political efficacy" of rhetoric that draws on personal narrative "is tied to its resolute integrity as personal experience," even that which is intimate.[19]

Through the most essentially feminine role of mother, Truth challenges the dichotomy between public authority and womanhood. She boldly defines herself as a powerful female and a mother, Nell Irvin Painter remarks, resisting the classification of sexual object even as she bares her breast. Truth's status as a mother, usually exclusively part of a woman's private and domestic persona, becomes a public antislavery argument as Truth responds to her audience's hostile challenge. She turns the usually private action of exposing her breast to nurse children into a public statement about the injustices of slavery, which prevent the slave mother from nourishing her own children. Marshaling the forceful image of mother—embodied not only in her words but in her physical presence—she positions the African American woman in both the public and private spheres, redefining what it means to be genuinely female. For African American women, Truth implies, the role of mother bridges the gap between public and private, giving women a unique source of public, rhetorical, and essentially female power. Truth's formulation reveals the importance of motherhood for African American women as a role that grants them an agency that transcends the boundaries of the domestic sphere and that challenges racist stereotypes. Emphasizing the role of mother, bell hooks notes, African American women aim to "shift the focus of attention away from sexuality" and to "prove their value and worth." And African American women's definitions of motherhood, Collins remarks, are part of their efforts "to define and value [their] own experiences" and to resist society's representations of them. By controlling the terms that characterize this aspect of their lives, Collins remarks, African American women make motherhood "a site where Black women express and learn the power of self-definition, the importance of valuing and respecting [them]selves, the necessity of self-reliance and independence, and a belief in Black women's empowerment."

Society may try to control the ways in which African American womanhood is represented, but through the role of mother, Truth and other African American women find a means to resist these definitions and articulate alternatives.[20]

In her famous speech to the Woman's Rights Convention in Akron in 1851, Truth—like Stewart and Douglass before her—mounts a strong challenge to conventional definitions of femininity, demonstrating that they privilege white women's experiences while denying those of African American women. Truth calls upon her audience to examine the exclusive confines of "True Womanhood," voicing her experience as a slave woman:

> She said she was a woman, and had done as much work in the field as any man here. She had heard much about equality of the sexes, but would not argue that question. (*Tribune* version)

> I am a woman's rights. I have as much muscle as any man, and can do as much work as any man. I have plowed and reaped and husked and chopped and mowed, and can any man do more than that? I have heard much about the sexes being equal; I can carry as much as any man, and can eat as much too, if I can get it. I am as strong as any man that is now. (*Bugle* version)

> I have plowed and planted and gathered into barns, and no man could head me—and ar'n't I a woman? I could work as much and eat as much as a man (when I could get it), and bear de lash as well—and ar'n't I a woman? (*National Anti-Slavery Standard* version [Gage])[21]

Truth exposes the hypocrisy of white antebellum society, which represents white women as inviolate while sanctioning physical labor for oppressed slave women whose experience is ignored in definitions of femininity. Disclosing her personal history, Truth proposes a new view of womanhood that privileges strength and the ability to survive hardship.

Harriet Jacobs similarly grounds her commentary on femininity in her experiences as a female slave, appropriating traditional conceptions of womanhood in contexts that expose the ways in which these standards are applied narrowly and hypocritically in antebellum society. Like Truth, Jacobs articulates the experiences of the female slave to complicate simplistic definitions of female virtue. In her 1861 narrative *Incidents in the Life of a Slave Girl,* Jacobs reveals that antebellum society's purported respect for female sexual purity is limited to white women only. Describing the abuse of her master, Dr. Flint, who continually threatens her in an effort to make her succumb to his sexual advances, Jacobs reveals antebellum hypocrisy about womanhood through her narrative, challenging an ideology that respects white women but allows African American women to be exploited. Jacobs's experience serves to defy the pervasive stereotype of the promiscuous African American woman—her "soul revolt[s]" at Dr. Flint's attempts "to corrupt the pure principles [her] grandmother had instilled" (*ILSG,* 27).[22] She reveals, though, that others do not share this concern for her virtue. Describing her vulnerability, she also exposes the way racism limits antebellum society's true respect for gender: "Where could I turn for protection? . . . [T]here is no shadow of law to protect [the slave girl] from insult, from violence, or even from death; all these are inflicted by fiends who bear the shape of men. The mistress, who ought to protect the helpless victim, has no other feelings towards her but those of jealousy and rage" (*ILSG,* 27–28).

Through the character of her mistress, Mrs. Flint, Jacobs also reverses traditional antebellum formulations of gender that contrast virtuous white "True Women" with their impure African American counterparts. Although Mrs. Flint "possesse[s] the key to her husband's character" and "might have used this knowledge to counsel and to screen the young and the innocent among her slaves," she has "no sympathy" for them (*ILSG,* 31). In a revealing passage, Jacobs describes Mrs. Flint's "grief" upon hearing of her husband's conduct toward the slave girl:

> She felt that her marriage vows were desecrated, her dignity insulted; but she had no compassion for the poor victim of her husband's perfidy. She pitied herself as a martyr; but she was incapable of feeling for the condition of shame and misery in which her unfortunate, helpless slave was placed.
> . . . I could not blame her. Slaveholders' wives feel as other women would under similar circumstances. . . .
> . . . I pitied Mrs. Flint. (*ILSG,* 33–34)

The forgiving and sympathetic Jacobs is the "True Woman," an ideal the petty and selfish Mrs. Flint fails to attain. Undermining traditional associations of "True Womanhood" with whiteness, Jacobs appropriates antebellum ideals in a context that questions their very basis. By investing antebellum ideals of femininity with the potential to overturn conventional beliefs about gender and race, Jacobs effects what Burke calls a "re-individuation" of a cultural "form," in which a rhetor deploys a resonant form while shifting its original content. Through this process, Burke explains, a rhetor can marshal the connotations of the original form while redefining its implications for the audience.[23] Jacobs re-individuates a fundamental topos of antebellum society, challenging her audience's conventional notions of femininity.

Jacobs's portrayal of the slaveholding Mrs. Flint as "unfeminine" is, in some aspects, similar to the efforts of white women abolitionists to represent southern white women as violating norms of gender through their support of slavery and to contrast them with white women abolitionists. Jacobs's characterization of Mrs. Flint is in some ways reminiscent of Lydia Maria Child's account of Miss G., for example, who sells her female slave to a male acquaintance who intends to exploit the slave sexually. Yet there are important differences to be noted.

Representing their white female opponents as "unfeminine," white women abolitionists do not question the association of "True Womanhood" and whiteness.
Indeed, their arguments depend upon the assumption that southern white
women were violating their "natural" femininity by upholding slavery. For
Jacobs, though, the juxtaposition of virtuous slave women and unfeminine white
women undermines the associations of white women and "True Womanhood."
And, in Jacobs's story, white southern women are not contrasted solely with
white northern women, rendering African American women invisible. Jacobs
assumes agency and validates her own experiences in her descriptions of Mrs.
Flint's behavior.

In her portrayal of her successful resistance to Dr. Flint's sexual advances,
Jacobs asserts a definition of womanhood that, in contrast with traditional antebellum formulations, is strong, defiant, and self-assured. When Flint tells her he
has a right to "do as [he] likes with [her]" and even to kill her, she responds, "You
have tried to kill me, and I wish you had; but you have no right to do as you like
with me" (*ILSG*, 39). Jacobs appropriates the ideal of the virtuous woman who
would rather die than submit to impurity in a context that gives her agency. Her
virtuous nature does not render her passive or weak but gives her the ability to
actively resist Flint, boldly defending herself verbally.[24] She reveals through her
descriptions of her experiences with Flint that any abstract ideal of feminine submission is unrealistic given the actual oppression faced by African American
women. She cannot afford to be deferential or helpless; not only does she fight
her corruption, but she relies on her intellect and her ability to argue. Continually bettering—and belittling—Flint, she counters all of his persuasive attempts.
When he asks whether she "would like to be sold," she answers that she "would
rather be sold to any body than to lead such a life as [she] did" (*ILSG*, 35). When
he threatens her with jail, she remarks, "There would be more peace for me
there than there is here" (*ILSG*, 40). Jacobs demonstrates that the ideal woman
may need to be bold and independent. Because of the hypocrisy of antebellum
society, the vulnerable slave woman cannot even depend upon other women: "I
gained nothing by seeking the protection of my mistress . . . the power was still
all in [my master's] own hands" (*ILSG*, 34). Through the narrative of her resistance to Flint, Jacobs redefines ideal womanhood and reveals that feminine virtue
need not exclude boldness, defiance, and self-reliance. Furthermore, she proves
through her successful verbal opposition to Flint that a virtuous woman may also
be a rhetor.

Although Dr. Flint does not succeed in making her his mistress, Jacobs cannot
remain "uncorrupted" in antebellum terms. She becomes the lover of Mr. Sands, an
unmarried white man, eventually giving birth to two children. Explaining her
offense, Jacobs seems to conform to traditional antebellum notions of female morality, creating a self-conscious and apologetic ethos: "And now, reader, I come to a period
in my unhappy life, which I would gladly forget if I could. The remembrance

fills me with sorrow and shame" (*ILSG*, 53). But Jacobs is not merely endorsing antebellum society's ideals here. As we have seen, Jacobs suggests that resistance to sexual victimization is not just a way to be "pure" in white America's view, but a means of controlling one's own destiny and of resisting the exploitation with which African American women were constantly threatened. These implications of African American women's control of their own sexuality are reinforced by Jacobs's description of the particulars of the affair. She presents herself, Yellin maintains, not as "a passive female victim" of a lover, but as "an effective moral agent." Jacobs takes responsibility for her actions, noting that she does not "screen [her]self behind the plea of compulsion from a master," nor does she "plead ignorance or thoughtlessness" (*ILSG*, 54). In contrast, as Yellin remarks, she describes her affair with Mr. Sands as "a mistaken tactic in the struggle for freedom."[25] This formulation is significant, complicating the traditional stereotype that an African American woman's sexual behavior is determined solely by her libido and presenting an image of a female slave who assumes control over her own body. Jacobs explains the complicated feelings that lead to the liaison with Sands: "So much attention from a superior person was, of course, flattering. . . . I also felt grateful for his sympathy. . . . It seems less degrading to give one's self, than to submit to compulsion. There is something akin to freedom in having a lover who has no control over you" (*ILSG*, 54–55). In this description, Jacobs is not the passive victim of a more powerful man. She is a strong woman with agency who must make a difficult moral decision in a specific circumstance.

Significantly, too, although Jacobs expresses deep regret for the affair, it ironically presents her with a means of assuming power in her relationship to Dr. Flint. Her resulting pregnancy, in fact, foils Dr. Flint's plan to remove her to a secluded house away from town, where, isolated from her grandmother, he could "succeed at last in trampling his victim under his feet" (*ILSG*, 53). Thus even as Jacobs maintains that her affair with Sands might be sinful in abstract terms, she implies that it was, in her particular circumstances, the more moral course, allowing her to avoid becoming the mistress of a married man whom she despises. Jacobs's narrative suggests that abstract ideals fall short as a measure of the conduct of women whose lives do not conform to the narrow standards on which "True Womanhood" is based. She makes this argument explicit in the text, contending that female slaves should not be judged by standards that are undermined by slavery. Even though the memory of her sin "haunt[s]" her, she challenges the strict code that would pronounce her a corrupted woman: "I feel that the slave woman ought not to be judged by the same standard as others" (*ILSG*, 56). Arguing for a more complex view of female morality that accounts for the experiences of slave women, Jacobs appeals directly to her female readers: "O, ye happy women, whose purity has been sheltered from childhood, who have been free to choose the objects of your affection, whose homes are protected by law, do not judge the poor desolate slave girl too severely!" (*ILSG*, 54). The particular circumstances of white women's lives, Jacobs reveals, are not "universal" to all women. She exposes how white privilege—and not merely "natural" feminine virtue—protects white women while leaving their African American countrywomen vulnerable.

Inserting the personal in public rhetoric that addresses national policy, African American women abolitionists undermine the notion that private experience must be separated from the public sphere. In the experiences of slave women in particular, Lauren Berlant and Karen Sánchez-Eppler argue, sexuality is not just private but part of a system of oppression and exploitation with national implications.[26] Bringing the "outsider-within" perspective to the public sphere, African American female abolitionists challenge rigid formulations of public argument and add a powerful new dimension to national discourse.

"THINK OF YOUR SABLE SISTERS": THE BONDS OF WOMANHOOD AND SLAVE WOMEN'S EXPERIENCES

Jacobs's entreaty to female readers of her narrative to refrain from judging slave women suggests that, just as white women abolitionists profess "sympathy" with their oppressed "sisters," so African American women invoke the presumed bonds between women of different races in their antislavery rhetoric. In other words, they appeal to white women's ostensible sympathy for other women to argue against slavery. In particular, African American female abolitionists focus on two key aspects of womanhood—women's status as mothers and their vulnerability to sexual abuse. Yet they go beyond suggesting that these common concerns of women transcend the boundaries of race. They also stress their division from white women, emphasizing the unique ways in which motherhood and sexual abuse affect their lives. Their rhetoric, it might seem, fits the Burkeian model, in which division and identification are interconnected. In particular, Burke notes that sympathy depends upon the paradoxical interplay of "cooperation and division" and the human desire for "vicarious sharing" of the experiences of those from whom we are divided.[27]

Yet Burke's paradigm cannot entirely explain African American women's appeals to white women's sympathy. For Burke, although division is the fundamental human condition, rhetoric seeks to transcend difference by appealing to identification, particularly through ostensibly "universal" or "ultimate" themes that invoke a realm purportedly beyond division. Humans' sense of being divided from one another never disappears; without it, Burke stresses, there is no need for rhetoric. But although division is a structuring principle of rhetoric for Burke, he proposes that it serves as the incitement to persuasion that depends upon an ultimate transcendence of difference.[28] For African American women abolitionists, though, difference serves a rhetorical function unaccounted for in Burke's terms. Difference is not simply a means to identification in their rhetoric; it is a fundamental component of their persuasion about issues such as motherhood and sexual abuse.

As an alternative to Burke's model, I propose that difference and identification form a *defining tension* that structures African American women abolitionists' appeals to sympathy. On the one hand, they ask white women readers to identify with African American women, particularly slaves, based on women's status as mothers and their vulnerability to sexual abuse. At the same time, though, they stress within these general concerns the unique experiences of African American women, always reminding their audiences of their differences from white women. This defining tension is aptly captured in a comment from Harriet Jacobs's *Incidents in the Life of a Slave Girl*. Women who are enslaved, she remarks, "have wrongs, and sufferings, and mortifications peculiarly their own" (*ILSG*, 77). Jacobs emphasizes slave women's status as females whose experiences are dependent upon their gender. But Jacobs also implies that the concerns that are "peculiarly their own" are unique because of their race. Both identification and difference are crucial and interconnected components of African American women's discussions of female concerns.

The implications of their rhetoric are significant, particularly when we recall the limitations of the "rhetoric of sympathy" of white women abolitionists. When white women feature "universal" concerns of women, we have discovered, they often privilege white women's experiences and ignore those of women of color. For African American women, emphasizing the real distinctions that divide them from white women implicitly serves to critique this "universalist" rhetoric. In addition, they assume through their persuasion the authority to define themselves and their concerns—an authority that contrasts sharply with the invisibility of African American women in white women's rhetoric of sympathy. By articulating and defining African American women's particular experiences, they assume the agency to create their own images of womanhood. Their frequent emphasis on their own personal experiences, too, contrasts sharply with white women's abstract rhetoric that often romanticizes or overlooks the lives of African American women.

Motherhood, as we have seen, is a powerful topos that allows African American women abolitionists to define themselves and articulate their particular experiences. Their appeals to motherhood are informed by the defining tension between identification and difference, simultaneously appealing to white women beyond the bonds of race and emphasizing the particular experiences of African American women. Consider, for example, Sarah Douglass's article "A Mother's Love," written for the *Liberator*'s "Ladies' Department." Douglass begins with a short poem that invokes motherhood's transcendent power: "All other passions change / With changing circumstances . . . / . . . A mother's fondness reigns / Without a rival, and without an end." But although she appeals to the influence of motherhood on all women, her focus on slave women reveals that the maternal experiences of slaves are unique. She apostrophizes, "And dost thou, poor slave, feel this holy passion? Does thy heart swell with anguish, when thy helpless infant is torn from thy arms, and carried thou knowest not whither? when thou hast no hope left that thou shalt ever see his innocent face again? Yes, I know thou dost feel all this."[29] Like white women abolitionists, Douglass reveals that slavery interferes with women's maternal duties. Unlike her white counterparts, though, who appeal to white women to recognize their common bond with the slave mother, Douglass highlights the perspective of the slave mother herself. It is the singular experiences of the female slave, not her likeness to white women, that are central for Douglass. Asking white women to sympathize with the slave mother, she also critiques the foundations on which this sympathy is based. The poem with which she begins does not, despite its seemingly "universal" tone, capture the pain that accompanies motherhood for female slaves. Indeed, the poem ignores the experiences of the slave mother, who is cruelly denied the ideals it expresses. Juxtaposing the slave mother's concerns with the poem's abstract sentiments, Douglass gives voice to the slave woman's unique experiences of motherhood.

Appealing directly to white women, Douglass again invokes a defining tension between presumably universal bonds of womanhood and the distinct experiences of slave women. After describing the experiences of a slave mother forced by her mistress to neglect her child as she works in the field, Douglass asks, "American Mothers! can you doubt that the slave feels as tenderly for her offspring as you do for yours? Do your hearts feel no throb of pity for her woes? Will you not raise your voices, and plead for her emancipation—her immediate emancipation?"[30] Douglass evokes the transcendent appeal of motherhood that, she suggests, should spur white women to argue against slavery. At the same time, though, the negative form of her questions constitutes a challenge to white women. She suggests, indeed, that they *do* doubt that slave mothers share their feelings, that they *can* ignore the sufferings of slave women. White women, she insinuates, define motherhood in terms of white women's concerns, ignoring those of other women. As she asks them to acknowledge slave women's maternal feelings, she also challenges them to consider that their experiences of motherhood are not universal and to recognize how their white-centered definitions of maternity ignore the oppression and sufferings of their countrywomen.

In *Incidents in the Life of a Slave Girl*, Jacobs draws on her own experiences as a slave mother to both appeal to white women and to challenge their narrow views. In a letter to her white Quaker friend Amy Post in 1857, Jacobs explains her intentions in writing the narrative: "I have placed myself before you to be judged as a woman whether I deserve your pity or contempt—I have another object in view—it is to come to you just as I am a poor Slave Mother—not to tell you what I have heard but what I have seen—and what I have suffered—and if their [sic] is any sympathy to give—let it be given to the thousands—of of [sic] Slave Mothers that are still in bondage—suffering far more than I have—let it plead for their helpless Children."[31] Jacobs's terms are notable, revealing the defining tension between identification and difference that structures her relationship to white female readers. She wishes to be "judged as a woman," suggesting the presumed bonds of womanhood that will link white readers to her. At the same time, though, she has "another object"—she wishes to articulate her particular experiences as "a poor Slave Mother." Significantly, she does not automatically assume that white women will have sympathy for her plight—*if* her narrative evokes sympathy, she remarks, it should be for women who are still enslaved.

In her preface to the text, Jacobs's direct appeal to white female readers is similarly informed by identification and difference, the bonds of womanhood and the particular experiences of the female slave. "I have not written my experiences in order to attract attention to myself," Jacobs remarks. "Neither do I care to excite sympathy for my own sufferings. But I do earnestly desire to arouse the women of the North to a realizing sense of the condition of two millions of women at the South, still in bondage, suffering what I suffered, and most of them far worse. . . . Only by experience can any one realize how deep, and dark, and foul is that pit of abominations" (*ILSG*, 1–2). Jacobs wants to evoke both "sympathy"—presumably an instinctive reaction of one woman to another—and "a realizing sense" of the condition of slave women. The latter impulse suggests that white women's sympathy may often be limited, that the supposedly instinctive bonds that link women do not preclude those who are privileged from ignoring the situations of those who differ from them. Emphasizing her vantage point as a former slave, Jacobs stresses that white women's sympathy will be abstract and useless if it is not accompanied by a recognition of the concrete conditions that make slave women's lives different from white women's. Her deferential ethos—reminiscent of the self-denying professions of both African American male abolitionists and white women abolitionists—heightens her message that slavery can only be understood through personal narratives. She does not give particulars because she wishes to attract attention to herself but because experience is central to the force of her antislavery rhetoric.

In Jacobs's descriptions of slave mothers' particular sufferings, she creates images of African American motherhood that challenge both racist stereotypes and white-centered notions of ideal femininity. As Truth's offer to bare her maternal breasts demonstrates, through motherhood African American women can articulate definitions of themselves and their femininity that empower them. Jacobs's descriptions of the effects on slave mothers of the slave auctions that take place on New Year's Day is a case in point. She begins by drawing a contrast in rather abstract terms:

> O, you happy free women, contrast *your* New Year's day with that of the poor bond-woman! With you it is a pleasant season. . . . Children bring their little offerings, and raise their rosy lips for a caress. They are your own, and no hand but that of death can take them from you.
>
> But to the slave mother New Year's day comes laden with peculiar sorrows. She sits on her cold cabin floor, watching the children who may all be torn from her the next morning; and often does she wish that she

and they might die before the day dawns. She may be an ignorant creature, degraded by the system that has brutalized her from childhood; but
she has a mother's instincts, and is capable of feeling a mother's agonies.
(*ILSG,* 16)

These comments, akin in some ways to the abstract rhetoric of white women abolitionists, seem to universalize motherhood. With the exception of the slave
mother's wish for death, the description portrays the female slave in general terms
that de-emphasize her personal experiences in favor of her "mother's instincts." But
Jacobs does not leave her readers with this merely abstract portrayal of the slave
mother's New Year's day. She narrates a particular event she has witnessed, in
which a slave woman pleads with a trader to tell her where her children have been
sold. Jacobs vividly describes the woman's "wild, haggard face" and her wish for
God to kill her now that her children are gone (*ILSG,* 16). In this narrative, Jacobs
presents an image of African American motherhood that challenges racist and
proslavery stereotypes of slave mothers as unconcerned about their children. Her
description also empowers rather than objectifies or erases the slave woman. She is
bold, defying the slave system as she confronts the trader about her children's
whereabouts. Motherhood, in Jacobs's narrative, gives African American women
agency that arises from their particular oppressive circumstances and that contrasts
with abstract—and white-centered—definitions of femininity.

Other African American women abolitionists also feature the particular maternal experiences of slave women in ways that sharply differentiate female slaves from
white women and give them a unique sense of agency. In an 1859 speech of Sarah
Remond in Warrington, England, the wish for death alluded to in Jacobs's description of the slave mother's New Year's Day becomes a reality for a slave named
Margaret Garner, who, after escaping from her master, is threatened with capture
and a return to slavery. Remond's description of Garner paradoxically draws on idealized notions of womanhood and challenges abstract notions of maternity:

[She] determined to be free or die in the attempt. She was born a slave,
and had suffered in her own person the degradation that a woman could
not mention. She got as far as Cincinnati with her children. . . . The slaveholder found her; as he appeared at the door she snatched up a knife and
slew her first-born child, but before the poor frenzied creature could pro-
ceed further in her dread object, the hand of the tyrant was on her, when
she called to the grandmother of the children to kill the others, as she preferred to return them to the bosom of God rather than they should be
taken back to American slavery.[32]

In Remond's narrative, maternal devotion depends upon a paradoxical tension
between overarching ideals and the demands of particular circumstances. Remond
suggests that the extreme action of infanticide is, in terms of the transcendent values
of motherhood, not antithetical to Garner's true affection for her children, but an
example of pure maternal devotion. For Garner, the power of motherhood overrides

all earthly concerns. But in Remond's story, Garner's ultimate devotion to her children is revealed in particular and shocking circumstances that directly confront her audience with the limitations of abstract definitions of motherhood. Killing her children, Garner may paradoxically represent an idealized notion of maternal instincts, but her extreme actions separate her fundamentally from women who will never be driven to such a response.[33]

White female abolitionists also narrate stories of female slaves who take extreme actions, we will recall, risking death rather than separation from their families or killing their children in their attempts to protect them from slavery. In these narratives, white women abolitionists grant a particular agency to African American women even as they espouse views that depend on "romantic racialism," portraying African Americans as more instinctual and less rational than whites. Like her white counterparts, Remond gives the female slave a unique form of agency through her narrative, but it is notable that Garner's decision to kill her children is represented not as an instinctual decision but as a rational choice. Garner may be "frenzied," in Remond's terms, but she has her wits about her, calling to her children's grandmother for assistance in killing her children when she is restrained. And Remond's description of her choice indicates that it is based on her rational weighing of her options—"to return [her children] to the bosom of God" or to allow them to be "taken back to American slavery." In contrast to the slave mothers of white women's rhetoric, who act from instinct in their resistance, Garner is empowered by her own will to defy oppression.

Remond's reference in her narrative of Margaret Garner to "the degradation that a woman could not mention" suggests another topos featured by African American female abolitionists—the sexual abuse of slave women. Like their representations of motherhood, their discussions of slave women's sexual oppression are informed by a defining tension between identification and difference. Remond's description of Garner's sexual abuse is reminiscent of the rhetoric of her white female counterparts, who similarly use oblique and modest terms to allude to this theme. This similarly "feminine" tone notwithstanding, African American women abolitionists engage this topic very differently from their white counterparts. As we have discovered, white women abolitionists' descriptions of the sexual abuse of female slaves are often abstract, ignoring the women slaves themselves and shifting attention onto white southern women. African American women, on the other hand, focus both on white women audience members and on the direct victims of the abuse. While they entreat white women to sympathize with female slaves—and thus to become involved in the fight against slavery—they delineate the differences between slave women's experiences and white women's everyday lives, demonstrating that a "universal" description of womanhood necessarily minimizes the needs and concerns of those who are oppressed.

In speeches to English audiences in 1859, Remond frequently describes slave women's sexual oppression, simultaneously inviting the instinctual sympathy of white women for female slaves while suggesting that this sympathy must not ignore the particular experiences of slave women. In a speech in London, Remond asserts that white women are connected by the bonds of womanhood to abused slave women: "She pleaded especially on behalf of her own sex. Words were inadequate to express the depth of the infamy into which they were plunged by the cruelty and licentiousness of their brutal masters. If English women and English wives knew the unspeakable horrors to which their sex were exposed on Southern plantations, they would freight every westward gale with the voice of their moral indignation, and demand for the black woman the protection and rights enjoyed by the white."[34] Remond implies that women's sympathy for their oppressed sisters is automatic, but she also indicates that the particular abuses to which female slaves are exposed have been at best ignored and at worst erased in discussions of slavery. "English women and English wives" do *not* realize the conditions of American female slaves; their potential for sympathy notwithstanding, they have been able to overlook particulars such as sexual abuse that sharply divide slave women's lives from those of free white women.

In particular, Remond reveals, the sexual abuse of female slaves demonstrates that the qualities associated with womanhood, despite the rhetoric that would propose that they are universal, are attributed only to white women. Speaking in Bristol, Remond "call[s] especially upon the women of England to sympathize upon the atrocious wrongs of the colored women of America, who are sold for the basest purposes, their value on the auction-block being raised by every quality of beauty, talent, piety, and goodness which should have commanded the respect and tenderness of their fellow-creatures."[35] The very attributes that supposedly define the ideal woman are for the slave woman features that increase her vulnerability to sexual oppression. Thus these aspects of ideal femininity are, in antebellum society, valued only in white women; and the assumption that the "True Woman" gains respect is based only on white women's lives and experiences. Through the topos of sexual abuse, Remond reveals that qualities associated with womanhood are, in antebellum society, not universal but racially constructed.

In her London speech, Remond combines the force of images of motherhood and sexual abuse to explicitly reveal the limits of a "universal" rhetoric that purports to define women's experiences. She responds in particular to a specific proslavery contention. Apologists for slavery often claimed that southern slaves lived more comfortably and contentedly than laborers either in the North or in other countries. A few nights before Remond's speech, in fact, actress Lola Montez claimed in a speech on slavery that American slaves were better off than the laborers of other countries.[36] In Remond's response to Montez's charge, she reveals that comparisons of the lives of female slaves to those of women laborers in other countries—even those who work under oppressive conditions—ignore particular aspects of slave women's lives that need to be acknowledged, specifically their lack of control over their bodies and their children. The account of the speech for American readers of the *National Anti-Slavery Standard* relates, "[Remond] knew something of the trials and toils of the women of England—how, in the language of Hood, they were made to 'stitch, stitch, stitch,' till weariness and exhaustion overtook them. But there was this immeasurable difference between their condition and that of the slavewoman—that their persons were free and their progeny their own; while the slavewoman was the victim of the heartless lust of her master, and the children whom she bore were his property."[37] Identification of women's experiences, Remond reveals, has limits. Those who too broadly associate all women's encounters with oppression in fact may ignore significant features of slave women's lives that must be named and recognized if the African American woman is to assume the agency to define herself. Indeed, as Montez's contentions reveal, broad associations of women's experiences of oppression may downplay the cruelties of slavery in proslavery apologies.

Harriet Jacobs also reveals in her antislavery rhetoric that abstract arguments about womanhood that ignore particulars of slave women's experiences, particularly the horrors of sexual abuse, are often part of defenses of slavery. In an 1853 letter to the editor of the *New-York Daily Tribune,* published anonymously and signed "A Fugitive Slave," Jacobs enters an ongoing debate about the appropriate response of women to the question of slavery. New York newspapers in 1852 published an appeal to southern women by various eminent Englishwomen, exhorting them to help end slavery. Julia Tyler, wife of former President John Tyler, wrote a response on January 24, 1853, entitled "To the Duchess of Sutherland and the Ladies of England," which was published in many southern newspapers and magazines, including the *Richmond Enquirer* and the *Southern Literary Messenger.* In an argument akin to Montez's, Tyler proposes that southern slavery is relatively benign in contrast with the condition of poor English factory workers, claiming that "the negro of the South lives sumptuously in comparison with the 100,000 of the white population of London." She also maintains that because a woman's proper sphere is "literally and emphatically, that of her family," southern women cannot become involved with a political issue such as slavery.[38]

In her letter to the *Tribune,* Jacobs responds to Tyler's position by discussing the exploitation of women slaves. Jacobs counters Tyler's abstract contentions about women's appropriate response to slavery with particulars that reveal that Tyler's general statements, by avoiding the true experiences of women slaves, minimize slavery's horrors. Jacobs opens by underscoring her personal approach to the debate: "I became very much interested in some of the articles and comments written on Mrs. Tyler's Reply to the Ladies of England. Being a slave myself, I could not have felt otherwise." Jacobs offers women's personal narratives to refute Tyler's general claims, demonstrating the centrality of experience to the rhetoric of the African American woman and authorizing her text through her own experiences as a slave. She notes that although "Mrs. Tyler said that slaves were never sold only under very peculiar circumstances," these "peculiar circumstances" are not specified. Jacobs offers to supply these omitted details: "Let one whose particular sufferings justifies [*sic*] her in explaining it for Mrs. Tyler."[39] Jacobs features an ironic tone to assert her authority to respond to Tyler. Seemingly assuming Tyler's good motives, Jacobs suggests that she can educate Tyler about slavery. Her response reveals implicitly, though, that Tyler's omission of the details of slavery is due less to ignorance than to her complicity with the institution.

To illustrate the "peculiar circumstances"—ironically appropriating Tyler's terms—"under which slaves are sold," Jacobs offers the example of an "innocent" and "beautiful" female slave whom she refers to as her sister.[40] Her master tries to seduce her, leading the slave to ask her mother for "refuge from her persecutor." Rendering personal the abstract question of the sale of slaves—which Tyler minimizes through her claim that this occurrence is relatively rare—Jacobs recounts that the young woman is forced to submit to her master when he threatens to sell her mother if she refuses. Jacobs appeals directly to white female readers, asking them to identify with the slave through their common role of mother: "Oh, Christian mothers! you that have daughters of your own, can you think of your sable sisters without offering a prayer to that God who created all in their behalf?" Jacobs suggests that the bonds that link women will "naturally" evoke sympathy from white women at the thought of these horrors. But—drawing on the defining tension between identification and difference—she also reveals that, from their privileged position, they can (and often do) ignore the particulars of slave women's experiences. Jacobs ironically reveals the limits of white women's sympathy by forcing her audience to recognize the oppression that faces the female slave in her narrative: "Can you, Christian, find it in your heart to despise her? Ah, no! not even Mrs. Tyler; for though we believe that the vanity of a name would lead her to bestow her hand where her heart could never go with it, yet, with all her faults and follies, she is nothing more than a *woman*."[41] Turning the tables on her opponent, Jacobs also reverses traditional formulations of sympathy. The bonds of womanhood, she suggests, should not lead to abstract rhetoric such as Tyler's that ignores slavery's horrors or the distinct experiences of slave women, but to an acknowledgment of the particular aspects of the lives of white women's "sable sisters."

As we have seen, white women abolitionists often focus in their rhetoric of sympathy on the effects of slavery not on female slaves but on white women. In their appeals to white women, African American women similarly invoke their concern for other white women. But their rhetoric differs subtly from that of their white counterparts. White female abolitionists focus primarily on the white southern woman while ignoring the plight of the female slave; they emphasize, for example, the white woman whose husband fathers his slaves' children while ignoring the slave women who are thereby abused. In their version of this narrative, African American female abolitionists make no such omission. In Jacobs's letter to the *Tribune,* she describes the consequences of her sister's abuse for the slaveholder's wife: "The most sincere affection that his heart was capable of, could not make him faithful to his beautiful and wealthy bride the short time of three months, but every stratagem was used to seduce my sister. Mortified and tormented beyond endurance, this child came and threw herself on her mother's bosom."[42] The white woman's pain is merely implied, while Jacobs's sister's anguish is vividly described.

African American female abolitionists suggest, in fact, that the sexual abuse of slave women links them closely with white female slaveholders. This identification does not, as in the rhetoric of white female abolitionists, sublimate the experiences of the female slave to that of the white women. In contrast, in a reversal of the conventional emphasis on white women's lives, the female slave's experience becomes the norm against which white women's experiences are judged. Consider, for example, Jacobs's striking commentary in her letter to the *Tribune:*

> There is a strong rivalry between a handsome mulatto girl and a jealous and *faded* mistress. . . . Would you not think that Southern Women had cause to despise that Slavery which forces them to bear so much deception practiced by their *husbands?* . . . [A] slaveholder seldom takes a white mistress, for she is an expensive commodity, not submissive as he would like to have her, but more apt to be tyrannical; and when his passion seeks another object, he must leave her in quiet possession of all the gewgaws that she has sold herself for. But not so with his poor *slave victim,* that he has robbed of everything . . . she must be torn from the little that is left to hold her to life, and sold by her *seducer* and *master.*[43]

Jacobs's identification of the white southern woman and the slave woman empowers the female slave, making her experience the standard against which the actions of white women are judged. White women are "expensive commodities" who "sell themselves" for "gewgaws," while the slave woman, although in more oppressive circumstances, is more feminine than her white mistress. The slave woman does not choose her abuse—she does not, to use Jacobs's words, "sell herself"—and thus, despite her exploitation by white slaveholders, she has an identity apart from this oppression, in contrast to white southern women.

Remond also evokes an ironic reversal of the usual standard that measures African American women's lives against the experiences of white women. In her anecdotes of light-skinned female slaves, white women are associated physically with slave women, complicating the connection of whiteness with privilege and freedom. In her London speech, Remond mentions the "auction of a woman who was recommended on account of her being undistinguishable by complexion from the white race." The inherent message—that slavery's particular horrors include the selling of women who are "almost" white—is more explicit in Remond's speech in Warrington:

> In the open market place women are exposed for sale—their persons not always covered. Yes, I can tell you English men and women, that women are sold into slavery with cheeks like the lily and the rose, as well as those that might compare with the wing of the raven. They are exposed for sale, and subjected to the most shameful indignities. The more Anglo-Saxon blood that mingles with the blood of the slave, the more gold is poured out

when the auctioneer has a woman for sale, because they are sold to be con-
cubines for white Americans. They are not sold for plantation slaves.[44]

Remond's remarks are in some ways troubling, seeming to suggest that the abuse of
light-skinned slaves is more horrifying than that of those whose complexion is akin
to "the wing of the raven." But Remond's comments, directed at a white audience,
can also be seen as challenging her listeners to recognize the arbitrariness of racial
boundaries and the associations that accompany them. White privilege, usually seen
as natural and often "invisible," is revealed to be precarious in Remond's account.
And white female listeners are called upon to measure their own lives against that
of the light-skinned slave rather than the reverse, to recognize that the white privilege that structures their everyday lives is not "natural" but the result of arbitrary
societal racial divisions.

It is notable that, in their appropriations and redefinitions of the conventions associated with True Womanhood and the topoi of motherhood and sexual
abuse, African American female abolitionists demonstrate a more critical approach
toward essentialist definitions of gender than their white female counterparts.
Their experiences become sites for interrogating essentialist categories such as
womanhood or motherhood, and they reveal the ways in which essentialism
serves to mask features of the everyday lives of African American women.

"GIVE WOMAN A CHANCE TO SET THE WORLD RIGHT SIDE UP AGAIN": SCRIPTURAL ARGUMENTS

Christianity gave African American women an avenue through which to assume
responsibilities outside the domestic sphere. Although they, like their white female
counterparts, faced restrictions based on antebellum conventions, such as Paul's dictates against women's speaking and the opposition of many male leaders to women's
religious leadership, important features of African American Christianity allowed
them to assume agency to create strong religious arguments against slavery and for
women's public role in abolition. In contrast to traditional formulations favored by
white Americans, scholars note, African American Christianity is grounded in
experience, particularly enslavement and oppression, the hope of liberation offered
by Christ, and the immediate revelation of God in human lives—and the resulting
personal connection to the divine—through conversion.[45] Religious stories and biblical heroes, Lawrence Levine explains, are "not confined to a specific time or place,
but [are] appropriate to almost every situation." For African American women in
particular, Jacquelyn Grant argues, "the Bible must be read and interpreted in the
light of Black women's own experience of oppression and God's revelation within
that context."[46]

The centrality of experience that underlies their rhetoric about womanhood
and sympathy, then, also informs African American women's Christianity in
general and their readings of Scripture in particular. Thus although they, like
their white counterparts, engage the passages of the Bible that are traditionally

interpreted as restricting women's speaking and activism, their arguments depend less upon abstract hermeneutical strategies and more upon measuring the Bible against experience and personal revelation of God's will. Although their arguments at times share features with those of white women such as the Grimké sisters, this emphasis on the intimate connection of Scripture to personal experience distinguishes their rhetorical strategies from those of white women abolitionists.

In her farewell address in Boston in 1833, Maria Stewart draws upon the power of biblical example and its relevance to daily life in order to validate her public speaking. Stewart evokes biblical women who helped to liberate their peoples or who were connected with redemption through Christ, connecting their actions directly to her own position: "What if I am a woman; is not the God of ancient times the God of these modern days? Did he not raise up Deborah, to be a mother, and a judge in Israel [Judg. 4:4]? Did not queen Esther save the lives of the Jews? And Mary Magdalene first declare the resurrection of Christ from the dead? Come, said the woman of Samaria, and see a man that hath told me all things that ever I did, is not this the Christ?" (*MWS*, 68). This argument in some ways anticipates Angelina Grimké's *Appeal to the Christian Women of the South*—published three years after Stewart's speech—in which she argues for her right to speak from the "rule of justice" based on the precedent set by women of the Bible. Both women, in fact, draw on the heroines Esther and Deborah. Yet while Grimké emphasizes the particulars of the biblical stories—the names of kings, for example—Stewart focuses more on the general message of empowerment of women. Her strategy suggests the immediacy of biblical example to the African American tradition; for Stewart, these biblical heroines do not merely set an abstract precedent but are a compelling source of guidance for everyday life. And, through her personal challenge—"What if I am a woman?"—Stewart makes her own connection to these biblical forebears immediate, placing herself directly into the company of these women.

In the context of this biblical precedent, Stewart's question—"What if I am a woman?"—resonates at two levels. Stewart suggests to her audience that her gender should not matter, citing the examples of biblical women empowered by God whose actions have relevance for contemporary women's lives. But Stewart's subsequent discussion suggests another meaning for the question. Noting that many ancient traditions believed women had special religious insight, she implies that her audience should not dismiss women's spiritual inspiration: "If such women . . . have once existed, be no longer astonished then . . . that God at this eventful period should raise up your own females to strive, by their example both in public and private, to assist those who are endeavoring to stop the strong current of prejudice that flows so profusely against us at present. No longer ridicule their efforts. . . . For God makes use of feeble means sometimes, to bring about his most exalted purposes" (*MWS*, 69). Stewart proposes that women can claim a special connection to God, who often specifically chooses them as instruments for divine purposes. Her challenge—"What if I am a woman?"—suggests that her womanhood grants her a particular relationship with God like that revealed in the lives of women empowered by God throughout history. Women may be considered weak, Stewart implies, but they can assume a divine power that grants them authority to act in the public sphere.

In her Akron speech, Truth, in effect, answers Stewart's question. Biblical precedent, Truth argues, shows that women are connected literally and fundamentally to the Word in the person of Christ:

> She learned also from the new Gospel that man had nothing to do with bringing Jesus into the world, for God was his father, but woman was his mother. Jesus respected woman, and never turned her away. By woman's influence the dead was raised, for when Lazarus died Mary and Martha, full of faith and love, came to Jesus and besought him to raise their brother to life. He did not turn them away, but "Jesus wept," and Lazarus came forth. (*Tribune* version)

> The Lady has spoken about Jesus, how he never spurned woman from him, and she was right. When Lazarus died, Mary and Martha came to him with faith and love and besought him to raise their brother. And Jesus wept—and Lazarus came forth. And how came Jesus into the world? Through God who created him and woman who bore him. Man, where is your part? (*Bugle* version)

> "Den dat little man in black dar [a clergyman], he say woman can't have as much right as man 'cause Christ wa'n'nt a woman. *Whar did your Christ come from?*"
>
> Rolling thunder could not have stilled that crowd as did those deep, wonderful tones, as she stood there with outstretched arms and eye of fire. Raising her voice still louder, she repeated—
>
> "Whar did your Christ come from? From God and a woman. Man had not'ing to do with him." (*National Anti-Slavery Standard* version [Gage])[47]

Undermining traditional arguments that equate Christ's masculinity with male prerogative and authority, Truth demonstrates both that women play a significant role in Christ's ministry and that woman—unlike man—had a role in Christ's creation. Significantly, Truth does not refer to Mary but to "a woman," a semantic choice that universalizes women's role in Christianity. Mary's central role in Christ's presence on earth is not just part of a particular narrative, but a sign of women's personal connection to Jesus.

Truth's statement that man has "nothing to do" with Christ is significant. The idea that Christianity depends fundamentally upon "God and a woman" elucidates her empowering view of women's relationship to the divine and to biblical authority. The centrality of conversion in the African American tradition—an experience that is fundamental to Truth's Christianity—allows women to connect on a personal level with God. A woman who had experienced such a conversion,[48] Truth asserts that man does not have to stand between women and their religious obligations or biblical interpretations. Her own approach to Scripture as a result of this conversion illustrates her suggestion that women must measure biblical truths against their personal experiences of—and relationships to—God. Her explanation of her theological views in her 1850 *Narrative of Sojourner Truth* suggests that her philosophy depends upon her personal experiences of God rather than on traditional theology or literal interpretations of the Bible. Faced with inconsistencies in the Bible as well as with discrepancies when she compares biblical passages to "the witness within her," Truth determines that "the spirit of truth spoke in [the Bible], but that the recorders of those truths had intermingled with them ideas and suppositions of their own."[49] In her own life as well as in the biblical examples she cites, a direct connection between "God and a woman" allows women to interpret—and find empowerment in—the Bible.

Although Truth maintains that she does not take the Bible literally, she does not ignore its power and resonance as a source of spiritual guidance. As her reference to Mary suggests, she draws upon biblical example and its relevance to women's experiences in her theology. In a particularly powerful passage in her Akron speech, she addresses the issue of Eve's precedent for women. Far from proving that women are inferior or that they cannot assume authority, Eve's sin demonstrates the opposite:

> She said she could not read, but she could hear. She had heard the Bible read, and was told that Eve caused the fall of man. Well, if woman upset the world, do give her a chance to set it right side up again. (*Tribune* version)

> I can't read, but I can hear. I have heard the bible and have learned that Eve caused man to sin. Well if woman upset the world, do give her a chance to set it right side up again. (*Bugle* version)

> She took up the defence of Mother Eve. I cannot follow her through it all. . . . [S]he ended by asserting "that if de fust woman God ever made was strong enough to turn de world upside down all her one lone, all dese togeder," and she glanced her eye over us, "ought to be able to turn it back and git it right side up again, and now dey is asking to, de men better let 'em." (*National Anti-Slavery Standard* version [Gage])[50]

Truth's reversal of the usual significance of Eve's sin is reminiscent in some ways of Angelina Grimké's comment in her *Letters to Catherine* [sic] *Beecher* that since woman was the first "transgressor" and "victim of power," she has a right to determine the laws that will govern her. But, in contrast with Grimké's abstract, somewhat academic argumentation, Truth's image of a strong first woman able to "upset the world" is an immediate and compelling example that can be directly applied to everyday life. If, as in the account of Eve's sin, a woman could "upset the world," contemporary women have the power and the responsibility to take a personal stake in the events of that world, to influence public affairs and to set the world "right side up again."

Similarly, Scripture is, in Stewart's rhetoric, not a source of abstract rules but a text that must be measured against the immediate demands of women's lives. Consider, for example, Stewart's response to the Pauline proscriptions against public speaking in her farewell address in Boston: "St. Paul declared that it was a shame for a woman to speak in public, yet our great High Priest and Advocate did not condemn the woman for a more notorious offense than this; neither will he condemn this worthless worm. The bruised reed he will not break. . . . Did St. Paul but know of our wrongs and deprivations, I presume he would make no objections to our pleading in public for our rights" (*MWS,* 68). Stewart's response to Paul's injunctions is twofold. Using an argument *a fortiori,* she initially argues from the premise that her public speaking might, in general, be wrong. However, she maintains that because Christ did not denounce a woman for a greater sin, he would not censure her for her transgression—particularly because of her ostensible weakness as a woman.

Her next statement, however, suggests that, given the present circumstances, her public persuasion does not violate Christian morality. Paul is not, in this representation, a distant authority. Building on the premise of African American Christianity that biblical figures are not confined to a particular historical place or time, Stewart makes Paul hypothetically present, giving his opinion of her role. When the demands of the present are taken into account, she asserts, even Paul would validate her right to persuade publicly. Significantly, Stewart's strategy here is connected to her white female counterparts' strategies of dissociation. As we have seen, white female abolitionists often separate the particular from the general in Paul's injunctions to women, arguing that aspects of Paul's counsel that are related to specific historical circumstances are less relevant than his general message. Stewart's strategy depends, in effect, upon a reversal of this maneuver—differentiating the particular and the general, she elevates the particular. The demands of her specific circumstances, Stewart asserts, override Paul's general advice. For Stewart, as for other African American women, personal experience and immediate concerns are central to the interpretation of the Bible and to its role in women's lives.

ANSWERING THE CALL: THE AFRICAN AMERICAN FEMALE PROPHET

If, as Truth and Stewart establish, God may call contemporary women as religious leaders and speakers, among the roles they may assume is that of prophet. As in the rhetoric of African American men and white women, certain features of the traditional jeremiadic form resonate in the prophetic discourse of African American female abolitionists. Yet there are unique features of the jeremiadic rhetoric of African American women abolitionists as well. Race and gender shape the prophetic rhetoric of Stewart, Sarah Douglass, Truth, and Frances Ellen Watkins in particular ways.

In her lecture at Franklin Hall, Stewart places herself in a prophetic role: "Methinks I heard a spiritual interrogation—'Who shall go forward, and take off the reproach that is cast upon the people of color? Shall it be a woman?' And my heart made this reply—'If it is thy will, be it even so, Lord Jesus!'" (MWS, 45).[51] Like her African American male and white female colleagues, Stewart proposes that she is answering a divine call, assuming agency through God's inspiration. Notably, though, Stewart suggests that God calls her particularly because of her status both as a woman and as a person of color. Her reference to her race connects her jeremiadic rhetoric to that of her African American male counterparts. Drawing on the notion that African Americans are a chosen people whose liberation is part of God's redemption of American society, Stewart implies that her race grants her the agency to advocate for her suffering people.

But Stewart also refers to her gender, distinguishing her prophetic rhetoric both from that of African American male and white female abolitionists. White women do not suggest that their gender empowers them uniquely as prophets, and their language, for the most part, does not evoke their femininity. Even when Sarah Grimké features the feminine image of Christ as a mother hen in her *Epistle to the Clergy of the Southern States,* she does not explicitly connect this image of a feminine redeemer to her role as a female prophet. Stewart, though, authorizes her prophetic rhetoric on the basis of her gender as well as her race. Just as she suggests in her farewell address that women can be especially empowered to help end prejudice, Stewart maintains that God may specifically call African American women as prophets. If a prophetic rhetor's ethos depends upon his or her unique position in society—both removed from society and connected to it— Stewart suggests that the African American woman prophet can draw a particular authority from the intersections of race and gender in her experience. She is called by God not despite but because of her status as an African American woman.

As we have discovered through David Walker's speech to the MGCA, African American rhetors may direct their prophetic persuasion at African American audiences. This form of the African American jeremiad, Walker's speech demonstrates, uses jeremiadic themes—the prophetic lamentation of society's sins and a call for fundamental change—to empower African Americans in the fight against slavery. Individual actions of African Americans, Walker implies, have impact on the community and ultimately on society as a whole. Similarly, Stewart's prophetic rhetoric in her speech at Franklin Hall exhorts African Americans to turn away from ignorance and improve themselves as a way to fight for the advancement of the race. She begins with a challenge: "Why sit ye here and die? If we say we will go to a foreign land, the famine and the pestilence are there, and there we shall die. If we sit here, we shall die. Come let us plead our cause before the whites . . . if they kill us, we shall but die" (*MWS*, 45). Echoing the language of 2 Kings 3–4, part of the narrative of the prophet Elisha's deliverance of Israel from Syria, Stewart suggests that African Americans have to take an active role in the struggle against oppression. They should neither remove themselves from the United States (as counseled by colonizationists) or wait for aid from outside the community; they must actively and assertively "plead their cause." It is significant that the words Stewart features are spoken in the biblical narrative by four lepers, who enter the city where the Syrians have set up camp in order to find food. Risking their lives, they find the camp abandoned and they nourish themselves unharmed (2 Kings 5–8). In this story, the lowest in society take decisive action to help themselves and are protected by God, a message that would clearly resonate for Stewart's African American audience.

Similarly, in her speech at the African Masonic Hall, Stewart directly exhorts African Americans to take action to fight their oppression. "I would ask," she challenges, "is it blindness of mind, or stupidity of soul, or the want of education that has caused our men who are 60 or 70 years of age, never to let their voices be heard, nor their hands be raised in behalf of their color? Or has it been for the fear of offending the whites? If it has, O ye fearful ones, throw off your fearfulness, and come forth in the name of the Lord, and in the strength of the God of Justice, and make yourselves useful and active members in society" (*MWS*, 57). Stewart's tone is less directly militant than that of her mentor Walker. Implicitly, though, she invokes the militant jeremiadic theme of her male counterparts— the oppressed will rise and demand their rights even in the face of violence. Although, as in all prophetic rhetoric, Stewart implies that God is ultimately the force behind this deliverance, she grants African Americans the agency to take a fundamental role in executing God's plan.

Stewart's assertion that she is answering a divine call to speak also connects her prophetic rhetoric to that of her African American male counterparts as well as to that of white female abolitionists. As we have found, the prophetic stance of one who is a vessel for God's message allows rhetors in marginalized positions in society to offer rhetoric that is harsh and critical of society while deflecting attention from their own motives and maintaining a posture of goodwill toward their audiences. Stewart's assertion of her unique authority demonstrates that this status as God's messenger need not remove authority from the jeremiadic rhetor; rather, the rhetor can be empowered through this role. The African American woman prophet who is called by God does not argue abstractly against sin; she assumes agency to struggle for the end of oppression in her community. Through this role of a messenger of God's will, she is connected to the powerful tradition of African American women's community activism. In her speech at Franklin Hall, for example, Stewart quotes Jer. 29:18 to indicate that her divine call is to aid her people; addressing her "beloved brethren," she asserts, "It is for [woman's] sake and yours that I have come forward and made myself a hissing and a reproach among the people" (*MWS*, 48). Although she places herself in the tradition of divinely inspired prophets, she does not deflect attention from her own authority. By contrast, her assertion that she must speak on behalf of her people places her in an influential public role in her community.

Even when Stewart maintains, as she does in her speech to the Afric-American Female Intelligence Society, that God speaks through her, she reveals her personal strength. Discussing her tract *Religion and the Pure Principles of Morality* and the opposition it received, she claims, "It is the word of God, though men and devils may oppose it" (*MWS*, 52). Stewart may suggest that she is a vessel for a divine message, but she also claims the power inherent in prophetic language. "Be not offended because I tell you the truth," she tells her audience, "for I believe that God has fired my soul with a holy zeal for his cause" (*MWS*, 52). Notably, Stewart echoes the same biblical passage that Angelina Grimké features in her *Appeal to the Christian Women of the South*—Paul's challenge to the Galatians, "Am I therefore become your enemy, because I tell you the truth?" (Gal. 4:16). Yet Grimké sublimates her own voice as she appropriates these words, remarking, "well may [abolitionists] say with the apostle, 'am I then your enemy because I tell you the truth,' and warn you to flee from impending judgments" (*ACW*, 64). By contrast, in Stewart's speech, the words of Paul become her own. She is the prophet inspired to bring the truth to her audience, Stewart asserts, placing herself in a central public role. The difference between Grimké's and Stewart's use of Paul's words is significant. In Stewart's speech, the biblical words are no longer part of a separate text to which the rhetor refers—they become a part of the immediate context. Stewart's appropriation of Paul's words suggests the relevance of the Bible to everyday life in the African American tradition and African American women's testing of biblical passages against their own experiences. Notably, these features of her religious background allow her to assume a more authoritative voice than her white colleague Angelina Grimké.

The notion that the messenger for God's will need not be self-effacing or deferential is illustrated vividly in Stewart's farewell address in Boston. In this speech, she claims that God "hath unloosed [her] tongue, and put his word into [her] mouth" (*MWS*, 67). On its own, this assertion may seem self-denying, suggesting that she has no agency in creating her persuasion. But Stewart's subsequent words reveal otherwise: "[God] hath clothed my face with steel, and lined my forehead with brass. He hath put his testimony within me, and engraven his seal on my forehead. . . . [W]ith these weapons I have indeed set the fiends of earth and hell at defiance" (*MWS*, 67–68). Referring to Rev. 9:4, Stewart implies that although her words may originate beyond her, they are weapons that she uses against her enemies, potentially in a holy battle. The female prophet, then, can assume a powerful authority and can even take on the traditionally male role of warrior. It is notable that Stewart does not call explicitly for the violence that her mentor Walker predicts; her words focus on God's call to her rather than on her advocacy of others' militant action. This difference suggests a feature of African American women's jeremiadic rhetoric identified by David Howard-Pitney, who notes that expectations of what is appropriate for women often influence the jeremiadic rhetoric of African American female orators. Yet Stewart's militant imagery also challenges Howard-Pitney's claim that African American women rhetors often soften potentially harsh aspects of jeremiadic messages and cast them in a less confrontational form.[52] She may not be as direct in her call for divinely inspired violence as Walker, but she does not avoid conflict. Placing herself in a role that is fundamentally confrontational—and that, in its reference to warfare, is not traditionally feminine—she espouses a radical and militant vision.

In her jeremiadic rhetoric, Sojourner Truth also adopts the ethos of one who delivers God's message, using this seemingly self-denying position to assert her personal strength as a speaker. The *Narrative of Sojourner Truth* relates her words to a religious "camp-meeting": "*I am going to stay here and stand the fire,* like Shadrach, Meshach, and Abednego! And Jesus will walk with me through the fire, and keep me from harm." God's protection is not abstract for Truth. Drawing on the immediacy of African American Christianity, Christ is present with her, giving her a power transcending human considerations. Threatened at another religious gathering by a mob of "wild young men, with no motive but that of entertaining themselves by annoying and injuring the feelings of others," Truth bravely confronts them, miraculously calming the crowd and preaching to them. Olive Gilbert, the *Narrative*'s transcriber, relates, "It seemed to her to be given her at the time to answer them with truth and wisdom beyond herself."[53] The *Narrative* represents the preacher and abolitionist speaker Truth as a prophet whose authority comes from divine inspiration. Yet it is clear that this authority gives her a powerful earthly agency, allowing her to confront those who are skeptical and even potentially violent.

The balance in Stewart's and Truth's rhetoric between their submission to God's ultimate authority and their articulation of a vision of African American agency is reminiscent of the rhetoric of Walker and Frederick Douglass, who both set forth a radical vision of God's redemption of the oppressed and suggest the need for African American revolt. In this aspect of their prophetic rhetoric, they draw on the tensions within Christianity between submission to God's will and the militant empowerment of the oppressed to fight for freedom. Although Stewart does not call explicitly for violent action, she similarly draws on these competing forces within Christianity in her jeremiadic rhetoric. Speaking to the Afric-American Female Intelligence Society of America, Stewart remarks, "Were our blessed Lord and Saviour, Jesus Christ, upon the earth, I believe he would say of many that are called by his name, 'O, ye hypocrites, ye generation of vipers, how can you escape the damnation of hell [Matthew 23:33].' I have enlisted in the holy warfare, and Jesus is my captain; and the Lord's battle I mean to fight, until my voice expire in death. I expect to be hated of all men, and persecuted even unto death, for righteousness and the truth's sake" (*MWS,* 52).

Stewart features two references to the book of Matthew here that illustrate the tendencies within Christianity toward submission and revolution. She combines Jesus' harsh condemnation of the scribes and Pharisees—"Ye serpents, ye generation of vipers, how can you escape the damnation of hell?" (Matt. 23:33)—with both a reference to herself as a holy warrior and an allusion to the Beatitudes, which refers to those "persecuted for righteousness' sake" (Matt. 5:10). Like her male counterparts, Stewart draws on the paradoxical forces within Christianity to empower her rhetoric and give it multiple layers of significance.

The tensions within Christianity also inform the rhetoric of retribution of African American men, who both invoke God's punishment of white America and profess concern for their audiences' welfare. In this way, they introduce themes of vengeance and violence while seeming to remove their own motives from the punishments they describe. Nonetheless, as we have discovered, their professions of concern for their audience notwithstanding, they assume the authority through these predictions to articulate a radical vision of the future in which contemporary power relations are overturned through violent revolution. In the rhetoric of African American women such as Stewart and Truth, this duality is also present, although in a slightly different form. In particular, African American women abolitionists often overtly emphasize their compassion for their audiences and leave their suggestions of punishment implicit. In an 1832 piece for the *Liberator* entitled "Cause for Encouragement," for example, in which she praises Garrison's account of the Second Annual Convention of the People of Color in Philadelphia, Stewart apostrophizes, "O, ye southern slaveholders! We will no longer curse you for your wrongs; but we will implore the Almighty to soften your hard hearts towards our brethren, and to send them a speedy deliverance."[54] Explicitly calling neither for violence nor destruction, Stewart seems to profess forgiveness. Yet she, like Walker, invokes through the Old Testament phrase "hard hearts" the enslavement of the Israelites under Pharaoh and implies God's ultimate punishment for white America's sins against African Americans—a theme with potentially violent implications.

Similarly, in her speech at the Masonic Hall, Stewart invokes jeremiadic themes through an appeal to white listeners for assistance: "Let me entreat my white brethren to awake and save our sons from dissipation and our daughters from ruin. Lend the hand of assistance . . . so shall our curses upon you be turned into blessings; and though you should endeavor to drive us from these shores, still we will cling to you the more firmly" (*MWS*, 63). Stewart's supplicatory tone contrasts with Walker's more perfunctory declarations that he wishes white Americans no ill will—declarations that are, we will recall, followed by predictions of violent destruction. And, significantly, by referring to African Americans' "curses" on white America, Stewart undercuts her professions of compassion with an acknowledgment of the very real anger felt by African Americans toward the society that oppresses them. This sentiment, presumably, could lead to violence if their wrongs are not addressed. Stewart also obliquely condemns the colonization movement and suggests that African Americans will resist efforts to drive them from the country. In Stewart's vision, white America can be saved only by embracing African Americans and deserving their allegiance.

Like Stewart, Truth assumes an ostensibly forgiving and compassionate tone in her jeremiadic rhetoric that nonetheless invokes potentially violent themes. Speaking at an anti-slavery celebration in Framingham, Mass., Truth remarks, "The white people owed the colored race a big debt, and if they paid it all back, they wouldn't have any thing left for seed. (Laughter.) All they could do was to repent, and have the debt forgiven them. The colored people had labored and suffered for the white people . . . and why did they hate them? Even the blood of one man, Abel, did not call from the ground in vain."[55] Truth's message resonates on a variety of levels. She suggests that the "debt" whites owe African Americans is so large that they cannot repay it, yet she also evokes the endless forgiveness of Christianity, in which all debts can be erased. And her call for whites to repent is given a radical context through the biblical allusion to the blood of Abel. This reference is featured in Jesus' denunciation of the scribes and Pharisees, in which Christ predicts that they will be responsible for the blood of the prophets, beginning with Abel (Matt. 23:35, Luke 11:51). Featuring the language of Christ's harsh denunciation of the hypocrites of his society, Truth suggests that the sinners of her time are also guilty and deserve the wrath of a savior who exposes hypocrisy and vindicates the wrongs perpetrated against the oppressed. Significantly, Truth's biblical allusion is reminiscent of Stewart's evocation of Christ's words to the scribes and Pharisees in her speech to the Afric-American Female Intelligence Society of America. This biblical narrative, which reveals that the compassionate savior is nonetheless capable of wrath, draws on the militant potential inherent in Christ's teachings.

In an 1853 speech at the First Congregational Church in New York, Truth more explicitly evokes the potential for violent retribution as she professes forgiveness toward whites. Relating her feelings—past and present—about slaveholders, she suggests both Christian charity and apocalyptic warnings:

> She had learnt of Jesus and had become strengthened, and if they all had learned religion of Jesus and were of one mind, what would become of the slave-holder? How stood the case between them? . . .
>
> She used to say she wished God would kill all the white people. . . . Her mother had taught her to pray to make her master good, and she did so, but she was tied up and whipped till the blood trickled down her back, and she used to think if she was God she would have made them good, and if God were she, she would not allow it.
>
> . . . What could they say on the Day of Judgment in reply to the question "why do they hate us?" She did not wish unduly to ridicule the whites, but the blood and sweat and tears drawn from the black people were sufficient to cover the earth all over the United States. Still she desired to advocate their cause in a Christian spirit and in one of forgiveness, and had high hopes of their success.[56]

Truth's declarations are reminiscent of David Walker's assertions that he does not wish for the destruction that he foretells for white America. Truth is less aggressive than Walker, who explicitly predicts apocalyptic violence, but her reference to the Day of Judgment suggests an apocalyptic message of retribution that would evoke images of harsh punishment for her audience. Truth cleverly describes her past feelings about whites to refer to a violent punishment while seemingly disavowing it. In addition, her focus on her life story grounds her predictions of divine vengeance not in abstract theoretical principles, but in her actual experience of oppression. She is a prophet whose authority to call for radical change comes from both her status as a divine messenger and from her own personal history. Truth not only suggests the defining tension of Christianity, in which the victim becomes the victor; she embodies it. A former slave who assumes authority through her oppression, Truth reveals that that through Christianity "the humblest may stand forth"—in Frederick Douglass's words—with a particular prophetic authority.

In their jeremiadic rhetoric, African American female abolitionists also feature the topos marshaled by their male counterparts of African Americans as God's "chosen people" whose deliverance from oppression is central to America's redemption. Their rhetoric demonstrates the flexibility of this commonplace, which can be deployed in contexts that do not directly challenge white Americans as well as in more radical and even militant arguments. Sarah Douglass's remarks in her pseudonymous essays for the *Liberator* illustrate the less confrontational use of this theme. In "To a Friend," she remarks, "God is on our side. With the eye of faith, I pierce the veil of futurity . . . no wailing is heard, no clanking chains; but the voice of peace and love and joy is wafted to my ear by every breeze." In the short, contemplative 1832 essay "Moonlight," Douglass adopts more explicitly biblical language, placing African Americans in the scriptural role of the chosen people and suggesting God's eventual vindication of them. Douglass remarks that at moonlight, "Hope whispers,—'The time is not far distant, when the wronged and enslaved children of America shall cease to be a "by-word and a reproach" among their brethren.'"[57] In both of these examples, Douglass articulates a future vision of equality and freedom for African Americans, but she mentions neither the punishment of the oppressors nor the means by which this revolution will be effected. Her quote from "Moonlight," which describes the condition of African Americans in the language of Ps. 44:13–14, which laments the present condition of Israel and anticipates future deliverance, connects her people to the enslaved Israelites, a theme also marshaled by Walker in his *Appeal*. Unlike Walker, though, who refers to the Egyptians' punishment for their enslavement of God's chosen people, Douglass does not directly condemn the oppressors.

In an 1857 speech to the New York City Anti-Slavery Society, Frances Ellen Watkins similarly evokes the theme of God's chosen people—in her case, in New Testament language—to suggest the deliverance of African Americans without directly confronting white America. "God is on the side of freedom," Watkins declares, "and any cause that has God on its side, I care not how much it may be trampled upon, how much it may be trailed in the dust, is sure to triumph. The message of Jesus Christ is on the side of freedom, 'I come to preach deliverance to the captives, the opening of the prison doors to them that are bound.' The truest and noblest hearts in the land are on the side of freedom."[58] Watkins's jeremiadic theme of deliverance draws power from the immediacy of scriptural example inherent in African American Christianity and from the powerful language of Christ's terminology, which promises victory to the disenfranchised. Like Sarah Douglass, Watkins emphasizes the empowerment of the oppressed rather than the punishment of the oppressors. Yet we should not assume that merely because this rhetoric is less confrontational than that of male jeremiadic rhetors such as Walker, it is ineffectual. Just as Frederick Douglass's statement that "the humblest may stand forth" is an indirect yet forceful assertion of African Americans' particular influence, Sarah Douglass and Frances Ellen Watkins suggest that African Americans can assume a divinely sanctioned authority.

Nor should we assume that because Sarah Douglass and Watkins do not directly criticize white America in their jeremiadic rhetoric, African American women all eschew radical or militant formulations of the "chosen people" theme. Stewart and Truth, in fact, employ the topos of God's chosen people to directly condemn white Americans and to call for their divinely ordained punishment. In their jeremiadic arguments—which are neither indirect, forgiving, nor mild—these African American female abolitionists are as vehement as their male counterparts. In *Religion and the Pure Principles of Morality,* Stewart predicts divine retribution in harsh tones reminiscent of her mentor Walker:

> Oh, America, America, foul and indelible is thy stain! Dark and dismal is the cloud that hangs over thee, for thy cruel wrongs and injuries to the fallen sons of Africa. The blood of her murdered ones cries to heaven for vengeance against thee. . . .
>
> O, ye great and mighty men of America, ye rich and powerful ones, many of you will call for the rocks and mountains to fall upon you, and to hide you from the wrath of the Lamb [Revelation 6:16], and from him that sitteth upon the throne; whilst many of the sable-skinned Africans you now despise will shine in the kingdom of heaven. . . . [O]ur cry shall come up before the throne of God. . . . Vengeance is [God's], and he will repay. (*R,* 39–40)

Quoting Rev. 6:15–16—"the great men, and the rich men . . . and the mighty men . . . said to the mountains and rocks, Fall on us, and hide us from the face of him that sitteth on the throne, and from the wrath of the Lamb"—Stewart militantly asserts that America must end slavery or face dire consequences.

When Truth deploys the jeremiadic topos of God's justice for his "chosen people," she, too, does not mince words. In her speech to the antislavery gathering in Framingham, she directly invokes God's eventual vindication of African

Americans—and, through the language of Revelation, evokes the apocalyptic punishment of the oppressors. A reporter for the *Liberator* conveys her message: "The promises of Scripture were all for the black people, and God would recompense them for all their sufferings in this world. One day they would meet the poor slave in heaven, 'his robes washed white in the blood of the lamb,' coming 'through much tribulation,' ('you know who that means,' said Sojourner; 'it don't mean you; white folks don't suffer tribulation; it means the black people, and those friends who have suffered with them,') to peace and joy in the kingdom."[59] Truth's citation of Revelation—in particular, the prophecy that those who "came out of great tribulation" will have robes washed "white in the blood of the Lamb" (7:14)—warns that God's ultimate and violent justice awaits those who do not try to end slavery. Both Truth's and Stewart's references to Revelation, like those of Walker and Frederick Douglass, suggest the unique potential of apocalyptic biblical language in the African American jeremiad, which empowers rhetors—even women, presumably expected to appear non-aggressive—to feature militant themes.

"TRUE BORN AMERICANS"

As we have seen, African American male abolitionists often feature the language and topoi of the American Revolution in antislavery rhetoric that is, in Gary Woodward's terms, "advisory," highlighting dissent and confrontation between rhetor and audience, "challeng[ing] conventional attitudes," and often shocking audiences by boldly revealing their hypocrisy. African American female abolitionists similarly marshal language and topoi that invoke the American Revolution to condemn slavery and the country's failure to live up to its promise. Due to conventions of antebellum femininity, though, their rhetoric conforms more readily to the approach Woodward calls "adaptory," which emphasizes the shared beliefs of audience and rhetor and avoids direct conflict with the audience.[60] In their adaptory arguments, African American women abolitionists focus on the qualities that connect them to the country rather than emphasizing the exclusion from American society that is a central theme of the rhetoric of their male counterparts. Like their male colleagues, they compare African Americans' desire for liberty to the sentiments of the heroes of the American Revolution. Yet in contrast to their male colleagues' confrontational use of this theme, they frequently encourage their audiences to identify with them and to grant them credibility based on a patriotic common bond.

Yet even in their adaptory rhetoric, African American women abolitionists implicitly suggest the more radical advisory antislavery arguments made by their male counterparts. While overtly emphasizing connection, African American women insinuate that Americans are hypocritical if they allow slavery to persist in a land ostensibly devoted to freedom—and even subtly suggest the militant argument that African Americans may revolt against tyranny as the Americans did against the British. Indirectly, then, their seemingly accommodating adaptory rhetoric poses challenges as militant as those of their male colleagues. In addition, their suggestion of radical themes within forms that are overtly advisory demonstrates that the advisory and adaptory traditions can be seen as opposite ends of a continuum. Discourse does not necessarily fit completely into one or the other category, and thus although it is useful to draw on these two categories to highlight broad features of persuasive texts, we also should view them as interrelated. The adaptory rhetoric of African American women, in particular, reveals that rhetoric can overtly conform to an ostensibly conciliatory model while implicitly or indirectly incorporating confrontational strategies.

Stewart's Franklin Hall speech demonstrates the way in which a patriotic and sympathetic ethos can suggest militant arguments. Discussing the racism that prevents African Americans from pursuing all but menial careers, Stewart defends her boldness: "I can but die for expressing my sentiments: and I am as willing to die by the sword as the pestilence; for I am a true born American; your blood flows in my veins, and your spirit fires my breast" (*MWS,* 46). Similarly, addressing the claim of a colonizationist text that African Americans were "a ragged set, crying for liberty," Stewart appeals to the inspiration of American values: "I reply to it, the whites have so long and so loudly proclaimed the theme of equal rights and privileges, that our souls have caught the flame also, ragged as we are" (*MWS,* 47). As a woman, Stewart chooses not to directly advocate militant resistance to oppression. Yet appealing to connection with her audience based on her American identity, Stewart implicitly justifies militant—even violent— action. As "true born Americans" inspired with the spirit of liberty, African Americans will not be submissive when their rights are denied; they are willing even to die to gain freedom. She turns the charge that African Americans are a "ragged set, crying for liberty" into a comparison with white Americans, implicitly suggesting the insurgent status of the patriots that rebelled against England. Thus she implies that American history and America's bold rhetoric of equality inspire African Americans to fight for freedom, even to take potentially violent action. Like her male counterparts, she evokes America's own founding mythology of revolution and resistance to empower African Americans.

Stewart also explicitly compares the situation of contemporary African Americans with that of the Founding Fathers. In contrast to her male counterparts, however, she ostensibly directs her criticism toward African Americans rather than toward white society. In part, this strategy can be attributed to the fact that many among her audience were African American. Her call to them to adopt what she calls a "spirit of virtuous emulation" of the leaders of the American Revolution empowers them to take action against oppression and to assert their rights in American society. In addition, her tactic of addressing African Americans rather than confronting white America directly allows her to suggest militant themes while seemingly avoiding overt confrontation with American society. She asks,

> Did the pilgrims, when they first landed on these shores, quietly compose
> themselves and say, "The Britons have all the money and all the power,

and we must continue their servants forever?" Did they sluggishly sigh and say, "Our lot is hard, the Indians own the soil, and we cannot cultivate it?" No; they first made powerful efforts to raise themselves, and then God raised up those illustrious patriots, WASHINGTON and LAFAYETTE, to assist and defend them. And, my brethren, have you made a powerful effort? Have you prayed the legislature for mercy's sake to grant you all the rights and privileges of free citizens, that your daughters may rise to that degree of respectability which true merit deserves, and your sons above the servile situations which most of them fill? (*MWS*, 49)

Rather than explicitly criticize white society's oppression of African Americans, Stewart appeals to her audience to strive to follow the lead of America's Founding Fathers. Yet although this strategy allows her to avoid directly criticizing white America, her underlying message has militant implications—particularly for the African American members of her audience. Following the precedent of the American Revolution, Stewart suggests, leads one to fight those who have "all the power" and make a "powerful effort" to gain civil rights. Endorsing white society's history and values allows her to promote the African American fight for freedom and equality, a struggle that will involve bold action.

Although she affirms white America's ideals, Stewart implies the hypocrisy of a nation founded on liberty that enslaves African Americans. Yet she adopts a more indirect approach than her male colleagues who articulate this theme. In *Religion and the Pure Principles of Morality*, Stewart couches her potentially militant argument in what appears to be commentary on the plight of African American men:

Did every gentleman in America realize, as one, that they had got to become bondmen, and their wives, their sons, and their daughters, servants forever, to Great Britain, their very joints would become loosened, and tremblingly would smite one against another; their countenance would be filled with horror, every nerve and muscle would be forced into action, their souls would recoil at the very thought, their hearts would die within them, and death would be far more preferable. Then why have not Afric's sons the right to feel the same? Are not their wives, their sons, and their daughters, as dear to them as those of the white man's? (*R*, 38–39)

On the surface, Stewart's comparison appeals to connection with white Americans, who should be sympathetic to the effects of slavery on "Afric's sons." Her commentary frames the ideals of the American Revolution in terms of the obligation of men to their families, allowing her to exhort her audience as an antebellum woman focused on domestic relations. Yet Stewart's message has militant undertones. Invoking the revolt of Americans against British oppression, she reaches beyond domestic concerns to suggest precedent for violent resistance. In fact, her domestic argument becomes a call to arms—the oppression of their families demands that African American men take action.

Stewart's use of the term "Afric's sons" is notable. African American abolitionists may emphasize their status as Americans and may draw on ideals and
mythology associated with America's history, but they also suggest the influence
of their African heritage on their struggle for their rights. Stewart implies that
the tradition of rising from oppression is not just an American phenomenon.
Although she speaks as a "true born American" due all the rights of an American citizen, she also emphasizes her African heritage, appealing throughout her
speeches to "the sons and daughters of Africa." In many of her speeches and
writings, Stewart refers to the prediction of Ps. 68: 31, "Ethiopia shall soon
stretch out her hands unto God," to empower African Americans to act. In her
Franklin Hall address, for example, this prediction provides ultimate hope in the
face of injustice and prejudice: "It is true, that the free people of color throughout these United States are neither bought nor sold, nor under the lash of the
cruel driver; many obtain a comfortable support; but few, if any, have an opportunity of becoming rich and independent. . . . As servants, we are respected; but
let us presume to aspire any higher, our employer regards us no longer. And
were it not that the King eternal has declared that Ethiopia shall stretch forth her
hands unto God, I should indeed despair" (*MWS*, 47). Not just Americans, but
many peoples can claim the power of revolution, Stewart emphasizes. In her
speech to the Afric-American Female Intelligence Society, for example, she
describes the revolutionary actions of the Greeks, the French, the Poles, and—
significantly, in light of her emphasis on African heritage—the Haitians (*MWS*,
53–54). Direct resistance to oppression links African Americans to other Americans but it also transcends their status as Americans, connecting them to the traditions of other nations and to their African heritage.[61]

In *Incidents in the Life of a Slave Girl*, Harriet Jacobs features the tradition of
revolution through exclusively American images. Yet she, too, asserts the right
of African Americans to take potentially militant action against oppression.
Jacobs connects her personal experience fighting her enslavement to the situation
of the Founding Fathers. While she is in hiding, awaiting the chance to escape,
Dr. Flint threatens her relatives in order to force her to return; and, she relates,
"despairing of [her] having a chance to escape, they advised [her] to return to
[her] master" (*ILSG*, 99). But Jacobs could not be persuaded to return to the tor-
ment she endured at the hands of her oppressor. She describes her determination
to gain her freedom: "When I started upon this hazardous undertaking, I had
resolved that, come what would, there should be no turning back. 'Give me liberty, or give me death,' was my motto" (*ILSG*, 99). Jacob's reference to Patrick
Henry's famous words implicitly connects her cause and her tenacity to those of
the Founding Fathers, creating a fundamentally American ethos that appeals to
her audience to understand her plight and her decision to run away. More generally, though, Jacobs implies that fundamental American principles underlie
slaves' resistance to their oppression—even if that resistance leads to violence or
death. As does Stewart, Jacobs suggests that the example of the Founding Fathers

does not resonate merely for white Americans or for men. African American women, as "true born Americans," also inherit this tradition, a tradition they appropriate in their antislavery rhetoric.

In her 1859 speech in Warrington, Sarah Remond features similar language to generalize Jacobs's claim about her own right to escape oppression. She asserts, "'Liberty or death' [is] the motto of the American slave; and there were from 30,000 to 40,000 who had escaped into Canada in spite of the overwhelming obstacles that presented themselves."[62] As in Jacobs's narrative, the language of the American Revolution does not just arouse antislavery indignation but also sanctions physical action against slavery. Through Patrick Henry's aphorism—separated from its author and placed into a new context that empowers slaves—Remond, like Jacobs, suggests that the American tradition of rising up against oppression sanctions slaves' attempts to escape as well as potentially violent resistance to slavery.

Remond also refers to America's founding texts—particularly the Declaration of Independence—in this speech, contending that white America's professions of freedom and equality ring hollow in light of their oppression of both free African Americans and slaves. She remarks that "the American people, beyond all others, were making greater professions of liberty than any other nation" and offering on "any 4th of July" speeches and references to the Declaration of Independence, while at the same time in the country there is "an iron despotism crushing out the intellect, aye, the very souls of men and women." Yet even as she condemns white America for its hypocrisy concerning the Declaration of Independence, she suggests that this text is a powerful weapon against injustice. She invokes and recontextualizes the language of the Declaration, separating its words from contextual factors that would limit its application to exclude those of African descent. This document, Remond argues, articulates God-given truths that not only all Americans but all human beings are bound to honor: "That God gave the right of liberty, and the right to pursue happiness as they listed, no one before her would question—nor that a right so sacred no one could take from another without infringing the higher law of God; therefore, they believed that every man and woman who dared to take from another a right so sacred, was a usurper of freedom, and should receive the indignation of every honest heart, and that the moral feeling of mankind should be arrayed against the sinner and the sin."[63] In Remond's argument, like in those of her male colleagues, the power of the Declaration does not belong solely to white America. It transcends any context that might limit it to assume the status of universal truth, and thus the oppressed can harness its influence to condemn American slavery. Like David Walker, Remond exposes the inconsistencies between America's language and the oppression within American society. And she, like Walker, reveals strikingly that America's language does not resonate for white America alone.

Remond's condemnation of white Americans for their hypocrisy suggests that, in some cases, African American female abolitionists, like their male colleagues, feature rhetoric that is more advisory than adaptory when they appropriate the themes and language of the American Revolution. It is true that because that Remond's primary audience for the speech is British, she does not confront Americans directly. Yet the text of her speech, which was reported in the *Liberator,* reached an American audience; and it seems likely that Remond would expect Americans to read an account of her speech, since antebellum editors regularly reprinted articles and accounts of speeches from both foreign and domestic papers. Remond does, then, challenge white American forcefully although somewhat indirectly. Indeed, as we have seen in the rhetoric of African American male abolitionists, indirection need not compromise a rhetor's power. In terms of the continuum of rhetoric that ranges from adaptory to advisory, then, Remond's confrontation of white America favors the latter model.

In her 1857 speech to the New York City Anti-Slavery Society, Frances Ellen Watkins creates even more explicitly advisory arguments about America's founding, featuring America's history and principles while directly chastising American oppression of African Americans. Watkins aggressively marshals topoi associated with the American Revolution to expose American hypocrisy. As did her cousin William J. Watkins three years earlier in his editorial "Who are the Murderers?" she features the case of escaped slave Anthony Burns, invoking the imagery of the American Revolution ironically to condemn American oppression in general and the Fugitive Slave Law in particular:

> A few months since a man escaped from bondage and found a temporary shelter almost beneath the shadow of Bunker Hill. Had that man stood upon the deck of an Austrian ship . . . he would have found protection. Had he been wrecked upon an island or colony of Great Britain, the waves of the tempest-lashed ocean would have washed him deliverance. . . . But from Boston harbour, made memorable by the infusion of three-penny taxed tea, Boston in its proximity to the plains of Lexington and Concord, Boston almost beneath the shadow of Bunker Hill and almost in sight of Plymouth Rock, he is thrust back from liberty and manhood and reconverted into a chattel. . . . Ye [southern] bloodhounds, go back to your kennels . . . when [the fugitive's] stealthy tread is heard in the place where the bones of the revolutionary sires repose, the ready North is base enough to do your shameful service.[64]

Watkins's juxtaposition of the sites of the American Revolution with the plight of the fugitive who hides nearby condemns America's inconsistency. But her irony goes further. The American Revolution is not the glorious harbinger of liberty of traditional American rhetoric; it is a sham. Her description of the events of Boston Harbor—a conflict over "three-penny taxed tea"—undermines traditional epideictic rhetoric of America's founding, recasting it in terms that expose America's shallow commitment to liberty. In contrast to William J. Watkins's use of precedent from the American Revolution to justify abolitionists' resistance to Burns's capture, she offers no explicit call for violence. Yet her withering scorn for America's professed mission as a nation founded on liberty establishes an argument every bit as confrontational as her cousin's, challenging Americans to examine America's patriotic rhetoric in light of slavery's influence in both the South and the North.

THE FEMALE TRICKSTER

Frances Ellen Watkins's ironic revision of the story of Boston Harbor is a form of signifying, appropriating and recreating a seminal narrative of America's historical mythology in a way that collapses its authority. As we have seen, African American female rhetors marshal various strategies related to signifying—irony, indirection, a dual language that explicitly suggests one meaning while encoding an alternate implicit meaning, and appropriation and revision of white America's texts. Claudia Mitchell-Kernan asserts that although signifying is employed by women as well as men, highly aggressive forms of signifying are difficult for women to deploy "because other social norms require more circumspection in their verbal behavior."[65] Yet, in some cases, women may need to call on the subversive use of language more readily than their male counterparts, particularly as a form of resistance in situations in which men could employ physical force. Compare, for example, the experiences of Frederick Douglass and Harriet Jacobs as related in their autobiographical writing. Douglass wins his battle with the slave-breaker Covey by physically subduing his oppressor (*N*, 64–65); Jacobs resists Dr. Flint through a series of verbal acts involving both overt opposition and covert manipulation of language. From her hiding place in her grandmother's attic, Jacobs tricks Flint through cleverly constructed letters into believing that she is in the North, sending him on fruitless searches as she watches from her "peeping-hole" (*ILSG*, 116, 128–32). Jacobs's strategies—which recall the linguistic manipulation of the trickster figure of African American folklore—demonstrate that the language of the dominant group can be exploited by women as well as men, revising its meaning to reverse or undermine the dominant group's power.[66] Writing to Dr. Flint from her hiding place, Jacobs uses information from the *New York Herald,* a newspaper devoted to upholding societal institutions such as slavery, in order to appear to be in the North. Jacobs comments on her appropriation of this text of the dominant group: "For once, the paper that systematically abuses the colored people, was made to render them a service" (*ILSG*, 128). Verbal trickery, Jacobs's narrative suggests, can be a powerful and often necessary resource for the African American woman.

We will recall that Jacobs marshals an ironic tone in her 1853 letter to the editor of the *New-York Daily Tribune,* published anonymously and signed "A Fugitive Slave," which responds to Julia Tyler's letter "To the Duchess of Sutherland and the Ladies of England" defending slavery. Like Frederick Douglass's tone in his letter to his former master Auld, Jacobs adopts a tone of exaggerated politeness toward Tyler. Jacobs responds to Tyler's omission of any details of slavery in her letter by ironically suggesting that she can be helpful to Tyler, educating her through the personal experiences of a former slave. Jacobs's comment that she "became very much interested" in the conversation initiated by Tyler's letter has an ironic dual meaning. The word "interested" suggests explicitly that she finds the discussion engaging, yet its alternate meaning—that she is personally connected to the topic—implies that she is particularly authorized to address this subject. Underscoring this latter meaning, she remarks, "Being a slave myself, I could not have felt otherwise."[67] Jacobs's elucidation of women's particular experiences in her letter is an inherently ironic act. She ironically suggests that Tyler's omission of specifics is the result of a lack of information, yet it is clear that Tyler's motives are in fact more sinister. Ignoring details, Tyler avoids the very real consequences of her proslavery argument on the lives of those who are enslaved. But Jacobs does not allow Tyler to maintain this strategic ignorance; confronting her (and other white Americans) with the details of slavery, she forces them to acknowledge the particulars that they wish to neglect. Her exaggerated tone of goodwill toward Tyler and her "helpful" ethos ironically highlight the precariousness of Tyler's vague defenses of slavery. White America may try to erase the details of slavery, but African American rhetors will not allow them to do so.

Relying on her personal experience, Jacobs also signifies on the stereotypical notion that African Americans are not capable of abstract reasoning. At the outset, she claims that she does not offer argument, only the "truth," her personal observations on the effect of slavery on women. Playing on the assumption that those of African descent are only capable of narration, she defends her credibility: "You will not say that it is fiction, for had I the inclination I have neither the brain or talent to write it."[68] Her ostensible narration, though, implicitly encodes the arguments that she claims she will not make. Relating the experiences of female slaves, she indirectly but strongly indicts Tyler for her comments both on slavery and on women's role in abolition. Describing the effects of slavery on women who are seduced, forced to bear their masters' children, and sold, Jacobs implicitly condemns Tyler for her cold-hearted disregard for enslaved women.

Jacobs also uses linguistic manipulation and appropriation to present antislavery arguments in *Incidents in the Life of a Slave Girl*. In the chapter "The Church and Slavery," Jacobs describes the desire of her uncle Fred to learn to read because he could "serve God better if he could only read the Bible" (*ILSG*, 72). She remarks, "There are thousands, who, like good uncle Fred, are thirsting for the water of life; but the law forbids it, and the churches withhold it. They send the Bible to heathen abroad, and neglect the heathen at home" (*ILSG*, 73). Jacobs's deployment of the term "heathen" would have specific antebellum connotations. The "heathen" nature of Africans was often offered in defense of the system of slavery, which, advocates argued, exposed them to the Christian religion.[69] Jacobs, however, reverses this usual meaning: "I am glad that missionaries go out to the dark corners of the earth; but I ask them not to overlook the dark corners at home. Talk to American slaveholders as you talk to savages in Africa.

Tell *them* it is wrong to traffic in men. Tell them it is sinful to sell their own children. . . . Tell them they are answerable to God for sealing up the Fountain of Life from souls that are thirsting for it" (*ILSG,* 73). Appropriating the terms of the dominant group, Jacobs alters their usual connotations, ironically demonstrating that the true "heathens" are unchristian "American slaveholders." Furthermore, her remarks discredit the proslavery argument that slaveholders bring religion to their slaves, revealing that they keep their slaves from a true knowledge of Christianity.

Like her male counterparts, who appropriate, parody, and revise various influential texts of white America, Jacobs also signifies on a key text of the dominant culture, the 1857 decision of Chief Justice Roger Taney in the Dred Scott case. A particular passage of Taney's opinion came to epitomize the case and its ominous implications: "[Those of African descent] had for more than a century before been regarded as . . . so far inferior that they had no rights which the white man was bound to respect." In her narrative, Jacobs appropriates Taney's words while discussing her opposition to paying for her freedom after she has escaped to the North: "It seemed not only hard, but unjust, to pay for myself. I could not possibly regard myself as a piece of property. . . . I knew the law would decide that I was [Dr. Flint's] property . . . but I regarded such laws as the regulations of robbers, who *had no rights that I was bound to respect*" (*ILSG,* 187; emphasis added). Appropriating Taney's key words in a context that inverts their meaning, Jacobs undermines Taney's authority and the system that regards her as "property." Reversing their cultural roles, Jacobs tries Taney, finding against him and the legal system he represents. The words of the chief justice, Jacobs suggests, may foster injustice, but they can also be appropriated by—and can empower—the ex-slave.

Although scholars note Sojourner Truth's use of humor and sarcasm in her oratory,[70] her wit cannot be fully understood without reference to the strategies of signifying, through which she appropriates her society's terms to undermine dominant perceptions of African American women and to establish new interpretations of antebellum ideals and texts. Her ironic challenges to the Cult of True Womanhood and her appropriation and reinterpretation of biblical texts illustrate how her wit and humor are informed by the power of signifying. Truth also marshals the trope of signifying to offer statements with ironic double meanings. In her Akron speech, Truth features a practical analogy to argue that women should be allowed to fulfill their potential:

> All she could say was, that if she had a pint of intellect and man a quart, what reason was there why she should not have her pint *full.* [Roars of laughter.] (*Tribune* version)

> As for intellect, all I can say is, if woman have a pint and man a quart—why can't she have her little pint full? You need not be afraid to give us

our rights for fear we will take too much, for we can't take more than our
pint'll hold. (*Bugle* version)

——◆◆◆——

"Den dey talks 'bout dis ting in de head. What dis dey call it?" "Intellect,"
whispered some one near. "Dat's it, honey. What's dat got to do with
woman's rights or niggers' rights? If my cup won't hold but a pint and
yourn holds a quart, wouldn't ye be mean not to let me have my little half-
measure full?" (*National Anti-Slavery Standard* version [Gage])

In this passage, Karlyn Kohrs Campbell remarks, Truth seemingly avoids the question of "women's mental capacity to affirm the right to equality of opportunity."[71]
Campbell's interpretation accounts for Truth's surface meaning, yet Truth implicitly and ironically engages the issue of women's intellectual power. Ostensibly
assuming women's inferiority, Truth assumes an agency that belies this stereotype.
Instead of pleading with men to grant her condescension, she demands it without
humility, reversing the traditional roles of the inferior female and the superior male.
Furthermore, her ironic request to men implicitly reveals the inherent contradictions in the stereotype of the mentally inferior woman. In all three accounts, Truth
uses a hypothetical construction that challenges her audience to examine why, if
women are inferior, men should worry that they will develop their lesser intellectual
powers. Truth implies that *if* women were truly men's intellectual subordinates,
men would not demonstrate the alarm that arises over women's rights, suggesting
that male anxiety is actually based on a sense that women are *not* inferior. The *Bugle*
account particularly underscores this interpretation, revealing male insecurity
through an explicit reference to men's fear.

As we have seen, signifying is a complex rhetorical strategy that places
African American rhetoric and white American discourse in a dialectical relationship. Reigning notions of authority, agency, power, and ownership of language are problematized as African American rhetors appropriate and revise
traditional language, reverse conventional assumptions to undermine white
hegemony, and engage in dialogue with white discourse. On a larger scale, these
features of signifying epitomize the power the rhetoric of African American
female abolitionists as well as their African American male and white female
colleagues. As they speak and write, they do more than claim the potential of
language to grant agency to the oppressed and insert new voices, experiences,
and perspectives into American discourse. They also significantly *transform* that
discourse, infusing it with new meanings and fashioning it into a tool of resistance to oppression. This capacity of rhetoric is the empowering converse to Frederick Douglass's statement that "there comes no *voice* from the enslaved" (*FDP,*
2:259). As Douglass asserts in an 1891 speech in Washington, D.C., "It is often
asked . . . what have such men as Garnet, Ward, Remond and others done for the
colored race? . . . They have only talked; but talk is itself a power" (*FDP,* 5:476).

Over a century later, the words of bell hooks similarly underscore the transformatory power inherent in language: "In the mouths of black Africans in the so-called 'New World,' English was altered, transformed, and became a different speech. Enslaved black people . . . put together their words in such a way that the colonizer had to rethink the meaning of English language. . . . Using English in a way that ruptured standard usage and meaning . . . made English into more than the oppressor's language."[72]

6

Rhetoric and Empowerment
The Marginalized Abolitionists and Beyond

The discourse of the marginalized abolitionists reveals vividly the relationships between slavery and silence, freedom and rhetoric. Although slavery was abolished with the Emancipation Proclamation, its legacy has persisted in institutionalized racism, denial of civil rights, and injustice. At the end of the nineteenth century, the ongoing connection between oppression and silence—the fact that, in Frederick Douglass's words, "there comes no *voice* from the enslaved" (*FDP*, 2:259)—was frighteningly illustrated by the suppression of discussion about the horrors of lynching. As Ida B. Wells comments in her 1893 speech "Lynch Law in All Its Phases," the white press remained silent on the subject and there was no public discussion of the widespread crime. When periodicals such as the *Memphis Free Speech,* of which Wells was half owner, attempted to publicize these atrocities, opponents responded with violence, destroying the newspaper's offices. But Wells understood that her antilynching rhetoric was necessary to effect change. As long as "those who commit the murders write the reports," she remarks, there could be "no adequate demand for justice." Extending the implications of Samuel Cornish and John Russwurm's statement in the first issue of *Freedom's Journal* that they "wish to plead [their] own cause," Wells suggests that if African Americans allow others to speak for them, the result will be not only the misrepresentations identified by Cornish and Russwurm but violence and murder. Defending her antilynching editorial—which became the "excuse" for the mob that destroyed the *Memphis Free Speech*'s offices—she asserts, "I could no longer hold my peace, and I feel, yes, I am sure, that if it had to be done over again . . . I would do and say the very same again."[1]

Many changes have taken place in American society in the century since Wells courageously fought lynching. Yet African Americans continue to face oppression, and the associations between silence and slavery, rhetoric and freedom continue to resonate for those who are marginalized. In a paper delivered at the 1977 Modern Language Association conference, Audre Lorde discusses silence, speech, and empowerment in the context of her experiences with the threat of breast cancer:

> In becoming forcibly and essentially aware of my mortality . . . what I most regretted were my silences. . . . To question or to speak as I believed

could have meant pain, or death. But we all hurt in so many different ways. . . . Death, on the other hand, is the final silence. . . . And I began to recognize a source of power within myself. . . .

I was going to die, if not sooner than later, whether or not I had ever spoken myself. My silences had not protected me. Your silence will not protect you. But for every real word spoken . . . I had made contact with other women . . . bridging our differences. . . .

Each of us is here now because in one way or another we share a commitment to language and to the power of language, and to the reclaiming of that language which has been made to work against us.[2]

These remarks demonstrate that the challenges facing the marginalized abolitionists continue to be relevant, particularly for African American activists and rhetors such as Lorde. Like their abolitionist predecessors, these contemporary rhetors realize that they must not allow themselves to be silenced. At the same time, they need to find ways to assume agency through rhetoric, to, in Lorde's terms, "reclaim" the language that "has been made to work against" them.

For Frederick Douglass, Wells, Lorde, and other African American rhetors whose work spans the period from the mid nineteenth to the late twentieth centuries, rhetoric is fundamental to the struggle for freedom. As we have found, marginalized abolitionists adopt a variety of discursive tools, drawing on traditional rhetorical approaches, revising conventional persuasive categories, and developing alternative strategies. The influence of their rhetoric reaches beyond the antebellum period, creating a legacy that activists of later eras extend. The flexible, empowering rhetorical strategies of rhetors such as Frederick Douglass, Charles Remond, Maria Stewart, and Sojourner Truth continue to be effective as they evolve in response to the changes of society. In four influential speeches of different eras—Wells's "Lynch Law in All Its Phases"; Archibald Grimké's "The Shame of America, or the Negro's Case Against the Republic," first delivered in 1919 before the American Negro Academy; Malcolm X's 1964 speech "The Ballot or the Bullet"; and Audre Lorde's 1979 "The Master's Tools Will Never Dismantle the Master's House," a paper delivered at the Second Sex Conference in New York—we can discover the legacy of the marginalized abolitionists, the continuing relationship between rhetoric and freedom, and the power of discourse for those who are oppressed in American society.

SELF-HELP DISCOURSE: CONTINUITY AND CHANGE

The self-help rhetoric of African American male and female abolitionists demonstrates that this discourse need not be individualistic or conciliatory. In fact, African American abolitionists often marshal this genre to argue forcefully against racism and for radical and even militant societal change. African American discourse of other periods also engages the theme of self-help; yet societal change may alter a rhetor's approach. The empowering implications of education identified by David Walker or the solidarity among African Americans evoked by Maria Stewart's self-help persuasion, for example, may seem, during certain periods, to be useless or impracticable means for advancing the race.

The extreme climate of violence in the South during the 1890s, for example, led Ida B. Wells to question the effectiveness of self-help. In "Lynch Law," she explains the transformation in her perspective from support to rejection of self-help as a form of struggle against oppression. She notes that she, too, had once "believed the condition of the masses gave large excuse for the humiliations and proscriptions under which [African Americans] labored; that when wealth, education and character became more general among [them], the cause being removed the effect would cease, and justice be accorded to all alike." Because of this belief, she supported the cause of self-help in her activism: "Wherever I went among the people, I gave them . . . my honest conviction that maintenance of character, money getting and education would finally solve our problem." In her home of Memphis, she relates, this approach seemed to be a success; African Americans lived in "nice homes" and supported one another's businesses. Yet when three African American men who owned and ran the "People's Grocery," a prosperous business in an African American section of town, were lynched, "there was a rude awakening." Not only would self-help not protect African Americans, but prosperity could in fact lead to violence. Wells remarks, "It was our first object lesson in the doctrine of white supremacy; an illustration of the South's cardinal principle that no matter what the attainments, character or standing of an Afro-American, the laws of the South will not protect him against a white man."[3]

Wells, then, rejects her abolitionist forebears' focus on self-help as a form of activism. It is important to note, though, that elements of her critique of white society are connected to the self-help discourse of abolitionists such as William Whipper and Charles Lenox Remond. Whipper, as we have seen, acknowledges that white prejudice will not end because of African Americans' moral uplift and that, in fact, "the man of color in this country" who is "a truly noble being" is given neither respect nor equal rights in American society. We will recall also that Whipper, Alfred Niger, and Augustus Price's outline of the goals of the AMRS proposes that it is hypocritical for Americans to ask African Americans to elevate themselves while society continues to hold them down.[4] African American abolitionists may have felt that self-help had an important role to play in the struggle against oppression, but they did not assume that it was an easy remedy for prejudice or that it should substitute for agitation to change laws. Wells's rejection of self-help is not necessarily an abandonment of the principles of her abolitionist forebears; alternatively, it can be seen as a practical approach in response to extreme circumstances. In light of the ever-present threat of lynching, African Americans could not afford to emphasize measures such as thrift, economy, and education as the sole means of achieving equality—nor could they ignore violent incidents in which whites murdered those who elevated themselves.

Without laws to prevent lynching, the African American community could not achieve equality, with or without self-help.

In addition, Wells's rejection of self-help should be viewed in the context of the rhetoric of contemporary spokesmen such as Booker T. Washington. Washington's well-publicized accommodationist message, which rejected the struggle for political rights, was seen by many—as it frequently is today—as the epitome of self-help discourse. Because rhetoric such as Washington's suggested a polarization between self-help and political rights, rhetors like Wells, who argued for political change, would naturally distance themselves from self-help messages.[5]

Although Wells reaches a different conclusion about self-help than her predecessor Sarah Douglass, there is also an important similarity between the two women's perspectives on moral uplift. Douglass emphasizes her own experience as the force that impels her to endorse self-help; the danger to free African Americans in the North convinces her that she must work for the elevation of the race.[6] Wells, too, features the events in her home of Memphis to vivify the transformation in her view of self-help, similarly drawing on the interplay of thought and experience that is an important component of the rhetoric of African American women. Wells's and Douglass's reactions to the threats of violence in their immediate communities differ, but each reveals that her life experiences and her perspectives on self-help are fundamentally interconnected.

Whereas Wells focused on altering the laws of her society, Malcolm X argued that trying to change white society was not the answer to African Americans' oppression. His agenda of black nationalism proposed that African Americans needed to be independent from whites and to take control of their own communities. This perspective is reminiscent of the view of many African American abolitionists who by the 1840s and 1850s felt that they needed to reject the leadership of white reformers and to pursue community-oriented activism. Just as a focus on moral elevation was part of the drive for independence among African American abolitionists, Malcolm X's definition of black nationalism in his famous speech "The Ballot or the Bullet" is replete with self-help themes. "The social philosophy of black nationalism," he asserts, "only means that we have to get together and remove the evils, the vices, alcoholism, drug addiction, and other evils that are destroying the moral fiber of our community. We ourselves have to lift the level of our community . . . to a higher level." Like his militant abolitionist forebear Walker, Malcolm X stresses that the goal of moral uplift is not to emulate white America, to adopt its values, or to convince whites that African Americans deserve equality. In fact, he specifically rejects such attempts at accommodation: "Don't change the white man's mind; you can't change his mind. And that whole thing about appealing to the moral conscience of America—America's conscience is bankrupt. . . . We've got to change our own minds about each other. . . . We have to come together with warmth so we can develop unity and harmony."[7] Malcolm X's use of the rhetoric of self-help in a militant speech demonstrates the enduring radical potential of the rhetoric of moral reform.

Although rhetors like Wells may reject messages of moral reform, believing that it is useless under certain circumstances, Malcolm X's rhetoric reveals that this form remains relevant to the struggle against oppression.

The crucial role of self-help rhetoric in African American activism of different eras also helps counter a common perception about contemporary discourse. The American public, Cornel West notes, frequently associates African American self-help rhetoric with the discourse of conservatives such as Shelby Steele or Stanley Crouch. Americans often believe, then, that African American proponents of self-help necessarily advocate the elimination of affirmative action and welfare and focus on primarily "individualistic" solutions to racial problems. Yet West asserts that self-help rhetoric need not be exclusively conservative. Indeed, reformers such as Jesse Jackson integrate self-help into a larger agenda that includes protest against societal injustice, community-based activism, and governmental programs to fight oppression.[8] African American self-help rhetoric from the antebellum period to the black nationalism of the 1960s places contemporary discourse in context, demonstrating that contemporary self-help rhetoric need not be a conservative form and that the messages of moral reform of leaders such as Jesse Jackson are part of a long tradition of progressive African American discourse.

RHETORIC AND RACE

As we have seen, African American abolitionists frequently feature race in their rhetoric, naming racial differences and thereby taking control of the terms that define race, revealing the arbitrary nature of such classifications, and demonstrating how purportedly race-neutral categories such as "womanhood" are in fact racially defined. America has always been and continues to be a society in which race influences social and political policy, national discourse, and the everyday lives of all Americans. As in the time of the marginalized abolitionists, contemporary white Americans often ignore the racial dimensions of their lives and beliefs, and race continues to be an "invisible" or unnamed factor in discussions that implicitly engage racial issues. African American rhetors such as Archibald Grimké and Audre Lorde draw on strategies related to those of their abolitionist predecessors to marshal the power of race in their discourse.

In "The Shame of America," Archibald Grimké, like his predecessor Walker, emphasizes the physical characteristics that are often associated with racial difference, taking control of the terms that define race. Walker, we will recall, highlights African American physical characteristics to reveal the absurdity of American discussions of racial difference, arguing ironically that in spite of their "*improminent noses* and *woolly heads,*" African Americans have the same underlying feelings as whites (*DWA,* 4–5). Grimké, too, draws on traditional markers of race—skin and hair—but, in a reversal of Walker's strategy, uses them to describe whites. Grimké appropriates an essentialist discourse about race, making "whiteness" the fundamental category that defines white Americans. "A white man is a white man," Grimké argues, "whether he lives in the North or in the South. . . . Scratch the skin of Republican or Democrat, of Northern white men or Southern white men, and you will find close to the surface race prejudice, American color-phobia. The difference, did you but know it, is not even epidermal, is not skin-deep. The hair is Democratic Esau's, and the voice is Republican Jacob's."[9] Grimké's act of exposing the usually invisible status of whiteness demonstrates that race influences the lives of all Americans, not just people of color. Notably, he reverses arguments about African Americans—that the color of the skin is a marker of fundamental identification, that it is relevant to define people by referring to their hair—revealing that racial categories are not only arbitrary, but can be appropriated and redefined by those who are oppressed. His strategy differs from that of his predecessor Walker but is based on similar assumptions—that racial categories are not eternal and that people of color can assume agency by taking control of the discourse of race.

Grimké also marshals a strategy that recalls the discourse of his predecessors Frederick Douglass and Charles Lenox Remond, who feature Britain as a pur-portedly "race-neutral" realm that contrasts with race-stratified American soci-ety. By 1919, it would seem, the resonance of the contrast between Britain and America, evoked by the memory of the Revolution, would have waned. Yet after World War I, references to Europe, where African American soldiers fought, were particularly relevant. Grimké argues, "The Negro went [to France] and saw—saw the incredible meanness and malice of his own country by the side of the immense genius for Liberty and Brotherhood of France. There he found himself a man and brother regardless of his race and color." Like Douglass and Remond, Grimké suggests that travel to an ostensibly nonracist realm demon-strates the arbitrary nature of American racism. In contrast to Douglass, though, who, we will recall, maintains that he "went back to America, almost forgetting that he was a black man" (*FDP*, 3:279), Grimké suggests that African Americans' experiences in France make them *more* conscious of racial difference in a way that empowers them to fight oppression. The African American soldier, he asserts, "has come back not as he went but a New Negro. He has come back to challenge injustice in his own land. . . . From his brave black lips I hear the ring-ing challenge, 'This is my right . . . I have come back to claim all that belongs to me of industrial and political equality and liberty.'"[10] Grimké suggests a new def-inition of equality that does not mean that one has to ignore race. In fact, after one is treated as an equal, one gains racial pride.

Grimké's revisions of the travel rhetoric of Douglass and Remond are sig-nificant, demonstrating a shift in African American discourse about race that is relevant to contemporary discussions. Douglass's and Remond's comments about Britain suggest that, in an ideal situation, Americans should forget about racial distinctions. But Douglass's rhetoric also shows that he had conflicting feelings about ignoring racial difference—he castigated Remond, we will recall, for saying he "would not speak as a colored man, but as *a man*."[11] Douglass's contrasting statements about the awareness of race demonstrate the tensions and anxiety experienced by Americans of all races about difference. Americans are conflicted about the relationship of the awareness of race to equality, and they wonder whether racial distinctions must be ignored or acknowledged in order to achieve a genuinely egalitarian society. Grimké, it seems, comes to terms with the conflict experienced by Douglass, revealing that racial pride is inherent in true equality.

Malcolm X's assertions in "The Ballot or the Bullet" also recall Douglass's rhetoric about race. Douglass emphasizes the "colored-white" dichotomy in an 1853 speech in New York to the AFASS, asserting the power to name and discuss racial difference. Douglass, we will recall, posits that if he were "a white man, speaking before and for white men," he would have "a smooth sea," adding that "the Hungarian, the Italian, the Irishman, the Jew and the Gentile" are all welcomed in America while African Americans find "neither justice, mercy nor religion" (*FDP,* 2:424–25). By taking control of the terms that define race, Douglass assumes agency to challenge American perceptions of racial difference. In particular, by mentioning the identification of Americans with white immigrants, Douglass suggests that the category of "whiteness" is arbitrary and can be questioned. Speaking over a hundred years later, Malcolm X poses a similar challenge about whiteness, making his critique of American racial categories even more explicit than his forebear:

> I don't even consider myself an American. . . . Those Hunkies that just got off the boat, they're already Americans; Polacks are already Americans; the Italian refugees are already Americans. Everything that came out of Europe, every blue-eyed thing, is already an American. And as long as you and I have been over here, we aren't Americans yet. . . .
>
> No, I'm not an American. I'm one of the twenty-two million black people who are the victims of democracy. . . . So, I'm not standing here speaking to you as an American. . . . I'm speaking as a victim of this American system.[12]

Like Douglass, Malcolm X exposes America's selective attention to racial difference.

Malcolm X's claim that he is "a victim of this American system" is also reminiscent of Douglass's description of America's treatment of African Americans. In his 1853 speech, Douglass remarks, "If I do not misinterpret the feelings of my white countrymen generally, they wish . . . to have nothing whatever to do with us, unless it may be to coin dollars out of our blood. Our position here is anomalous, unequal, and extraordinary" (*FDP,* 2:425). Both Douglass and Malcolm X draw attention to their alienation from American society. There is, however, an important difference in the implications of this alienation. Douglass suggests that African Americans are considered "aliens" in their "native land," but he emphasizes their ultimate ties to America, which is "the soil of [their] birth," "a country which has known [them] for centuries" (*FDP,* 2:425). Malcolm X, though, asserts that he does not consider himself an American—a statement his definition of

African Americans, "Africans who are in America," underscores.[13] This difference in the rhetoric of Douglass and Malcolm X can be attributed in part to the
latter's more militant views of race in America. In addition, we might speculate
that, in the context of the threatening rhetoric of the white-dominated antebellum colonization movement, Douglass and his colleagues would not want to
renounce their status as Americans. In the 1960s, the racism that fueled the colonization movement continued to exist (as it persists today), but arguments that
African Americans should be expatriated were no longer part of mainstream
white discourse.

For African American women, the phenomena that Douglass and Malcolm
X challenge—white Americans' selective attention to racial difference and the
alienation of African Americans from American society—have particular implications. As we have discovered, when white women claim an identification with
African American women, they often erase the experiences of African American
women. Assuming that their experiences represent those of all women, they
privilege definitions of womanhood that depend fundamentally on whiteness.
African American women are thus doubly alienated from American society
through race and gender. Like abolitionists such as Stewart and Truth, African
American women of the twentieth century challenge white women's narrow
definitions of women's issues and articulate expanded definitions of womanhood
that accommodate their perspectives. In particular, African American women
often challenge white feminism both for its refusal to acknowledge how racial difference influences women's lives and for its emphasis on white women's concerns.

In "The Master's Tools Will Never Dismantle the Master's House," Audre
Lorde directly confronts her white female audience with the ways in which their
discourse fails to acknowledge race—and in fact perpetuates racism. Like
African American female abolitionists such as Maria Stewart and Sarah Douglass,
Lorde adopts the "outsider-within" viewpoint described by Patricia Hill Collins,
which allows her to see "the contradictions between the dominant group's
actions and ideologies" and to offer perspectives that challenge conventional
views. Lorde comments, for example, on the analogy white feminists frequently
make between marriage and prostitution: "Poor women and women of Color
know there is a difference between the daily manifestations of marital slavery
and prostitution because it is our daughters who line 42nd Street. If white american
feminist theory need not deal with the differences between us, and the resulting
difference in our oppressions, then how do you deal with the fact that the women
who clean your houses and tend your children while you attend conferences on
feminist theory are, for the most part, poor women and women of Color?"[14]
Those who minimize difference for the sake of identification, Lorde argues,
actually ignore the real oppression African American women face. And, just as
Stewart and Lorde emphasize how the domestic ideal of womanhood excludes
those women who work in other women's houses or in the fields, Lorde
scathingly reveals how academic feminists exclude poor women and women of

color from their discourse, ignore their concerns in favor of "theory," and even contribute to their oppression by maintaining classist and racist power relations.

Lorde in fact extends the message of her abolitionist predecessors that distinctions must be acknowledged in discussions of women's experiences. Just as Archibald Grimké suggests that an awareness of race can be beneficial to society, so she maintains that difference can be a source of strength in the feminist movement. In contrast to common perceptions, difference should be valued as a source of power: "As women, we have been taught either to ignore our differences, or to view them as causes for separation and suspicion rather than as forces for change. Without community there is no liberation. . . . But community must not mean a shedding of our differences, nor the pathetic pretense that these differences do not exist." Reminiscent of Grimké, who suggests that American equality does not require Americans to ignore racial distinctions, Lorde argues that feminist community must coexist with discussions about difference.[15]

This lesson—that equality and community do not require what has come to be called "color-blindness"—provides important context for contemporary discussions about race. Public debates about equality are often based on the assumption that American society will only be egalitarian when it transcends race. Yet various scholars argue that, in fact, "color-blindness" is an ideal that erases the particular experiences of African Americans, and that true societal equality demands a recognition of racial difference.[16] These assertions take on new meaning when placed in a historical context that includes Frederick Douglass and Remond's perspective of "forgetting" race after their travels to Britain; Douglass's conflicts about highlighting race; and Archibald Grimké's, Malcolm X's, and Lorde's assertions in very different eras and contexts of the value of race consciousness. Debates in contemporary American society about the awareness of race and the challenges posed by African Americans to white America's conceptions of race are not new, but engage longstanding issues.

RHETORIC AND REVOLUTION

Since the antebellum period, America's founding texts, such as the Declaration of Independence, and themes related to the Revolution and the Founding Fathers have continued to be popular in American discourse and to resonate for marginalized rhetors. In addition, other discourse has been added to the canon of texts considered to be evocative of fundamental American values, such as Lincoln's Gettysburg Address and the "Star-Spangled Banner." Those rhetors who have followed the African American abolitionists have drawn on this canon to argue against the oppression of American society. Like their predecessors, they appropriate America's language and themes both to challenge American society and to demonstrate that the marginalized can draw on the influence of the language of those who are in power, refashioning it to create rhetorical tools to fight against their oppressors.

African American abolitionists, we have found, feature both adaptory, or overtly conciliatory, and advisory, or more directly confrontational, arguments. Both of

these forms, which are not discrete but rather represent opposite ends of a continuum, have empowered African American rhetors in a variety of eras, who draw
on the enduring influence of texts associated with America's patriotism and narratives of America's founding. In "Lynch Law," Ida B. Wells features both adaptory and advisory strategies in her appropriation of patriotic American rhetoric.
She begins the speech with famous words from Lincoln's Gettysburg Address,
the "Star-Spangled Banner," and the First Amendment to the Constitution,
redefining them in order to harshly confront white America with the realities of
lynching. "The observing and thoughtful must know," Wells relates, "that in one
section, at least, of our common country, a government of the people, by the people,
and for the people, means a government by the mob; where the land of the free
and the home of the brave means a land of lawlessness, murder and outrage; and
where liberty of speech means the license of might to destroy the business and
drive from home those who exercise this privilege contrary to the will of the
mob."[17] Like David Walker in his *Appeal*, Wells juxtaposes the rhetoric of fundamental American texts—America's "own language," in Walker's phrase—with
the realities of oppression that render the words meaningless. As Walker tells
Americans to "compare [their] own language" with the "cruelties and murders"
perpetrated by white America against African Americans (*DWA*, 75), Wells
reveals the tension between rhetoric and reality, confronting white Americans
with their hypocrisy.

Wells also appropriates white America's language in a less directly confrontational manner. She ends her speech with the first verse of "Star-Spangled
Banner," declaring that she looks forward to a time when "every member of this
great composite nation will be a living, harmonious illustration of the words, and
all can honestly and gladly join in singing" the anthem.[18] Yet this argument
should not be viewed as conciliatory. Wells is not appealing to her audience to
acknowledge her as an American deserving of rights; she, like African American male abolitionists such as David Walker or Frederick Douglass, assumes her
rightful status as an American—both explicitly, by confidently articulating an
inclusive vision of American society, and implicitly, by claiming the words of the
National Anthem. And Wells's rhetoric has another connection to that of her
abolitionist forebears. Wells's appropriation of the National Anthem is ironic in
light of the sentiments of its author, Francis Scott Key, who, as a colonizationist,
would presumably have rejected—or at least questioned—African Americans'
claim to America's promises. Yet Wells shows that in her rhetoric, like in that of
her predecessors, the discourse of white America assumes an influence that
extends beyond the control of individual authors. Just as abolitionists such as
William Whipper and William Watkins appropriate the language of the slaveholder and colonizationist Thomas Jefferson, separating his words from his
motives and elevating them to the level of universal truths, so Wells marshals the
power of Key's lyrics, an influence that extends beyond their immediate historical
context.

As in Whipper's and Watkins's appropriations of Jefferson's language, Wells's use of the words of the "Star-Spangled Banner" in two contexts demonstrates two key aspects of African American rhetors' deployment of the canon of American texts. On the one hand, they honor the ideals these texts embody— freedom, justice, and liberty—and they elevate these ideals to a status that transcends the motives of those who wrote them. On the other hand, they continually remind Americans that these words are not abstract, that they must be tested against the realities of American society. These two tendencies in their appropriation of American discourse form a defining tension that balances text and context. American texts are not the property of any one group or person; all can claim their power, which extends beyond the situation in which they were written. At the same time, though, the words are not removed from the context of American society. Rather, they embody standards against which Americans are judged.

Archibald Grimké's "The Shame of America" also embodies this defining tension between text and context. Grimké tests America's rhetoric of equality against the realities of oppression experienced by African Americans. In language strongly reminiscent of Walker's citation and commentary on the Declaration of Independence, he offers a striking phrase-by-phrase interpretation of the preamble to the Constitution:

> "We the people!" From the standpoint of the Negro, what grim irony; "establish justice"! What exquisitely cruel mockery . . . "to promote the general welfare"! What studied ignoring of an ugly fact; "and secure the blessings of liberty to ourselves and posterity"! What masterly abuse of noble words to mask an equivocal meaning, to throw over a great national transgression an air of virtue, so subtle and illusive as to deceive the framers themselves into believing in their own sincerity. . . . The muse of history, dipping her iron pen in the generous blood of the Negro, has written large across the page of that Preamble, and the face of the Declaration of Independence, the words, "sham, hypocrisy."[19]

Strikingly, Grimké suggests that America's treatment of African Americans rewrites the Preamble and the Declaration. America's texts are challenged and even altered by the realities of American society.

Yet even as he explicitly argues that the lofty sentiments of the Preamble and the Declaration are meaningless in light of the oppression African Americans face, Grimké implicitly creates a new meaning that empowers African Americans. The "noble words" of these documents no longer valorize abstract American ideals; in Grimké's reformulation, their meaning resides in their contrast with America's actions. But even as he claims that the words "sham, hypocrisy" should obliterate the Preamble and the Declaration, he points to the transcendent significance of the ideals they embody. They are, in fact, enduring standards against which American society must continually be judged. This defining tension that balances text and context is reiterated in Grimké's discussions of "the fathers of the Republic," particularly Washington and Jefferson. Grimké remarks that these men "had very fine words for liberty," but chastises them for their unwillingness to "translat[e] them into action" that would free African Americans.[20] Explicitly, Grimké argues that their words lose their meaning when put into the context of their authors' deeds. Implicitly, though, Grimké posits that their words have a significance that transcends them as individuals. Washington's and Jefferson's language, no longer controlled by them, becomes a tool that Grimké uses against these Founding Fathers. Their discourse extends beyond these authors, empowering even those whom they excluded from its promises.

As we have found, various African American abolitionists draw the language and heritage of the American Revolution to advocate—both implicitly and explicitly—militant antislavery action. Both Harriet Jacobs and Sarah Remond, we will recall, feature Patrick Henry's aphorism "liberty or death" to endorse physical resistance to slavery. Malcolm X similarly appropriates this phrase in "The Ballot or the Bullet" to advocate militant African American action to overcome oppression. Significantly, Malcolm X translates Patrick Henry's phrase into the words of his title—words that have, in their own right, entered into American popular consciousness. Explaining that many African Americans have become disillusioned with the nonviolence of the Civil Rights movement, Malcolm X remarks, "There's new strategy coming in. It'll be Molotov cocktails this month, hand grenades next month, and something else next month. It'll be ballots, or it'll be bullets. It'll be liberty, or it will be death." Later in the speech, he reiterates, "If it's necessary to form a black nationalist army, we'll form a black nationalist army. It'll be the ballot or the bullet. It'll be liberty or it'll be death."[21] Extending Jacobs's and Remond's advocacy of resistance, Malcolm X argues that proactive violence may also be necessary if rights are not granted to African Americans.

Malcolm X's advocacy of the "ballot or the bullet" is also reminiscent of the perspective of African American abolitionists such as David Walker and Frederick Douglass about the use of violence to fight oppression. In their jeremiadic rhetoric and their rhetoric that appropriates themes associated with the American Revolution, we will recall, Walker and Douglass call for Americans to take action that will forestall violence, although they acknowledge that eventual bloodshed is probably inevitable. Indeed, the very fact that they use persuasion to fight oppression demonstrates that they do not see violence as the only answer. Hoping to change American society through rhetoric, they nonetheless anticipate its limitations. Paradoxically, a militant discourse foreshadows its own end, when only violence can bring about change. Malcolm X's rhetoric also relies on these assumptions—that rhetoric can be a peaceful means for change, but that it may ultimately become powerless, leaving physical resistance as the only solution. "We will work with anybody," he asserts, "anywhere, at any time, who is genuinely interested in tackling the problem head-on, nonviolently as long as the enemy is nonviolent, but violent when the enemy gets violent."[22] Like his predecessors,

Malcolm X both values rhetoric as a force for societal transformation and acknowledges that in American society, founded on revolution, change by any means necessary often involves violence. From the Revolution to the Civil War to the violent confrontations of the Civil Rights era, the tensions within American society between rhetoric and revolution persist.

TELLING THE "BLACK TRUTH": SIGNIFYING

Just as African American abolitionists signified in ways that allowed them, in Audre Lorde's words, to "reclaim that language which has been made to work against" them, so African American rhetors of other eras marshal strategies related to signifying that enable them to use the language of the oppressor to fight oppression. In a manner reminiscent of his predecessors David Walker and Frederick Douglass, Archibald Grimké signifies on Thomas Jefferson's *Notes on the State of Virginia,* particularly his famous pronouncement that he "trembles for his country" when he anticipates God's justice for slavery. Grimké asserts,

> The author of the Declaration of Independence said once that he trembled for his country when he remembered that God was just. And he did well to do so. But while he was about it he might have quaked a little for himself. For he was certainly guilty of the same crime against humanity, which had aroused in his philosophic and patriotic mind such lively sensations of anxiety. . . . Said Jefferson on paper: "We hold these truths to be self-evident, that all men are created equal . . ." while on his plantation he was holding some men as slaves, and continued to hold them as such for fifty years thereafter, and died at the end of a long and brilliant life, a Virginia slaveholder. And yet Thomas Jefferson was sincere, or fancied that he was, when he uttered those sublime sentiments. . . . This inconsistency between the man's magnificence in profession and his smallness in practice, between the grandeur of what he promised and the meanness of what he performed . . . is essentially and emphatically an American national trait, a national idiosyncrasy.[23]

Grimké signifies in various ways in this passage. Seemingly complimentary descriptions of Jefferson are juxtaposed with language that undermines Jefferson's authority. Jefferson's comments on slavery were apt, "sublime sentiments," promises of "grandeur"; in context of his actions, though, Grimké reveals the limits of Jefferson's discretion and the shallow nature of his concern. Jefferson's career was "brilliant," Grimké notes, but his subsequent words suggest that this assessment is belied by the realities of Jefferson's life, his "smallness" and "meanness" when it came to translating words into action. Recontextualizing Jefferson's remarks, Grimké suggests that they are fundamentally important, but for a particular reason—they reveal America's inherent hypocrisy about race.

Grimké's portrayal of Jefferson as an enduring symbol of American "inconsistency" about race reveals the continuing resonance of this national figure in the American consciousness. Although, in the twentieth century, Jefferson's comments on race in his *Notes on the State of Virginia* are no longer referred to as a source for American racial thought, Jefferson continues to be a figure of fascination for historians and the public, who debate the contradictions between his words about slavery and his actions. His continuing resonance as a figure who embodies many of America's continuing anxieties about race has been underscored recently by discoveries that DNA evidence links him to the descendents of his slave Sally Hemings. Although discussion of Jefferson's liaison with Hemings and his fathering of children by her have circulated since Jefferson's time, until recently many white Americans refused to believe that Jefferson could embody such fundamental contradictions about race. Discounting the oral histories passed down through generations of Hemings's descendents, most white historians revealed both their inability to listen to alternative voices in American society and their investment in an image of Jefferson that precluded the possibility of a sexual relationship with Hemings. African Americans, on the other hand, who know firsthand that American society is founded on many contradictions about race, have long been skeptical of white historians' denials. Like Grimké, they have been aware of the inconsistencies of figures like Jefferson, disparities that are not anomalous but that reveal pervasive tensions in American society.[24] Grimké's signifying on Jefferson's words demonstrates that the history of American race relations is not static, but is part of an ongoing dialogue that recontextualizes canonical American texts about race. His rhetoric, like that of Douglass and Walker before him, also challenges white Americans to examine critically the sentiments of America's founders and to acknowledge that American society has always embodied fundamental tensions about race.

Grimké also signifies on the words of another American figure, Supreme Court Chief Justice Roger Taney's assertion in his opinion on the Dred Scott case that Americans of African descent "had no rights which the white man was bound to respect." In her narrative, we will recall, Harriet Jacobs signifies on this phrase, appropriating it to describe her sentiments toward unjust American laws. Grimké adopts a different strategy as he quotes and recontextualizes Taney's words. "Taney," he comments, "argued that black men had no rights in America which white men were bound to respect. The downright brutality of that opinion was extremely shocking to some sensitive Americans, but it was no more so than was the downright brutality of the facts, which it reflected with brutal accuracy. The fell apparition of American inhumanity, which those words conjured up from the depths of an abominable past and from that of a no less abominable present, was indeed black, but it was no blacker than the truth."[25] Taney's infamous words, Grimké maintains, are indeed "brutal," but not because they *create* an injustice that is new in American society but because they *reflect* the stark realities of American race relations. Placed into this context, Taney does not embody anomalous racial hatred that has been alleviated; on the contrary, his words reveal an enduring truth about American "brutality" toward African Americans.

Notably, Grimké employs a resonant double meaning to describe Taney's comments. The truth that Taney reveals is, in Grimké's words, "black." On the one hand, of course, this description connotes the somber state of American race relations. But Grimké suggests another meaning. If one is to understand America's ongoing problems with race, Grimké implies, one cannot limit one's study to whites' perspectives. It is also necessary to hear African American voices discussing the realities of American injustice—to listen to the "black truth" as well as to whites' views. Those who merely listen to white America will see Taney's decision as a "shocking" anomaly, but Grimké relates the "black truth," the larger context of American injustice that inform Taney's comments. When African Americans engage in dialogue with white America's texts—a fundamental component of signifying—new truths, "black truths," are revealed.

Speaking over a half century later, Audre Lorde similarly reframes the words and assumptions of white women, placing their perspectives into a new context. Her signifying reveals, in effect, the "black truth"—the views of African American women that are often ignored by white feminists. In a move reminiscent of Frederick Douglass's casting of his invitation to speak at a Fourth of July celebration as an ironic representation of American hypocrisy, Lorde turns her own presence at an academic feminist conference into an indictment of white feminism:

> Why weren't other women of Color found to participate in this conference? Why were two phone calls to me considered a consultation? Am I the only possible source of names of Black feminists? . . .
>
> In academic feminist circles, the answer to these questions is often, "We did not know who to ask." But that is the same evasion of responsibility, the same cop-out, that keeps Black women's art out of women's exhibitions, Black women's work of out most feminist publications except for the occasional "Special Third World Women's Issue," and Black women's texts off your reading lists.[26]

Lorde challenges white feminists, recasting their assumptions in a larger context that reveals the limitations of their theoretical perspectives. In the context of African American women's continuing marginalization in the feminist movement, the invitation to Lorde to speak is tokenism, the assumption that Lorde can represent the views of all African American women is reductionism, and the limited interest of feminists in African American women's literature and art is a substitute for real inclusion of African American women's perspectives. Lorde reveals to her audience the "black truth" in both senses. She exposes the problems that pervade feminism; and, by articulating the perspectives of African American women, she challenges white feminists' perspectives and suggests that they must engage new views in order to be truly inclusive.

"THE HUMBLEST MAY STAND FORTH": LANGUAGE, FREEDOM, AND THE "MASTER'S TOOLS"

The empowering discursive strategies of African American rhetors recall the dual meaning of Frederick Douglass's statement that "the humblest may stand forth." Like Douglass, rhetors such as Wells, Archibald Grimké, Malcolm X, and Lorde negotiate their marginal position in society and assume agency to argue against oppression. Yet the second meaning of Douglass's words is perhaps even more resonant. These rhetors demonstrate that the marginalized have a *particular* authority in American society, that the "humblest" emerge as uniquely powerful rhetors precisely because of their position in society. Their efforts illustrate William G. Allen's assertions in 1852 that the most influential oratory originates in oppression, and that the passage from slavery into freedom is linked to the transition from silence to rhetoric.[27] The rhetoric of the marginalized abolitionists as well as those that followed them demonstrates that persuasion is itself an act of freedom. The "humblest" do not only "stand forth" in order to persuade; by persuading, they are also "standing forth," assuming agency.

To "stand forth" through persuasion, marginalized rhetors must create persuasive strategies that are empowering. As we have found, in order to examine this discourse on its own terms, we must challenge—but not reject out of hand—conventional theoretical perspectives. This position problematizes one of Lorde's most famous polemical pronouncements: "*The master's tools will never dismantle the master's house.* They may allow us temporarily to beat him at his own game, but they will never enable us to bring about genuine change."[28] Lorde's assertion cannot fully account for the complex persuasion of the marginalized abolitionists and African American rhetors of other eras. These rhetors draw on conventional categories and modes of persuasion, appropriating their power. They also challenge and revise fundamental assumptions about traditional rhetoric, revealing ways that we must rethink conventional theories to account for the persuasion of those who are marginalized in society. In fact, we might say that the strategies of the marginalized abolitionists and those who followed them demonstrate that, paradoxically, the oppressed often assume agency by taking the master's language, texts, and premises and using them against the master. As bell hooks maintains, "We take the oppressor's language and turn it against itself. We make our words a counter-hegemonic speech, liberating ourselves in language." Henry Louis Gates similarly comments in a 1997 speech in San Francisco,

> We turn the tools of the master back on the master. . . . [T]o reverse Audre Lorde, my dear friend . . . who said famously that you can't dismantle the master's house with the master's tools, I say, you can only dismantle the master's house with the master's tools. Our whole tradition was based on beating the white boy at his own game. That is the way it was said when I was growing up. . . . Frederick Douglass said you have to steal a little learning from the white man, and you have to beat him at his own game. We're the only group of slaves in the history of human beings who invented a literature out of their enslavement. . . . [W]e took the scraps of knowledge and turned it into a great tradition.[29]

The relationship between marginalized rhetors and the language of the oppressor is, like that of the relationship of freedom and rhetoric, paradoxical. For Douglass and for other rhetors, freedom lay—in Gates's terms—in "turning the tools of the master back on the master." And by doing so, by deploying their society's discursive tools as well as by challenging, expanding, and revising them, these rhetors reveal the limits of the master's control of language. The master's tools are not static, nor are they solely the property of those in power. And, if conventional categories can be appropriated and refashioned by the oppressed, the master's house is also more vulnerable than the master might assume. The persuasion of the "humblest" reveals that rhetoric, which is often used against those who are marginalized, can also be a weapon to fight oppression.

As the persuasion of Wells, Archibald Grimké, Malcolm X, and Lorde reveals, in the struggle to use rhetoric to gain freedom, marginalized rhetors draw on and revise not only the master's tools but also the discourse of those who have preceded them. Their rhetoric must be viewed in context of their predecessors, whose persuasion is part of the foundation on which they build. At the same time, the relationship between their discourse and that of their forebears is not static. The rhetoric of the marginalized abolitionists, as well as that of activists who followed them, becomes for later rhetors a dynamic framework that is continually expanding. In articulating her own relationship to Malcolm X, Lorde expresses this connection. Speaking in 1982 at the Malcolm X Weekend at Harvard University, Lorde identifies herself as "an inheritor of Malcolm," one who works "in his tradition" with "the ghost of his voice through [her] mouth." But she also maintains that as she builds on her predecessor's rhetoric, she creates a new context that will influence those who come after her:

> As Malcolm stressed, we are not responsible for our oppression, but we must be responsible for our own liberation. It is not going to be easy, but we have what we have learned and what we have been given that is useful. We have the power those who came before us have given us, to move beyond the place where they were standing. . . . Malcolm X does not live in the dry texts of his words as we read them; he lives in the energy we generate and use to move along the visions we share with him. We are making the future as well as bonding to survive the enormous pressures of the present, and that is what it means to be a part of history.[30]

Like Malcolm X before her, Lorde creates a legacy for those who are just now gaining their voices—and for those who have yet to "stand forth."

Notes

CHAPTER 1

1. See the Abbrevations section for citations of quotations from Frederick Douglass's works.

2. This brief overview of Douglass's career will be amplified in chapter 3.

3. AASS, *Proceedings,* 30; May, *Some Recollections,* 92; Oliver Johnson, *William Lloyd Garrison,* 255.

4. AASS, *Second Annual Report,* 28, 50; AASS, *Sixth Annual Report,* 27–35, 44–47; AASS, *First Annual Report,* 26; AASS, *Fifth Annual Report,* 25–30.

5. See, for example, AASS, *First Annual Report,* 6–12, 15, 27–31, 62–64; AASS, *Second Annual Report,* 76–82; AASS, *Fifth Annual Report,* 35; AASS, *Sixth Annual Report,* 3–4.

6. For traditional historical accounts, see Kraditor, *Means and Ends;* Friedman, *Gregarious Saints;* Barnes, *Antislavery Impulse;* Griffin, *Their Brothers' Keepers;* Walters, *Antislavery Appeal;* Dumond, *Antislavery.* For studies of particular white male abolitionists, see Nye, *William Lloyd Garrison;* Merrill, *Against Wind and Tide;* Yacovone, *Samuel Joseph May;* Abzug, *Passionate Liberator;* Thomas, *Theodore Weld;* Goodheart, *Abolitionist;* Gougeon, "Emerson and Abolition"; Jackson, "Emerson"; Albrecht, "Conflict and Resolution"; Funk, "Henry David Thoreau." For biographies of Douglass, see Huggins, *Slave and Citizen;* McFeely, *Frederick Douglass;* Quarles, *Frederick Douglass;* Ronald K. Burke, *Frederick Douglass.*

7. Scholars such as Shirley Logan, Drema Lipscomb, Charles Nero, Robbie Walker, and Carla Peterson revise and extend traditional views of antebellum rhetoric in their work on the persuasion of African American rhetors. See Logan, "Literacy"; Logan, *With Pen and Voice;* Logan, *"We Are Coming";* Lipscomb, "Sojourner Truth"; Nero, "Oh, What I Think"; Robbie Jean Walker, *Rhetoric of Struggle;* Peterson, *"Doers of the Word."* This book enters into the scholarly inquiry engaged by these studies.

8. Quarles, *Black Abolitionists;* Pease and Pease, *They Who Would Be Free;* Levesque, "Black Abolitionists"; Dick, *Black Protest;* Hersh, *Slavery of Sex;* Lerner, *Grimké Sisters;* Lumpkin, *Emancipation.*

9. See, for example, Jacobs, *Courage and Conscience;* Yellin and Van Horne, *Abolitionist Sisterhood;* Samuels, *Culture of Sentiment;* Yellin, *Women and Sisters;* Yee, *Black Women Abolitionists;* Campbell, *Man;* Logan, *"We Are Coming";* Jeffrey, *Great Silent Army.*

10. See Mills, *Cultural Reformations;* Clifford, *Crusader for Freedom;* Karcher, *First Woman;* Sterling, *Ahead;* Taylor, *Women;* Pasternak, *Rise Now;* Schor, *Henry Highland Garnet;*

Ronald K. Burke, *Samuel Ringgold Ward;* Hunter, *To Set the Captives Free;* Painter, *Sojourner Truth;* Lipscomb, "Sojourner Truth"; Mabee and Newhouse, *Sojourner Truth;* Stetson and David, *Glorying in Tribulation;* Richardson, "What If I Am a Woman?"; Andrews, "Changing Moral Discourse"; Garfield and Zafar, *Harriet Jacobs.*

11. See, for example, Sekora, "Mr. Editor"; Andrews, *Critical Essays;* Stephens, "Frederick Douglass"; Lampe, *Frederick Douglass.*

12. See, for example, Venet, *Neither Ballots,* 4–7, 12–19; Hewitt, "Social Origins"; Hansen, *Strained Sisterhood;* Hansen, "Boston Female"; Swerdlow, "Abolition's Conservative Sisters"; Williams, "Female Antislavery Movement"; Soderlund, "Priorities and Power"; Boylan, "Benevolence"; Winch, "You Have Talents"; Ripley et al., *BAP,* 3:17–18, 3:35–40; Jacobs, "David Walker and William Lloyd Garrison," 7–9; George, "Widening the Circle."

13. Welter, *Dimity Convictions;* Smith-Rosenberg, *Disorderly Conduct;* Baym, *American Women Writers;* Brown, *Domestic Individualism;* Ryan, *Women in Public;* Giddings, *When and Where I Enter;* Sterling, *We Are Your Sisters;* Deborah Gray White, *Ar'n't I a Woman?*

14. Gates, *Signifying,* xix.

15. Kenneth Burke, *Grammar;* Kenneth Burke, *Rhetoric;* Bercovitch, *American Jeremiad;* Zulick, "Agon of Jeremiah."

16. Edwin Ardener, "Belief"; Edwin Ardener, "Problem"; Shirley Ardener, introduction to *Perceiving;* Shirley Ardener, "Nature"; Kramarae, *Women and Men.*

17. Campbell, *Man;* Yellin, *Women and Sisters;* Collins, *Black Feminist Thought;* hooks, *Ain't I A Woman.*

18. Howard-Pitney, *Afro-American Jeremiad;* Moses, *Black Messiahs;* Grant, *White Women's Christ;* Connor, *Conversions;* Gates, *Signifying;* Gates, *Figures;* Mitchell-Kernan, "Signifying"; Abrahams, *Deep Down;* Abrahams, *Singing.*

19. Kimberly K. Smith, *Dominion of Voice;* Warren, *Culture of Eloquence;* Browne, *Angelina Grimké.* Other studies that focus on the role of public argument in American history include Jasinski, "Feminization of Liberty"; McDorman, "Challenging Constitutional Authority"; Zarefsky and Gallagher, "From 'Conflict'"; Bush, *American Declarations;* Levander, *Voices of the Nation;* Eberly, *Citizen Critics.*

20. For Habermas's notion of the public sphere, see Habermas, *Structural Transformation;* Habermas, "Public Sphere." Critiques include Benhabib, "Models of Public Space"; Fraser, "Rethinking the Public Sphere"; Phillips, "Spaces of Public Dissension"; Baker, "Critical Memory"; Dawson, "A Black Counterpublic?"

21. Fraser, "Rethinking the Public Sphere," 122–32; Gring-Pemble, "Writing Themselves," 43; Baker, "Critical Memory," 16–26; Dawson, "A Black Counterpublic?" 210–11.

22. For late-eighteenth-century and early-nineteenth-century African American antislavery writings and speeches, see Porter, *Early Negro Writing.*

23. Hinks, *To Awaken,* 92. On the activism of the late 1820s, see also Pease and Pease, *They Who Would Be Free,* 22–27; Ripley et al., *BAP,* 3:6–7.

24. Dennett, "Eloquence"; Blassingame, "Editorial Method," lxxvi–lxxx.

25. Blassingame, Ripley et al., and Ceplair are editors of *The Frederick Douglass Papers, The Black Abolitionist Papers,* and *The Public Years of Sarah and Angelina Grimké,* respectively.

26. Kenneth Burke, *Grammar,* 323–25.

27. Until recently, many scholars questioned Jacobs's authorship, suggesting that Child in fact wrote the narrative. Jean Fagan Yellin, however, demonstrates that Jacobs in fact wrote the text, asking for Child's assistance after a publisher expressed interest in her manuscript if she could obtain an introduction by Child. Yellin adds that Child's editorial assistance did change Jacobs's original text, particularly through her alteration of Jacobs's initial ending. See Yellin, introduction to *Incidents,* xxi-xxii.

28. Clarence E. Walker, *Deromanticizing Black History,* xvi-xviii.

29. Allen, "Orators," 232.

CHAPTER 2

1. Hayden White, *Metahistory,* 5.

2. My summary of traditional historical accounts throughout this section draws from various works, including Dumond, *Antislavery;* Dillon, *Slavery Attacked;* Aptheker, *Abolitionism;* Friedman, *Gregarious Saints;* Barnes, *Antislavery Impulse;* Kraditor, *Means and Ends;* Walters, "Boundaries"; Walters, *Antislavery Appeal;* Scott, "Abolition"; Cain, *William Lloyd Garrison;* Perry, *Radical Abolitionism;* Woodward, "John Brown's Raid"; Merrill, *Against Wind and Tide.*

3. Hayden White, *Metahistory,* 5.

4. AASS, *First Annual Report,* 39–40.

5. My discussion in this and the next section of African American abolition is informed by the following sources: Franklin and Moss, *From Slavery to Freedom;* Nash, *Forging Freedom;* Horton and Horton, *Black Bostonians;* Horton and Horton, "Affirmation of Manhood"; Jacobs, "David Walker and William Lloyd Garrison"; Pease and Pease, *They Who Would Be Free;* Ripley et al., *Witness For Freedom;* Ripley et al., *BAP,* 3:3–69; Quarles, *Black Abolitionists;* Levesque, "Black Abolitionists"; Yee, *Black Women Abolitionists;* Dick, *Black Protest;* Berry and Blassingame, *Long Memory;* Hinks, *To Awaken;* James Brewer Stewart, "Modernizing the 'Difference'"; Carol Wilson, "Active Vigilance."

6. After the passage of the 1850 Fugitive Slave Law, African American interest in emigration to establish an independent nation resurfaced, although emigrationists disagreed over potential destinations. Yet most African Americans remained committed to staying in the United States. For a more complete discussion of African American attitudes toward emigration and colonization in the antebellum period, see Cain, *William Lloyd Garrison,* 50; Ripley et al., *Witness for Freedom,* 2–3, 20–21; Pease and Pease, *They Who Would Be Free,* 20–26, 255–77; Quarles, *Black Abolitionists,* 7–8, 215–22; Yee, *Black Women Abolitionists,* 67, 105; Berman E. Johnson, *Dream Deferred,* 7; Kinshasa, *Emigration vs. Assimilation;* Miller, *Search.*

7. Quotations from David Walker's *Appeal* are cited in the text as indicated in the Abbreviations section.

8. Hinks, *To Awaken,* 108–9, 174–80.

9. Garrison and Garrison, *William Lloyd Garrison,* 1:147–48.

10. Hayden White, *Metahistory,* 5–7.

11. *Emerson's Antislavery Writings,* 53, 74, 80. Emerson somewhat overstated his earlier detachment from slavery; in 1846, he had become angered at the kidnapping of a runaway slave who had escaped to Boston. See *Emerson's Antislavery Writings,* 45–46.

12. For Douglass's articulation of his position on women's rights, see "The Rights of Women," *NS,* 28 July 1848. For an analysis of the complexities of Douglass's view of women's role in the antislavery movement, see Hamilton, "Frederick Douglass."

13. The African American connection to the Free Soil Party is complicated. Certain African American leaders believed that, given the weakness of the Liberty Party, the Free Soil Party was the most effective alternative to the Whigs and the Democrats. However, many members of the Free Soil Party opposed civil rights for African Americans and believed that labor in the western territories should be free and *white.* See Pease and Pease, *They Who Would Be Free,* 198–200; Dick, *Black Protest,* 103–13; Friedman, *Gregarious Saints,* 180–82.

14. Angelina Grimké to Theodore Dwight Weld and John Greenleaf Whittier, August 20 [1837], Weld, Weld, and Grimké, *Letters,* 1:429–30.

15. hooks, *Ain't I A Woman,* 12–13, 123–27; Giddings, *When and Where I Enter,* 6, 52–55; Valerie Smith, *Not Just Race,* xiii–xiv. See also Loewenberg and Bogin, *Black Women,* 18.

16. M. [Stephen A. Myers], Editorial, *Northern Star and Freeman's Advocate,* 3 Mar. 1842.

17. Carol Wilson, "Active Vigilance," 116.

18. Augustus William Hanson to William Lloyd Garrison, 3 November 1838, *BAP,* 3:284; "Resolutions by a Committee of Philadelphia Blacks, Presented at the Brick Wesley African Methodist Episcopal Church, Philadelphia, Pennsylvania, 14 October 1850," *BAP,* 4:68–69.

19. Although popular accounts of the Underground Railroad since Emancipation have suggested that white activists played leading roles, historians have discovered that this depiction is inaccurate. In fact, African American leadership was primary to its success—a fact that was acknowledged by white abolitionists such as James Birney. See Quarles, foreword to *Underground Rail Road,* v; Buckmaster, *Let My People Go,* 37, 75–76; Berry and Blassingame, *Long Memory,* 65; Berman E. Johnson, *Dream Deferred,* 26; Hunter, *To Set the Captives Free,* 152. For an investigation of the Underground Railroad as well as the reasons for much of the mythology surrounding it, see Gara, *Liberty Line.*

20. Pease and Pease, *They Who Would Be Free,* 206–7.

21. "Speech by James McCune Smith, Delivered at the First Colored Presbyterian Church, New York, New York, 8 May 1855," *BAP,* 4:292.

22. On these activities, see Boylan, "Benevolence"; Chambers-Schiller, "Good Work."

23. Ripley et al., *Witness for Freedom,* 12.

24. Samuel E. Cornish, "Responsibility of Colored People in the Free States," *Colored American,* 4 Mar. 1837.

25. See Cooper, "To Elevate"; Fordham, *Major Themes,* 33–56; Kinshasa, *Emigration,* 45–62. For notable exceptions to this traditional perspective, see Quarles, *Black Abolitionists,* 102; Hinks, *To Awaken,* 109, 198; Horton and Horton, *In Hope of Liberty,* 228; Horton, *Free People of Color,* 55. For further discussion of this reevaluation of self-help rhetoric, see Bacon, "Rethinking the History."

26. In addition to the primary sources cited, my discussion in this section of antebellum religious and scientific justifications for slavery is informed by various studies, including Pease and Pease, *They Who Would Be Free;* Levine, *Black Culture;* Jordan, *White over Black;* Genovese, *Roll, Jordan, Roll;* Frederickson, *Black Image;* Jenkins, *Pro-Slavery Thought;* Tise, *Proslavery;* McKivigan and Snay, "Introduction."

27. Priest, *Bible Defence,* v; Cartwright, *Essays,* 5, 8–9.

28. See, for example, Bledsoe, "Liberty and Slavery"; Stringfellow, "Bible Argument," 479–80, 513–15.

29. Jefferson, *Notes,* 137–43; Cartwright, *Essays,* 15–20; Fitzhugh, *Sociology;* Nott, *Types of Mankind,* 131; Dew, *Review,* 30–31.

30. Samuel Cartwright, "Natural History of the Prognathous Species of Mankind," *Day-Book,* 10 Nov. 1857; Cartwright, *Essays,* 12; [Fitzhugh], *Slavery Justified,* 3, 9–10.

31. Samuel E. Cornish and John B. Russwurm, "To Our Patrons," *FJ,* 16 Mar. 1827.

32. Scholarship on *Freedom's Journal* and the language of the editorials in the paper suggest that there were both white and African American subscribers and readers; see Pease and Pease, *They Who Would Be Free,* 24; Penn, *Afro-American Press,* 27; Gross, *"Freedom's Journal,"* 242, 250; Detweiler, *Negro Press,* 36; Bell, *Survey,* 11; Cornish and Russwurm, "To Our Patrons"; Samuel E. Cornish and John B. Russwurm, "Prospectus," *FJ,* 16 Mar. 1827.

33. Cornish and Russwurm, "To Our Patrons." Throughout its run, the paper experienced various shifts and tensions, including a modification in editorial focus and changes in editorship. The last issue of *Freedom's Journal* was published in March 1829. For further discussion of *Freedom's Journal,* see Gross, *"Freedom's Journal"*; Penn, *Afro-American Press,* 26–30; Clint C. Wilson, *Black Journalists,* 25–30; Pease and Pease, *They Who Would Be Free,* 24–26; Wolseley, *Black Press,* 17–18; Detweiler, *Negro Press,* 35–39; Wesley, "Negroes of New York," 70–72; Bell, *Survey,* 10–12.

34. For further discussion of African American literary societies, see McHenry, "Dreaded Eloquence"; McHenry, "Forgotten Readers"; Bacon and McClish, "Reinventing the Master's Tools."

35. In addition to the primary sources cited in this section, my discussion of prejudice within the abolition movement draws from various secondary sources, including Friedman, *Gregarious Saints;* Stewart, *Holy Warriors;* Pease and Pease, *They Who Would Be Free;* Quarles, *Black Abolitionists;* Sterling, *Ahead of Her Time;* Hall, "Massachusetts Abolitionists"; Ripley et al., *Witness for Freedom;* Andrews, *To Tell a Free Story;* Sekora, "Black Message"; Sekora, "Mr. Editor"; Winter, *Subjects of Slavery.*

36. Frederickson, *Black Image,* 101–2.

37. W. [William J. Watkins], "One Thing Thou Lackest," *Frederick Douglass' Paper,* 10 Feb. 1854.

38. "Speech by Theodore S. Wright, Delivered at the Bleecker Street Church, Utica, New York, 20 October 1836," *BAP,* 3:186; Benjamin F. Roberts to Amos A. Phelps, 19 June 1838, *BAP,* 3:269–70.

39. Pease and Pease, *They Who Would Be Free,* 69; Lydia Maria Child, "Letter to Dr. Channing," *Lib,* 2 Apr. 1836; Quarles, *Black Abolitionists,* 49. For Weston's comment, see Yee, *Black Women Abolitionists,* 37.

40. Communipaw [James McCune Smith], Letter, *Frederick Douglass' Paper,* 26 Jan. 1855.

41. Sekora, "Black Message," 496.

42. Sekora, "Black Message," 496; Sekora, "Mr. Editor," 611.

43. Blassingame, introduction to *FDP,* lii.

44. "Speech by John S. Rock, Delivered at the Meionaon, Boston, Massachusetts, 5 March 1860," *BAP,* 5:61.

45. Blassingame, introduction to *FDP,* xlviii-xlix; Lampe, *Frederick Douglass,* x, 57–65, 88; Jefferson, *Notes,* 139.

46. Andrews, *Critical Essays,* 3; Lane, *Narrative,* iii; Wright, "Life and Adventures."

47. Baker, "Critical Memory," 16–26; Dawson, "A Black Counterpublic?" 210–11.

48. Samuel E. Cornish, "Why We Should Have a Paper," *Colored American,* 4 Mar. 1837.

49. Jermain Wesley Loguen to Frederick Douglass, March 1855, *BAP,* 4:271.

50. Pease and Pease, "Boston Garrisonians," 36. See also Quarles, "Breach."

51. Fredrick Douglass, "Our Paper and Its Prospects," *NS,* 3 Dec. 1847.

52. In 1851, Douglass and white abolitionist Gerrit Smith decided to merge the *North Star* with Smith's *Liberty Party Paper,* creating *Frederick Douglass' Paper. Douglass' Monthly* was created for foreign subscribers. For further discussion of Douglass's editorial career, see Wolseley, *Black Press,* 21–24; Detweiler, *Negro Press,* 40–42; Wilson, *Black Journalists,* 36–38; Penn, *Afro-American Press,* 67–70.

53. In addition to the primary sources I cite throughout this chapter, my discussion of the "Cult of True Womanhood" is informed by Smith-Rosenberg, *Disorderly Conduct;* Baym, *American Women Writers;* Cott, *Bonds of Womanhood;* Welter, *Dimity Convictions;* Sklar, *Catharine Beecher;* Campbell, *Man,* 1:9–11, 1:39.

54. See, for example, Clinton, *Other Civil War,* 34; Ginzburg, *Women,* 17.

55. M. A. H., "Appeal," 433.

56. "On the Duties," 59, 61–62, "Domestic Duties," 6; "Fragments," 154; Bolles, "Influence of Women," 268–69.

57. G., "How Ought Woman," 511, 515.

58. Beecher, *Essay on Slavery,* 100, 102; "Domestic Duties," 6; G., "How Ought Woman," 511; "Women of '76," 98.

59. Cmiel, *Democratic Eloquence,* 96–106.

60. "On the Duties," 62–63.

61. All biblical quotations are taken from the King James Version, the standard antebellum translation. Although the King James Version was the target of reformers in the period from the 1820s to the Civil War, its defenders effectively fought off these attacks (Cmiel, *Democratic Eloquence,* 96–106, 121).

62. "On the Duties," 64.

63. Perrine, *Women,* 10; Peck, *True Woman,* 292, 345–46.

64. Hale, "Ought Ladies," 89.

65. Beecher, *Essay on Slavery,* 102–3. Beecher's opinions on slavery and abolition were complex; see Sklar, *Catharine Beecher,* 133–34; Browne, *Angelina Grimké,* 88–94.

66. Beecher, *Essay on Slavery,* 103–5, 100–101, 128–29, 137, 145; "Pastoral Letter: The General Association of Massachusetts to the Churches Under Their Care," *New England Spectator,* 12 July 1837, reprint in *PY,* 211.

67. My discussions in this section of women's antislavery activities and of abolitionists' perspectives on women's roles draws from the work of various scholars; see Friedman, *Gregarious Saints;* Sánchez-Eppler, *Touching Liberty,* 14–49; Chambers-Schiller, "Good Work"; Van Broekhoven, "Let Your Names"; Hansen, "Boston Female"; Soderlund, "Priorities and Power"; Hewitt, "Social Origins."

68. For contemporary accounts of women's antislavery fairs, see Sarah Forten to Elizabeth Whittier, 25 December 1836, *BAP*, 3:201–5; Lydia Maria Child, "Massachusetts Anti-Slavery Fair," *NASS*, 16 Dec. 1841; Amy Post, "An Appeal in Behalf of the Western New York Anti-Slavery Fair," *NS*, 21 Sept. 1849.

69. Van Broekhoven, "Let Your Names," 179–80. Van Broekhoven notes that as legislators began to receive more petitions and to notice the number of female names, the act became the subject of dispute, declining by the early 1840s ("Let Your Names," 184–90).

70. Female Anti-Slavery Society of Chatham-Street Chapel, *Constitution,* 10; Forten, *Address,* 13.

71. AASS, *Second Annual Report,* 50–51; "The Ladies of Boston and Providence," *Lib,* 18 Apr. 1835.

72. Ohio State Anti-Slavery Society, "Declaration of Sentiments," *Lib,* 16 May 1835; New-York Young Men's Anti-Slavery Society, *Preamble and Constitution,* 8. See also Massachusetts Anti-Slavery Society, "Quarterly Meeting of the Massachusetts Anti-Slavery Society, Sept. 28, 1835," *Lib,* 3 Oct. 1835; Cambridgeport Anti-Slavery Society, "Constitution of the Cambridgeport Anti-Slavery Society," *Lib,* 29 Aug. 1835.

73. Boston Female Anti-Slavery Society, *Report,* 3; Female Anti-Slavery Society of Chatham-Street Chapel, *Constitution,* 4. See also Providence Ladies' Anti-Slavery Society, "Constitution of the Providence Ladies' Anti-Slavery Society," *Lib,* 25 Apr. 1835; South Reading [Massachusetts] Female Anti-Slavery Society, "Preamble and Constitution of the South Reading Female A. S. Society," *Lib,* 26 Mar. 1836.

74. William Lloyd Garrison, "Christian Heroism," *Lib,* 19 Sept. 1835. For an extended analysis of the gendered rhetoric of the "Ladies' Department," see Bacon, "*Liberator*'s 'Ladies' Department'."

75. Lydia Maria Child to Lucretia Mott, 5 March 1839, *Lydia Maria Child,* 106–7; "Proceedings of the Woman's Rights Convention, Held at the Unitarian Church, in the City of Rochester, August 2, 1848, to Consider the Rights of Woman: Politically, Religiously, and Industriously," *Lib,* 15 Sept. 1848.

76. AASS, *Sixth Annual Report,* 45.

77. See Swerdlow, "Abolition's Conservative Sisters"; Taylor, *Women,* 17–18, 27–42.

78. See Cmiel, *Democratic Eloquence,* 57–71, for a discussion of this phenomenon.

79. Friedman, *Gregarious Saints,* 131–32, 142–44.

80. Angelina Grimké to Sarah Grimké, 27 September 1835, *PY,* 27–28; Sarah Grimké, diary entry, 25 September 1835, *PY,* 27.

81. For a discussion of the reaction to this work, see Karcher, "Rape," 60; Karcher, *First Woman,* 190–92; Clifford, *Crusader for Freedom,* 103–4.

82. Lydia Maria Child, "To the Readers of the Standard," *NASS,* 20 May 1841.

83. Hansen, "Boston Female," 47; Boylan, "Benevolence," 120.

84. Frankenberg, *White Women,* 1–17, 49, 176–97.

85. In addition to the primary sources cited in this section, my discussions of how traditional notions of gender influenced antebellum African American women and of the work and experiences of African American female abolitionists draws from various secondary sources, including Yee, *Black Women Abolitionists*; Richardson, introduction to *Maria W.*

Stewart; Boylan, "Benevolence"; Giddings, *When and Where I Enter;* Loewenberg and Bogin, *Black Women,* 1–36; Connor, *Conversions;* Russell, *Render Me My Song;* Deborah G. White, *Ar'n't I a Woman?* Sterling, *We Are Your Sisters;* Sterling, *Speak Out;* Hall, "Massachusetts Abolitionists."

86. hooks, *Ain't I A Woman,* 7; "Advancing!" *Lib,* 9 July 1831.

87. Angelina Grimké to Jane Smith, 22 March 1837, *PY,* 125–26. Grimké presumably refers to the Ladies' New York City Anti-Slavery Society, the central citywide organization.

88. Yee, *Black Women Abolitionists,* 18–19; Sterling, *Ahead,* 47.

89. "Essay by 'A Colored Woman' [November 1839]," *BAP,* 3:326.

90. Sterling, *Ahead,* 47. For the accounts on which Sterling bases this conclusion, see "Ladies' Anti-Slavery Convention," *Lib,* 2 June 1837; "Ladies' Convention," *Lib,* 2 June 1837.

91. Hansen, "Boston Female," 58.

92. hooks, *Ain't I A Woman,* 88–92; Yee, *Black Women Abolitionists,* 3.

93. Yee, *Black Women Abolitionists,* 4.

94. Ibid.

95. Ophelia, Letter, *FJ,* 22 Aug. 1828; S., "Female Tenderness," *FJ,* 27 July 1827.

96. "Duties of Wives," *FJ,* 21 Feb. 1829; "Female Temper," *FJ,* 20 Apr. 1827.

97. John B. Russwurm, "Our Dorcas Society," *FJ,* 9 Jan. 1829; John B. Russwurm, "Another Celebration!!!" *FJ,* 15 Aug. 1828.

98. Matilda, Letter, *FJ,* 10 Aug. 1827.

99. Terborg-Penn, "Black Male Perspectives," 28–29. See also Perkins, "Black Women," 321.

100. "Speech by Charles Lenox Remond, Delivered at Marlboro Chapel, Boston, Massachusetts, 29 May 1844," *BAP,* 3:443; Frederick Douglass, "Rights of Women," *NS,* 28 July 1848; hooks, *Ain't I A Woman,* 89–91; Hamilton, "Frederick Douglass."

101. Hine, *Hine Sight,* 51; see also Guy-Sheftall, "Black Feminism," 348–52.

102. Mary Ann Shadd, Letter, *NS,* 23 Mar. 1849; Barbara Ann Stewart [*sic*], Letter, *Frederick Douglass' Paper,* 1 June 1855.

103. Quotations from Maria Stewart's works are cited in the text as indicated in the Abbreviations section.

104. Beecher, *Essay on Slavery,* 108.

105. Afric-American Female Intelligence Society of Boston, "Constitution of the Afric-American Female Intelligence Society of Boston," *Lib,* 7 Jan. 1832.

106. See Coleman, *Tribal Talk,* 107–34; Wilmore, "Black Religious Traditions," 290–91.

107. "Speech by Sarah M. Douglass, Delivered Before the Female Literary Society of Philadelphia, Philadelphia, Pennsylvania [June 1832]," *BAP,* 3:117.

CHAPTER 3

1. Cornish and Russwurm, "To Our Patrons."

2. Cornish and Russwurm, "To Our Patrons"; Cornish and Russwurm, "Prospectus."

3. For biographical information included in this section, I am indebted to the following sources: Ripley et al., *BAP;* Jacobs, "David Walker and William Lloyd Garrison"; Jacobs, "David Walker: Boston Race Leader"; Wilentz, introduction to *David Walker's Appeal;* Wiltse, introduction to *David Walker's Appeal;* Aptheker, *"One Continual Cry";* Usrey, "Charles

Lenox Remond"; Horton and Horton, *Black Bostonians;* Quarles, *Black Abolitionists;* Quarles, *Frederick Douglass;* Pease and Pease, *They Who Would Be Free;* Lessl, "William Whipper"; Wheaton and Condit, "Charles Lenox Remond."

4. Southern legislatures passed laws banning "incendiary works" from being brought to the South, and southern politicians appealed to Boston's mayor, protesting Walker's work and suggesting he should be punished. See Aptheker, *"One Continual Cry,"* 47–48; Wilentz, introduction to *David Walker's Appeal,* xix; Jacobs, "David Walker: Boston Race Leader," 104–5. Janet Duitsman Cornelius notes that Walker's *Appeal* was often cited by proslavery southerners as evidence that slaves should not be taught to read, and its publication was among the factors leading to harsh legislation to keep slaves illiterate (*"When I Can Read,"* 31–33). For a summary of the reaction to Walker's *Appeal* in the northern press, see Jacobs, "David Walker: Boston Race Leader," 105–6.

5. Although he does not deny the possibility that Walker was murdered, Peter Hinks notes that no evidence exists to support this conclusion and that "available sources . . . strongly support a natural death from a common and virulent urban disease of the nineteenth century [consumption]" (*To Awaken,* 269–70).

6. The AMRS was an outgrowth of the African American convention movement of the early 1830s, organized to bring together African American leaders of different cities to discuss issues such as emigration, education, prejudice, and moral reform; see *Minutes of the Fifth Annual Convention,* 4–5, 25–31.

7. Douglass wrote a third and final version of his life story, *Life and Times of Frederick Douglass,* published in 1881.

8. For an extension of my argument in this section that considers African American self-help rhetoric of other periods as well, see Bacon, "Rethinking the History."

9. Shirley Ardener, introduction to *Perceiving;* viii-ix; Shirley Ardener, "Nature," 21, 28; Kramarae, *Women and Men,* 3.

10. Whipper, *Address Delivered in Wesley Church,* 115–16.

11. Watkins, *Address Delivered Before the Moral Reform Society,* 165; *Minutes of the Fifth Annual Convention for the Improvement of the Free People of Colour in the United States, BAP,* 3:149.

12. *Minutes of the Fifth Annual Convention for the Improvement of the Free People of Colour, BAP,* 3:147–48, 150.

13. "Speech by William Whipper, Delivered Before the Colored Temperance Society of Philadelphia, Philadelphia, Pennsylvania, 8 January 1834," *BAP,* 3:125–26.

14. Bower and Ochs, *Rhetoric of Agitation,* 20.

15. Ibid., 26–27.

16. Hinks, *To Awaken,* 108–9.

17. "Address, Delivered Before the [Massachusetts] General Colored Association at Boston, by David Walker," *FJ,* 20 Dec. 1828.

18. "Speech by Andrew Harris, Delivered at the Broadway Tabernacle, New York, New York, 7 May 1839," *BAP,* 3:294–95; "Speech by Peter Paul Simons, Delivered Before the African Clarkson Association, New York, New York, 23 April 1839," *BAP,* 3:289; "Testimony by Charles Lenox Remond, Delivered at the Massachusetts State House, Boston, Massachusetts, 10 February 1842," *BAP,* 3:369.

19. Blassingame, introduction to *FDP,* xlviii.

20. Blassingame, introduction to *FDP,* xxii; Fisher, *Human Communication,* 143–44.

21. Weal, "Force of Narrative," 105.

22. Ibid., 113.

23. See Andrews, "Frederick Douglass," for a discussion of the influence of preaching on Douglass's oratory.

24. Kenneth Burke, *Rhetoric,* 98.

25. My references throughout this study to African Americans' *appropriation, recasting,* or *reinvention* of texts and discourse associated with white Americans are not intended to imply that these acts were illegitimate or that African Americans were "taking" something not properly or naturally theirs. Nor do I mean that African Americans were merely "borrowing" forms of language but that they were transforming and redefining them. I use these terms to emphasize the ways that discourse that was often used to disenfranchise African Americans could be deployed in ways that gave them power. This disruption of "the oppressor's language," as bell hooks explains, is a radical act of resistance (*Teaching to Transgress,* 169–70; see also Gates, *Figures in Black,* 57; Gates, *Signifying Monkey,* xxii–xxv; Bacon and McClish, "Reinventing the Master's Tools," 21).

26. Blassingame, introduction to *FDP,* xxx.

27. For Burke's discussion of "mystery," the rhetorical forms invoked by hierarchy, and the relation of identification and difference, see his *Rhetoric,* 22, 45–46, 114–127, 137–42, 208–12.

28. Ibid., 124.

29. Ibid., 140.

30. Kenneth Burke, *Grammar,* 122, 271–72; Kenneth Burke, *Rhetoric,* 328.

31. On this point, see Levine, *Black Culture,* 49; Genovese, *Roll, Jordan, Roll,* 163–67, 192–93, 242, 254; Cone, *God of the Oppressed,* 138–39, 224–25; Coleman, *Tribal Talk,* 107–34.

32. William J. Watkins, Letter, *Boston Herald,* 23 Apr. 1853.

33. Cmiel, *Democratic Eloquence,* 56–82, 94–122.

34. Charles Lenox Remond to the West Newbury Anti-Slavery Society, 16 Sept. 1842, *Lib,* 7 Oct. 1842.

35. See Frederickson, *Black Image,* 90–96.

36. Kenneth Burke, *Rhetoric,* 208–12.

37. Frankenberg, *White Women,* 147.

38. Jefferson, *Notes,* 143.

39. Frankenberg, *White Women,* 6–7, 17–18; Frankenberg, "Introduction," 1–4; Crenshaw, "Color-Blind Dreams," 110–11; Aanerud, "Whiteness," 37–38; Fine et al., preface to *Off White,* vii–viii.

40. Levine, *Black Culture,* 85–86; "Ironical Defence of Drunkenness," *Lib,* 18 June 1831.

41. Fanuzzi, "Trouble," 27–28.

42. "Testimony by Charles Lenox Remond," *BAP,* 3:368.

43. Ibid., *BAP,* 3:368–69.

44. See, for example, American Colonization Society, *African Colonization,* 23–24; Clay, *Speech . . . 1847,* 22; Jefferson, *Notes,* 87.

45. According to the report in the New York *Herald,* many African Americans were also in the audience; see John Blassingame's headnote to the speech, *FDP,* 2:423.

46. Frankenberg, *White Women,* 49; see also McIntosh, "White Privilege," 291–92.

47. Frankenberg, *White Women,* 152, 188; see also Crenshaw, "Color-Blind Dreams," 107; Crenshaw, "Color Blindness," 285–87.

48. "Grand Anti-Slavery Convention at Cincinnati," *Lib,* 6 May 1853. Douglass's vehement denunciation of Remond connects to the larger battle between Douglass and the Garrisonians over Douglass's independence and his publication of the *North Star.* Douglass's repudiation of Garrisonian principles led to a feud between Douglass and Garrison's supporters such as Remond, with both sides sharply criticizing the other. See Quarles, "Breach," 151; Pease and Pease, "Boston Garrisonians," 37–38.

49. "Speech by Charles Lenox Remond, Delivered at Mozart Hall, New York, New York, 13 May 1858," *BAP,* 4:382.

50. My discussion of the American jeremiad in this section is informed by the work of various scholars, including Bercovitch, *American Jeremiad;* Ritter, "American Political Rhetoric"; Murphy, "Time of Shame"; Zulick, "Agon of Jeremiah."

51. On the resonance of the identification with the Israelites in African American Christianity, see Raboteau, "African-Americans"; Coleman, *Tribal Talk,* 128.

52. Howard-Pitney, *Afro-American Jeremiad,* 12–15, 186; Moses, *Black Messiahs,* 31–38, 50, 228.

53. Howard-Pitney, *Afro-American Jeremiad,* 13; Moses, *Black Messiahs,* 29, 51.

54. "Address, Delivered Before the [Massachusetts] General Colored Association."

55. Ibid.

56. Kenneth Burke, *Rhetoric,* 328.

57. Bercovitch, *American Jeremiad,* 25.

58. A Colored Baltimorean [William Watkins], Letter, *Lib,* 4 June 1831.

59. See also Ronald K. Burke, *Frederick Douglass,* 82–88, for a discussion of this speech as an example of jeremiadic rhetoric.

60. See Wills, *Inventing America,* xvi-xxii; Wills, *Lincoln,* 86–89, 100–103, 109–10; Bush, *American Declarations,* 33–36.

61. Samuel Cartwright, "Education," 884; Bledsoe, "Liberty and Slavery," 323–24; U. S. Congress, *Annals,* 16th Cong., 1st. sess., 1384.

62. Condit and Lucaites, *Crafting Equality,* 69–98; Gary Woodward, *Persuasive Encounters,* 28–30, 39.

63. Gary Woodward, *Persuasive Encounters,* 34–38.

64. Ibid., 39.

65. Kimberly K. Smith, *Dominion of Voice,* 11–50.

66. Whipper, *Address Delivered in Wesley Church,* 114.

67. Exegesis of the Constitution by African American abolitionists is a complex topic that is beyond the scope of this discussion. On African American abolitionists' varying perceptions of the Constitution, see Dick, *Black Protest,* 54–77. On the use of the Constitution by African American abolitionists after the Dred Scott decision, see McDorman, "Challenging Constitutional Authority."

68. A Colored Baltimorean [William Watkins], Letter, *Genius of Universal Emancipation,* July 1831.

69. Ibid.

70. The date of Douglass's speech itself has ironic resonance. It was given on July 5, which had been celebrated in the 1820s both to commemorate emancipation in New York and as a protest against whites' celebration of July Fourth in a nation in which slavery persisted (Quarles, "Antebellum Free Blacks," 235).

71. On Douglass's simultaneous evocation and critique of America's ideals in this speech, see also Bush, *American Declarations,* 49–50; Stephens, "Frederick Douglass."

72. Perelman and Olbrechts-Tyteca, *New Rhetoric,* 293.

73. Ibid., 218–19.

74. "Speech by Charles Lenox Remond, Delivered at Marlboro Chapel," *BAP,* 3:443.

75. W. [William J. Watkins], "Who Are the Murderers?" *Frederick Douglass' Paper,* 2 June 1854.

76. On the work of African American abolitionists in Britain, see Quarles, *Black Abolitionists,* 117–118, 129–42; Pease and Pease, *They Who Would Be Free,* 48–67; Fisch, *American Slaves.* As these scholars demonstrate, African American abolitionists' idealistic descriptions of the British Isles did not always correspond to their actual experiences as transatlantic travelers. British abolitionists and audiences often responded patronizingly to African American abolitionists and were not infrequently made uneasy or angry by them.

77. Kenneth Burke, *Rhetoric,* 273–74, 298.

78. "Speeches of O'Connell and Remond," *Lib,* 31 July 1840.

79. Charles Lenox Remond to Thomas Cole, 2 Oct. 1840, *Lib,* 30 Oct. 1840.

80. "Testimony by Charles Lenox Remond," *BAP,* 3:370.

81. Gates, *Figures,* xxi, 236–50; Abrahams, *Deep Down,* 51–52, 264; Mitchell-Kernan, "Signifying," 314; Gates, *Signifying,* xxv-xxvi, 40, 48–54, 70–124.

82. Gates, *Figures,* 48; Gates, *Signifying,* xix.

83. Frederick Douglass, "To My Old Master," *NS,* 8 Sept. 1848.

84. Levine, *Black Culture,* 121–33; Abrahams, *Singing the Master,* 107–16.

85. Mitchell-Kernan, "Signifying," 314.

86. Douglass, "To My Old Master."

87. Ibid.

88. Gates, *Figures,* 117.

89. Douglass, "To My Old Master."

90. Ibid.

91. Mitchell-Kernan, "Signifying," 318–21.

92. Ibid., 322.

93. Gates, *Figures,* 17, 236; Gates, *Signifying,* 103–24..

94. Jefferson, *Notes,* 138–43.

95. On this passage, see also McHenry, "Forgotten Readers," 153.

96. Jefferson, *Notes,* 163.

97. Clay, *Address,* 7, 13–14; Clay, *Speech . . . 1827,* 6, 12; American Colonization Society, *View,* 5–6; "Thirty-First," 81.

98. For the original text of Clay's speech, see American Colonization Society, *View,* 5–6.

99. Ibid., 5.

100. Frederick Douglass, "Letter to Henry Clay," *NS,* 3 Dec. 1847; Clay, *Speech . . . 1847,* 22.

101. Clay, *Speech . . . 1847,* 21–22; Douglass, "Letter to Henry Clay."

102. Clay, *Speech . . . 1847,* 22; Douglass, "Letter to Henry Clay."

103. Clay, *Speech . . . 1847,* 22; Douglass, "Letter to Henry Clay."

104. Clay, *Speech . . . 1847,* 23; Douglass, "Letter to Henry Clay."

105. For further exploration of the connections among language, power, enslavement, and freedom, see Warren, *Culture of Eloquence,* 120–31; Wardrop, "'While I Am Writing'"; Lampe, *Frederick Douglass,* 9.

CHAPTER 4

1. Angelina Grimké to Amos A. Phelps, 17 August 1837, *PY,* 279; Abby Kelley, "Letter to Elizur Wright, Jr.," *Lib,* 6 Sept. 1839.

2. Oliver Johnson, *William Lloyd Garrison,* 254–57; May, *Some Recollections,* 92.

3. In addition to the primary sources cited in this section, I am indebted to the following sources for biographical information on these abolitionists: Cromwell, *Lucretia Mott;* Karcher, "Rape"; Karcher, *First Woman;* Karcher, *Lydia Maria Child,* 135–45; Clifford, *Crusader for Freedom;* Ceplair, introduction to *PY;* Lerner, introduction to *Feminist Thought;* Yellin, *Women and Sisters;* Sterling, *Ahead;* Hersh, *Slavery of Sex;* Melder, "Abby Kelley."

4. In contrast to other Christian denominations in antebellum America, Quakers allowed women to preach because they believed spiritual inspiration did not depend upon gender. Yet women still found themselves in a subordinate position in the Quaker religion, denied equal status in decision-making processes. On women's role in the Quaker religion, see Yellin, *Women and Sisters,* 51; Greene, introduction to *Lucretia Mott,* 9.

5. Lydia Maria Child to Anne Whitney, 25 May 1879, *Lydia Maria Child,* 558; Lydia Maria Child to Louisa Loring [March? 1837], *Lydia Maria Child,* 64.

6. Angelina Grimké, diary entry, 6 February 1829, *PY,* 17–18; Angelina Grimké to Jane Smith, 4 February 1837, *PY,* 116; Angelina Grimké to Sarah Grimké [27 September 1835], *PY,* 28; Angelina Grimké to Sarah Grimké, 19 [July 1836], *PY,* 34.

7. Sarah Grimké, diary entry, 25 September 1835, *PY,* 27.

8. See also Campbell, *Man,* 1:12, on the contrasting requirements of femininity and rhetorical credibility and on the deployment of a "feminine style."

9. Edwin Ardener, "Belief," 2, 14; Shirley Ardener, "Nature," 21; Kramarae, *Women and Men,* 3.

10. Shirley Ardener, introduction to *Perceiving,* xvii.

11. See also Bacon, "*Liberator*'s 'Ladies' Department,'" 10–13.

12. Shirley Ardener, introduction to *Perceiving,* xiii.

13. hooks, *Ain't I A Woman,* 7–8, 52–54; Frankenberg, *White Women,* 71–75.

14. Abby Kelley, "A Row in Millbury" [letter to William Lloyd Garrison], *Lib,* 10 Sept. 1841.

15. Ibid.

16. "New England Anti-Slavery Convention," *Lib,* 9 June 1854.

17. Kelley, "Letter to Elizur Wright, Jr."

18. Kenneth Burke, *Rhetoric,* 140–41.

19. Beecher, *Essay on Slavery,* 101–2; Putnam, *Address,* 11–12.

20. Ginzburg, *Women,* 18; see also Clinton, *Other Civil War,* 54; Hersh, "Am I Not a Woman," 277.

21. Clarkson, "To Mrs. Angelina E. Grimké and Sarah M. Grimké," *Religious Intelligencer,* 11 Feb. 1837.

22. Sarah and Angelina Grimké, "Letter to 'Clarkson,'" *Friend of Man,* 5 Apr. 1837.

23. Quotations from Sarah Grimké's works are cited in the text as indicated in the Abbreviations section.

24. Grimké's counterargument is, however, problematic, based on racist and anti-Semitic tendencies (*E,* 98–100).

25. Kenneth Burke, *Rhetoric,* 298–99, 277–78.

26. Quotations from Angelina Grimké's works are cited in the text as indicated in the Abbreviations section.

27. Browne, *Angelina Grimké,* 60–63.

28. Arthos, "My Voice," 128.

29. Quotations from Lydia Maria Child's works are cited in the text as indicated in the Abbreviations section.

30. Beecher, *Essay on Slavery,* 102. Beecher's advice was not lost on her famous sister. As Gillian Brown suggests in her discussion of *Uncle Tom's Cabin,* the appeal to mothers whose families are corrupted by slavery allowed Harriet Beecher Stowe to discuss political questions by framing them as domestic concerns (*Domestic Individualism,* 13–38).

31. Browne, *Angelina Grimké,* 14.

32. Grimké revised the letters for their publication in book form. Quotes in this study are from the revised text.

33. Angelina Grimké to Jane Smith, June [1837], *PY,* 146.

34. Hoganson, "Garrisonian Abolitionists," 558–60.

35. Karcher, *First Woman,* 420; Karcher, introduction to *Lydia Maria Child,* 145.

36. hooks, *Ain't I A Woman,* 125–26; see also Sánchez-Eppler, *Touching Liberty,* 14–23.

37. This text was comprised of a series of fifteen letters written in response to the request of Mary S. Parker, president of BFASS, that Sarah Grimké describe the history of women's oppression in society and argue for women's equality. The first letter was published in the *New England Spectator,* and the entire series appeared in the *Liberator* in 1837. It was published in tract form by the AASS in 1838.

38. Kenneth Burke, *Rhetoric,* 130.

39. "American Anti-Slavery Society," *Lib,* 19 May 1853.

40. See also Sánchez-Eppler, *Touching Liberty,* 19, on the way white female abolitionists assumed agency to speak while silencing slave voices.

41. Yellin, *Women and Sisters,* 3–26.

42. This work was first published in 1835 in two volumes, with the second edition published as one volume in 1838. My citations in this chapter refer to the earlier edition.

43. Yellin, *Women and Sisters,* 21–25.

44. Clinton, *Other Civil War,* 41–42; Ginzburg, *Women,* 4, 18; Boylan, "Timid Girls," 791.

45. Quotations from *Lucretia Mott: Her Complete Speeches and Sermons* are cited in the text as indicated in the Abbreviations section.

46. I have borrowed here from Gillian Brown's analysis of *Uncle Tom's Cabin* (*Domestic Individualism,* 13–16).

47. Stowe, *Key,* 257.

48. hooks, *Ain't I A Woman,* 126.

49. See, for example, Edmund Ruffin's 1853 thesis that the domestic life of "laborers"— as opposed to that of capitalists—is more efficient under a system such as slavery that, instead of encouraging individual family units, concentrates domestic efforts (*Political Economy,* 82–85).

50. See, for example, Jefferson, *Notes,* 139; Priest, *Bible Defence,* 238, 265–66; Cartwright, "On the Caucasians," 727–28. This assumption is also illustrated in Harriet Beecher Stowe's *Uncle Tom's Cabin,* particularly in the views of Marie St. Clare (262, 268). I am indebted to Joseph Moldenhauer for suggesting this connection.

51. See also Child's comments about Mandingo mothers in her children's essay "Kindness of the Africans," 111–18.

52. Lydia Maria Child, "A, B, C, of Abolition: For Those Who Have Not Yet Examined the Subject," *NASS,* 12 Aug. 1841. Child reprinted her series of these columns in her 1836 *Anti-Slavery Catechism.*

53. See Levander, *Voices of the Nation,* 19; Sánchez-Eppler, *Touching Liberty,* 3.

54. Angelina Grimké to Theodore Dwight Weld, August 12 [1837], Weld, Weld, and Grimké, *Letters,* 1:417; Sarah and Angelina Grimké to Theodore Dwight Weld, September 20, 1837, Weld, Weld, and Grimké, *Letters,* 1:448.

55. Nathaniel P. Rogers, "The National Anti-Slavery Standard," *NASS,* 6 May 1841; Child, "To the Readers."

56. Oliver Johnson, *William Lloyd Garrison,* 255; May, *Some Recollections,* 92; Angelina Grimké to William Lloyd Garrison, 30 August 1835, *Lib,* 19 Sept. 1835.

57. Kenneth Burke, *Rhetoric,* 22, 118, 124.

58. "Angelina E. Grimké," *Lib,* 2 March 1838.

59. Ibid.

60. Ibid.

61. Angelina Grimké, diary entry, October 1835, *PY,* 31; Child, "To the Readers."

62. Perelman and Olbrechts-Tyteca, *New Rhetoric,* 4–6; Frank, "New Rhetoric," 314–15.

63. Mailloux, "Rhetorical Hermeneutics," 629, 631; Mailloux, "Rhetorical Hermeneutics Revisited," 238–42.

64. Perelman and Olbrechts-Tyteca, *New Rhetoric,* 218–19.

65. Mailloux, "Rhetorical Hermeneutics Revisited," 242.

66. Perelman and Olbrechts-Tyteca, *New Rhetoric,* 293–96.

67. Ibid., 293.

68. Ibid., 411–24.

69. Lydia Maria Child, "To Abolitionists," *NASS,* 20 May 1841.

70. Lydia Maria Child, "Speaking in the Church." *NASS*, 15 July 1841.

71. Abby Kelley, "The Woman Question," *Lib*, 27 Mar. 1840.

72. For more discussion of this aspect of jeremiadic authority, see Zulick, "Agon of Jeremiah," 127–28.

73. Ibid., 133–35, 139.

74. Angelina Grimké, "Speech at Pennsylvania Hall, May 16, 1838," *PY*, 318–19, 321.

75. Ibid., 321. For another discussion of Grimké's use of prophetic strategies in this speech, see Campbell, *Man*, 1:29–33.

76. Angelina Grimké, "Speech at Pennsylvania Hall," *PY*, 319–20. See also Browne, *Angelina Grimké*, 139–65, for analysis of Grimké's symbolic use of the mob's violence in this speech.

77. Woodward, *Persuasive Encounters*, 22, 47.

78. Lydia Maria Child to Samuel May Jr., 26 Feb. 1860, *Lydia Maria Child*, 342.

79. Kramarae, *Women and Men*, 143–44.

80. Campbell, *Man*, 1:13.

81. Perelman and Olbrechts-Tyteca, *New Rhetoric*, 159.

82. Kramarae, *Women and Men*, 144.

83. *American Slavery As It Is*, 52–53, 57.

84. See, for example, Priest, *Bible Defence*, 107–59; Bledsoe, "Liberty and Slavery," 337–46; Stringfellow, "Bible Argument," 462–78.

85. Lydia Maria Child, "The Third Political Party," *NASS*, 24 June 1841; Kenneth Burke, *Rhetoric*, 28.

86. Lydia Maria Child, "A Slaveholder's Argument," *NASS*, 14 Apr. 1842.

87. Ibid.

88. Lydia Maria Child, "A, B, C, of Abolition: For Those Who Have Not Yet Examined the Subject," *NASS*, 5 Aug. 1841.

CHAPTER 5

1. "Speech by Sarah P. Remond, Delivered at the Red Lion Hotel, Warrington, England, 2 February 1859," *BAP*, 1:446.

2. "Colored Men's State Convention," *Frederick Douglass' Paper*, 14 Sept. 1855.

3. I am indebted to the following sources for biographical information on the abolitionists featured in this chapter: Richardson, "What If I Am a Woman?"; Richardson, introduction to *Maria W. Stewart;* Halford Ross Ryan, "Maria W. Miller Stewart," 310; Leeman, "Frances Ellen Watkins Harper," 171–72; Giddings, *When and Where I Enter*, 49–54; Campbell, *Man*, 1:17–22, 1:33; Ripley et al., *BAP;* Yellin, introduction to *Incidents;* Yellin, *Women and Sisters*, 77–96; Fitch, "Sojourner Truth"; Painter, "Difference"; Painter, *Sojourner Truth;* Washington, introduction to *Narrative;* Lipscomb, "Sojourner Truth"; Mabee and Newhouse, *Sojourner Truth;* Stetson and David, *Glorying in Tribulation;* Robbie Jean Walker, "Sojourner Truth," 332–33; Andrews, *To Tell*, 239–63; Russell, *Render Me My Song*, 9–11; Mullen, "Runaway Tongue," 249–54; Soderlund, "Priorities and Power"; Winch, "You Have Talents"; Porter, "Sarah Parker Remond."

4. Collins, *Fighting Words*, 14–32.

5. Collins, *Black Feminist Thought,* 24–29; Collins, *Fighting Words,* 8, 205; see also hooks, *Ain't I A Woman,* 160.

6. "Speech by Sarah M. Douglass," *BAP,* 3:116–17.

7. See Carol Wilson, *Freedom at Risk.* Given Douglass's choice of words, it seems likely that she refers to kidnappers. Marie Lindhorst and Dorothy Sterling suggest alternatively that Douglass alludes to restrictive legislation against African Americans proposed in Pennsylvania (but not passed) in 1831–32 (Lindhorst, "Politics," 266–68; Sterling, *We Are Your Sisters,* 126).

8. Collins, *Black Feminist Thought,* 28.

9. Terborg-Penn, "Black Male Perspectives," 30; see also Perkins, "Black Women," 323–25.

10. Logan, *"We Are Coming,"* 42–43.

11. "Philadelphia Woman's Association," *NS,* 9 Mar. 1849.

12. Watkins, "Our Greatest Want," 160.

13. Shirley Ardener, introduction to *Perceiving,* xvii.

14. Collins, *Black Feminist Thought,* 11–12.

15. Zillah [Sarah Douglass], "To a Friend," *Lib,* 30 June 1832.

16. "Lecture by Sojourner Truth," *New-York Daily Tribune,* 8 Nov. 1853.

17. William Hayward, Letter, *Lib,* 15 Oct. 1858.

18. Ibid.

19. Collins, *Black Feminist Thought,* 105–7; Arthos, "My Voice," 128.

20. Painter, "Difference," 155; hooks, *Ain't I A Woman,* 70; Collins, *Black Feminist Thought,* 118.

21. "The Rights of Woman. Ohio Woman's Rights Convention," *New-York Daily Tribune,* 6 June 1851; "Women's Rights Convention. Sojourner Truth," *Anti-Slavery Bugle,* 21 June 1851; Frances Dana Gage, "Sojourner Truth," *NASS,* 2 May 1863. Because it is difficult to accurately determine the content of Truth's speech, I analyze parallel passages from three often varying accounts by eyewitnesses and reporters—the 1851 reports in the *New-York Daily Tribune* and the *Anti-Slavery Bugle* and the 1863 report of Frances Dana Gage, a women's rights activist and the convention's president, which was published in the *National Anti-Slavery Standard.* Gage's account is the most famous, and her text has frequently been featured to the exclusion of others. Recent scholarship, however, suggests that an exclusive focus on Gage's account—which was written twelve years after the speech was given—is problematic. Scholars question the accuracy of various details of Gage's version, including whether Truth indeed posed the famous question "Ar'n't I a woman?"—a query that does not appear in other accounts—and Gage's rendering of Truth's words in stereotypical southern slave dialect. See Mabee and Newhouse, *Sojourner Truth,* 67–82; Painter, *Sojourner Truth,* 164–75; Stetson and David, *Glorying in Tribulation,* 112, 118–119; Fitch, "Sojourner Truth," 421.

22. Quotations from Jacobs's narrative *Incidents in the Life of a Slave Girl* are cited in the text as indicated in the Abbreviations section.

23. Kenneth Burke, *Counter-Statement,* 148–49.

24. On the place of language in the battle between Jacobs and Flint, see also Levander, *Voices of the Nation,* 94–97; Sale, "Critiques from Within," 708.

25. Yellin, introduction to *Incidents,* xxx; see also Berlant, "Queen of America," 555.

26. Berlant, "Queen of America," 550–54; Sánchez-Eppler, *Touching Liberty,* 91.

27. Kenneth Burke, *Rhetoric,* 130.

28. Ibid., 22–25.

29. Zillah [Sarah Douglass], "A Mother's Love," *Lib,* 28 July 1832.

30. Ibid.

31. Jacobs to Amy Post, 9 Oct. 1853, *ILSG,* 242.

32. "Speech by Sarah P. Remond, Delivered at the Music Hall, Warrington, England, 24 January 1859," *BAP,* 1:437.

33. The experiences of Margaret Garner inspired Toni Morrison's novel *Beloved;* see Elizabeth Kastor, "Toni Morrison's 'Beloved' Country: The Writer and Her Haunting Tale of Slavery," *Washington Post,* 5 Oct. 1987.

34. "Lola Montez Reviewed by Miss Remond," *NASS,* 9 July 1859.

35. "Miss Remond in Bristol," *NASS,* 24 Sept. 1859.

36. "Lola Montez on American Slavery," *NASS,* 9 July 1859.

37. "Lola Montez Reviewed by Miss Remond."

38. Julia Gardiner Tyler, "To the Duchess of Sutherland and the Ladies of England," *Richmond Enquirer,* 28 Jan. 1853.

39. [Harriet Jacobs], "Letter From a Fugitive Slave," *New-York Daily Tribune,* 21 June 1853.

40. Jacobs explains in a letter to Amy Post that the woman was actually a friend with whom she grew up (Jacobs to Post, *ILSG,* 236).

41. [Jacobs], "Letter From a Fugitive Slave."

42. Ibid.

43. Ibid.

44. "Lola Montez Reviewed by Miss Remond"; "Speech by Sarah P. Remond, Delivered at the Music Hall, Warrington, England," *BAP,* 1:438.

45. Cone, *God of the Oppressed,* 17–18, 32–36, 108–13, 142; Grant, *White Women's Christ,* 211–20; Connor, *Conversions,* 4; Levine, *Black Culture,* 35–37; Genovese, *Roll, Jordan, Roll,* 252–55; Coleman, *Tribal Talk,* 107–34.

46. Levine, *Black Culture,* 31; Grant, *White Women's Christ,* 212.

47. "The Rights of Woman"; "Women's Rights Convention"; Gage, "Sojourner Truth."

48. For Truth's account of her conversion, see Truth and Gilbert, *Narrative,* 48–51.

49. Ibid., 86–88.

50. "The Rights of Woman"; "Women's Rights Convention"; Gage, "Sojourner Truth."

51. On Stewart's religious rhetoric, including her jeremiadic persuasion, see also Peterson, *"Doers of the Word,"* 57–73.

52. Howard-Pitney, *Afro-American Jeremiad,* 83–86, 112.

53. Truth and Gilbert, *Narrative,* 90, 93, 95.

54. Maria W. Stewart, "Cause for Encouragement," *Lib,* 14 July 1832.

55. "Proceedings of the Anti-Slavery Celebration at Framingham, July 4, 1854," *Lib,* 14 July 1854.

56. "Address by a Slave Mother," *New-York Tribune,* 7 Sept. 1853.

57. Zillah [Sarah Douglass], "To a Friend"; Zillah [Sarah Douglass], "Moonlight," *Lib,* 7 Apr. 1832.

58. "New York City Anti-Slavery Society. Fourth Anniversary," *NASS,* 23 May 1857.

59. "Proceedings of the Anti-Slavery Celebration at Framingham, July 4, 1854."

60. Woodward, *Persuasive Encounters,* 28–30, 35–37.

61. On the ways Stewart incorporates in her rhetoric both an appeal to African heritage and an assertion of African Americans' rights in America, see Logan, *"We Are Coming,"* 23–43.

62. "Speech by Sarah P. Remond, Delivered at the Music Hall, Warrington, England," *BAP,* 1:438.

63. Ibid., *BAP,* 1:437.

64. "New York City Anti-Slavery Society."

65. Mitchell-Kernan, "Signifying," 328.

66. On Jacobs as trickster, see also Beardslee, "Through Slave Culture's Lens," 48–52.

67. [Harriet Jacobs], "Letter From a Fugitive Slave," *New-York Daily Tribune,* 21 June 1853.

68. Ibid.

69. See Woodson, *Education of the Negro,* 18–19.

70. Fitch and Mandziuk, *Sojourner Truth,* 34–46; Lipscomb, "Sojourner Truth," 235.

71. "The Rights of Woman"; "Women's Rights Convention"; Gage, "Sojourner Truth"; Campbell, "Style," 435.

72. hooks, *Teaching to Transgress,* 170.

CHAPTER 6

1. Wells, "Lynch Law," 751–54; Cornish and Russwurm, "To our Patrons."

2. Lorde, *Sister Outsider,* 41–43. For discussion of Lorde's commentary on silence and speech, see Olson, "On the Margins."

3. Wells, "Lynch Law," 747–51.

4. "Speech by William Whipper, Delivered Before the Colored Temperance Society of Philadelphia, Philadelphia, Pennsylvania, 8 January 1834," *BAP,* 3: 126; *Minutes of the Fifth Annual Convention for the Improvement of the Free People of Colour in the United States, BAP,* 3:147.

5. On Wells's opinion of Booker T. Washington's views, see her autobiography *Crusade for Justice,* 265. It is important to note that although self-help rhetoric of the 1890s and early twentieth century is frequently identified with Washington's accommodationist approach, this form of discourse was also marshaled at this time by rhetors with very different perspectives, such as W. E. B. Du Bois. See Bacon, "Rethinking the History," 71–72.

6. "Speech by Sarah M. Douglass," *BAP,* 3:114.

7. Malcolm X, "Ballot," 997.

8. West, *Race Matters,* 49–59; see also Bacon, "Rethinking the History," 73–74.

9. Archibald Grimké, "Shame," 689.

10. Ibid., 688.

11. "Grand Anti-Slavery Convention at Cincinnati," *Lib,* 6 May 1853.

12. Malcolm X, "Ballot," 987–88.

13. Ibid., 994.

14. Lorde, *Sister Outsider,* 112.

15. Ibid. For further discussion of Lorde's view of difference as a means of "reclaiming language" and empowering those who are marginalized, see Olson, "Liabilities."

16. Flagg, "Antidiscrimination," 590; Frankenberg, *White Women,* 152, 188; Crenshaw, "Color-Blind Dreams," 102–8; Crenshaw, "Color Blindness," 285–87.

17. Wells, "Lynch Law," 747.

18. Ibid., 760.

19. Archibald Grimké, "Shame," 674–75.

20. Ibid., 675.

21. Malcolm X, "Ballot," 993, 998.

22. Ibid., 999.

23. Archibald Grimké, "Shame," 671–72.

24. For the traditional perspectives of white historians, see Ellis, *American Sphinx,* 303–7; Dabney, *Jefferson Scandals.* For the alternative (and ultimately validated) beliefs of African Americans, see Gordon-Reed, *Thomas Jefferson;* Don Terry, "DNA Results Confirmed Old News About Jefferson, Blacks Say," *New York Times,* 10 Nov. 1998, late edition, A18. For analysis of what the controversy about Jefferson and Hemings reveals about American attitudes about race, see French and Ayers, "Strange Career"; Annette Gordon-Reed, "Why Jefferson Scholars Were the Last to Know," *New York Times,* 3 Nov. 1998, late edition, A27; Boyce, "Slaves of the Past."

25. Archibald Grimké, "Shame," 677.

26. Lorde, *Sister Outsider,* 113.

27. Allen, "Orators," 232.

28. Ibid., 112.

29. hooks, *Teaching to Transgress,* 175; Gates, "Address."

30. Lorde, *Sister Outsider,* 134, 144.

Bibliography

PRIMARY SOURCES

Newspapers

Anti-Slavery Bugle, Salem, Ohio, 21 June 1851.

Boston Herald, 23 Apr. 1853.

Colored American, New York, 4 Mar. 1837.

Day-Book, New York, 10 Nov. 1857.

Frederick Douglass' Paper, Rochester, N.Y., 10 Feb. 1854–14 Sept. 1855.

Freedom's Journal, New York, 16 Mar. 1827–21 Feb. 1829.

Friend of Man, Utica, N.Y., 5 Apr.1837.

Genius of Universal Emancipation, Baltimore, July 1831.

Liberator, Boston, 4 June 1831–11 Mar. 1859.

National Anti-Slavery Standard, New York, 6 May 1841–2 May 1863.

New-York Tribune, 6 June 1851–8 Nov. 1853.

North Star, Rochester, N.Y., 3 Dec. 1842–21 Sept. 1849.

Northern Star and Freeman's Advocate, Albany, N.Y., 3 Mar. 1842.

Religious Intelligencer, New Haven, Conn., 11 Feb. 1837.

Richmond Enquirer, 28 Jan. 1853.

Books, Tracts, Articles, Speeches, and Collections

Allen, William G. "Orators and Oratory." In *Lift Every Voice: African American Oratory, 1787–1900,* edited by Philip S. Foner and Robert James Branham, 229–46. Tuscaloosa: University of Alabama Press, 1998.

American Anti-Slavery Society. *Fifth Annual Report of the Executive Committee of the American Anti-Slavery Society.* New York, 1838.

———. *First Annual Report of the American Anti-Slavery Society.* New York, 1834.

———. *Proceedings of the American Anti-Slavery Society, at its Second Decade, Held in the City of Philadelphia, Dec. 3rd, 4th and 5th, 1853.* New York, 1854.

———. *Second Annual Report of the American Anti-Slavery Society.* New York, 1835.

———. *Sixth Annual Report of the Executive Committee of the American Anti-Slavery Society.* New York, 1839.

American Colonization Society. *African Colonization. An Enquiry into the Origin, Plan, & Prospects of the American Colonization Society.* Fredericksburg, Va., 1829.

———. *A View of Exertions Lately Made for the Purpose of Colonizing the Free People of Colour, in the United States, in Africa, or Elsewhere.* Washington, D.C., 1817.

American Slavery As It Is: Testimony of a Thousand Witnesses. New York, 1839.

Beecher, Catharine E. *An Essay on Slavery and Abolitionism, with Reference to the Duty of American Females.* Philadelphia, 1837.

Bledsoe, Albert Taylor. "Liberty and Slavery: Or, Slavery in the Light of Moral and Political Philosophy." In *Cotton is King, and Pro-Slavery Arguments: Comprising the Writings of Hammond, Harper, Christy, Stringfellow, Hodge, Bledsoe, and Cartwright, on This Important Subject,* edited by E. N. Elliott, 269–458. Augusta, Ga., 1860.

Bolles, John A. "The Influence of Women on Society." *Ladies' Magazine and Literary Gazette* 4 (1831): 256–69.

Boston Female Anti-Slavery Society. *Report of the Boston Female Anti-Slavery Society; With a Concise Statement of Events, Previous and Subsequent to the Annual Meeting of 1835.* Boston, 1836.

Cartwright, Samuel. "The Education, Labor, and Wealth of the South." In *Cotton is King, and Pro-Slavery Arguments: Comprising the Writings of Hammond, Harper, Christy, Stringfellow, Hodge, Bledsoe, and Cartwright, on This Important Subject,* edited by E. N. Elliott, 879–96. Augusta, Ga., 1860.

———. *Essays, Being Inductions Drawn from the Baconian Philosophy Proving the Truth of the Bible and the Justice and Benevolence of the Decree Dooming Canaan to be Servant of Servants.* Vidalia, La., 1843.

Child, Lydia Maria. *An Appeal in Favor of That Class of Americans Called Africans.* 1833. Reprint, New York, 1836.

[———]. *Authentic Anecdotes of American Slavery.* 2 vols. Newburyport, Mass., 1835.

———. *Correspondence Between Lydia Maria Child and Governor Wise and Mrs. Mason, of Virginia.* Boston, 1860.

———. "Kindness of the Africans." *Juvenile Miscellany,* 3d ser., 5 (November–December 1833): 111–18.

———. *Lydia Maria Child: Selected Letters, 1817–1880.* Edited by Milton Meltzer, Patricia G. Holland, and Francine Krasno. Amherst: University of Massachusetts Press, 1982.

———. *The Patriarchal Institution, as Described by Members of its Own Family.* New York, 1860.

———. *The Right Way the Safe Way, Proved by Emancipation in the British West Indies and Elsewhere.* 1860. Reprint, New York, 1862.

Clay, Henry. *An Address, Delivered to the Colonization Society of Kentucky, at Frankfort, December 17, 1829.* Lexington, Ky., 1829.

———. *Speech of the Hon. Henry Clay at the Mass Meeting in Lexington, Ky., on Saturday, November 13, 1847.* Philadelphia, 1847.

———. *Speech of the Hon. Henry Clay, Before the American Colonization Society, in the Hall of the House of Representatives, January 20, 1827.* Washington, D.C., 1827.

Dennett, John R. "Eloquence at Second-Hand." *Nation* 2 (11 January 1866): 43.

Dew, Thomas R. *Review of the Debate in the Virginia Legislature of 1831 and 1832*. Richmond, 1832. Reprint in *Slavery Defended: The Views of the Old South,* edited by Eric L. McKitrick, 20–33. Englewood Cliffs, N.J.: Prentice-Hall, 1963.

"Domestic Duties." *Godey's Lady's Book* 12 (1836): 6.

Douglass, Frederick. *The Frederick Douglass Papers, Series One: Speeches, Debates, and Interviews*. 5 vols. New Haven, Conn.: Yale University Press, 1979–92.

———. *My Bondage and My Freedom*. 1855. Reprinted in *Autobiographies,* edited by Henry Louis Gates Jr., 103–452. New York: Library of America, 1994.

———. *Narrative of the Life of Frederick Douglass, An American Slave: Written by Himself.* 1845. Reprinted in *Autobiographies,* edited by Henry Louis Gates Jr., 1–102. New York: Library of America, 1994.

Emerson, Ralph Waldo. *Emerson's Antislavery Writings*. Edited by Len Gougeon and Joel Myerson. New Haven, Conn.: Yale University Press, 1995.

Female Anti-Slavery Society of Chatham-Street Chapel. *Constitution and Address of the Female Anti-Slavery Society of Chatham-Street Chapel*. New York, 1834.

[Fitzhugh, George]. *Slavery Justified; by a Southerner*. Fredericksburg, Va., 1860.

———. *Sociology for the South or the Failure of Free Society*. 1854. Reprinted in *Ante-Bellum: Writings of George Fitzhugh and Hinton Rowan Helper on Slavery,* edited by Harvey Wish, 41–95. New York: Capricorn, 1960.

Forten, James, Jr. *An Address Delivered Before the Ladies' Anti-Slavery Society of Philadelphia, on the Evening of the 14th of April, 1836*. Philadelphia, 1836.

"Fragments." *Godey's Lady's Book* 32 (1846): 154–55.

G. "How Ought Woman to Be Educated?" *Ladies' Magazine and Literary Gazette* 5 (1832): 508–15.

Garrison, Wendell Phillips, and Francis Jackson Garrison. *William Lloyd Garrison, 1805–1879: The Story of His Life Told by His Children*. 4 vols. New York, 1885–89.

Grimké, Angelina. *Appeal to the Christian Women of the South*. 1836. Reprinted in *The Public Years of Sarah and Angelina Grimké: Selected Writings 1835–1839,* edited by Larry Ceplair, 36–79. New York: Columbia University Press, 1989.

———. *Letters to Catherine* [sic] *E. Beecher, in Reply to an Essay on Slavery and Abolitionism, Addressed to A. E. Grimké*. 1838. Reprinted in *The Public Years of Sarah and Angelina Grimké: Selected Writings 1835–1839,* edited by Larry Ceplair, 146–204. New York: Columbia University Press, 1989.

Grimké, Archibald. "The Shame of America, Or the Negro's Case Against the Republic." In *Negro Orators and Their Orations,* edited by Carter G. Woodson, 671–89. Washington, D.C.: Associated Publishers, 1925.

Grimké, Sarah M. *An Epistle to the Clergy of the Southern States*. 1836. Reprinted in *The Public Years of Sarah and Angelina Grimké: Selected Writings 1835–1839,* edited by Larry Ceplair, 90–115. New York: Columbia University Press, 1989.

———. *Letters on the Equality of the Sexes, and the Condition of Woman, Addressed to Mary S. Parker, President of the Boston Female Anti-Slavery Society*. 1838. Reprinted in *The Public Years of Sarah and Angelina Grimké: Selected Writings 1835–1839,* edited by Larry Ceplair, 204–72. New York: Columbia University Press, 1989.

Grimké, Sarah Moore, and Angelina Emily Grimké. *The Public Years of Sarah and Angelina Grimké: Selected Writings 1835–1839*. Edited by Larry Ceplair. New York: Columbia University Press, 1989.

Hale, S[arah] J[ane]. "Ought Ladies to Form Peace Societies?" *Godey's Lady's Book* 21 (1840): 88–89.

Jacobs, Harriet A. *Incidents in the Life of a Slave Girl: Written by Herself.* Edited by Lydia Maria Child. 1861. Reprint, edited by Jean Fagan Yellin. Cambridge: Harvard University Press, 1987.

Jefferson, Thomas. *Notes on the State of Virginia.* 1787. Reprint, edited by William Peden. Chapel Hill: University of North Carolina Press, 1955.

Johnson, Oliver. *William Lloyd Garrison and His Times; Or, Sketches of the Anti-Slavery Movement in America, and of the Man Who Was its Founder and Moral Leader.* Boston, 1885.

Lane, Lunsford. *The Narrative of Lunsford Lane, Formerly of Raleigh, N.C.* 3d ed. Boston, 1845.

Lorde, Audre. *Sister Outsider: Essays and Speeches.* Freedom, Calif.: Crossing Press, 1984.

M. A. H. "An Appeal to the Enlightened and Philanthropic Gentlemen of the United States." *Ladies' Magazine and Literary Gazette* 6 (1833): 433–47.

Malcolm X. "The Ballot or the Bullet." In *The Voice of Black America: Major Speeches by Negroes in the United States, 1797–1971,* edited by Philip S. Foner, 985–1001. New York: Simon and Schuster, 1972.

May, Samuel J. *Some Recollections of Our Antislavery Conflict.* 1869. Reprint, New York: Arno Press, 1968.

Mott, Lucretia. *Lucretia Mott: Her Complete Speeches and Sermons.* Edited by Dana Greene. Lewiston, N.Y.: Edwin Mellen, 1980.

New-York Young Men's Anti-Slavery Society. *Preamble and Constitution of the New-York Young Men's Anti-Slavery Society.* New York, 1834.

Nott, Josiah. *Types of Mankind.* 1854. Reprinted in *Slavery Defended: The Views of the Old South,* edited by Eric L. McKitrick, 126–38. Englewood Cliffs, N.J.: Prentice-Hall, 1963.

"On the Duties of Wives." *Christian Monitor* 2.4 (1806): 58–78.

Peck, Jesse T. *The True Woman; Or, Life and Happiness at Home and Abroad.* New York, 1857.

Perrine, Matthew La Rue. *Women Have a Work To Do in the House of God: A Discourse Delivered at the First Annual Meeting of the Female Missionary Society for the Poor of the City of New-York and its Vicinity, May 12, 1817.* New York, 1817.

Porter, Dorothy, ed. *Early Negro Writing 1760–1837.* Boston: Beacon Press, 1971.

Priest, Josiah. *Bible Defence of Slavery; Or the Origin, History, and Fortunes of the Negro Race.* Louisville, Ky., 1851.

Putnam, John M. *An Address Delivered at Concord, N. H., Dec. 25, 1835, Before the Female Anti-Slavery Society of that Place.* Concord, 1836.

Ripley, C. Peter, et al., eds. *The Black Abolitionist Papers.* 5 vols. Chapel Hill: University of North Carolina Press, 1985–92.

Stewart, Maria W. *Maria W. Stewart, America's First Black Woman Political Writer: Essays and Speeches.* Edited by Marilyn Richardson. Bloomington: Indiana University. Press, 1987.

———. *Religion and the Pure Principles of Morality, the Sure Foundation on Which We Must Build.* 1831. Reprinted in *Maria W. Stewart, America's First Black Woman Political Writer: Essays and*

Speeches, edited by Marilyn Richardson, 28–42. Bloomington: Indiana University Press, 1987.

Stowe, Harriet Beecher. *The Key to Uncle Tom's Cabin.* 1854. Reprint, New York: Arno Press, 1969.

———. *Uncle Tom's Cabin: Or, Life Among the Lowly.* 1852. Reprint, New York: Penguin Books, 1981.

Stringfellow, Thornton. "The Bible Argument: Or, Slavery in the Light of Divine Revelation." In *Cotton is King, and Pro-Slavery Arguments: Comprising the Writings of Hammond, Harper, Christy, Stringfellow, Hodge, Bledsoe, and Cartwright, on This Important Subject,* edited by E. N. Elliott, 459–546. Augusta, Ga., 1860.

"Thirty-First Anniversary of the American Colonization Society." *African Repository and Colonization Journal* 24 (1848): 79–88.

Truth, Sojourner, and Olive Gilbert. *Narrative of Sojourner Truth.* 1850. Reprint, edited by Margaret Washington. New York: Vintage Books, 1993.

U.S. Congress. *Annals of the Congress of the United States, 1789–1824.* Washington, D.C., 1834–56.

Walker, David. *David Walker's Appeal, in Four Articles; Together with a Preamble, to the Coloured Citizens of the World, But in Particular, and Very Expressly, to Those of the United States of America.* 3d ed. 1830. Reprint, edited by Charles M. Wiltse. New York: Hill and Wang, 1965.

Watkins, Frances Ellen. "Our Greatest Want." *Anglo-African Magazine* 1 (May 1859): 160.

Watkins, William. *Address Delivered Before the Moral Reform Society, in Philadelphia, August 8, 1836.* 1836. Reprinted in *Early Negro Writing 1760–1837,* edited by Dorothy Porter, 155–66. Boston: Beacon Press, 1971.

Weld, Theodore Dwight, Angelina Grimké Weld, and Sarah Grimké. *Letters of Theodore Dwight Weld, Angelina Grimké Weld, and Sarah Grimké, 1822–1844.* Edited by Gilbert H. Barnes and Dwight L. Dumond. 2 vols. New York: D. Appleton-Century, 1934.

Wells, Ida B. *Crusade for Justice: The Autobiography of Ida B. Wells.* Edited by Alfreda M. Duster. Chicago: University of Chicago Press, 1970.

———. "Lynch Law in All Its Phases." In *Lift Every Voice: African American Oratory, 1787–1900,* edited by Philip S. Foner and Robert James Branham, 745–60. Tuscaloosa: University of Alabama Press, 1998.

Whipper, William. *An Address Delivered in Wesley Church, on the Evening of June 12, Before the Colored Reading Society of Philadelphia, for Mental Improvement.* 1828. Reprinted in *Early Negro Writing 1760–1837,* edited by Dorothy Porter, 105–19. Boston: Beacon Press, 1971.

"The Women of '76." *Godey's Lady's Book* 30 (1845): 97–102.

Wright, Elizur, Jr. "The Life and Adventures of a Fugitive Slave." *Quarterly Anti-Slavery Magazine* 1.4 (July 1836): 375–93.

SECONDARY SOURCES

Newspapers

New York Times, 3–10 Nov. 1998.

Washington Post, 5 Oct. 1987.

Books, Articles, and Speeches

Aanerud, Rebecca. "Fictions of Whiteness: Speaking the Names of Whiteness in U.S. Literature." In *Displacing Whiteness: Essays in Social and Cultural Criticism,* edited by Ruth Frankenberg, 35–59. Durham, N.C.: Duke University Press, 1997.

Abrahams, Roger D. *Deep Down in the Jungle: Negro Narrative Folklore from the Streets of Philadelphia.* 2d ed. New York: Aldine Publishing Co., 1970.

———. *Singing the Master: The Emergence of African American Culture in the Plantation South.* New York: Pantheon Books, 1992.

Abzug, Robert R. *Passionate Liberator: Theodore Dwight Weld and the Dilemma of Reform.* New York: Oxford University Press, 1980.

Albrecht, Robert C. "Conflict and Resolution: 'Slavery in Massachusetts.'" *ESQ* 19 (1973): 179–88.

Andrews, William L. "The Changing Moral Discourse of Nineteenth-Century African American Women's Autobiography: Harriet Jacobs and Elizabeth Keckley." In *De/Colonizing the Subject: The Politics of Gender in Women's Autobiography,* edited by Sidonie Smith and Julia Watson, 225–41. Minneapolis: University of Minnesota Press, 1992.

———, ed. *Critical Essays on Frederick Douglass.* Boston: G. K. Hall, 1991.

———. "Frederick Douglass, Preacher." *American Literature* 54 (1982): 592–97.

———. *To Tell a Free Story: The First Century of Afro-American Autobiography, 1760–1865.* Urbana: University of Illinois Press, 1986.

Aptheker, Herbert. *Abolitionism: A Revolutionary Movement.* Boston: Twayne Publishers, 1989.

———. *"One Continual Cry": David Walker's* Appeal to the Colored Citizens of the World *(1829–1830), Its Setting and Its Meaning.* New York: Humanities Press, 1965.

Ardener, Edwin. "Belief and the Problem of Women." In *Perceiving Women,* edited by Shirley Ardener, 1–17. New York: Wiley, 1975. First published in *The Interpretation of Ritual: Essays in Honour of A. I. Richards,* edited by J. S. La Fontaine (London: Tavistock Publications, 1972), 135–58.

———. "The 'Problem' Revisited" In *Perceiving Women,* edited by Shirley Ardener, 19–27. New York: Wiley, 1975.

Ardener, Shirley. Introduction to *Perceiving Women.* New York: Wiley, 1975.

———. "The Nature of Women in Society." In *Defining Females: The Nature of Women in Society,* edited by Shirley Ardener, 9–48. London: Croom Helm, 1978.

Arthos, John, Jr. "'My Voice is Bound to the Mass of My Own Life': Private and Public Boundaries in Feminist Rhetoric." *Southern Communication Journal* 63 (1998): 113–30.

Bacon, Jacqueline. "The *Liberator*'s 'Ladies' Department,' 1832–37: Freedom or Fetters?" In *Sexual Rhetoric: Media Perspectives on Sexuality, Gender and Identity,* edited by Meta G. Carstarphen and Susan Zavoina, 3–19. Westport, Conn.: Greenwood Publishing Group, 1999.

———. "Rethinking the History of African-American Self-Help Rhetoric: From Abolition to Civil Rights and Beyond." In *Advances in the History of Rhetoric: Histories of and Futures for Rhetorical Education, A Collection of Selected Papers Presented at ASHR Conferences in 1998,* vol. 3, edited by Richard Enos, 67–76. Fort Worth, Tex.: American Society for the History of Rhetoric, 1999.

Bacon, Jacqueline, and Glen McClish. "Reinventing the Master's Tools: Nineteenth-Century African-American Literary Societies of Philadelphia and Rhetorical Education." *Rhetoric Society Quarterly* 30.4 (fall 2000): 19–47.

Baker, Houston A., Jr. "Critical Memory and the Black Public Sphere." In *The Black Public Sphere: A Public Culture Book,* edited by Black Public Sphere Collective, 7–37. Chicago: University of Chicago Press, 1995.

Barnes, Gilbert Hobbs. *The Antislavery Impulse, 1830–1844.* New York: D. Appleton-Century, 1933.

Baym, Nina. *American Women Writers and the Work of History, 1790–1860.* New Brunswick, N.J.: Rutgers University Press, 1995.

Beardslee, Karen E. "Through Slave Culture's Lens Comes the Abundant Source: Harriet A. Jacobs's *Incidents in the Life of a Slave Girl." MELUS* 24.1 (spring 1999): 37–58.

Bell, Howard Holman. *A Survey of the Negro Convention Movement, 1830–1861.* 1953. Reprint, New York: Arno, 1969.

Benhabib, Seyla. "Models of Public Space: Hannah Arendt, the Liberal Tradition, and Jürgen Habermas." In *Habermas and the Public Sphere,* edited by Craig Calhoun, 73–98. Cambridge, Mass.: MIT Press, 1992.

Bercovitch, Sacvan. *The American Jeremiad.* Madison: University of Wisconsin Press, 1978.

Berlant, Lauren. "The Queen of America Goes to Washington City: Harriet Jacobs, Frances Harper, Anita Hill." *American Literature* 65 (1993): 549–74.

Berry, Mary Frances, and John W. Blassingame. *Long Memory: The Black Experience in America.* New York: Oxford University Press, 1982.

Blassingame, John W. "Editorial Method." In *The Frederick Douglass Papers, Series One: Speeches, Debates, and Interviews,* lxxiii–lxxxv. vol. 1. New Haven, Conn.: Yale University Press, 1979.

———. Introduction to *The Frederick Douglass Papers, Series One: Speeches, Debates, and Interviews.* vol. 1. New Haven, Conn.: Yale University Press, 1979.

Bower, John Waite, and Donovan J. Ochs. *The Rhetoric of Agitation and Control.* New York: Random House, 1971.

Boyce, Nell. "Slaves of the Past." *New Scientist,* 21 November 1998, 60.

Boylan, Anne M. "Benevolence and Antislavery Activity among African American Women in New York and Boston, 1820–1840." In *The Abolitionist Sisterhood: Women's Political Culture in Antebellum America,* edited by Jean Fagan Yellin and John C. Van Horne, 119–37. Ithaca, N.Y.: Cornell University Press, 1994.

———. "Timid Girls, Venerable Widows and Dignified Matrons: Life Cycle Patterns among Organized Women in New York and Boston, 1797–1840." *American Quarterly* 38 (1986): 779–97.

Brown, Gillian. *Domestic Individualism: Imagining Self in Nineteenth-Century America.* Berkeley: University of California Press, 1990.

Browne, Stephen Howard. *Angelina Grimké: Rhetoric, Identity, and the Radical Imagination.* East Lansing: Michigan State University Press, 1999.

Buckmaster, Henrietta. *Let My People Go: The Story of the Underground Railroad and the Growth of the Abolition Movement.* 1941. Reprint, Columbia: University of South Carolina Press, 1992.

Burke, Kenneth. *Counter-Statement.* 1931. Reprint, Berkeley: University of California Press, 1968.

———. *A Grammar of Motives.* 1945. Reprint, Berkeley: University of California Press, 1969.

———. *A Rhetoric of Motives.* 1950. Reprint, Berkeley: University of California Press, 1969.

Burke, Ronald K. *Frederick Douglass: Crusading Orator for Human Rights.* New York: Garland Publishing, 1996.

———. *Samuel Ringgold Ward, Christian Abolitionist.* New York: Garland Publishing, 1995.

Bush, Harold K., Jr. *American Declarations: Rebellion and Repentance in American Cultural History.* Urbana: University of Illinois Press, 1999.

Cain, William E, ed. *William Lloyd Garrison and the Fight against Slavery: Selections from the Liberator.* Boston: Bedford Books, 1995.

Campbell, Karlyn Kohrs. *Man Cannot Speak for Her.* 2 vols. Westport, Conn.: Greenwood Press, 1989.

———. "Style and Content in the Rhetoric of Early Afro-American Feminists." *Quarterly Journal of Speech* 72 (1986): 434–45.

Ceplair, Larry. Introduction to *The Public Years of Sarah and Angelina Grimké: Selected Writings 1835–1839.* New York: Columbia University Press, 1989.

Chambers-Schiller, Lee. "'A Good Work among the People': The Political Culture of the Boston Antislavery Fair." In *The Abolitionist Sisterhood: Women's Political Culture in Antebellum America,* edited by Jean Fagan Yellin and John C. Van Horne, 249–74. Ithaca, N.Y.: Cornell University Press, 1994.

Clifford, Deborah Pickman. *Crusader for Freedom: A Life of Lydia Maria Child.* Boston: Beacon Press, 1992.

Clinton, Catherine. *The Other Civil War: American Women in the Nineteenth Century.* New York: Hill and Wang, 1984.

Cmiel, Kenneth. *Democratic Eloquence: The Fight over Popular Speech in Nineteenth-Century America.* New York: William Morrow and Co., 1990.

Coleman, Will. *Tribal Talk: Black Theology, Hermeneutics, and African/American Ways of "Telling the Story."* University Park: Pennsylvania State University Press, 2000.

Collins, Patricia Hill. *Black Feminist Thought: Knowledge, Consciousness, and the Politics of Empowerment.* New York: Routledge, 1990.

———. *Fighting Words: Black Women and the Search for Justice.* Minneapolis: University of Minnesota Press, 1998.

Condit, Celeste Michelle, and John Louis Lucaites. *Crafting Equality: America's Anglo-African Word.* Chicago: University of Chicago Press, 1993.

Cone, James H. *God of the Oppressed.* Minneapolis, Minn.: Seabury Press, 1975.

Connor, Kimberly Rae. *Conversions and Visions in the Writings of African-American Women.* Knoxville: University of Tennessee Press, 1994.

Cooper, Frederick. "To Elevate the Race: The Social Thought of Black Leaders." *American Quarterly* 24 (1972): 604–25.

Cornelius, Janet Duitsman. *"When I Can Read My Title Clear": Literacy, Slavery, and Religion in the Antebellum South.* Columbia: University of South Carolina Press, 1991.

Cott, Nancy F. *The Bonds of Womanhood: "Woman's Sphere" in New England, 1780–1835.* New Haven, Conn.: Yale University Press, 1977.

Crenshaw, Kimberlé Williams. "Color-Blind Dreams and Racial Nightmares: Reconfiguring Racism in the Post–Civil Rights Era." In *Birth of a Nation'hood: Gaze, Script, and Spectacle in the O. J. Simpson Case,* edited by Toni Morrison and Claudia Brodsky Lacour, 97–168. New York: Pantheon Books, 1997.

———. "Color Blindness, History, and the Law." In *The House That Race Built: Black Americans, U.S. Terrain,* edited by Wahneema Lubiano, 280–88. New York: Pantheon Books, 1997.

Cromwell, Otelia. *Lucretia Mott.* Cambridge: Harvard University Press, 1958.

Dabney, Virginius. *The Jefferson Scandals: A Rebuttal.* Lanham, Md.: Madison Books, 1981.

Dawson, Michael C. "A Black Counterpublic? Earthquakes, Racial Agenda(s), and Black Politics." In *The Black Public Sphere: A Public Culture Book,* edited by the Black Public Sphere Collective, 199–227. Chicago: University of Chicago Press, 1995.

Detweiler, Frederick G. *The Negro Press in the United States.* Chicago: University of Chicago Press, 1922.

Dick, Robert C. *Black Protest: Issues and Tactics.* Westport, Conn.: Greenwood Press, 1974.

Dillon, Merton L. *Slavery Attacked: Southern Slaves and their Allies, 1619–1865.* Baton Rouge: Louisiana State University Press, 1990.

Dumond, Dwight Lowell. *Antislavery: The Crusade for Freedom in America.* Ann Arbor: University of Michigan Press, 1961.

Eberly, Rosa A. *Citizen Critics: Literary Public Spheres.* Urbana: University of Illinois Press, 2000.

Ellis, Joseph J. *American Sphinx: The Character of Thomas Jefferson.* New York: Alfred A. Knopf, 1996.

Fanuzzi, Robert. "The Trouble with Douglass's Body." *American Transcendental Quarterly* 13 (1999): 27–49.

Fine, Michelle, et al. Preface to *Off White: Readings on Race, Power, and Society.* New York: Routledge, 1997.

Fisch, Audrey A. *American Slaves in Victorian England: Abolitionist Politics in Popular Literature and Culture.* Cambridge: Cambridge University Press, 2000.

Fisher, Walter R. *Human Communication as Narration: Toward a Philosophy of Reason, Value, and Action.* Columbia: University of South Carolina Press, 1997.

Fitch, Suzanne Pullon. "Sojourner Truth." In *Women Public Speakers in the United States, 1800–1925: A Bio-Critical Sourcebook,* edited by Karlyn Kohrs Campbell, 421–33. Westport, Conn.: Greenwood Press, 1993.

Fitch, Suzanne Pullon, and Roseann M. Mandziuk. *Sojourner Truth as Orator: Wit, Story, and Song.* Westport, Conn.: Greenwood Press, 1997.

Flagg, Barbara J. "Antidiscrimination Law and Transparency: Barriers to Equality?" In *Critical White Studies: Looking Behind the Mirror,* edited by Richard Delgado and Jean Stefancic, 589–91. Philadelphia: Temple University Press, 1997.

Fordham, Monroe. *Major Themes in Northern Black Religious Thought, 1800–1860.* Hicksville, N.Y.: Exposition Press, 1975.

Frank, David A. "The New Rhetoric, Judaism, and Post-Enlightenment Thought: The Cultural Origins of Perelmanian Philosophy." *Quarterly Journal of Speech* 83 (1997): 311–31.

Frankenberg, Ruth. "Introduction: Local Whitenesses, Localizing Whiteness." In *Displacing Whiteness: Essays in Social and Cultural Criticism,* edited by Ruth Frankenberg, 1–33. Durham, N.C.: Duke University Press, 1997.

———. *White Women, Race Matters: The Social Construction of Whiteness.* Minneapolis: University of Minnesota Press, 1993.

Franklin, John Hope, and Alfred A. Moss Jr. *From Slavery to Freedom: A History of African Americans.* 7th ed. New York: Alfred A. Knopf, 1994.

Fraser, Nancy. "Rethinking the Public Sphere: A Contribution to the Critique of Actually Existing Democracy." In *Habermas and the Public Sphere,* edited by Craig Calhoun, 109–42. Cambridge, Mass.: MIT Press, 1992.

Frederickson, George M. *The Black Image in the White Mind: The Debate on Afro-American Character and Destiny, 1817–1914.* New York: Harper and Row, 1971.

French, Scot A., and Edward L. Ayers. "The Strange Career of Thomas Jefferson: Race and Slavery in American Memory, 1943–1993." In *Jeffersonian Legacies,* edited by Peter S. Onuf, 418–56. Charlottesville: University Press of Virginia, 1993.

Friedman, Lawrence J. *Gregarious Saints: Self and Community in American Abolitionism, 1830–1870.* Cambridge: Cambridge University Press, 1982.

Funk, Albert A. "Henry David Thoreau's 'Slavery in Massachusetts.'" *Western Speech* 36 (1972): 159–68.

Gara, Larry. *The Liberty Line: The Legend of the Underground Railroad.* Lexington: University of Kentucky Press, 1961.

Garfield, Deborah M., and Rafia Zafar, eds. *Harriet Jacobs and* Incidents in the Life of a Slave Girl*: New Critical Essays.* Cambridge: Cambridge University Press, 1996.

Gates, Henry Louis, Jr. "Address at Benefit for 'Back on Track,'" San Francisco, 28 January 1997. Radio broadcast on *City Arts and Lectures,* KQED, San Francisco, 18 March 1997.

———. *Figures in Black: Words, Signs, and the "Racial" Self.* New York: Oxford University Press, 1987.

———. *The Signifying Monkey: A Theory of Afro-American Literary Criticism.* New York: Oxford University Press, 1988.

Genovese, Eugene D. *Roll, Jordan, Roll: The World the Slaves Made.* New York: Pantheon Books, 1974.

George, Carol V. R. "Widening the Circle: The Black Church and the Abolitionist Crusade, 1830–1860." In *Antislavery Reconsidered: New Perspectives on the Abolitionists,* edited by Lewis Perry and Michael Fellman, 75–95. Baton Rouge: Louisiana State University Press, 1979.

Giddings, Paula. *When and Where I Enter: The Impact of Black Women on Race and Sex in America.* New York: William Morrow and Co., 1984; New York: Bantam Books, 1985.

Ginzburg, Lori D. *Women and the Work of Benevolence: Morality, Politics, and Class in the Nineteenth-Century United States.* New Haven, Conn.: Yale University Press, 1990.

Goodheart, Lawrence B. *Abolitionist, Actuary, Atheist: Elizur Wright and the Reform Impulse.* Kent, Ohio: Kent State University Press, 1990.

Gordon-Reed, Annette. *Thomas Jefferson and Sally Hemings: An American Controversy.* Charlottesville: University Press of Virginia, 1997.

Gougeon, Len. "Emerson and Abolition: The Silent Years, 1837–1844." *American Literature* 54 (1982): 560–75.

Grant, Jacquelyn. *White Women's Christ and Black Women's Jesus: Feminist Christology and Womanist Response.* Atlanta: Scholars Press, 1989.

Greene, Dana. Introduction to *Lucretia Mott: Her Complete Speeches and Sermons.* Lewiston, N.Y.: Edwin Mellen, 1980.

Griffin, Clifford S. *Their Brothers' Keepers: Moral Stewardship in the United States, 1800–1865.* New Brunswick, N.J.: Rutgers University Press, 1960.

Gring-Pemble, Lisa M. "Writing Themselves into Consciousness: Creating a Rhetorical Bridge between the Public and Private Spheres." *Quarterly Journal of Speech* 84 (1998): 41–61.

Gross, Bella. *"Freedom's Journal* and the *Rights of All." Journal of Negro History* 27 (1932): 241–86.

Guy-Sheftall, Beverly. "Black Feminism in the United States." In *Upon These Shores: Themes in the African-American Experience, 1600 to the Present,* edited by William R. Scott and William D. Shade, 347–66. New York: Routledge, 2000.

Habermas, Jürgen. "The Public Sphere: An Encyclopedia Article." Trans. Sara Lennox and Frank Lennox. *New German Critique* 1.3 (Fall 1974): 49–55.

———. *The Structural Transformation of the Public Sphere.* Trans. Thomas Burger and Frederick Lawrence. Cambridge, Mass.: MIT Press, 1989.

Hall, Robert L. "Massachusetts Abolitionists Document the Slave Experience." In *Courage and Conscience: Black and White Abolitionists in Boston,* edited by Donald M. Jacobs, 75–99. Bloomington: Indiana University Press, 1993.

Hamilton, Cynthia. "Frederick Douglass and the Gender Politics of Reform." In *Liberating Sojourn: Frederick Douglass and Transatlantic Reform,* edited by Alan J. Rice and Martin Crawford, 73–92. Athens: University of Georgia Press, 1999.

Hansen, Debra Gold. "The Boston Female Anti-Slavery Society and the Limits of Gender Politics." In *The Abolitionist Sisterhood: Women's Political Culture in Antebellum America,* edited by Jean Fagan Yellin and John C. Van Horne, 45–65. Ithaca, N.Y.: Cornell University Press, 1994.

———. *Strained Sisterhood: Gender and Class in the Boston Female Anti-Slavery Society.* Amherst: University of Massachusetts Press, 1993.

Hersh, Blanche Glassman. "'Am I Not a Woman and a Sister?': Abolitionist Beginnings of Nineteenth-Century Feminism." In *Antislavery Reconsidered: New Perspectives on the Abolitionists,* edited by Lewis Perry and Michael Fellman, 252–83. Baton Rouge: Louisiana State University Press, 1979.

———. *The Slavery of Sex: Feminist-Abolitionists in America.* Urbana: University of Illinois Press, 1978.

Hewitt, Nancy A. "The Social Origins of Women's Antislavery Politics in Western New York." In *Crusaders and Compromisers: Essays on the Relationship of the Antislavery Struggle to the Antebellum Party System,* edited by Alan M. Kraut, 205–33. Westport, Conn.: Greenwood, 1983.

Hine, Darlene Clark. *Hine Sight: Black Women and the Re-Construction of American History.* Brooklyn, N.Y.: Carlson Publishing, 1994.

Hinks, Peter P. *To Awaken My Afflicted Brethren: David Walker and the Problem of Antebellum Slave Resistance.* University Park: Pennsylvania State University Press, 1997.

Hoganson, Kristin. "Garrisonian Abolitionists and the Rhetoric of Gender, 1850–1860." *American Quarterly* 45 (1993): 558–95.

hooks, bell. *Ain't I A Woman: Black Women and Feminism*. Boston: South End Press, 1981.
———. *Teaching to Transgress: Education as the Practice of Freedom*. New York: Routledge, 1994.

Horton, James Oliver. *Free People of Color: Inside the African-American Community*. Washington, D.C.: Smithsonian Institution Press, 1993.

Horton, James Oliver, and Lois E. Horton. "The Affirmation of Manhood: Black Garrisonians in Antebellum Boston." In *Courage and Conscience: Black and White Abolitionists in Boston,* edited by Donald M. Jacobs, 127–53. Bloomington: Indiana University Press, 1993.

———. *Black Bostonians: Family Life and Community Struggle in the Antebellum North*. New York: Holmes and Meier, 1979.

———. *In Hope of Liberty: Culture, Community and Protest among Northern Free Blacks, 1700–1860*. New York: Oxford University Press, 1997.

Howard-Pitney, David. *The Afro-American Jeremiad: Appeals for Justice in America*. Philadelphia: Temple University Press, 1990.

Huggins, Nathan Irvin. *Slave and Citizen: The Life of Frederick Douglass*. Boston: Little, Brown and Co., 1980.

Hunter, Carol M. *To Set the Captives Free: Reverend Jermain Wesley Loguen and the Struggle for Freedom in Central New York, 1835–1872*. New York: Garland Publishing, 1993.

Jackson, Wendell. "Emerson and the Burden of Slavery." *College Language Association Journal* 25 (1981): 48–55.

Jacobs, Donald M. "David Walker and William Lloyd Garrison: Racial Cooperation and the Shaping of Boston Abolition." In *Courage and Conscience: Black and White Abolitionists in Boston,* edited by Donald M. Jacobs, 1–20. Bloomington: Indiana University Press, 1993.

———. "David Walker: Boston Race Leader, 1825–1830." *Essex Institute Historical Collections* 107 (1971): 94–107.

———, ed. *Courage and Conscience: Black and White Abolitionists in Boston*. Bloomington: Indiana University Press, 1993.

Jasinski, James. "The Feminization of Liberty, Domesticated Virtue, and the Reconstitution of Power and Authority in Early American Political Discourse." *Quarterly Journal of Speech* 79 (1993): 146–64.

Jeffrey, Julie Roy. *The Great Silent Army of Abolitionism: Ordinary Women in the Antislavery Movement*. Chapel Hill: University of North Carolina Press, 1998.

Jenkins, William Sumner. *Pro-Slavery Thought in the Old South*. Chapel Hill: University of North Carolina Press, 1935.

Johnson, Berman E. *The Dream Deferred: A Survey of Black America, 1840–1896*. Dubuque, Iowa: Kendall/Hunt, 1993.

Jordan, Winthrop D. *White over Black: American Attitudes toward the Negro, 1550–1812*. Chapel Hill: University of North Carolina Press, 1968.

Karcher, Carolyn L. *The First Woman in the Republic: A Cultural Biography of Lydia Maria Child*. Durham, N.C.: Duke University Press, 1994.

———, ed. *A Lydia Maria Child Reader*. Durham, N.C.: Duke University Press, 1997.

———. "Rape, Murder, and Revenge in 'Slavery's Pleasant Homes': Lydia Maria Child's Antislavery Fiction and the Limits of Genre." In *The Culture of Sentiment: Race, Gender, and Sentimentality in Nineteenth-Century America,* edited by Shirley Samuels, 58–72. New York: Oxford University Press, 1992.

Kinshasa, Kwando M. *Emigration vs. Assimilation: The Debate in the African American Press, 1827–1861.* Jefferson, N.C.: McFarland and Co., 1988.

Kraditor, Aileen S. *Means and Ends in American Abolitionism: Garrison and His Critics on Strategy and Tactics, 1834–50.* 1969. Reprint, Chicago: Ivan R. Dee, 1989.

Kramarae, Cheris. *Women and Men Speaking: Frameworks for Analysis.* Rowley, Mass.: Newbury House Publishers, 1981.

Lampe, Gregory P. *Frederick Douglass: Freedom's Voice, 1818–1845.* East Lansing: Michigan State University Press, 1998.

Leeman, Richard W. "Frances Ellen Watkins Harper, 1825–1911, Poet, Author, Abolitionist, Lecturer, Reform Leader." In *African-American Orators: A Bio-Critical Sourcebook,* edited by Richard W. Leeman, 171–80. Westport, Conn.: Greenwood Press, 1996.

Lerner, Gerda. *The Grimké Sisters from South Carolina: Pioneers for Woman's Rights and Abolition.* New York: Schocken Books, 1967.

———. Introduction to *The Feminist Thought of Sarah Grimké.* New York: Oxford University Press, 1998.

Lessl, Thomas M. "William Whipper, c.1804–1876, Businessman, Abolitionist, Reform Activist." In *African-American Orators: A Bio-Critical Sourcebook,* edited by Richard W. Leeman, 375–83. Westport, Conn.: Greenwood Press, 1996.

Levander, Caroline Field. *Voices of the Nation: Women and Public Speech in Nineteenth-Century American Literature and Culture.* Cambridge: Cambridge University Press, 1998.

Levesque, George A. "Black Abolitionists in the Age of Jackson: Catalysts in the Radicalization of American Abolition." *Journal of Black Studies* 1 (1970): 187–201.

Levine, Lawrence W. *Black Culture and Black Consciousness: Afro-American Folk Thought from Slavery to Freedom.* New York: Oxford University Press, 1977.

Lindhorst, Marie. "Politics in a Box: Sarah Mapps Douglass and the Female Literary Association, 1831–1833." *Pennsylvania History* 65 (1998): 263–78.

Lipscomb, Drema R. "Sojourner Truth: A Practical Public Discourse." In *Reclaiming Rhetorica: Women in the Rhetorical Tradition,* edited by Andrea A. Lunsford, 227–45. Pittsburgh: University of Pittsburgh Press, 1995.

Loewenberg, Bert James, and Ruth Bogin, eds. *Black Women in Nineteenth-Century American Life: Their Words, Their Thoughts, Their Feelings.* University Park: Pennsylvania State University Press, 1976.

Logan, Shirley Wilson. "Literacy as a Tool for Social Action among Nineteenth-Century African American Women." In *Nineteenth-Century Women Learn to Write,* edited by Catherine Hobbs, 179–96. Charlottesville: University Press of Virginia, 1995.

———. *"We Are Coming": The Persuasive Discourse of Nineteenth-Century Black Women.* Carbondale: Southern Illinois University Press, 1999.

———, ed. *With Pen and Voice: A Critical Anthology of Nineteenth-Century African-American Women.* Carbondale: Southern Illinois University Press, 1995.

Lumpkin, Katharine Du Pre. *The Emancipation of Angelina Grimké.* Chapel Hill: University of North Carolina Press, 1974.

Mabee, Carleton, and Susan Mabee Newhouse. *Sojourner Truth: Slave, Prophet, Legend.* New York: New York University Press, 1993.

Mailloux, Steven. "Rhetorical Hermeneutics." *Critical Inquiry* 11 (1985): 620–41.

———. "Rhetorical Hermeneutics Revisited." *Text and Performance Quarterly* 11 (1991): 233–48.

McDorman, Todd F. "Challenging Constitutional Authority: African American Responses to *Scott v. Sandford.*" *Quarterly Journal of Speech* 83 (1997): 192–209.

McFeely, William S. *Frederick Douglass.* New York: W. W. Norton and Co., 1991.

McHenry, Elizabeth. "'Dreaded Eloquence': The Origins and Rise of African American Literary Societies and Libraries." *Harvard Library Bulletin,* n.s. 6.2 (spring 1995): 32–56.

———. "Forgotten Readers: African-American Literary Societies and the American Scene." In *Print Culture in a Diverse America,* edited by James P. Danky and Wayne A. Wiegand, 149–72. Urbana: University of Illinois Press, 1998.

McIntosh, Peggy. "White Privilege and Male Privilege: A Personal Account of Coming to See Correspondences through Work in Women's Studies." In *Critical White Studies: Looking Behind the Mirror,* edited by Richard Delgado and Jean Stefancic, 291–99. Philadelphia: Temple University Press, 1997.

McKivigan, John R., and Mitchell Snay. "Introduction: Religion and the Problem of Slavery in Antebellum America." In *Religion and the Antebellum Debate over Slavery,* edited by John R. McKivigan and Mitchell Snay, 1–32. Athens: University of Georgia Press, 1999.

Melder, Keith. "Abby Kelley and the Process of Liberation." In *The Abolitionist Sisterhood: Women's Political Culture in Antebellum America,* edited by Jean Fagan Yellin and John C. Van Horne, 231–48. Ithaca, N.Y.: Cornell University Press, 1994.

Merrill, Walter M. *Against Wind and Tide: A Biography of William Lloyd Garrison.* Cambridge: Harvard University Press, 1963.

Miller, Floyd J. *The Search for a Black Nationality: Black Emigration and Colonization, 1787–1863.* Urbana: University of Illinois Press, 1975.

Mills, Bruce. *Cultural Reformations: Lydia Maria Child and the Literature of Reform.* Athens: University of Georgia Press, 1994.

Mitchell-Kernan, Claudia. "Signifying." In *Mother Wit from the Laughing Barrel: Readings in the Interpretation of Afro-American Folklore,* edited by Alan Dundes, 310–28. Englewood Cliffs, N.J.: Prentice-Hall, 1973.

Moses, Wilson Jeremiah. *Black Messiahs and Uncle Toms: Social and Literary Manifestations of a Religious Myth.* University Park: Pennsylvania State University Press, 1982.

Mullen, Harryette. "Runaway Tongue: Resistant Orality in *Uncle Tom's Cabin, Our Nig, Incidents in the Life of a Slave Girl,* and *Beloved.*" In *The Culture of Sentiment: Race, Gender, and Sentimentality in Nineteenth-Century America,* edited by Shirley Samuels, 244–64. New York: Oxford University Press, 1992.

Murphy, John M. "'A Time of Shame and Sorrow': Robert F. Kennedy and the American Jeremiad." *Quarterly Journal of Speech* 76 (1990): 401–14.

Nash, Gary B. *Forging Freedom: The Formation of Philadelphia's Black Community, 1720–1840.* Cambridge: Harvard University Press, 1988.

Nero, Charles I. "'Oh, What I Think I Must Tell This World!': Oratory and Public Address of African-American Women." In *Black Women in America,* edited by Kim Marie Vaz, 261–75. Thousand Oaks, Calif.: Sage Publications, 1995.

Nye, Russel B. *William Lloyd Garrison and the Humanitarian Reformers.* Boston: Little, Brown and Co., 1955.

Olson, Lester C. "Liabilities of Language: Audre Lorde Reclaiming Difference." *Quarterly Journal of Speech* 84 (1998): 448–70.

———. "On the Margins of Rhetoric: Audre Lorde Transforming Silence into Language and Action." *Quarterly Journal of Speech* 83 (1997): 49–70.

Painter, Nell Irvin. "Difference, Slavery, and Memory: Sojourner Truth in Feminist Abolitionism." In *The Abolitionist Sisterhood: Women's Political Culture in Antebellum America,* edited by Jean Fagan Yellin and John C. Van Horne, 139–58. Ithaca: Cornell University Press, 1994.

———. *Sojourner Truth: A Life, A Symbol.* New York: W. W. Norton and Co., 1996.

Pasternak, Martin B. *Rise Now and Fly to Arms: The Life of Henry Highland Garnet.* New York: Garland Publishing, 1995.

Pease, Jane H., and William H. Pease. "Boston Garrisonians and the Problem of Frederick Douglass." *Canadian Journal of History* 11.2 (September 1967): 29–48.

———. *They Who Would Be Free: Blacks' Search for Freedom, 1830–1861.* New York: Atheneum, 1974.

Penn, I. Garland. *The Afro-American Press, and its Editors.* Springfield, Mass., 1891.

Perelman, Chaim, and Lucie Olbrechts-Tyteca. *The New Rhetoric: A Treatise on Argumentation.* Trans. John Wilkinson and Purcell Weaver. Notre Dame, Ind.: University of Notre Dame Press, 1969.

Perkins, Linda. "Black Women and Racial 'Uplift' prior to Emancipation." In *The Black Women Cross-Culturally,* edited by Filomina Chioma Steady, 317–34. Rochester, Vt.: Schenkman Books, 1981.

Perry, Lewis. *Radical Abolitionism: Anarchy and the Government of God in Antislavery Thought.* Ithaca, N.Y.: Cornell University Press, 1973.

Peterson, Carla L. *"Doers of the Word": African-American Women Speakers and Writers in the North, 1830–1880.* New York: Oxford University Press, 1995.

Phillips, Kendall R. "The Spaces of Public Dissension: Reconsidering the Public Sphere." *Communication Monographs* 63 (1996): 231–48.

Porter, Dorothy B. "Sarah Parker Remond, Abolitionist and Physician." *Journal of Negro History* 20 (1935): 287–93.

Quarles, Benjamin. "Antebellum Free Blacks and the 'Spirit of '76.'" *Journal of Negro History* 61 (1976): 229–42.

———. *Black Abolitionists.* New York: Oxford University Press, 1969.

———. "The Breach between Douglass and Garrison." *Journal of Negro History* 23 (1938): 144–54.

———. Foreword to *The Underground Rail Road,* by William Still. 1871. Reprint, Chicago: Johnson, 1970.

————. *Frederick Douglass.* 1948. Reprint, New York: Atheneum, 1969.

Raboteau, Albert J. "African-Americans, Exodus, and the American Israel." In *African-American Christianity: Essays in History,* edited by Paul E. Johnson, 1–17. Berkeley: University of California Press, 1994.

Richardson, Marilyn. Introduction to *Maria W. Stewart, America's First Black Woman Political Writer: Essays and Speeches.* Bloomington: Indiana University Press, 1987.

————. "'What If I Am a Woman?' Maria W. Stewart's Defense of Black Women's Political Activism." In *Courage and Conscience: Black and White Abolitionists in Boston,* edited by Donald M. Jacobs, 191–206. Bloomington: Indiana University Press, 1993.

Ripley, C. Peter, et al., eds. *Witness for Freedom: African American Voices on Race, Slavery, and Emancipation.* Chapel Hill: University of North Carolina Press, 1993.

Ritter, Kurt W. "American Political Rhetoric and the Jeremiad Tradition: Presidential Nomination Acceptance Addresses, 1960–1976." *Central States Speech Journal* 31 (1980): 153–71.

Russell, Sandi. *Render Me My Song: African-American Women Writers from Slavery to the Present.* New York: St. Martin's Press, 1990.

Ryan, Halford Ross. "Maria W. Miller Stewart, 1803–1879, Essayist, Educator." In *African-American Orators: A Bio-Critical Sourcebook,* edited by Richard W. Leeman, 311–17. Westport, Conn.: Greenwood Press, 1996.

Ryan, Mary P. *Women in Public: Between Banners and Ballots, 1825–1880.* Baltimore, Md.: Johns Hopkins University Press, 1990.

Sale, Maggie. "Critiques from Within: Antebellum Projects of Resistance." *American Literature* 64 (1992): 695–718.

Samuels, Shirley, ed. *The Culture of Sentiment: Race, Gender, and Sentimentality in Nineteenth-Century America.* New York: Oxford University Press, 1992.

Sánchez-Eppler, Karen. *Touching Liberty: Abolitionism, Feminism, and the Politics of the Body.* Berkeley: University of California Press, 1993.

Schor, Joel. *Henry Highland Garnet: A Voice of Black Radicalism in the Nineteenth Century.* Westport, Conn.: Greenwood Press, 1977.

Scott, Donald M. "Abolition as a Sacred Vocation." In *Antislavery Reconsidered: New Perspectives on the Abolitionists,* edited by Lewis Perry and Michael Fellman, 51–74. Baton Rouge: Louisiana State University Press, 1979.

Sekora, John. "Black Message / White Envelope: Genre, Authenticity, and Authority in the Antebellum Slave Narrative." *Callaloo* 10 (1987): 482–515.

————. "'Mr. Editor, If You Please': Frederick Douglass, *My Bondage and My Freedom,* and the End of the Abolitionist Imprint." *Callaloo* 17 (1994): 608–26.

Sklar, Kathryn Kish. *Catharine Beecher: A Study in American Domesticity.* New York: W. W. Norton and Co., 1973.

Smith, Kimberly K. *The Dominion of Voice: Riot, Reason, and Romance in Antebellum Politics.* Lawrence: University Press of Kansas, 1999.

Smith, Valerie. *Not Just Race, Not Just Gender: Black Feminist Readings.* New York: Routledge, 1998.

Smith-Rosenberg, Carroll. *Disorderly Conduct: Visions of Gender in Victorian America.* New York: Alfred A. Knopf, 1985.

Soderlund, Jean R. "Priorities and Power: The Philadelphia Female Anti-Slavery Society." In *The Abolitionist Sisterhood: Women's Political Culture in Antebellum America,* edited by Jean Fagan Yellin and John C. Van Horne, 67–88. Ithaca, N.Y.: Cornell University Press, 1994.

Stephens, Gregory. "Frederick Douglass' Multiracial Abolitionism: 'Antagonistic Cooperation' and 'Redeemable Ideas' in the July 5 Speech." *Communication Studies* 48 (1997): 175–94.

Sterling, Dorothy. *Ahead of Her Time: Abby Kelley and the Politics of Antislavery.* New York: W. W. Norton and Co., 1991.

———, ed. *We Are Your Sisters: Black Women in the Nineteenth Century.* New York: W. W. Norton and Co., 1984.

———, ed. *Speak Out in Thunder Tones: Letters and Other Writings by Black Northerners, 1787–1865.* Garden City, N.Y.: Doubleday, 1973.

Stetson, Erlene, and Linda David. *Glorying in Tribulation: The Lifework of Sojourner Truth.* East Lansing: Michigan State University Press, 1994.

Stewart, James Brewer. *Holy Warriors: The Abolitionists and American Slavery.* New York: Hill and Wang, 1976.

———. "Modernizing the 'Difference': The Political Meanings of Color in the Free States, 1776–1840." *Journal of the Early Republic* 19 (winter 1999): 691–712.

Swerdlow, Amy. "Abolition's Conservative Sisters: The Ladies' New York City Anti-Slavery Societies, 1834–1840." In *The Abolitionist Sisterhood: Women's Political Culture in Antebellum America,* edited by Jean Fagan Yellin and John C. Van Horne, 31–44. Ithaca, N.Y.: Cornell University Press, 1994.

Taylor, Clare. *Women of the Anti-Slavery Movement: The Weston Sisters.* New York: St. Martin's Press, 1995.

Terborg-Penn, Rosalyn. "Black Male Perspectives on the Nineteenth-Century Woman." In *The Afro-American Woman: Struggles and Images,* edited by Sharon Harley and Rosalyn Terborg-Penn, 28–42. Port Washington, N.Y.: Kennikat Press, 1978.

Thomas, Benjamin P. *Theodore Weld: Crusader for Freedom.* New Brunswick, N.J.: Rutgers University Press, 1950.

Tise, Larry E. *Proslavery: A History of the Defense of Slavery in America, 1701–1840.* Athens: University of Georgia Press, 1987.

Usrey, Miriam L. "Charles Lenox Remond, Garrison's Ebony Echo, World Anti-Slavery Convention, 1840." *Essex Institute Historical Collections* 106 (1970): 112–25.

Van Broekhoven, Deborah Bingham. "'Let Your Names Be Enrolled': Method and Ideology in Women's Antislavery Petitioning." In *The Abolitionist Sisterhood: Women's Political Culture in Antebellum America,* edited by Jean Fagan Yellin and John C. Van Horne, 179–99. Ithaca, N.Y.: Cornell University Press, 1994.

Venet, Wendy Hammand. *Neither Ballots nor Bullets: Women Abolitionists and the Civil War.* Charlottesville: University Press of Virginia, 1991.

Walker, Clarence E. *Deromanticizing Black History: Critical Essays and Reappraisals.* Knoxville: University of Tennessee Press, 1991.

Walker, Robbie Jean, ed. *The Rhetoric of Struggle: Public Address by African American Women.* New York: Garland Publishing, 1992.

———. "Sojourner Truth, c. 1797–1883, Lecturer, Abolitionist, Women's Rights Speaker." In *African-American Orators: A Bio-Critical Sourcebook,* edited by Richard W. Leeman, 332–40. Westport, Conn.: Greenwood Press, 1996.

Walters, Ronald G. *The Antislavery Appeal: American Abolitionism after 1830.* Baltimore, Md.: Johns Hopkins University Press, 1976.

———. "The Boundaries of Abolitionism." In *Antislavery Reconsidered: New Perspectives on the Abolitionists,* edited by Lewis Perry and Michael Fellman, 3–23. Baton Rouge: Louisiana State University Press, 1979.

Wardrop, Daneen. "'While I Am Writing': Webster's 1825 Spelling Book, the Ell, and Frederick Douglass's Positioning of Language." *African American Review* 32 (1998): 649–60.

Warren, James Perrin. *Culture of Eloquence: Oratory and Reform in Antebellum America.* University Park: Pennsylvania State University Press, 1999.

Washington, Margaret. Introduction to *Narrative of Sojourner Truth.* 1850. Reprint, New York: Vintage-Random, 1993.

Weal, Bruce W. "The Force of Narrative in the Public Sphere of Argument." *Journal of the American Forensic Association* 22 (1985): 104–14.

Welter, Barbara. *Dimity Convictions: The American Woman in the Nineteenth Century.* Athens: Ohio University Press, 1976.

Wesley, Charles H. "The Negroes of New York in the Emancipation Movement." *Journal of Negro History* 24 (1939): 65–103.

West, Cornel. *Race Matters.* Boston: Beacon Press, 1993.

Wheaton, Patrick G., and Celeste M. Condit. "Charles Lenox Remond (1810–1873), Abolitionist, Reform Activist." In *African-American Orators: A Bio-Critical Sourcebook,* edited by Richard W. Leeman, 302–10. Westport, Conn.: Greenwood Press, 1996.

White, Deborah Gray. *Ar'n't I a Woman? Female Slaves in the Plantation South.* New York: W. W. Norton and Co., 1985.

White, Hayden. *Metahistory: The Historical Imagination in Nineteenth-Century Europe.* Baltimore, Md.: Johns Hopkins University Press, 1973.

Wilentz, Sean. Introduction to *David Walker's Appeal, in Four Articles; Together with a Preamble, to the Coloured Citizens of the World, But in Particular, and Very Expressly, to Those of the United States of America.* 3d ed. 1830. Reprint, New York: Hill and Wang, 1995.

Williams, Carolyn. "The Female Antislavery Movement: Fighting against Racial Prejudice and Promoting Women's Rights in Antebellum America." In *The Abolitionist Sisterhood: Women's Political Culture in Antebellum America,* edited by Jean Fagan Yellin and John C. Van Horne, 159–77. Ithaca, N.Y.: Cornell University Press, 1994.

Wills, Garry. *Inventing America: Jefferson's Declaration of Independence.* New York: Doubleday, 1978.

———. *Lincoln at Gettysburg: The Words That Remade America.* New York: Simon and Schuster, 1992.

Wilmore, Gayraud S. "Black Religious Traditions: Sacred and Secular Themes." In *Upon These Shores: Themes in the African-American Experience, 1600 to the Present,* edited by William R. Scott and William D. Shade, 285–99. New York: Routledge, 2000.

Wilson, Carol. "Active Vigilance Is the Price of Liberty: Black Self-Defense against Fugitive Slave Recapture and Kidnapping of Free Blacks." In *Antislavery Violence: Sectional,*

Racial, and Cultural Conflict in Antebellum America, edited by John R. McKivigan and Stanley Harrold, 108–27. Knoxville: University of Tennessee Press, 1999.

———. *Freedom at Risk: The Kidnapping of Free Blacks in America, 1780–1865.* Lexington: University Press of Kentucky, 1994.

Wilson, Clint C., II. *Black Journalists in Paradox: Historical Perspectives and Current Dilemmas.* Westport, Conn.: Greenwood Press, 1991.

Wiltse, Charles M. Introduction to *David Walker's Appeal, in Four Articles; Together with a Preamble, to the Coloured Citizens of the World, But in Particular, and Very Expressly, to Those of the United States of America.* 3d ed. 1830. Reprint, New York: Hill and Wang, 1965.

Winch, Julie. "'You Have Talents—Only Cultivate Them': Philadelphia's Black Female Literary Societies and the Abolitionist Crusade." In *The Abolitionist Sisterhood: Women's Political Culture in Antebellum America,* edited by Jean Fagan Yellin and John C. Van Horne, 101–18. Ithaca, N.Y.: Cornell University Press, 1994.

Winter, Kari J. *Subjects of Slavery, Agents of Change: Women and Power in Gothic Novels and Slave Narratives, 1790–1865.* Athens: University of Georgia Press, 1992.

Wolseley, Roland E. *The Black Press, U.S.A.* Ames: Iowa State University Press, 1971.

Woodson, Carter Godwin. *The Education of the Negro prior to 1861: A History of the Education of the Colored People of the United States from the Beginning of Slavery to the Civil War.* 1919. Reprint, Brooklyn, N.Y.: A and B, n.d.

Woodward, C. Vann. "John Brown's Raid and the Abandonment of Nonviolence." In *The Abolitionists: Reformers or Fanatics?* edited by Richard O. Curry, 97–106. New York: Holt, Rinehart, and Winston, 1965. First published as "John Brown's Private War" in *America in Crisis,* edited by Daniel Aaron (New York: Alfred A. Knopf, 1952), 110–30.

Woodward, Gary. *Persuasive Encounters: Case Studies in Constructive Confrontation.* New York: Praeger, 1990.

Yacovone, Donald. *Samuel Joseph May and the Dilemmas of the Liberal Persuasion, 1797–1871.* Philadelphia: Temple University Press, 1991.

Yee, Shirley J. *Black Women Abolitionists: A Study in Activism, 1828–1860.* Knoxville: University of Tennessee Press, 1992.

Yellin, Jean Fagan. Introduction to *Incidents in the Life of a Slave Girl: Written by Herself.* 1861. Reprint, Cambridge: Harvard University Press, 1987.

———. *Women and Sisters: The Antislavery Feminists in American Culture.* New Haven, Conn.: Yale University Press, 1989.

Yellin, Jean Fagan, and John C. Van Horne, eds. *The Abolitionist Sisterhood: Women's Political Culture in Antebellum America.* Ithaca, N.Y.: Cornell University Press, 1994.

Zarefsky, David, and Victoria J. Gallagher. "From 'Conflict' to 'Constitutional Question': Transformations in Early American Public Discourse." *Quarterly Journal of Speech* 76 (1990): 247–61.

Zulick, Margaret D. "The Agon of Jeremiah: On the Dialogic Invention of Prophetic Ethos." *Quarterly Journal of Speech* 78 (1992): 125–48.

Index

"A, B, C, of Abolition" (Child), 163–64
Abel. *See* Cain and Abel
abolitionism: alternate histories of, 15–25; bibliographic and textual problems with texts on, 11; boundaries for study of, 10–12; dispute between abolitionists and supporters of slavery on, 114; and elimination of prejudice and segregation, 21, 23, 27–29; factions within, 18; gradual abolition, 16; historical studies of, 3–4; inaugural motifs of, 15–16; kneeling slaves as emblems of, 126–27; rhetoric of generally, 1–14; secondary issues included in, 18, 19–21; and self-help or racial uplift, 23–24, 48–49, 52, 53–60, 168–75, 221–22; speeches by abolitionists generally, 11–12; transitional motifs of, 17–21; and violent antislavery action, 18–19, 21, 22; and women's rights, 18, 19–21, 47–48, 123, 135–36, 165–66, 167. *See also* African American abolitionists; African American female abolitionists; African American male abolitionists; female abolitionists; white female abolitionists; white male abolitionists; and specific abolitionists
Abrahams, Roger, 9, 97
ACS. *See* American Colonization Society (ACS)
Adam and Eve, 143–46, 199–200
adaptory rhetoric, 85–86, 209–10, 214, 228–29
advisory rhetoric, 86, 87, 89, 209, 210, 214, 228–29
AFASS. *See* American and Foreign Anti-Slavery Society (AFASS)
Africa, 108, 133–34, 173, 211–12, 216–17
Afric-American Female Intelligence Society, 49, 169, 176–77, 203, 204–5, 212
African American abolitionists: and alternative histories of abolition movement, 10, 16–17; American Anti-Slavery Society membership for, 3; appropriation by, 65,

91, 97–108, 176, 216–18, 229–30, 246n. 25; in 1820s, 10, 16, 26; in eighteenth century, 16; and elimination of prejudice and segregation, 21, 23, 27–29; and England, 31, 93–97, 225, 248n. 76; and fugitive slaves, 21–22, 214; goals of, 27; influence of, on white abolitionists, 17, 22; and jeremiadic form, 8–9, 77–84, 154, 200–209; organizations of, 5, 10, 13, 16, 23, 27, 32, 52; rhetoric of generally, 4–14, 17; secondary role of in national antislavery organizations, 19, 23, 27, 29; and self-help, 23–24, 48–49, 52, 53–60, 168–75, 221–22; and vigilance committees, 22, 23. *See also* African American female abolitionists; African American male abolitionists; and specific abolitionists
African American female abolitionists: and African American male abolitionists, 45, 47–48; appropriation by, 176, 216–18; and Cult of True Womanhood, 45–46, 113, 175–86, 192, 217–18; defining tension in appeal to sympathy by, 187; and feminist studies, 8–9; and gender roles, 46–48; indirect rhetorical strategies of, 215–19; and integrated female antislavery organizations, 42, 44–45; intersection of sexism and racism for, 43–50, 165–66, 175–86; invisibility of, 43–44; and motherhood, 180–82, 186, 187–91; organizations of, 23, 42, 45, 49; outsider-within stance of, 176–86, 227; patriotic rhetoric of, 209–15; prophetic rhetoric of, 200–209; public speaking by, 11, 50, 165–74, 176–83, 190–93, 195–215, 217–18; religious rhetoric of, 50, 169–70, 196–200; revolutionary rhetoric of, 209–15, 228–29, 231; secondary role of in national antislavery organizations, 19, 27; self-determination of, 47, 48–50; self-help rhetoric of, 168–75, 221–22; and signifying, 215–19; on slave women, 44, 182–96; trickster role of, 215–19;